SYNTHETIST ART THEORIES

The publication of this book was made possible through financial assistance of the Netherlands Organization for the advancement of Pure Research (Z.W.O.)

DR. H. R. ROOKMAAKER

SYNTHETIST ART THEORIES

GENESIS AND NATURE
OF THE IDEAS ON ART
OF GAUGUIN
AND HIS CIRCLE

1959
SWETS & ZEITLINGER
AMSTERDAM

Printed by J. F. Duwaer & Zonen / Amsterdam

Up to the present there has existed a romantic notion according to which a true artist creates his work under a kind of divine inspiration and as it were unconsciously. He is endowed with a mysterious kind of insight into the reality of his own times, although he has no deeper discursive understanding even of what he is doing himself.

To the author such a proposition seems to be a fallacy, and this conviction is one of the reasons for the choice of the subject treated in this book. His study of the art-theoretical notions that were really alive among the artists of the eighteen-nineties will, he hopes, show that these artists were aware of what they were aiming at and what was involved in their search for a new style.

Another reason is that in studying modern art it has become increasingly clear that the art-theoretical ideas that are behind it cannot be understood properly if not studied in their genesis. In this respect the work of the group of artists that can be labelled together under the name of the Post-Impressionists, and especially Gauguin and his circle, seemed to him to be of primary importance. Their influence did not remain restricted to matters of style only, but was concerned with much wider issues.

A third reason for me to choose this field of investigation is that in the art-historical discipline to-day the iconological aspects of a work of art are becoming clearer as such, but at the same time they pose the problem of their theoretical and historical implications all the more emphatically. As precisely at the end of the last century the iconical in opposition to the imitative character proclaimed by artists and theorists alike became more and more apparent as its true basic impulse, a study of this art, and the ideas of the artists that created it, promised some elucidations. They turned out to be richer and deeper than I had hoped for.

I have to acknowledge my indebtedness to Dr. J. Q. van Regteren Altena, Professor of History of Art at the Amsterdam University, for his careful reading of my manuscript and for his many clarifying remarks. Many other scholars have helped me some way or another with my study of the subject treated in this book. I want to mention specifically: the late Prof. Dr. W. Ph. Pos, Prof. Dr. J. M. Romein, the late Dr. J. Suys, Prof. Dr. H. M. J. Oldewelt, Prof. Dr. A. H. van der Weel, all of the Amsterdam University; Prof. Dr. H. Dooyeweerd, Prof. Dr. D. H. Th. Vollenhoven, of the Free University, Amsterdam; Prof. Dr. J. P. A. Mekkes, Prof. Dr. H. van de Waal, of the University of Leyden; Prof. Dr. C. G. Seerveld, Belhaven College, Jackson, Miss.; Prof. Dr. E. H. Gombrich, of the Warburg Institute, London. Beside these who have advised me as only scholars of profound learning can do, there were those who helped me by lending or giving me books and other material. It would be impossible to name them all, but I wish to stress that without their generous aid this study would not have been possible.

Special mention must be made of Mr. H. de Jongste, who translated this book into English, not only for putting all his knowledge of the language as well as the subjects treated at my disposal, but also for the generous way in which he gave his time and energy to this work.

I may not pass over in silence the amiable help of the publisher of this book, Mr. R. J. Swets, and of Mr. H. van Krimpen, who looked after the lay-out and typography.

Thanks are also due to my wife, who has spent much of her energy in order to make this study ready for publication, as she has done all the type-writing and correcting.

CONTENTS

Booklet at the back, with notes (in letters)

We have refrained from incorporating reproductions in this book. Almost all the pictures that are more extensively dealt with can be found reproduced in Rewald's *Post-Impressionism* or in books on Gauguin that are equally easy to obtain.

INTRODUCTION

'After having proclaimed the omnipotence of scientific observation and deduction for eighty years with childlike enthusiasm, and after asserting that for its lenses and scalpels there did not exist a single mystery, the nineteenth century at last seems to perceive that its efforts have been in vain, and its boast puerile. Man is still walking about in the midst of the same enigmas, in the same formidable unknown, which has become even more obscure and disconcerting since its habitual neglect. A great many scientists and scholars to-day have come to a halt discouraged. They realize that this experimental science, of which they were so proud, is a thousand times less certain than the most bizarre theogony, the maddest metaphysical rêverie, the least acceptable poet's dream, and they have a presentiment that this haughty science which they proudly used to call 'positive' may perhaps be only a science of what is relative, of appearances, of 'shadows' as Plato said, and that they themselves have nothing to put on old Olympus, from which they have removed the deities and unhinged the constellations.' [a]

This is how Aurier characterizes the position about 1890, functioning as the spokesman for many of his generation. No wonder that they tried to strike out new paths and wanted to free themselves out of the quandary into which especially art had been brought by the exclusive positivistic focussing on visible things.

What was the state of affairs in the plastic arts? Was there any justification for fulminating against naturalism since academism reigned supreme, and—to quote Toynbee—, had changed from a creative minority into a ruling majority? Or are we to hold such pronouncements applicable only to the domain of literary art? True, there also prevailed a naturalism founded in the positivistic mentality, and, no doubt, Aurier stems from an environment of writers and poets. But our quotation is the initial part of an article on contemporary painting which enters more thoroughly into the subject of naturalistic pictorial art which was nothing but 'la copie myope des anecdotes sociales, l'imitation imbécile des verrues de la nature, la plate observation, le trompe-l'oeuil, la gloire d'être aussi fidèlement, aussi banalement exact que le daguerréotype.' [b]

It should not be supposed that in the period about 1890 there existed a criticism like this with respect to the impressionists, and that Aurier's strictures were levelled at them. For the impressionists were only just beginning to find a certain amount of recognition in these years, and were fighting their own battle against the prevailing taste. For the latter reason the newcomers felt some affinity with them and admired them. Only now did they get acquainted with this kind of art, although it had flourished since the seventies. For it should be borne in mind that the generation of artists of 1890 was very young—apart from a pioneer like Gauguin, who notwithstanding his passing through impressionism did not yet sharply oppose it. It was, however, impossible for them to see in the impressionism of Monet, Renoir, Sisley, and Pissarro the realization of their ideals. They were of too different a mind for this—for in their art they wanted to dig deeper than was compatible with a faithful representation of light and atmosphere, however brilliant it might be. Very soon they were to formulate their objections, but quite different from their attitude towards the naturalists, this criticism would not exclude their appreciation and admiration.

The art of the 'Salons'

This disqualified naturalism was properly speaking the art of the 'Salons' displayed at the great annual exhibitions in Paris. What were the aims of that large group who proudly called themselves 'academicians', a name that in the mouths of their adversaries was almost synonymous to the words 'bad, meaningless'. They prided themselves on continuing the great tradition of French pictorial art and on faithfully preserving the ancient principles, that is to say, those artistic principles that had been formulated by Raphael in the sixteenth century, and renewed as well as adapted to the French mind in the seventeenth century by Poussin, Vouet and Lebrun. Afterwards

2

they had been undermined by the rococo with its pastorals and courtly love-scenes and 'rendez-vous', to be renewed in the cool, manly classicism of the late eighteenth century.

This lofty tradition, this 'grand manner' did not only mean a particular way of painting, but chiefly a special kind of themes. The artist was expected to observe the required 'decorum'. So long as this 'decorum' was not violated, widely different techniques were permitted, provided the deviations from what was hall-marked were not too obvious. So, for instance, in the case of the debate around Courbet's work the academicians seem to have taken offence almost exclusively at his realistic themes, his attention for what they considered to be too trivial a kind of reality. This appears, a.o., from Couture's caricature of a realist, a man who chooses a pig's head as his model, painted in a technique which, after all, differs only very little from Courbet's.[1] The exalted myths of a remote past, especially that of the Greeks and the Romans, the great heroic events of history, the ideal man, beautiful in body and mind, such were the subjects worthy of art,[2] while as to beauty as such, its highest norm could be what the Greeks had bequeathed to us, for it was they who had formulated the ideals in such a pure and almost inimitable way. On the other hand, if we examine the works made at this time by the painters who ruled the 'Salons', we discover that these ideals were only rarely a concrete guiding principle. In reality academism was merely the acceptance of one single dogma, viz., that there are fixed rules for art, particular technical precepts that ought to be observed —especially as regards the method of drawing—and that this method can be learned.[3]

Consequently there is more than a little truth in Gauguin's statement 'au début du XIXième siècle, l'art n'est plus une langue comme autrefois, dans chaque pays, avec le souvenir des belles traditions. C'est en quelque sorte un volapuk formé avec des recettes. Un langage unique, enseigné par des professeurs brevétés, donnant l'assurance du parfait et d'une immense médiocreté. Ce volapuk se parle encore...'[c] This certainly holds for the classicistic painters in the narrower sense, for those who stuck most faithfully to the academic tradition proper, artists like Gleyre, Gerôme, and the proverbial Bouguereau. But on examining their work, we see that both in technique and in their themes they had not been left untouched by

3

what was the spirit of the age, and that they, too, were much more realistic than the classicists of the past. For one thing, they were no longer able to follow the anachronisms of the earlier painters, who represented the lofty events of the past in the contemporary style of clothing—now 'they knew better'.[4] They regretted the fact, but they acquiesced in it. And in the second place they followed nature much more closely, especially when painting the nude, in which case they based themselves less on the classical norms of ideal bodily beauty than on a well-chosen model.[d] Thus this art had degenerated into genre painting, reporting, as it were, every day incidents of a distant past, or giving us a glimpse of a quasi-ideal world in which nymphs and satyrs, gods and goddesses walk or fly about naked. Looking, e.g., at Bouguereau's 'Satyr and Nymphs'[5] we get the impression of seeing a snapshot taken in a nudist camp. The figures are represented in such naturalistic detail, so palpable are the beautiful people performing a round dance with their bodies bare, that it is difficult for us to take the title seriously. The same thing holds for 'Venus Toilet' painted by Baudry in 1859 (and bought by the Museum of Bordeaux): This Venus is certainly a beautiful woman, but a real one, of flesh and blood, standing bare in a (very naturalistically painted) wood. There is nothing left of the sculptural-idealizing and abstract-timeless quality of the genuinely classicistic nudes of the time of David.

There is no longer any belief in the classical themes, the allegorical figures or the ideal human figures that are painted. These subjects, which had a profound meaning for an artist like Rubens, because they were directly connected with his vision of life, are now no more than pretexts. Venuses, Magdalenes, and other themes in which beautiful naked women could be the artist's subjects without loss of decorum, or without shocking the public, were very much in favour. But it was precisely the naturalistic way of painting that often rendered them unpalatable and vulgar, rather bare than naked, more sensual than aesthetic. In this connection Gauguin even speaks of 'un Lupanar obligatoire'.[e] How great the deviation from the classical ideal might be can be experienced in the 'Madeleine' by Falguière, a sculpture which was on view at the 'Exposition centenale de l'art',[6] offering us nothing but the full-length portrait of a bare female dancer, whose body had been considerable deformed by the

4

corsets of those days. The title has to save the situation, and in that way the 'decorum' has been observed. But, the examples are as common as grass.

And finally, if contemporary themes were chosen, the result became frankly sentimental as the unreal embellishing gave rise to namby-pambyism. This is the case with 'Brother and Sister' by Bouguereau in the catalogue cited above,[6] depicting some too sweet children in too beautiful clothes and too neatly combed long hair, but with nothing of the aristocratic air and the naturalness based on a grand style of living which made such a theme convincing and truly beautiful in the hands of a painter like Reynolds.

However, also other tendencies could be discovered in the 'Salons' sometimes even flatly contrary to the classicistic tradition. But there was hardly question of a conflict, and a writer like Castagnary, an advocate of naturalism, asserted that he could comprise by this term 'the whole of the younger idealistic and realistic generation'.[7] The artists referred to in this context, Bastien-Lepage, Lhermitte, Roll and the like, were influenced in more than one respect by realists like Courbet, Manet, and even by the impressionists. But they mitigated this realism to such a degree that buyers at the 'Salons' should not be deterred. They continued the tradition of the painters of history who already in a previous period had come very near to photographic accuracy—recall Boissard de Boisdenier's 'La retraite de Moscou' of 1835, now in the Rouen Museum,[8] and similar works by Meisonnier, Neuville and Detaille, reconstructing the events very exactly in retrospect as an elaborate photographic record. Although the art of these realists within the 'Salons' was very naturalistic, it was rarely personal, and always adapted to the taste of the indispensable clients. This was one of the reasons why they were never attacked, however much their subjects must often have meant a violation of the academic 'decorum'. In this connection one might think of Gervex' scenes in hospitals, preferably representing operations, in a chill and would-be scientifically objective way, but not without a melodramatic accent.

In addition to the smooth surface of their paintings the firm position of these painters in the 'Salons' was also due to the fact that with their themes they remained within the prevailing social class, or, if 'lower class people' were represented, they viewed them with the eyes of this bourgeoisie. We might mention Dantan's studio-pieces: they satisfied the curiosity of those who wanted to know how things were done at the studios of the naturalistic sculptors, where images of living models were cast for the making of lay figures (and perhaps also for the production of works of art). Never was there any revolutionary sentiment in this art, and very rarely was there a hint at the contrast between the social classes in a socialistic spirit. Even if this should ever have happened, it would have been done in such a way that nobody's feelings could be hurt.

Perhaps there may have been a few genuinely good artists among these 'academicians' who, as we have seen, were in reality naturalists. It is possible that they will be re-discovered when the artistic tide turns and an art that is directed to the visual aspect of things has a stronger appeal than at the present day. However, it is still difficult for us to look at works of this kind with an open and unprejudiced mind, free from the excessive criticism made by the artists outside of the world of the 'Salons' and their adherents, the more so as in many cases they rightly poured out the vials of their wrath. But some of the works of Bastien-Lepage and of Lhermitte certainly testify to their originality and their daring. They are free of the empty display of technique intended to curry favour with the public that had lost taste and a genuine love of art. The above mentioned artists, e.g., are highly praised by van Gogh, who had got thoroughly acquainted with them when he was engaged at an art-dealer's.[9] [f] But he, too, has his criticism to offer, the gist of which is directed against the academic technique. This technique turns painting into applying a certain number of rules. 'Sans le savoir is die academie une maîtresse die verhindert dat er eene meer serieuze meer warme meer vruchtbare liefde in U wakker wordt.—Laat die maîtresse loopen en wordt tot over de ooren verliefd op uwe eigentlijke beminde dame nature of réalité . . . Elle renouvelle elle retrempe elle donne la vie! Cette dame Nature cette dame Réalité.' [g]

The very sharp condemnation of the arts of the 'Salons' by artists and critics not belonging to that circle is not to be explained, however, only from a different attitude. There is something else, which perhaps plays the decisive part. Aurier summarizes this in a masterly way in his discussion of the Salon of 1891, '. . . les flots d'articles de pur commerce ... il n'y serait point question d'art, point d'artistes, mais simplement d'une industrie de luxe ...' [h]

This criticism was not a novelty. In the course of the nineteenth century there had been repeated complaints about the low artistic level of the 'Salons'. Of course they came from those circles who wanted to go in another direction, or from those who had been seized by revolutionary ideas and opposed the leading social groups. No wonder that most of the criticism came from the socialists, or that Baudelaire wrote with reference to the 'Salons': 'la médiocreté ... règne plus que jamais ...' [i]

Yet there is a great difference between the older kind of criticism and that made at the end of the century. For a man like Baudelaire did not at all shun the task of subjecting the Salon-artists to an elaborate discussion. And in his comment on a picture by Tassaert he devotes many words of praise to it.[10] Yet this work, a very naturalistic representation of a market of female slaves, might certainly have been used by us as an example of an academism of a dubious kind. It would no doubt also have occasioned sharp criticism on the part of the generation of 1890. For it is true they had inherited Baudelaire's negative attitude with regard to the art of the Salons as a whole, but were not merely content with stating its bad quality. They tried to dig deeper and to lay bare the cause of this artistic decadence. Thus they came upon positivism, upon the fact that French culture was overgrown with the natural scientific mentality, and were induced to make a pronouncement like that of Aurier.

It was impossible for us to give an account of the artistic situation about 1890 without considering the art of the 'Salons'. For this art dominated the situation, and the new-comers in the artistic field of battle stood up against it. They linked up with an entirely different tradition which by the side of that of the painters of the 'Salons' had determined the artistic climate of the nineteenth century. In many respects this tradition held on to the French artistic achievements of the past, certainly in a more essential and in a deeper sense. It did not degenerate into the insipid banality of a photographic art without a trace of the artistic or even of good taste, although in the course of the century these figures in the margin of the official world of art

7

came just as well to manifest a growing tendency toward realism in their choice of themes.

In this study we propose to institute a thorough-going investigation of the theories advanced by the generation of 1890, which has created an art that has become decisive in every way for the twentieth century—witness the 'Fauves' in particular, who would have been unthinkable but for the men of 1890. The development of art in the circles outside of the 'Salons' became of such eminent historical importance that very often even apart from the far superior artistic quality of their creations, it is to us the nineteenth century proper. The art of the 'Salons' is, therefore, no more than a 'repoussoir' enabling us to get a better insight into the development which is our chief interest.

It should not be supposed, however, that outside of the 'Salons' there is only one single line of development to be discovered in the history of the art of the nineteenth century. For here, too, the state of affairs is very involved, and there are tendencies to be discovered which deviate from each other sometimes very strongly. A closer study of the genesis and the character especially of the theories on art of Gauguin and his circle will necessitate a sharp analysis, to prevent us from losing our way in the thick tangle of tendencies and movements that are more or less related to one another and sought to strike out new paths about 1890. It is especially imperative for us to distinguish their art and their ideas clearly from those of the symbolists, with whom they are too often classed together.

THE PRECURSORS OF THE SYNTHETISTS

David, Ingres, Gros, Géricault

The nineteenth century opened with the supremacy of classicism
under the undisputed leadership of *David*. More than ever before
the classicistic dogma of following the Greeks found adherence. As
a reaction to the art of the rococo, which had concentrated on the
erotic and the feminine elements, the artists now laid emphasis on
the masculine character. Their favourite subjects were taken from
Roman history and were concerned with examples of heroism,
patriotism, generosity and loyalty. They strove after formal lucidity
and balance. Again they adopted the principles of the 17th century
classicism as Poussin had defined them. Even more than David it was
to be *Ingres* who embodied this old ideal as far as the 19th century
is concerned, no doubt also because he worked on far into the century
and raised the classicistic torch high. This is why the discussions about
classicism were concentrated on his art. In his words and works he
continues to acknowledge the drawing, 'le dessin'—always a characteristic of the academic tradition—as the foundation of the
painter's work, although at times he could be very fascinating as a
colourist.

Gros and Géricault, too, considered the 'grande histoire' as the
highest aim of painting. Only, they were more inclined to follow the
baroque. The former, it is true, made desperate attempts to be a
classicist in the line of David, but often maintained a greater measure
of freedom in composition, a greater mobility in his figures and
groups. That which in his heart of hearts Gros would have liked to
do, was realized by *Géricault*, who followed him in the beginning

and always continued to admire him. He is out and out a romantic artist in the French acceptation of the term, but his relatedness to the Baroque is even more manifest than in anybody else. This does not only appear from the masters he admires and studies, Rubens and Michelangelo, but also from his strongly mobile compositions built on the diagonal. We are introduced into a heroic world in which powerful figures and noble animals move about. Following new tendencies in historical painting, which had already asserted themselves in the eighteenth century,[1] he also selects an event of contemporary history for his principal work. But notwithstanding his scrupulous accuracy of detail he does not fall into the error of a kind of photographic naturalism. After the manner of the baroque he strives after an ennobled summary of the meaning of an event. The history of this work 'Le radeau de la Méduse', of the year 1819, is extremely instructive in this respect. After first obtaining exact information on the facts, also by means of conversations with the survivors of the wreck of the French warship—a scandal that made a great stir—, he made experiments in his preliminary studies until the composition had reached the maximum of artistic effect.[2]

Constable, Turner

It is *Constable* who became very important for the further course of the events. In many respects he continues the tradition of such seventeenth century Dutch landscape painters as Ruysdael and Hobbema. But he aims at something new insofar as he tries to represent the changing aspects of nature—recall his studies of clouds—as exactly as possible, which betrays an almost scientific attitude,[3] which as such had bien alien to our great landscapists. For the purpose of noting the rapidly changing effects of the weather he developed a very direct and quick manner of painting, adding to the quasi-scientific tendency in his observation a marked subjective element which was also foreign to his predecessors. It is remarkable that the nineteenth century was to be a constant witness of this new and peculiar manner. In the very method of painting it made the tension palpable, as it were, between nature and freedom which has always dominated Humanism: [a] On the one hand there is a concentrated study of nature in its visible outward appearance; on the other, we find a strictly subjective manner of representing what has been observed.

This complex mentality later on found its most explicit realization in impressionism. Zola's well known pronouncement that the artist should represent 'un coin de la nature vu par un tempérament' [b] concisely formulated this.

We do not believe that one is justified in depreciating Constable's more elaborate finished works in favour of his rapidly painted sketches, in which what has just been said is most clearly manifest. Constable is certainly not likely to have belied his own nature when finishing the symphonic pictures and to explain this peculiarity one need not say that he yielded to the prevailing taste and to tradition.[4] But, as so often happens, the new tendency comes to the fore in its most unpurified form in a study and in a sketch. Also in the completed works the new elements were not lacking. Was it not the 'Haywain' in its elaborated version which opened the eyes of Delacroix at the Salon of 1824 to a new method of working in which the colours were put on the canvas unmixed, which procedure made them give the impression of freshness and naturalness?

The influence of Constable—and kindred artists like Bonington—on French painting, indirectly via Delacroix, and above all directly on the landscapists of the School of Fontainebleau, can hardly be overestimated. It is exactly the direct inspiration derived from nature, without any romantic admixtures, which has again and again been a guiding principle. *Turner's* influence was to remain much more restricted. This was also due to his much more pronounced subjectivity with respect to natural scenery. This is the consequence of his sense of composition, an academistic trait derived from Claude. His too great freedom in the realization of his effects, together with his always noticeable idealizing tendency after the manner of Claude Lorrain, caused his work to be less in line with the tendencies of the French painters. There is no doubt that he took a great interest in light and colour, but they remained a means to him for the expression of feeling, for making the dream acceptable.[5] There was always something in Turner's work that was not naturalistic. This striving to give more than nature as such we also find clearly formulated in Ruskin's work *Modern Painters,* devoted to Turner's art. Here, e.g., we read that Turner not only knew and studied the clouds, but 'to him ... the stormclouds seemed messengers of fate. He feared them, while he reverenced; nor does he ever introduce them without some

11

hidden purpose, bearing upon the expression of the scene he is painting.'[6]

Goya

We should not altogether leave Goya out of the picture, although we must not overestimate his direct influence. The problems of the artists about 1890, to be investigated in more detail in a later context, are concerned with the relation of a work of art to reality. They have rejected naturalism, but are by no means prepared to indulge in a fantastic art that has got detached from reality. It is precisely on this point that they might have made an appeal to Goya, although they have never done so, as far as we know. For Goya's art was not easily accessible. Some of them will no doubt have known about him because of what Baudelaire wrote about him, and possibly, via Delacroix in particular, there must have been some indirect influence. In this connection we refer to his famous print of the series of the 'Caprichos',[7] with the striking title 'El sueño de la razón produce monstruos'. It represents a man asleep, with his head on a table—behind him there are all kinds of monsters resembling bats, owls, and a cat. The title should not be translated by 'the *sleep* of reason produces monsters', as is done in Levitine's note—which, by the way, is a particularly important one—[8] but by 'the *dream* of reason produces monsters', which is the rendering given by Gombrich in his no less important article.[9] This term 'dream' (rêve) was in very frequent use among the generation of 1890. But in this case we find it for the first time applied to great art in the sense of the artist's mind being a creative spirit, who invents a whole world of images and symbols. This world is not the realm of fantasy, but bears the closest relation to the world in which the artist lives. This dream is not at all a means to escape from reality into the freedom of fantasy. On the contrary, the attempt is made to come to close grips with reality by means of an image.[c]

Gombrich shows that this method had already been applied by the English graphic artists and caricaturists of the latter half of the 18th century, men like Gillray, e.g. The dream, fantastic figures, ghosts, etc. are used to represent in an image things that cannot be rendered in a naturalistic way.[d] In this way an attempt is made to avoid the incongruity that has existed in the visual arts since the

12

Renaissance, because on the one hand the artists tried to represent everything in accordance with what the eye perceives, and on the other they stuck to the allegorical-symbolical method of the Middle Ages.[10] For in this way the spectator was shown things in the picture that had the appearance of being real, but that never occur together in such a context in actual reality. A simple example of such incongruity is the picture of an angel who is represented as a human being with wings. To interpret such an image naturalistically is mere folly. However, now that the world represented in the picture is called a dream, a fiction, the artist has become free to depart from the outward appearance of everyday reality. And exactly in this way he is able to satirize the events of the day all the more sharply, or to elucidate them critically in an image.

Also Goya's 'Caprichos', although they are the 'monstruos' of his 'sueño', are not really dream-castles, but works which in many cases bear the character of genre-pieces, if we only study their titles and descriptions. They are peeps into the daily life of Spain in Goya's days. It is true, already at an earlier period, viz. in the case of Tiepolo, we find 'capricci'—he sometimes also calls them 'scherzi di fantasia'— [11] but we think that Gombrich is right in discovering some connection between Goya's work and that of the English caricaturists, because the technique of both is new and certainly something different from that of Tiepolo. For Tiepolo really gives, either a world of fantasy, or simply a genre-piece. He does not know this element of the 'dream', i.e., the creative day-dream, in which there is always a vision of what is found in the immediate surroundings, however slight the naturalism of the representation might be.

Certainly new were the peculiar character and the contents of this vision which, by way of a pun, we had better call a 'day-mare' than a day-dream, and which Baudelaire characterized with the words 'Le monstrueux vraisemblable'. In fact, 'ces contorsions, ces faces bestiales, ces grimaces diaboliques sont pénétrées d'humanité'.[e] For in Goya's case even the strangest representations rarely make the impression that the artist is giving the reins to his imagination. Even in the case of that remarkable print entitled 'Quien lo creyera'—a significant inscription!—representing two fighting naked old hags, it seems that Baudelaire's interpretation, a summary of 'tous les vices que l'esprit humain peut concevoir' [f] is the only right one. In this

13

connection the very clearly non-naturalistic print opening the series 'Desastros de la guerra' is also characteristic.[12] Here the horror of war is summarized in a birdlike monster. It resembles a bird because there is no possibility of human contact with this kind of creatures, for we do not know and cannot predict their reactions. It is a symbol that we meet again in our own time in many ways—e.g., in drawings by Zadkine made during the last war.

Delacroix

Delacroix's influence reached the generation of 1890 in three different ways. In the first place, of course, there were his works, which, comparatively speaking, were within the reach of every painter. But by the side of this grand work he also left a number of no less fascinating writings, while Baudelaire's articles containing a brilliant analysis as well as an enthusiastic glorification of his art will certainly have been of great importance.[g] In many respects Baudelaire was the teacher of the generation of 1885-1890. But he would never have occupied that influential position with the artists among them, if he had never written about Delacroix's art. This is why Delacroix and Baudelaire belong together, and the influence of the one is not conceivable without that of the other.

When studying Delacroix's work the first thing that strikes us is the way in which colour is handled. It is so much different, so much more lively and fascinating than in the works of his contemporaries. Also Ingres, who, to be sure, had some qualities as a colourist, at times used bright and telling colours. But there is always this difference that those of Delacroix are, so to say, vibrant. This is the result of a very easy manner of painting. This striking technical quality of Delacroix's work has always fascinated artists. He did not discover this new technique without an effort. The examples of Rubens and Constable pointed the way, but his own studies and thought were after all necessary for him to attain to perfect mastery. Many passages in his 'Journal' and in his other writings dealing with this subject bear witness to all this. And they have not remained unknown to the artists. Van Gogh writes about them in his Nuenen period,[13] while Signac's book is one elaborate homage to the colourist Delacroix.[14]

Yet Delacroix never aimed at colour for the sake of colour, just as

14

an art for art's sake was foreign to him. The colouristic realization of his work was subservient to the effect he wanted to reach, namely, directness and fluency, in opposition to the painful accuracy with which Ingres as well as the Salon artists worked. In the rare cases of a certain ease and fluency of execution in the works of the latter we can nearly always trace it back to Delacroix's influence—we are referring to Decamps, Couture, and similar artists. Delacroix did not strive after romantic fire, the direct and unrestrained expression of the self, but, in his own formula, 'il faudrait faire ... des tableaux esquisses qui auraient la liberté et la franchise des croquis.' [h] A few days before he wrote this he had noted down in his Diary a criticism of painters whom he calls 'des prosateurs'—the classicists—, in which he makes the remark that 'le hasard a l'air d'avoir assemblé les tons et agencé les lignes de la composition. L'idée poétique ou expressive ne vous frappe pas au premier coup d'oeuil.' [i] So he is in search of a kind of ease and freedom of execution not implying casualness. And the sentence last quoted approaches much more closely that which he considers to be essential in this respect, viz., that the colour and the composition built up in a colouristic way should bear and underline the emotional expressiveness of the subject. He gave pregnant expression to this idea which frequently occurs later on with his admirers: [15] 'Il y a une impression qui résulte de tel arrangement de couleurs, de lumières et d'ombres etc.... C'est ce qu'on appellerait la musique du tableau ...' [k]

The vivid impression of reality that his paintings call up, and which immediately strikes the spectator as genuine and natural, has been achieved by means of a technique and a manner of execution which is not in the least naturalistic in the sense of the Salon painters. 'For', Delacroix says, 'l'imagination chez l'artiste ne se représente pas seulement tels ou tels objets, elle les combine pour la fin qu'il veut obtenir; elle fait des tableaux, des images qu'il compose à son gré.' [l] Therefore, his view of art embodies a strong urge for freedom in perfect agreement with the impression we get from his work. This freedom, however, is not licence, but aims at the poetic expression, the representation of reality. For, according to him, it is indeed right to compose a fine arrangement of lines and colours, 'mais si, à une composition déjà intéressante par le choix du sujet, vous ajoutez une disposition de lignes qui augmente l'impression, un

15

clair-obscur saisissant pour l'imagination, une couleur adaptée aux caractères, vous avez résolu un problème plus difficile, et, encore une fois, vous êtes supérieur: c'est l'harmonie et ses combinaisons adaptées à un chant unique.' [m]

So in Delacroix's art we witness two requirements that might contradict each other if they had not been brought to a synthesis in such a convincing way, viz, the inclination to develop harmonies of colour in full freedom and the demand to render reality in a pure and telling manner. That which Delacroix tries to define is something that in former centuries artists had done intuitively without raising so many problems. The artistic act representing reality without the inclusion of so many details of what was to be seen somewhere at a certain moment, now required more precise justification. For man's relation to nature had become problematic in all kind of ways, because either a freedom was sought that was detached from nature (in romanticism), or only the depiction of what the eye can perceive was thought to be meaningful (in a naturalistic conception). We might almost say that here Delacroix upholds an old painter's tradition which before him had found its most beautiful formulation in the works of Rubens and Rembrandt. He does so at a time that did not understand it any longer, and thus he hands it down to the next generation. As we hope to show, it is precisely at this point that we must look for the most positive value of the art and the theories of the synthetists at the end of the century.

So to Delacroix the great problem was that of the relation of a work of art to reality, because his observation and his manner were different from those of his contemporaries. 'Nos modernes', he says, 'ne peignent plus seulement les sentiments; ils décrivent l'extérieur, ils analysent tout.' [n] Yet he does not condemn a thorough study of nature, on the contrary, as may appear from his landscapes, his 'coins d'atelier', and his studies of the model. But we shall never find such a study as that after Mademoiselle Rose of 1821 in the Louvre used in the great compositions that can no longer be considered as studies. On the contrary, more than once he speaks of his experience that work done directly from nature is not really good, and that he only comes nearer to his ideal when he works out what he has found by directly studying nature, because 'mes intentions sont plus prononcées et les choses inutiles éloignées'.[o] For he abides by his

16

opinion that human interpretation, human feelings with respect to the facts of nature, to what the eye perceives in the strict sense of the word, are essential, both to human experience and to art. He may say as sharply as he can—and here he follows the motive of freedom of Humanistic Romanticism—that 'l'exécution la plus soignée dans les détails ne donnera pas cette unité qui résulte de je ne sais quelle puissance créatrice dont la source est indéfinissable,' p he certainly does not strive after the unrestrained expression of absolute freedom in the modern sense. He has certainly reflected on the relation of the sensorily given facts and that which is in the artist's mind as an ideal first, that which he creates according to his 'imagination'.[16] It can hardly cause any surprise that his answer is in line with eighteenth century philosophy q which has struggled with this problem from its strictly subjectivistic-sensualistic standpoint.[17] 'Le fait est comme rien, puisqu'il passe. Il n'en reste que l'idée; réellement même il n'existe que dans l'idée, puisqu'elle lui donne une couleur ... (C'est) ce qui s'y passe quand la faculté créatrice s'empare d'elle (l'idée) pour animer le monde réel (which is given in the 'faits passagers') et en tirer des tableaux d'imagination. Elle compose, c'est-à-dire qu'elle idéalise et choisit.' r

Thus Delacroix almost inevitably arrives at the thought which was to be in the centre of the meditations on the theory of art at the end of the century, viz., that the figures and the things represented in a work of art are mere signs, symbols. This is why Delacroix writes about painting: 'Ces figures, ces objets, qui semblent la chose même à une certaine partie de votre être intelligent, semblent comme un pont solide sur lequel l'imagination s'appuie pour pénétrer jusqu'à la sensation mystérieuse et profonde dont les formes sont en quelque sorte l'hiéroglyphe ...' s In direct contact with Delacroix Baudelaire was to express and elaborate this thought.

It now remains to make a few observations on Delacroix's subjects. Although at the end of the century his admirers have never criticized him in this, they have rarely followed him. For Delacroix represents reality very vividly and directly, but embodies it in images that have only rarely been derived from the reality about him. He remains entirely in line with the great generation of artists of pre-revolutionary times when he is engaged on historical and allegorical subjects or derives his inspiration from such authors as Walter Scott. In

17

this respect he certainly is much less in opposition to the art of his own time than he is in his execution. Consequently he has never been criticized on this point by his contemporaries, nor by his opponents. He belongs to his age by his striving after historical exactitude in dress and environment just like his contemporaries. He can no longer follow the older generations of painters in their way of depicting historical scenes with suits that had hardly anything to do with the way people dressed at the time of the event.[t] But his paintings never impress one as the depiction of costumes or of manners, an exact reconstruction of the past.

In this lies the essential difference between Delacroix and his contemporaries as to the handling of historical data. On the contrary, Delacroix is fully aware of the fact that a photographical reconstruction of the events has serious deficiencies. In the first place, because a picture has to bring to light the historical meaning of the event recorded, to interpret the latter and to suggest it in line and colour.[18] His treatise on this matter in his Diary of the 4th of October 1854 is well worth reading. But in addition, Delacroix wants to be modern above all, i.e., he wants to reflect the spirit of his own time. As a result the subject itself thus becomes a kind of metaphor of the view that his own time has of man and of human history. He, therefore, states that there is no point in producing a Greek Achilles. Not even Homer himself has done so, for as Delacroix rightly observes, Homer's Achilles was the hero who lived on in the imagination of the poet's contemporaries a long time after the death of the real Achilles with his whole generation and all their ideals. And perhaps in reality he had not at all been such a super-hero.[19]

This view for a great part explains the secret of Delacroix's paintings. Even now they do not in the least strike us as cold and too much photographically exact and soulless like those of Delaroche. It is true that a picture of the revolution of 1830 makes an impression that is hardly different from that of a work representing the capture of Constantinople or the battle of Taillebourg. For in all these paintings we have to deal with the same living human beings, animated by a similar spirit, which fact hardly renders the depiction historically exact but not less meaningful for this reason. Their meaning is to be sought in the fact that they reflect the contemporary spirit in various ways. No doubt it was this circumstance to which

18

Delacroix referred in his diary when he made a note saying that in his dictionary—which remained a project only—he must also devote a long article to philosophy: 'sans cette philosophie que j'entends, nulle durée pour le livre ou le tableau, ou plutôt nul existence.' [u] In short, a work of art must be based on a view of men and their actions, otherwise one will never achieve anything better than a photograph or a reporter's reconstruction after the event. This very important thought at the same time implied the severest criticism of the art of the Salons of his time.

In Delacroix's work the whole of the great artistic tradition of Western culture was as it were formulated anew and integrated into the contemporary pattern. The heritage of Constable, Goya, Géricault, who had done the same thing in their own way, with all their personal contributions and additions, was epitomized in a grand way and made alive and fertile for the future. But only Baudelaire's words were able to make the true import of all this clear to later generations.

Baudelaire

The great difference between the ideals of Baudelaire and those of his contemporaries, not only of the 'Salon' artists but also of those of the still highly esteemed school of Fontainebleau is clear when we read his elaborate criticism of them in the 'Salon of 1859'. Especially its conclusion in which he once more states his own wishes explicitly: 'Je désire être ramené vers les dioramas dont la magie brutale et énorme sait m'imposer une utile illusion... Ces choses, parce qu'elles sont fausses, sont infiniment plus près du vrai; tandis que la plupart de nos paysagistes sont des menteurs, justement parce qu'ils ont negligé de mentir.' [v] These desires appear to have been satisfied by Victor Hugo's drawings, in which Baudelaire discovered a 'magnifique imagination' [w], drawings which can in no way be called naturalistic, but rather romantic.

Yet Baudelaire did not strive after an excessive kind of imagination, disorderly, uncontrolled and unconnected with reality. On the contrary, he did not want to have absolutely free play, but truth, the full human truth, which he could not find in the naturalistic art of his time, because there was too little that is human in it, too little of a vision. But also Grandville's art, a kind of pre-

19

surrealism did not give him the truth he wanted. The latter sometimes succeeded in making beautiful and good things, but too often
he changed reality into an apocalypse, and turned the world upside
down.[20]

Baudelaire's attitude can be best understood by taking into account
that ultimately he stemmed from romanticism and had positivism by
his side. In his own person he felt the consequences of the former,
and he was too keenly aware of its faults, the 'désordre et étalages
sans pudeur'.[x] But he certainly did not like the other tendency to
be found in the works of the landscapists, and those of Courbet and
his followers, whose art derives from the same attitude towards nature
as positivistic philosophy. To him, the child of romanticism, this
positivism left too much to be desired. That is why he tried to avoid
the shortcomings of the one as much as those of the other. In some
way or other he attempted to satisfy these two fundamental requirements, viz., human freedom and subjectivity on the one hand, and
on the other the interest in the reality outside of man.

Baudelaire was perfectly aware of this situation. That romanticism
was the cause of many of his difficulties and of his inner depression,
he explicitly stated in the words of the autobiographical chief
character in his *Fanfarlo*: 'Plaignez-moi, ou plutôt plaignez-nous, car
j'ai beaucoup de frères de ma sorte; c'est la haine de tous et de nous
même qui nous a conduits vers ces mensonges. C'est par désespoir de
ne pouvoir être nobles et beaux suivant les moyens naturels que nous
nous sommes si bizarrement fardé le visage. Nous nous sommes tellement appliqués à sophistiquer notre coeur, nous avons tant abusé du
microscope pour étudier les hideuses excroissances et les honteuses
verrues dont il est couvert et que nous grossissons à plaisir, qu'il est
impossible que nous parlions le langage des autres hommes ... Nous
avons altéré l'accent de la nature, nous avons extirpé une à une les
pudeurs virginales dont était herissé notre intérieur d'honnête
homme. Nous avons psychologisé comme des fous qui augmentent
leur folie en s'efforçant de la comprendre ...—Malheur, trois fois
malheur aux pères infirmes qui nous ont fait rachitiques et mal
venus...' [y] More than lengthy theories this pronouncement by the
young Baudelaire may make it clear that the situation in which he
and his fellows of the same generation found themselves was the fruit
of the development of the eighteenth and the early part of the nine-

20

teenth century. To begin with, the value of the revelation in Holy Scripture and that of the traditional—Roman Catholic—faith with its certainties were denied and considered to be without any real importance. And then the attempt was made to regain an insight into reality through psychologistic epistemologies. Later on came Romanticism which laid even more emphasis on human subjectivity, and cultivated its expressions in all directions.

So this trend of events evidences the revival of the old Humanism [z] which had been thwarted in its development by the Reformation and the Counter-Reformation. By the end of the 17th century it had again begun to reflect upon its own starting point and its consequences. At first the effort was made to subject reality to human supremacy in a practicalistic way, with the aid of the insight and the knowledge gained by means of science and philosophy. When this scientialistic ideal concretized more and more, human freedom was endangered, for this science aimed at the formulation of universally valid laws in the sense of the natural sciences. In the name of this freedom a sharp reaction started, especially in Germany and England, and, under the influence of what was happening there, although a little later, also in France.[21]

The results were manifest in the situation in which we find Baudelaire. Although he certainly showed the influence of Christian (Roman Catholic) thinkers—recall, e.g., Xavier de Maistre [22]—he did not turn his back on the Humanistic past. On the contrary his starting-point remained the opposition of human freedom to nature. And this was also the reason why to him this reality—which he still viewed through the glasses of the eighteenth century French philosophers—was a strange and incomprehensible power, a world which was fitted into his conception only with difficulty, and which put up a strong resistance against that thirst after freedom which was the deepest and most central nodal point in his view of life.[aa] In this way the estrangement from reality arose, a feeling of 'l'hostilité de l'atmosphère',[ab] and the dread which expressed itself in 'die Klage einer früh in den Stürmen des Lebens verdorrten Seele über die Leere und Nichtigkeit des Daseins.'[ac] Perhaps it was more applicable to his own work than to that of Delacroix that 'tout cet oeuvre ... ressemble à un hymne terrible composé en l'honneur de la fatalité et

21

de l'irrémédiable douleur.' [ad] And most clearly perhaps he laid bare his heart in the final lines of 'Les Fleurs du Mal':

'O, Mort,
'Verse nous ton poison pour qu'il nous reconforte!
'Nous voulons, tant ce feu nous brûle le cerveau,
'Plonger au fond du gouffre, enfer, ou ciel qu'importe!
'Au fond de l'inconnu pour trouver du nouveau.' [ae]

For the very fact that this contact with reality had become problematical and this reality seemed to be a strange, mysterious power outside of man, his most personal basic experience of reality was that of a look into the abyss, into the abyss of death. As this reality in its eternal similarity—for thus eighteenth century scientists had represented it—oppressed him, he must look for new impulses and values 'au fond de l'inconnu' of this reality itself.[af]

Yet he rejected the consistent expression of freedom, as we have already stated. On the contrary, retaining a strongly pronounced subjectivism and laying great stress on human freedom in opposition to nature, he wanted to give nothing in his art but this very same reality. Baudelaire did not wish to be a dreamer building beautiful day-dreams by the side of an outside reality, erecting a paradisaic dream-palace to take refuge in. He wanted to look full in the eye of those oppressing and horrible depths that constituted his reality.[ag] He wanted to live in the world of his own times and to reflect it in his art. The demand for contemporaneousness, the reflection of the spirit motivating men, the expression of the heart as it really is, has always been the guiding line in all his critical and theoretical views of art. Or, as he put it himself: 'Qu'est-ce que l'art pur suivant la conception moderne? C'est créer une magie suggestive contenant à la fois l'objet et le sujet, le monde extérieur à l'artiste et l'artiste lui-même.' [ah]

It is this effort which is new, this search for a synthesis between the free experience of the strictly personal and the adherence to what reality has to offer. This synthesis is one of the fundamental characteristics of the theory of art advanced by the synthetists, as we hope to show later on. For it may be true that he wrote: 'Le romantisme [ak] n'est précisément ni dans le choix des sujets, ni dans la verité exacte, mais dans la manière de sentir', but he supplements this

22

sentence immediately with the following: 'Il faut donc, avant tout, connaître les aspects de la nature et les situations de l'homme, que les artistes du passé ont dédaignés ou n'ont pas connus.' ai

How did Baudelaire set about to effect such a synthesis? By means of the idea of the 'imagination' to which he devoted the best pages in his Salon of 1859. This imagination, 'la reine des facultés', comprises analysis and synthesis,al contains 'la sensibilité', but is more than that. It is the creative power of man, 'C'est l'imagination qui a enseigné à l'homme le sens moral de la couleur, du contour, du son et du parfum. Elle a créé, au commencement du monde, l'analogie et la métaphore. Elle décompose toute la création, et, avec les matériaux amassés et disposés suivant les règles dont on ne peut trouver l'origine que dans le plus profond de l'âme, elle crée un monde nouveau, elle produit la sensation du neuf. Comme elle a créé le monde—on peut bien dire cela, je crois, même dans un sens réligieux—,il est juste qu'elle le gouverne.' am If we study this passage, written in an almost religious rapture, philosophically, we are close to Kant's conception according to which in his 'reine Vernunft' man is supposed to create order in his chaotic sensory impressions. Or, perhaps, because we are dealing with a Frenchman, we may refer to Maine de Biran,[23] whose voluntaristic theories are related to those of Baudelaire in many respects. To the best of my knowledge Baudelaire was unacquainted with de Biran's work, or, at least he was not influenced by it to any noticeable degree.an It is even doubtful if Baudelaire carried his reflection so far, or lent to his thoughts on the 'imagination' such a far-reaching import. We are here much rather confronted with an art-theory as such, which (and this is typical of those days, as has already been observed in the case of Delacroix) is engaged in a penetrating study of the relation of man to reality in a way that is closely akin to the philosophical problem of epistemology.

However, we shall revert to Baudelaire's 'imagination' and read this passage: 'L'imagination est la reine du vrai, et le possible est une des provinces du vrai.' ao We must not take this pronouncement in a strictly literal sense, viz. with the implication that there are consequently more worlds 'possible' that can be created by the imagination in total freedom. By this 'possible' he much rather meant reality as understood by the 'doctrinaires en question' with whom he was carrying on a debate, the people who demand an artist to copy nature. The meaning of this passage in the theory of art must be conceived in the light of the statement made a little further on to the effect that 'la formule principale ... de la véritable esthétique' will be: 'Tout l'univers visible n'est qu'un magasin d'images et de signes auxquels l'imagination donnera une place et une valeur relative; c'est une espèce de pâture que l'imagination doit digérer et transformuler.' [ap] In this idea that reality is nothing but a 'dictionary' in which the true artists look for the elements that can be adapted to their conception Baudelaire not only very nearly approached Delacroix, who had advanced the same thought more than once,[24] but he had undoubtedly been influenced by the latter's world of thought, which fact he admitted himself.[25]

The criterion for the selection of the suitable facts from that 'dictionary' is that 'tout doit servir à illuminer l'idée génératrice et porter encore sa couleur originelle, sa livrée, pour ainsi dire.' [aq] And this 'idée génératrice' is undoubtedly the work of the imagination, or, as he indiscriminately called this faculty of the true artist, the work of 'le rêve', explicitly defined as a creative day-dream, 'une vision produite par une intense méditation.' [ar]

Here Baudelaire is one of the first writers who penetrated to the admission that an artist worthy of the name will attempt to make his work into something meaningful because it is related to his fundamental view of reality, to his view of life and the world. This relatedness to that which a man has very much at heart finds expression both in his choice of subject, and in the way in which the subject of his choice is realized, in his approach, in the composition and the execution. The one as well as the other must be relevant to this man, it must bear on his outlook and his fundamental attitude towards reality. In this way we shall perhaps be better able to understand such a pronouncement as the following, viz., that 'un tableau doit avant tout reproduire la pensée intime de l'artiste, qui domine le modèle, comme le créateur la création.' [as] It is quite understandable that especially Baudelaire—and the kindred spirit Delacroix—were the first to see this and that they even took it as the starting-point of their theory of art. For to them the relation between reality and a work of art had become problematic. This was partly due to the fact that to them reality itself was no longer something that was a matter of course, and partly because the starting-point was placed in the experience and the expression of what was peculiar to their own personality, in which the humanistically conceived freedom assumed a particular subjective form.

This explains why Baudelaire was always greatly and profoundly interested not only in the way in which a work had been realized, as to technique and composition, but also in the themes as such. To him l'art pour l'art did not at all mean that art ought to be abstract and purely aesthetical, as this phrase is often taken to mean nowadays.[at] In his final discussions of the landscapists in the Salon of 1859 he himself laid full emphasis on this thought, as we have seen. In this respect he even went great lengths, and for a moment wished back the romantic landscape, in which was found 'tout ce qu'il faudra inventer, si tout cela n'existait pas.' [au] Yet this is an exceptional passage, and much stronger is his call for subjects which have the heroism of his own times for their starting-point. As has already been said, his conception is determined by his yearning for reality, genuine, living reality, the desire to know it, to penetrate into it, to experience it passionately.[26]

How was such relevancy brought about, how was the artist to choose from that dictionary which comprises the whole of reality? For an answer Baudelaire called in the help of very ancient theories. They were to ensure a firm basis and relatedness to reality for the 'imagination' without risking the freedom inherent in it. This duality is typical and determinative. Baudelaire was perhaps as sharply opposed to the older romantics with whom he had notwithstanding so much in common and whose starting-point he wanted to modernize —recall the question on page 20 (note y)—as he was to naturalism. For he did not simply mean to realize the artist's subjectivity, the strictly personal.[27] He wanted something more; without giving this up he also wanted to attain to something that had universal validity, revealing a fixed and permanent truth and reality. As the Christian religion, in its real sence as the belief in God's revelation, had lost its hold on the culturally formative minds, it was necessary for them to know and understand the meaning of reality in some other way. This was also the aim of the positivists, which they tried to reach in their own way. But Baudelaire wanted something more; he wanted to get a deeper insight and a more comprehensive view than was afforded by the social and psycho-physical 'exterior' of things only. It is not sufficient for art, he says, to be merely a cultivation of form, for 'l'absence nette du juste et du vrai dans l'art équivaut à l'absence de l'art', because 'l'homme entier s'évanouit.' [av] That is why, he says, art should go hand in hand with science and philosophy, for otherwise it would mean suicide to art itself.[28]

So Baudelaire wanted to furnish the 'imagination' with a firm basis in its creative activity, enabling it to function as a means to reveal the essence of reality—this was no less than the absolutization of man's outlook to the deepest truth itself.[29] He clearly indicated the way in which this was done when he wrote: 'l'imagination est la plus scientifique des facultés, parce que seule elle comprend l'analogie universelle, ou ce qu'une réligion mystique appelle la correspondance.' [aw] And in these words he referred to the very old theories that have already been hinted at.

That very old tradition had come down to him especially via Swedenborg, the knowledge of whose work he had acquired chiefly in an indirect way, through Balzac and others. For Swedenborg had made a deep impression on the romantics by means of his strange theories which deviated so very much from the tendencies in the philosophy of the eighteenth century. They had been in very close contact with mysticistic movements,[30] which drew their inspiration from similar sources as Swedenborg did, whose views however succeeded in fascinating people most. At least this non-rationalistic, non-sensualistic tradition was summarized in his name. This conception gave a different answer to the question how we can attain to knowledge of the principles determining reality.

Swedenborg

Swedenborg came from the family of a Lutheran clergyman. He devoted the first part of his life to natural-scientific research.[31] Meanwhile very soon he began to long for a summarizing philosophical insight into the whole of the cosmos, so that we need not expect from him an elaborate and patient investigation of some particular phenomenon.[32] This brought him into close contact with the new insights that occupied the contemporary minds, especially with regard to epistemology. Locke became the determining influence, and like him, Swedenborg denied any innate knowledge, and was also an empiricist.[33] But no more that Locke did he find any firm basis in this. On the contrary, Swedenborg as well as Locke inferred from it that our knowledge shows a deficiency because it is entirely dependent on our (sensory) experience. And this is the starting-point of all of his further development, which is, as it were, an attempt to restore along a different road the lost certainty of human insight into the totality of the cosmic relations. It is an attempt to defend the Christian truth against the relativistic consequences of the rationalistic natural science which undermined any certainty. In this science God was reasoned away, and any firm content of truth was denied to this revelation. For his defensive purpose Swedenborg did not have recourse to the testimony of Holy Scripture itself, but sought for an equally rationalistic theory as Locke's to attain to an insight into the 'supernatural' and foundational truths. With a view to this he consulted mystical and Neo-platonic traditions.[34] Especially his allegorical way of interpreting the Bible made him closely approach the already very old attempts to synthesize the Platonic or Neo-platonic and the Christian heritage.[35]

According to Swedenborg it is an effect of the fall into sin that man has to rely on sensory experience in order to acquire knowledge. Things were originally different when man had a direct insight into the deeper relationships by means of a kind of radiation of the divine Light.[36] To an increasing degree Swedenborg also tried to acquire knowledge by means of the anima—about which he theorized in a way that is strongly suggestive of Plotinus [37]—and he more and more wanted to give up the unreliable knowledge gained by means of the senses.

In this way he drew up his theory of the 'Entsprechungen' or 'Correspondances' based on the agreement between things in different spheres: 'Omnia enim Divina sunt exemplaria, intellectualia, moralia et civilia sunt typi et imagines naturalia vero et physica sunt simulacra.' [ax] This was in itself the consequence of a Platonic, or rather a Plotinian thought, saying that all things in the different spheres are reflections, depictions of the ideas in the intelligible world.[38] Also Plotinus' conception of the meaning of the soul is found again in Swedenborg: 'l'âme ajoute aux quatre éléments la forme du monde dont elle leur fait don; mais c'est l'intelligence qui lui fournit des raisons séminales...' [ay] This might be a summary of Swedenborg's view although it really reflects Plotinus' thought. Swedenborg uses

27

this theory for the conclusion that 'consequently' the lower things agree with the higher ones, and 'so' what is lower can be used in order to arrive at the knowledge of what is higher.[39] Swedenborg's very close agreement with Plotinus may appear from the fact that he now starts talking of the Egyptian hieroglyphs, which are supposed to be no mere representations of natural things but to express the inner essence of things because they indicate the correspondances themselves. It is a 'conclusion' that occurs literally so in Plotinus.[40] Remarkably enough, though, Swedenborg continues to give a theory in explanation of the idolatry of the heathens but does not speak of art in general.

The inference might, therefore, be that the Renaissance had taken over the old theories which had from the outset already been directly related to art—recall Gombrich's article on the Icones Symbolae, which demonstrates the spread of these ideas especially in the 17th century [41]—and had been transmitted via Swedenborg to the 19th century without, however, being applied to art theory. Balzac was to draw the old conclusions again in his *Louis Lambert* [42] and they were to be worked out in full detail by Baudelaire. The latter made these theoretical ideas of art fruitful for the remainder of the 19th century. But maybe this reconstruction of the course of events is too bold and we should consider the possibility that Baudelaire had some personal acquaintance with the work of Plotinus and with that of other Neoplatonists, like Porphyry, or with that of the mystics.[43]

On the other hand it should be borne in mind that Swedenborg was much more accessible to these 19th century people than the old philosophers and mystics. For not only had his work been published in a French translation about 1820 by Moët and Hindmarsch, but Swedenborg struggled with the same problems as they did themselves and used these old theories for the same kind of purpose. He wanted to compose an epistemology which far transcended any natural-scientific limitation but was in actual fact equally rationalistic. The old ideas were formulated anew, as it were, within the cadre of the problems of the 18th century and detached from the scholastic or the Humanistic environment,[az] which was perfectly alien to men like Baudelaire. It enabled them to solve the tension between nature and freedom, or, to put it in another way, between the ideal of personality and that of science [ba] within the problems of their time. In such a way, at least, the two elements could be given their due in a kind of equilibrium—even though it was only a labile kind of equilibrium—and the artists were able to choose their own way of expressing their personality in freedom keeping up the appearance of its being founded in reality.

Thus we can agree with Evans who in his study on Balzac's *Louis Lambert* writes: 'L'éternel dialogue de l'idée et du fait, qui l'a toujours tourmenté, Balzac le résout finalement en faveur de l'idée, mais le fait subsiste, dans son oeuvre comme image de l'idée...[bb] We need not occupy ourselves here with a penetrating investigation of the depth of Swedenborg's actual influence, nor with the question whether Van der Elst is right in his assertion that Balzac really developed his theories independently and only cited Swedenborg as an authority to lend his own conception the required importance.[44] For it is clear that actuated by the impulse issuing from Swedenborg —and possibly also from other mystics—Balzac arrived at a theory which at least differed from theirs in that he had given up any reminiscences of a synthesis with (biblical) Christianity. If he borrowed directly he removed every element from Swedenborg's philosophy relating to God, the bible, heaven and hell, angels and devils.

Baudelaire (continued)

It is, of course, simply conceivable that Baudelaire got acquainted with such theories via Balzac, so after their purification of Christian and 'supernatural' admixtures. For it is well known that Balzac had a great influence on Baudelaire, especially in the latter's early years. The very search for a synthesis testifies to their spiritual affinity. This also explains why later on, at the end of the century, people again turned to Balzac, i.e., the Balzac of *Seraphita* and of *Louis Lambert*.[45]

However, Baudelaire had elaborated these ideas in a theory of art and made them accessible to posterity. One of the reasons for this accessibility was the fact that he divested his thoughts of their abstract philosophical character. In his Salon of 1859, when discussing the 'imagination' he hardly mentioned this theory and straightway applied it in his examination of the artist's method. But his exposition was charged with the driving power of his view of life, which imparts its force and influence to these passages. He also

29

summarized them in a poem entitled 'Correspondances' [46] for literary artists to derive their inspiration from. In this poem, by the way, Baudelaire elaborated an image taken from Balzac's *Les Lys dans la Vallée*.[47]

Baudelaire's ideas have had an enormous influence on the generation of 1890. First of all he considered the theory of 'correspondances' to be the foundation of the artistic possibility of suggesting one thing by means of another, a sound by a colour, a colour by a melody, etc., or, also, an idea by one of the means just mentioned. He thought this so essential and natural that it would be astonishing 'que le son ne pût pas suggérer la couleur, que les couleurs ne pûssent pas donner l'idée d'une mélodie, et que le son et la couleur fussent impropres à traduire des idées; les choses n'étant toujours exprimées par une analogie réciproque (another word for 'correspondance'), depuis le jour où Dieu a proféré le monde comme une complexe et indivisible totalité.' [bc] But Baudelaire wanted to dig even deeper. As Swedenborg has already taught us—so he says—that everything both in the spiritual realm and in that of nature has a signifying function, is 'correspondant', we must attain to 'cette vérité que tout est hiéroglyphique, et nous savons que les symboles ne sont obscurs que d'une manière relative, c'est-à-dire selon la pureté, la bonne volonté ou la clairvoyence native des âmes. Or, qu'est-ce qu'un poète —je prend le mot dans son acception la plus large—, si ce n'est un traducteur, un déchiffreur? Chez les excellents poètes il n'y a pas de métaphore, de comparaison ou d'épithète qui ne soit d'une adaptation mathématiquement exacte dans la circonstance actuelle, parce que ces comparaisons, ces métaphores et ces epithètes sont puisées dans l'inépuisable fonds de l'universelle analogie, et qu'elles ne peuvent être puisées alleurs.' [bd]

Just as had been done in the 17th century, as Gombrich has demonstrated, the aid of Neoplatonic theories was called in,[48] to give every image, or every comparison, every metaphor an ontical value far above mere playing or arbitrariness. But what is even more, in this way art became a means enabling us to get an insight into the deepest meaning of reality, into that which determines reality. Thus art became revelation. Baudelaire rarely says so 'expressis verbis', but it is very instructive to compare that part of his essay on Théophile Gautier in which he follows more or less closely a paragraph of Poe's

The Poetic Principle. Thus Baudelaire writes: 'C'est cet admirable, cet immortel instinct du Beau qui nous fait considérer la Terre et ses spectacles comme un aperçu, comme une correspondance du Ciel', [be] whereas Poe says that man's sense of beauty 'administers to his delight in the manifold forms, and sounds, and odours, and sentiments amid which he exists'. And Baudelaire continues: 'Le soif insatiable de tout ce qui est au delà, et que révèle la vie, est la preuve la plus vivante de notre immortalité',[bf] while in this part of his essay Poe apparently does not at all feel the need of any proof of his immortality but states that this joy in the beauty of things is not enough for man because he thirsts for something more important. 'This thirst belongs to the immortality of Man. It is at once a consequence and an indication of his perennial existance ... It is no mere appreciation of the Beauty before us, but a wild effort to reach the Beauty above. Inspired by an ecstatic prescience of the glories beyond the grave, we struggle by multiform combinations among the things and thoughts of Time to attain a portion of that Loveliness whose very elements perhaps appertain to eternity alone'. Of the latter we can 'attain to but brief and indeterminate glimpses' ... 'through the poem, through the music.' These thoughts are summarized in Baudelaire's translation as follows: 'C'est à la foi par la poésie et à travers la poésie, par et à travers la musique, que l'âme entrevoit les splendeurs situées derrière le tombeau',[bg] which is something more, because here, a little nearer to Christian thought, there is a reference to a fulness of reality revealed by art. That is why in Poe fine art evokes tears because we are aware that it does not yet attain to that fulness of 'Loveliness' that he has mentioned above. This may be called a purely Platonic way of thought. In Baudelaire, on the other hand, these tears are 'le témoignage d'une mélancolie irritée ... d'une nature exilée dans l'imparfait et qui voudrait s'emparer immédiatement, sur cette terre même, d'un paradis révélé.' [bh] The comparison of the words 'glimpses' and 'révélé' used in these quotations speaks volumes.[bi]

To summarize Baudelaire's view of art we might take as our point of departure his statement that the artist after his own heart 'l'imaginatif', says: 'Je veux illuminer les choses avec mon esprit et en projeter le reflet sur les autres esprits.' [bk] Here the starting-point is strictly subjective. The artist must not be ruled by a universally valid ideal outside himself or formulated by his predecessors.[bl] On the contrary, 'l'idéal, c'est l'individu redressé par l'individu.' [bm] But this does not mean that Baudelaire wishes the artist to let himself go in perfect freedom, to give the reins to his imagination. But he wants the work to be well-thought out and under perfect control. This thought is already to be found in his Salon of 1846,[49] but later on he was no doubt considerably strengthened in this opinion by his contact with Poe's work, especially with the latter's treatise on the poem 'The Raven'.[50] For Baudelaire is not interested in the artist's own subjectivity as such, so that the artist would fixate in his work what is strictly personal and peculiar. But his concern is the artist's personal *vision of reality*. He can give such a vision by means of the 'correspondances', and the relevant and appropriate images and comparisons will occur to him through his 'imagination'. For this purpose he makes use of the images that his mind has collected, images supplied to him by reality as if by a dictionary, and which he now produces from his remembrance. This remembrance, 'ce souvenir',[bn] is, therefore, the direct bond with reality which, as such, must never be copied. For then the artist would kill the thinking and feeling man in himself.[51]

Something new is the amply elaborated thought of the 'imagination'. In it Baudelaire combines ideas that flow to him from different sources, as, for instance, Swedenborg's philosophy. The knowledge of this philosophy he may owe to Balzac or to somebody else, and he combines it with the existing idea of 'le rêve', as a creative day-dream, an idea that is also found in Balzac,[52] and especially in Goya. Baudelaire would certainly have agreed with the latter's pronouncement with reference to his Capricho 43—the well-known work discussed at the beginning of this chapter—: 'La fantasía abandonada de la razón produce monstruos impossibles: unida con ella, es madre de las artes y origen de sus marabillas.' [bo], in which there is also the equalization of dream and imagination. And further, Delacroix is sure to have influenced the formation of Baudelaire's philosophy of the 'imagination'—thus we might almost call his theory—Delacroix, who generally uses this term and rarely uses the word 'Rêve'. Lastly, we should not forget the great influence Poe had in those days. There is a striking agreement between them when one compares for instance Baudelaire's ideas found in his Salon of

32

1859 with Poe's statement: 'That the imagination has not been unjustly ranked as supreme among the mental faculties appears from the intense consciousness, on the part of the imaginative man, that the faculty brings his soul often to a glimpse of things supernal and eternal.' [53]

It is remarkable that Baudelaire nowhere gives a theory of beauty in the narrow sense of the word. He did have a keen eye for the importance of colour and composition, even for the 'dessin' (drawing) in Ingres' sense, and there are few art critics before his time who realized as strongly as he did that a work of art is worthless if it is below the mark in this respect—one should read his treatise on colour in the Salon of 1846,[54]—but as soon as he goes on to speak about art, such terms as 'intimité', 'spiritualité', 'aspiration vers l'univers', etc. flow from his pen.[bp] He himself is aware of this and even explicitly mentions it. He says that he has devised many systems and rejected as many. So 'je me suis contenté de sentir; ... je préfère parler au nom du sentiment, de la morale et du plaisir.' [bq]

As soon as he really discusses an art which is important in his eyes, e.g., that of Delacroix, his thoughts try to penetrate deeply and to grasp the sense and meaning of this art, not exclusively in its artistic vehicles but in that which this art has to say. And the deeper such art penetrates, the more it satisfies the requirements that he, Baudelaire, posits with his own version of romanticism, the more he speaks of exactitude and truth. And then he even tries to fathom the depths of religion, which he considers as the fundamental relation of man to reality—the Creator and Norm-giver has practically already been excluded from his view, and consequently also redemption and joy. That is why this religion is not a joyful one. On the contrary. For the present we shall conclude our expositions of Baudelaire's views of art—it was not necessary to go into his literary work, or into his personality—by quoting his words on Delacroix, 'Mais pour expliquer ... que Delacroix seul sait faire de la religion, je ferai remarquer à l'observateur que, si ses tableaux les plus intéressants sont presque toujours ceux dont il choisit les sujets, c'est-à-dire ceux de fantaisie—néanmoins la tristesse sérieuse de son talent convient parfaitement à notre religion, religion profondément triste, religion de la douleur universelle, et qui, à cause de sa catholicité même,[br] laisse une pleine liberté à l'individu et ne demande pas mieux que

33

d'être célébrée dans le langage de chacun,—s'il connaît la douleur et
s'il est peintre.' [bs]

Edgar Allen Poe

We have already been in a position to say something about Edgar
Allen Poe's influence. Poe was a co-determinant of the climate in
which the artists worked about 1890. They were well-acquainted with
his work, since it had been made accessible to them in excellent
translations by Baudelaire. Indirectly the interest in Poe was in its
turn a factor working in favour of Baudelaire's influence, as the
latter prefixed many of his editions of Poe's works with an introduction. Of course we shall not enter into Poe's theories, nor into
his development,[55] but into that which may have struck his French
readers, into that strictly individual quality of Poe's that fascinated
them again and again.

It goes without saying that they will have been struck by the
eccentric nature of Poe's stories, on the one hand gruesome, strange,
exceptional, weird, and on the other hand never so fantastic that they
could not have happened like that in reality. Even the very sharp
analysis of the events whose every element was in itself no more than
natural contributed to the total effect of something grisly and
fantastic. It must have made a deep impression on those who sided
with Baudelaire or were influenced by him.[56] For here was something
that was properly speaking romantic, but never lost sight of reality.
And also, these stories were written in such a purely objective manner, sometimes almost in a cool and matter-of-fact way like a report
for a court of justice [57] (such reports, by the way, Poe had deliberately
allowed to influence him).[58] In such tales there was not a trace of
sentiment or of a personal emotional statement, and they must have
had a special appeal to those who wanted to retain the fundamental
characteristic of romanticism, namely, living out of human freedom,
but who rejected the romantic method.

Gautier concisely summarized this personal quality of Poe's in the
formula 'mathematiquement fantastique'.[59] Remarkably prophetic
were the words that the Goncourts wrote in their diary in the same
sense: 'Poe, une littérature nouvelle, la littérature du XXième siècle,
le miraculeux scientifique, la fabulation par A + B ... De l'imagination à coup d'analyse, Zadig juge d'instruction, Cyrano de Ber-

34

gerac élève d'Arago . . . enfin le roman de l'avenir appelé à faire plus l'histoire des choses qui se passent dans la cervelle de l'humanité que des choses qui se passent dans son coeur.' [bt]

This typically non-romantic trait in presentation and form, in the absence of any very personal expression of feeling, is very important. Mauclair,—and here we quote an author and critic belonging to the generation of 1890—therefore, writes about Poe: 'The tales of mystery treat of subjects without the aid of allegory, presented with all the relief belonging to the facts of real life; and the strangest of them always end with a plausible explanation. The artist in Poe shrinks from all gratuitous and illogical suppositions; he detests the melodramatic, just as he does over-charged style and fortuitous inspiration. Far from drawing his fantastic element from an arbitrary distortion of life, he makes it, on the contrary, grow out of a more careful study of what seems to the generality of people natural and commonplace.' [60] What is said here is exactly what these artists sought themselves. Poe pointed them the way, or at least, he showed that the synthesis they strove for was possible. True, Poe had something new to offer,—and this was something that had a strong appeal to those who sought so passionately for what was new, unheard of and unprecedented—but these qualities were after all new aspects of the reality in which we all live. That is why he is honoured for 'le sens profond qu'il a de cet aspect non encore observé de la nature et de l'humanité . . . le grotesque et l'horrible . . . le sens de l'Exception, le sens Spirituel de la Beauté dans l'intensité, et enfin le sens lyrique de la Science—voilà les trois plus glorieux titres de Poe à l'admiration éternelle'—thus Morice in 1889.[bu]

All this he attained by letting the imagination rooted in human freedom dominate over natural facts and events—something that ought to strike Gauguin too, who after all sought for the same thing. According to Morice he often quoted Poe's statement: 'C'est la matière qui est l'esclave de l'artiste, elle lui appartient.' [bv]

Also Carlyle and Schopenhauer influenced the formation of the art theory of the Synthetists. At the time with which we are now chiefly concerned, i.e., about the middle of the century, they both had finished their work, but in France they were pretty well unknown. Their influence, therefore, was felt later, but then in a very

35

direct way without any intermediaries, and without any artistic or pictorial tendency or figure that was affiliated with their work, while to a certain extent there was such a connection in the case of those we have discussed above: Balzac—and through his *Louis Lambert* and *Seraphita* [bw] also Swedenborg—Poe, and Baudelaire. Indirectly or directly they had something to do with the great French tradition which manifested itself in such a magnificent way in Delacroix.

Schopenhauer

The philosophy of Schopenhauer became increasingly better known in France in the course of the 19th century. The work of Ribot and other writers on philosophy, and that of translators, bore fruit. In a large measure Schopenhauer's work attracted so much attention and, consequently, influenced the circle of artists—most of them authors— chiefly because of the fact that his idealistic philosophy was really a theory of art, whereas his other treatises, his observations and remarks seem to be less 'Deutsch-gründlich' than those of the other great German philosophers. Whoever dips in an edition of translated fragments of 1880—*Pensées, Maximes et Fragments*,[61] a second edition —will understand that a writer who is read and presented in such a way was bound to appeal to the French. This holds especially for authors who were accustomed to deal with more or less theoretical works, it is true, but to whom the genuinely German and technically philosophical literature with its typical jargon and problems was too exacting, if only for their patience—apart from the question if they knew enough German or whether there were translations of these works available. As a result Schopenhauer became the connecting link between the German idealistic philosophy and this late 19th century literature. It seems that Moréas was the first to point their attention to him,[62] but whether this statement is correct or not, they were certainly willing to listen to Schopenhauer's thoughts. For Schopenhauer provided the desire of these artists to assign a very high place to art with the help of a philosophical justification, whereas through others—Baudelaire, Poe, Balzac, Swedenborg—they had become familiar with a world of thought ruled by Platonic ideas as well as by a strong subjectivism. For this combination is the most characteristic feature in Schopenhauer.

A look into his principal work *Die Welt als Wille und Vorstel-*

lung cannot but give the art-historian the impression that Schopenhauer tried to modernize and bring up to date the classicistic theories of Winckelmann and his followers—which were connected with the Enlightenment.[63] Already the introductory sentences of this book strongly remind us of the Kantian world of thought: 'Die Welt ist meine Vorstellung...' [bx] We shall not follow the elaboration of this philosophic theme any further here. For our purpose the most important part is his third chapter in which he combines the Kantian doctrine of the categories with Platonism by positing that the will—which he identifies with Kant's 'Ding an sich'—objectifies itself in different stages, in which we can recognise Plato's ideas, while in time and space we can find the principium individuationis.[64] As, however, all knowledge is dependent on the 'Satz vom Grunde', the concept of causality, to which the ideas are not subjected, the great problem becomes this: how can we know these ideas in order to get an insight into the true and profound meaning of reality? The answer is: 'Der, wie gesagt, mögliche, aber nur als Ausnahme zu betrachtende Uebergang von der gemeinen Erkenntnisz einzelner Dinge zur Erkenntnisz der Idee, geschieht plötzlich, indem die Erkenntnisz sich vom Dienste des Willes losreiszt, eben dadurch das Subjekt aufhört ein blosz individuelles zu sein und jetzt reines, willenloses Subjekt der Erkenntnisz ist, welches nicht mehr, dem Satze vom Grunde gemäsz, den Relationen nachgeht, sondern in fester Kontemplation des dargebotenen Objekts, auszer seinem Zusammenhange mit irgend andern, ruht und darin aufgeht... In solcher Kontemplation nun wird mit einem Schlage das einzelne Ding zur Idee seiner Gattung und das anschauende Individuum zum reinen Subjekt des Erkennens.' [by] These two statements of Schopenhauer's contain a summary of his epistemology, a development of his thoughts so full of jumps. But the important thing is that this stage, which is necessary for the knowledge of true reality detached from the principium individuationis, is attained in and through art, 'the work of a genius.' [65] Of art, whether pictorial art or literature, it may be said that 'Ihr einziger Ursprung ist die Erkenntnisz der Ideen, ihr einziges Ziel Mittheilung dieser Erkenntnisz', to which we should add that the 'Wesen des Genius besteht eben in der überwiegenden Fähigkeit solcher Kontemplation.' [bz] When these thoughts are worked out in more detail we come upon an artistic ideal of a strongly classicistic

37

stamp, for which Schopenhauer had been made enthusiastic especially by the work of Goethe and that of Fernow. We need not concern ourselves any further with this, as it did not have any strong appeal to a later generation, which had entirely outgrown the old classicism.

They will, however, have been struck by the fact that Schopenhauer declared art to be an eminent means to reveal deeper ideas of reality. It could penetrate deeper than the exact sciences without losing any of its certainty, and without losing sight of reality. And as there was question of genius, human freedom was preserved, and the artist was not forced into a strait-jacket of fixed norms and laws. The latter statement was valid in sofar as what followed about his clearly delineated artistic ideals was not taken too seriously.

What made the authors and poets about 1890 so very willing to listen to Schopenhauer as to a kindred soul, will no doubt have been his pessimism, his contempt for all that was 'ordinary' reality. 'Le monde, c'est l'enfer, et les hommes se partagent en âmes tourmentées et en diables tourmenteurs'—this is what they could read and sympathise with in the above-mentioned anthology.[ca] And pronouncements like those that will follow now, which from Schopenhauer's own theory are perhaps not so easy to defend, will have been highly appreciated by them, taught as they had been by Baudelaire and the others we have already mentioned: 'Un roman est d'un ordre d'autant plus noble et élevé qu'il pénètre dans la vie intérieure et qu'il a moins d'aventures... La tâche du romancier n'est pas de nous raconter de grands événements, mais de rendre les petites choses intéressantes,'[cb] or, to conclude: 'Le style est la physionomie de l'esprit.'[cb] We quote these pronouncements to explain why these men turned to Schopenhauer. For without his pessimism and without such less intrinsically philosophical opinions on art they would probably never have penetrated to Schopenhauer, even though he provided them with ever such a beautiful armature for the defence of their own views. For in the last analysis Schopenhauer's criticism of the German way of writing with its long paragraphs was also applicable to his own style which was no less cumbersome and obscure.[66]

For the same reason the influence of *Eduard von Hartmann* with his biologistic philosophy will not have been of much importance. In addition, we should not forget that he had no theory of art and no playful observations to offer by the side of his principal work. It will therefore have been rather a matter of fashion to speak about von Hartmann, although he was nearer to them in sofar as he really tried to work the exact data of natural science into his metaphysics. His tone and the totality of his conception, however, are by no means positivistic. He formulated his purpose in the demand to gain 'spekulative Resultate nach induktiv-naturwissenschaftlicher Methode', ᶜᶜ, so the effort to bring about a synthesis of the results of the idealistic philosophy with what positivism had yielded. We cannot help receiving the impression that in this procedure there is something laboured; there is something strained also in his passion for system in the sense of the earlier totality conceptions. However this may be, there is scarcely a trace of any real influence to be found, and it would be hardly conceivable at that. For notwithstanding the affinity of their striving, there was too great a difference in their environment, their intentions and direct aims for the artists to study Hartmann's abstruse principal work.

Carlyle

It cannot be surprising that Carlyle was a thinker who influenced the circle of the authors and artists of the last quarter of the century. Any one who studies his works enters into a world of thought which is in many respects related to that of Baudelaire and Schopenhauer. The agreement especially with the latter's work is striking, undoubtedly so, if these two are viewed on the level on which the above-mentioned artists will have considered them—for they were not interested in strictly technical-philosophical questions, no more will they have cared for problems of the history of philosophy. But what will certainly have rendered Carlyle more palatable than Schopenhauer is the form he had given to his ideas. His *Sartor Resartus* is in itself almost a work of art, fascinating and written in a richly imaginative style, playful, not in the least dry and strictly matter-of-fact in its logical argumentation. No doubt there is some scholarly pedantry, but it changes into playful wit owing to the somewhat bantering way in which Carlyle advances his thoughts. The very fact of his jotting down his views as if he hardly understands them himself and does not in the least take them seriously renders his work so attractive. We can, therefore, hardly be surprised

that Gauguin occupied himself with this book—Gauguin, too, liked
to make fun of what others took so seriously and what was at bottom
also near to his own heart, witness the dish in which he wrote 'Vive
la sintaize',[67] to which we hope to revert again. That Gauguin really
knew Carlyle's *Sartor Resartus* may appear from his portrait of
Meyer de Haan,[68] in which it lies on the table by the side of Milton's
Le Paradis Perdu.

The interest in Carlyle was especially roused by the work of Taine,
the positivistic philosopher who busied himself so much with art,
particularly in his *Histoire de la Littérature Anglaise* of 1864, and
L'idéalisme anglais, étude sur Carlyle of the same year. It would be
inconceivable for the symbolists and the synthetists not to have
immediately tried to know more of this author on reading the following quotation from the former work: 'Les faits saisis par cette
imagination véhémente s'y fondent comme dans une flamme... Les
idées, changées en hallucination, perdent leur solidité; les êtres
semblent des rêves... Le mysticisme entre comme une fumée dans
les parois surchauffées de l'intelligence qui craque.' [cd] What symbolist or synthetist would not have liked his own work to have been
written about in this way?

In his *Sartor Resartus* Carlyle writes about a German philosopher
Professor Teufelsdröck—who personified German idealistic philosophy, inclusive of Schopenhauer—who lives at Weissnichtwo in the
Wahngasse. Carlyle has happened to make the acquaintance of the
professor's remarkable philosophy of clothes, and lavishly quotes from
his confused notes and books. For Teufelsdröck may be muddle-
headed, his chief thoughts are perhaps not unimportant. And in this
disguise Carlyle explains his ideas in the most fantastic way. We
learn that he gets into a great crisis when he has been seized by the
'Spirit of Inquiry'. 'Thus must the bewildered Wanderer stand, as
so many have done, shouting question after question into the Sibyl-
Cave of Destiny, and receive no answer but an Echo. It is all a grim
Desert...' [69] 'From Suicide only a certain after-shine (Nachschein)
of Christianity held me'.[70] But when this mood has been on him, he
shakes himself loose and becomes aware of being a 'Child of Freedom'.[71] As such he does not turn his back upon reality, on the contrary, 'Yes here, in this poor miserable, hampered, despicable Actual,
wherein thou even now standest, here or nowhere is thy Ideal: work

it out therefrom; and working, believe, live, be free. Fool! The Ideal is in thyself, the Impediment too is in thyself: thy Condition is but the stuff thou art to shape that same Ideal out of: what matters whether such stuff be of this sort or that, so the Form thou give it be heroic, be poetic?' [72] Will not such a train of thought, expressing the same thing as Baudelaire had done in an entirely different way, have been exactly an answer to the questions which occupied the French artists so strongly in the late nineteenth century?

When we read on, we see that also in Carlyle there is the same combination of 'Imagination' and symbol as is found in Baudelaire, in which in a similar way man's freedom is upheld, and yet, at the same time, man's work is given a deep, very deep significance as the unveiling of truth. 'Fantasy' is 'the organ of the godlike' and 'Man thereby, though based, to all seeming on the small visible, does nevertheless extend down into the infinite deeps of the Invisible ...' [73] And this happens because he creates symbols in which there is 'concealment and yet revelation'. 'For it is here that Fantasy with her mystic wonderland plays into the small prose domain of Sense, and becomes incorporated therewith. In the Symbol proper, what we call a Symbol, there is ever, more or less distinctly and directly, some embodiment and revelation of the Infinite; the Infinite is made to blend itself with the Finite, to stand visible, and as it were attainable there ... He everywhere finds himself encompassed with Symbols ...: the Universe is but one vast Symbol of God; nay, if thou wilt have it, what is man himself but a symbol of God; is not all that he does symbolical; a revelation to Sense of the mystic god-given Force that is in him; a 'Gospel of Freedom', which he, the 'Messiah of Nature', preaches, as he can, by act and word?' [74]

The relation between nature investigated by science and the 'imagination' is like this: 'The understanding is indeed thy window, too clear thou canst not make it; but Fantasy is thy eye, with its colour-giving retina, healthy or diseased.' [75] In Carlyle, too, these thoughts are directly connected with the meaning of a work of art, in accordance with a very old tradition that started with Plotinus: 'Let but the Godlike manifest itself to Sense; let but Eternity look, more or less visibly, through the Time-Figure (Zeitbild)!' For this is found in a true work of art: 'in them wilt thou discern Eternity, looking through Time; the Godlike rendered visible.' [76]

41

With Carlyle we close the series of literati and theorists who influenced the world of thought of the generation of 1885 and 1890.
These figures showed the artists the way how to form their ideas on
art. In each of these writers we see old traditions appear in a new
dress, old ideas thought out in connection with the new spiritual
situation in which the attempt was made to overcome scientialistic
thought with its over-estimation of the natural-scientific method in
order to make room for human freedom.

Art in the realistic tradition

Turning to pictorial art again, we will first follow the line of
realism. It had its roots as early as the 18th century, as we have seen,
but it became something typically nineteenth century in the hands
of Gros and Géricault. In their works we find pictures of important
events of their own time which are exact representations but not
without some rhetoric in a baroque sense. The principal work of
Géricault, 'Le Radeau de la Méduse', is the grand and new formulation of this conception. The interest in reality itself is great,
also, or perhaps especially in its deviations, in its vehement
appearance as distinct from the commonplace. We are referring to
the portraits of lunatics that Géricault did in behalf of the scientific
study of his friend Dr. Georget.[77] It is especially the latter element
that is new, and more than the style it is precisely the subjects that
constitute the great and striking difference between this kind of art
and the baroque paintings of the 17th and the 18th centuries.

The next important artist in this tradition is *Daumier*. In principle and as a starting-point his art is one that is occupied with
everyday occurrences, politics, customs and social abuses. He is a
realist, but if anywhere it is here in this work that this term clearly
denotes something quite different in France from what it meant in
seventeenth century Holland. For here the artist does not in the least
try to contemplate lovingly the ordinary and the familiar about him,
to sing a song about the beautiful things presenting themselves to
his eyes; quite the other way round, according to Baudelaire here
are seen to 'défiler devant vos yeux, dans sa réalité fantastique et
saisissante, tout ce qu'une grande ville contient de vivantes mon-
struosités.' [ce] Daumier expressed his view of the politics of his time
with such conviction that many people can only look at the events

42

of his time through his glasses. He was a typical republican revolutionary. He not only exposed the personal frailties and faults (which he may have very shrewdly detected) of the various bearers of authority, but he did so in a manner that struck a blow at their office as such. For this office, this authority, Daumier had no respect. More than once one feels that he was concerned with their authority rather than with the individual personalities as such. He also mercilessly castigated what was bourgeois, all that did not wish or was unable to conform to the revolutionary style of living. And though more than once he hit the nail on the head, one asks oneself whether he did not pull down rather than build up, drag through the mire rather than show the relative nature of things in a truly humoristic vein.

The most important work for our subject is probably his series 'L'histoire ancienne'. In this series he disposes of every kind of classicism in such a radical way that it will no longer have been possible for an artist to paint a really classical 'Narcissus' of rare beauty in all seriousness and dignity after having seen, e.g., Daumier's 'Narcissus'. After all Daumier had reached his effects by thoroughly thinking out these stories from antiquity in a sober and realistic way and having them enacted by ordinary people whom he represented in a way directly opposite to the idealizing method. This is one of the causes why later on the classicistic subjects are no longer found, not even when it is possible to speak of a Renaissance of Classicism in the sense of R. Rey's book.[78] What would e.g. Seurat's art have been like if this strong realistic anti-classicist tendency in which this series of lithographs represents an important phase had not caused every classical subject as such to appear to be meaningless and untruthful, as something lifeless and unreal? There is no point in analysing this series in great detail here, but it is difficult to overestimate the importance of this work (be it in a negative sense) especially for the iconography of the art of the latter half of the century.

In *Constantin Guys* we find a man who as an illustrator and draughtsman directed all his energy to the easy, direct notation of the commonplace, the typical, life, manners and customs of people. With him every drawing was a summary of what he had seen, observed and retained in his mind. His importance for art history

43

was not great in spite of the long and extremely laudatory article that Baudelaire devoted to his work.[79] Together with Guys we might mention many other illustrators and draughtsmen like Gavarni, Monnier, etc.

The work of *Courbet* raised a good deal of dust in the middle of the century. Yet we may wonder what made it so remarkable. For, as has already been observed in our introduction, his method did not really differ so very much from that of the Salon artists.[80] His reform was chiefly concerned with the subjects treated. In his art there is no question of idealization, or of the interpretation of a subject from a particular idealizing or romanticizing point of view.[cf] It represents reality as it is seen, or at least experienced by the ordinary man— which Courbet was after all—and no more. This is, e.g., Delacroix's opinion, who when he made acquaintance with his work, wrote in his diary: 'J'ai été étonné de la vigueur et la saillie de son principal tableau; mais quel tableau! quel sujet! La vulgarité des formes ne ferait rien; c'est la vulgarité et l'inutilité de la pensée qui sont abominables; et même, si cette idée, telle quelle, était claire.'[cg] We need not discuss Delacroix's criticism in more detail, which partly follows from his own specific considerations—e.g., that a landscape should be in agreement with its figures so that the latter are truly standing in it—for its tenor is clear and shows at the same time that the name of 'realist' was well-chosen indeed. As a matter of fact Courbet himself expressed his views in the same spirit: 'La peinture est un art essentiellement concret et ne peut consister que dans la réprésentation des choses réelles et existantes. Un objet abstrait, non visible, n'est pas du domaine de la peinture. L'imagination dans l'art consiste à savoir trouver l'expression le plus complète d'une chose existente...'[ch] These few words clearly reveal a view of art which is entirely different from that of Baudelaire, notwithstanding the fact that the latter might have subscribed to the following pronounce-ment: 'Le beau, comme la vérité, est une chose relative au temps où l'on vit et à l'individu apte à le concevoir.'[ci] For us Courbet's special importance is that he approached art more nearly to reality and was more radical in killing any interest in allegories and in historical, mythological or literary subjects.

Thus he also pointed young painters the way who even ignored the social implications still found in Courbet's art in connection with his socialistic interest. Manet's 'Olympia' of 1864 is a good example of the way in which reality can be made the subject of a picture without any literary, social or other connotation. On the contrary, the new generation of painters, that of the naturalists, whose defender and literary equivalent was Zola, might even be said purposely to choose subjects that had never yet been deemed worthy of artistic interest. There is a marked preference for what is ugly, unbeautiful, vulgar—which in the eyes of the painter's contemporaries was certainly true in the case of the 'Olympia'.[81] Every kind of 'artistry' in the age-old sense of a certain idealization, heroizing or rhetoric is dropped. It was exactly this feature which made such art so difficult to understand; this constituted its novelty. For even Manet's technical reforms, with his insistence on brushwork, on paint, we would almost say, was after all not so very new. It was already found with Delacroix, or, in connection with Manet, we had better mention the great Spanish art of the 17th century.

The theoretical considerations bearing on this art are especially found in *Castagnary*, who calls it naturalism, to distinguish it from Courbet's realism. 'The naturalist school declares that art is the expression of life under all phases and all levels, and that its sole aim is to reproduce nature by carrying it to its maximum power and intensity; it is truth balanced with science. The naturalist school re-establishes the broken relation between man and nature.' Ultimately also this view is one that concentrated chiefly on the subjects. The following pronouncement clearly represents the way in which every view was rejected which follows from a conception of society deviating from the basic ideas of the great French revolution. These ideas had been formulated anew by the socialism and positivism of that time. 'This naturalistic art', Castagnary wrote, 'springs from our politics, which, by posing as a principle the equality of individuals and as a desideratum the equalizing of conditions, has caused false hierarchies and deceptive differentiations to disappear from the mind.'[82] Thus the artist was tightly bound to reality. But, showing the typical humanistic character of this movement, it was emphatically asserted that this conception would not and should not destroy the artist's freedom. 'It says to the artist: Be free!'[82] i.e., get rid of traditional forms and ideas with respect to the question as to what is, or is not, in accordance with the 'decorum' of art. It is

45

precisely this 'decorum' which used to play an important part in classicistic and baroque art,[83] but which now disappeared entirely.

The younger generation who at this very time began to find their feet, basing themselves on the work of Courbet and especially on that of Manet, still had quite different considerations originating in the art of the landscapist. They will now claim our attention.

French landscape

The French painters who in the early part of the 19th century concentrated on landscapes had to struggle free from an almost fossilized tradition. It is true, not so long ago some artists, such as Fragonard and Moreau l'Aîné, had set them an example, but they had to re-discover, as it were, the possibilities this genre offered to the painter. For the period preceding them was ruled by classicism, which was not particularly beneficial to this artistic genre, as it could only attach some importance to this division of painting if it was in accordance with Claude Lorrain, or better still, with Poussin. It is quite natural that by the side of Bonington also Constable became very important.[84] The magisterial 'Haywain', e.g., done by the latter, and exhibited at the Salon in Paris in the year 1824, proved that it was possible to practise the art of the landscapist in a fresh and direct way while reflecting the contemporary mind. More convincing than many words such paintings were a refutation of the prevailing view which, also in 1824, was formulated as follows: 'What would become of the landscapist's art if, through overtimidity, he feared to burst into the domain of history? What poetry, what high inspiration, could fire him, and sustain him in his labours? Continually trees and shrubs, and air and space and surface—what do I care for all these things if the artist does not throw upon these objects some sentiment of living animated nature, if he does not invest them alternately with sadness or serenity, violence or calm.' [85] No, to the young generation of painters visible nature was sufficient to quicken their inspiration, for it was precisely nature that fascinated them without all those side-reflections and rhetoric. They tried to express what lived in their hearts in accordance with the spirit of the times, which, after the manner of the French positivistic tradition [ck], or in a romantic vein, looked upon nature in itself as something significant that needed no justification.

46

Thus arose the new art of the landscapists such as Corot and others, mostly collectively designated by the term *'The School of Fontainebleau'*. They ware painters who were absorbed in the study of natural scenery in order to fixate nature in all its changing aspects. Their efforts were not concerned with the structure of the scenery as a whole in a particular part of the country, and that is why we can very well understand Baudelaire's criticism of Rousseau, e.g., 'Et puis il tombe dans le fameux défaut moderne, qui naît d'un amour aveugle de la nature, de rien que la nature; il prend un simple étude pour une composition.' [cl] And further: 'Je comprends qu'un esprit appliqué à prendre des notes ne puisse pas s'abandonner aux prodigieuses rêveries contenues dans les spectacles de la nature présente.' [cm]

To note down the visible effects of nature directly and quickly a new technique was necessary. *Corot* mentions it when he says that his academic teachers had not taught him how to draw. For he could not even represent what fascinated him because people—and we may add, the effect of nature—had already vanished before he had barely started to draw them. 'For the first time I essayed drawing in the mass, rapid drawing—the only drawing possible. I set myself to take in a group at a glance; if it stayed for a short time only at least I had got its character, its general unconscious attitude; if it remained long I could add the details...' [86]

And thus it may be said that these painters removed the veil cast over nature by Poussin and Lorrain, and rendered opaque by the methods of the 'faux classiques', and that they represented nature in its own beauty and value.[87] It has often been asserted, also in their own time,[88] that in the 19th century landscape painting became an important, if not the most important genre of pictorial art because of the desire to escape from the social and other problems connected with the growing industrialization. Perhaps we should look for a likelier and more positive reason to be found in a new view of life which sought to express itself in an entirely different manner and had already been manifest in Courbet and Castagnary. We shall not try to decide this point; possibly both factors cooperated in the same direction.

The new attitude towards landscape painting only gradually gained ground and its consequences were only slowly realized. Thus the painters of this first generation of the great French landscapists only rarely worked in the open 'sur le motif', and there remained a great deal of arrangement and composition in their art. Especially Corot often introduced such figures as Homer, Orpheus, women making music, etc., into his landscapes. A more striking feature is that these figures are really standing in the landscape and move in it in the same way as 'ordinary' people do in nature, whereas on the whole his women were painted in a much more naturalistic manner than was possible in the classical tradition after the manner of Poussin and Lorrain. They were really people of flesh and blood notwithstanding their occasional classical garments, like Orpheus, e.g., or the fact that they sometimes acted in a way which in a strictly realistic sense could not be defended—e.g., a half naked woman who has her hair dressed in the middle of a wood.[89]

Impressionism

The painters who are known by the name of *impressionists* started from these two traditions, viz. Courbet's and Manet's realism and that of the painters of the School of Fontainebleau. To them the great thing became noting down the changing aspects of the scenery painted immediately on the spot, while when they gave man a place in their art they represented him as he was in his daily occupations —e.g., while out boating or lounging at La Grenouillère. Degas, the figure-painter who associated himself with them, succeeded in making man as he behaved, as it were, unaware of the fact he was being portrayed, the chief subject of his work. Degas and also Manet distinguished themselves from the earlier realistic art by the directness of their vision, a building up of the composition in such a way that we seem to be confronted with a more or less accidental snapshot. In this they availed themselves of new principles of composition which they had found in Japanese art (to which we shall devote a special section below.)

It is possible that the landscapists had less difficulty in finding their way than figure painters like Manet and Degas, for the very reason that a landscape was considered to be of minor importance by the painters and critics of the world of the Salons, where the traditional formulation was in consequence far less strong and solid. As a matter of fact the school of Fontainebleau had already paved

48

the way to a certain extent. For the figure painters, however, there was a very firmly rooted tradition to combat, a view of art and its task which was still generally accepted in spite of the work of their predecessors and from which they could only struggle free with difficulty. For also Degas had done work in the classicistic spirit in his early years. That is why they talked and wrote much more often about their subject, and formulated their ideas in a much more articulate form. They embodied their view of man in their work, unhampered by the 'decorum' as it was understood by the ruling groups of their day. A landscape did not require any justification and this is why its devotees could concentrate on technical questions also in their meditations and conversations. On this point, therefore, they were attacked.[90] But already rather soon they had imitators even in the circle of the Salon painters. We are referring to a man like Bastien-Lepage.

Reverting to the figure-painters, especially to Degas, we find them very much aware of the new things they introduced in the domain of their subjects. This is directly reflected by Duranty's pamphlet of 1876 summarizing the new ideals of art as follows: 'Et ce que veut le dessin, dans ces modernes ambitions, c'est justement de reconnaître si étroitement la nature, de l'accoler si fortement, qu'il soit irréprochable dans tous les rapports des formes, qu'il sache l'inépuisable diversité des caractères. Adieu le corps humain, traité comme un vase, au point de vue du galbe décoratif; adieu l'uniforme monotonie de la charpente, de l'écorché saillant sous le nu; ce qu'il nous faut, c'est la note spéciale de l'individu moderne dans sons vêtement, au milieu de ses habitudes sociales, chez lui ou sur la rue. La donnée devient singulièrement aiguë, c'est l'emmanchement d'un flambleau avec le crayon, c'est l'étude des reflets moraux sur les physionomies et sur l'habit, l'observation de l'intimité de l'homme avec son appartement, du trait spécial que lui imprime sa profession, des gestes qu'elle entraîne à faire, des coupes d'aspect sous lesquelles il se développe et s'accentue le mieux.' [en] Indeed, this art was practised in a positivistic spirit so that Duranty was able to call even Diderot a witness to the fact that this art was undoubtedly founded in a French tradition.[91] It had been a tradition, however, which up till then had always been obliged to remain in the shade of what had been officially recognised as valuable. The once creative minority

49

had after all become a ruling majority, to speak with Toynbee, and was not likely to cede its place to this new trend straightway, a trend which carried on the ideals that had once fed the French revolution. With respect to politics these ideals lived on in revolutionary-republican and socialistic ideas. That is why properly speaking it is not surprising that in political and social matters most of these artists lived in this world of thought. But these are problems that need not concern us at this particular moment.

Japanese art

It would perhaps not be out of place to say a few words about the unquestionably great influence exercised by *Japanese art*. Especially in the circles of realists like Manet, Degas, and among the impressionists the interest in Japanese prints—we are not concerned now with pottery, clothes and small sculptures—was very great already soon after they had been discovered.[92] It would be possible that the analogous position occupied by the Japanese Okiyoye-art in its own country and that of the Frenchmen mentioned in theirs had some influence. For in both cases we are confronted with an art that has to maintain itself by the side of the art that is officially recognised and considered to be important. But although such an observation has sometimes been made,[92] we think it more likely that this interest was roused by the knowledge of having to do with artists who strove after a similar purpose: 'Une nouvelle esthétique, une esthétique plus libre, un dessin de premier jet, une exubérante fantaisie en même temps qu'une servilité de bon aloi à suivre la nature dans ses transformations les plus rapides', as Renan put it in 1888.[co] They will have been especially fascinated by the latter.[cp]

A far stronger appeal was made by this art to the generation that came to the fore in the eighties. For these artists sought for something absolutely new. It is true, they did not work in a naturalistic way, but nevertheless they left the bond with reality intact. The Japanese woodcuts are inspired by ordinary reality, but altogether lack the different characteristics of European naturalistic art, the sculptural quality of the figures, the representation of depth by means of perspective, the absorption in visible nature with its shadows, delicate shades of colour and such like things. Here art has the courage to simplify, to omit shadows as inessential, representing depth in a quite different way so that the picture-plane as such is not broken. This art is able to render the typical nature of things and living beings in their movements without surrendering to the very accidental aspects caused by the fall of the light and by the position with regard to surrounding objects. And yet it is an art that manages to present very unexpected views. But the latter are not due to the natural objects but to the artist who succeeds in arranging these natural objects on the surface of the paper in a perfectly new way.

And all this fitted in beautifully with the considerations and wishes of the artists of the eigtheen-eighties and the eigtheen-nineties. This is why we find the same terms used when they discussed Hokusai as when they formulated their own theoretical ideas on art: 'Il est évident qu'il y a deux hommes dans l'auteur de la Mangua: le naturaliste et l'idéaliste. Il ne faut pas s'étonner de ce dernier terme. Hokusai n'est pas seulement un amant de la nature visible; il est aussi rêveur, un peintre imaginatif.' [cq] And thus we need not be surprised that Ary Renan, whom we have quoted here, immediately points out an analogy with those artists whose conception of art we have already discussed, and who were so very important with respect to the formation of the new theory of art. After mentioning the names of Poe and Baudelaire Renan continues: 'N'est-ce pas une chose remarquable que de trouver chez un artiste de l'Extrême-Orient la réalisation plastique de ces rêves d'"au-delà', de ces songes nostalgiques que l'école la plus avancée de la literature anglaise et française a cru être seul à entrevoir?' [cr] The fact that he does not yet mention the painters is understandable, as there was then hardly any question of a school of artists equivalent to the literary men referred to (ca. 1888), or at least they had not yet clearly given public evidence of their existence.

THE GENESIS AND THE CHARACTER OF SYMBOLISM

If we wish to occupy ourselves especially with the theories of those artists working at the end of last century that we will comprise under the name of synthetists, it will be necessary to distinguish them sharply from another group working at the same time but with entirely different ideals. The latter group we will call that of the symbolists. In various respects they are related to the synthetists, but the differences between them are very marked and so fundamental that the two movements can certainly not be classed together. Symbolism also flourished in another environment, in closer contact with the poets, less far removed from artistic life in its more public manifestations. It will be necessary to examine its nature more closely in order to bring out more fully our view of the synthetists against its background.

William Blake

The first artist of any importance found outside of the 'academic' tradition in nineteenth century England was William Blake. In contrast with Turner and Constable and their followers Blake is not interested in nature as such. 'I assert for myself, that I do not behold the outward creation, and that to me it is hindrance and not action.' [1] His attitude towards reality is closely related to that of gnosticism, as he, too, held that the creation as such is evil, the enclosing of the infinite within the finite.[2] 'What is called corporeal nobody knows of; its dwellingplace is a fallacy, and its existence an imposture.' [3] He sharply opposes rationalism or scientialism, which had dominated the age of the Enlightenment and had certainly not lost its hold on the minds of the people yet. He considers all this as evil because it shuts off man from the life ruled by the 'Imagination'.

It is remarkable that we are again confronted with Swedenborg's influence. For not only does Blake take over the latter's theory of the correspondences but also the idea that man has lost the insight into them owing to his inordinate interest in what is material. For originally man was very well able to know the correspondences, namely in paradise—but we should not think of the historical paradise described in the Scriptures, but of a state or condition of man thus indicated in a mythologizing way (in accordance with the method used by Swedenborg to explain Genesis). Thus Blake writes:

'One day the world was a Paradise and Imagination was its principal Goddess. If the doors of perception were cleaned, everything would appear to men as it is: infinite. For man has closed himself up until he sees all things through the narrow chinks in his cavern.' [4]

We need not dwell on the Platonic image he uses, but would point out that both Swedenborg and Blake try to gain an insight into those things which the senses cannot give us a clear and true idea of, into the deeper reality which alone is true and genuine. According to Swedenborg this is achieved by a very direct contact with the world of the angels, in Blake it is the art based on the 'Imagination' which will point the way. Thus Blake says that his great task is 'to open the eternal worlds, to open the eternal eyes of Man inwards, into the worlds of Thought, into eternity, ever expanding in the bosom of God, the human Imagination.' Thus love and imaginative art are the redeeming powers of humanity.[5]

Art will have to start from the 'imagination' in order to grasp what is eternal and true. Or, perhaps, we must put it even more sharply—for here we find the same identification of the subjective view of man with truth and meaningful reality itself as in Baudelaire and Schopenhauer—by saying that the 'Imagination' itself embodies the eternal truth. Thus Blake says that in Paradise 'they are not talking of what is good and what is evil, or what is right or wrong, and puzzling themselves in Satan's labyrinth; but are conversing with eternal realities, as they exist in the human imagination.' [6] And therefore art will have to represent that true reality, not the material world in its 'vegetative' appearance. 'I question not my corporeal or vegetative Eye any more than I would question a Window concerning a sight. I look through it and not with it.' [7] And so he is able to say that in his imaginative art reality itself is represented, that it is a revelation of reality. For 'Vision or Imagination, is a representation of what actually exists, really and unchangeable.' [8] His art may be said to be allegorical only if it is borne in mind that to him this allegory represents reality itself and does not depict it indirectly: 'Allegory addressed to the intellectual powers while it is altogether hidden from the corporeal understanding (naturalistic scientialism we might say) is my definition of the most sublime poetry.' [9]

A closer study of his art (either of his pictures or of his poetry) shows that in a mythologizing way he describes the deeper forces and spirits determining society and the world about him.[10] These spiritual realities are personified and their mutual relations and struggles explained by having the personifications speak or act with each other. It appears that Blake's thought is contradictory,[a] because according to him the world comes into being by the interplay of opposing forces, by a 'Marriage of Heaven and Hell.' His mythologizing method is, for instance, very clearly manifested in the following passage about what we now call the industrial revolution. This revolution is a negative force, especially because 'the horses of instruction' (i.e. the science ideal) are let loose whose work consists in 'petrifying all the Human Imagination into rock and sand.' [11] In another passage industry is portrayed as follows:

'O Satan, my youngest born, art thou not Prince of the starry Hosts.
And of the wheels of Heaven, to turn the Mills day and night?
Get to thy Labours at the Mills and Leave me to my wrath
Thy work is eternal Death with Mills and Ovens and Cauldrons.' [12]

This is the way in which Blake's art is 'Imagination, vision, a revealing of the eternal, the Word made flesh, the Marriage of Heaven and Hell.' [13]

In a stylistic sense Blake's pictorial art might best be characterised as mannerism. True, there are different kinds of mannerism, and this term is not always used in a accurately defined sense. But there is certainly question of mannerism when an artist plays with forms proper to a way of representation which is no longer employed in its original meaning. Blake's figures are plastic whereas his drawing is often of a markedly graphic character. In many respects they remind us of the artistic method since the Renaissance. But they sometimes

54

display a remarkable kind of slimness and an excessive degree of stretch, moving often in a by no means ordinary supple manner giving rise to flowing and slightly rounded contours. Thus Blake— who was certainly influenced stylistically by Fussli—tries to make clear that he wants to express something spiritual, that his figures express more than mere reality on the corporeal and visible plane. This is also clear in his interpretation of biblical scenes,[14] in which he really succeeds more than once to bring home to us that those stories have a quite different meaning for him than that of historical events. They are only the embodiment of a deeper, a timeless truth. His intention is even clearer when he depicts persons not given in visible reality, like God, angels, or mythological visionary figures conceived by him like Enitharmon, etc.

So Blake operates with forms borrowed from the naturalistic (or classicistic) tradition, but he uses them for his frankly non-realistic purposes. Thus there arises a certain tension between the artistic means derived from naturalism and his decidedly anti-naturalistic [b] conception of art in connection with his non-realistic subjects. This remarkable state of affairs is always to be found with the symbolists discussed in this chapter: they use artistic means in the construction of their figures, the rendering of space, etc., that are connected with a view of life from which they have actually detached themselves.

John Ruskin

John Ruskin won fame by his *Modern Painters,* a work designed in defence of Turner's landscape art, but in his hands it developed into one of the most comprehensive views of art perhaps ever written. He does not build up a system, but supplies a truly admirable number of observations and reflections. He emphasizes the art of the landscapist, no doubt, and one might ask whether this is due to his purpose of defending a landscapist, or whether he really felt that the heart of contemporary art was in it. As a matter of fact he gives a classification of art reminiscent of the old theories,[15] in which the subject is decisive and according to which that art is thought to be the highest which depicts what is noblest. Later on, however, he occupies himself with 'the novelty of landscape' and tries to find out what can have caused the emphasis on this genre in the 19th century.[16] Finally he defines the peculiar character of this modern art of the landscapists [17] so that by this light he can examine the sublime reforms introduced by Turner in particular,[18] Turner, 'the first poet who has, in all their range, understood the grounds of noble emotion which exist in landscape.' [19]

What is the essential thing in art according to Ruskin? 'I say that the art is greatest which conveys to the mind of the spectator, by any means whatsoever, the greatest number of the greatest ideas; and I call an idea great in proportion as it is received by a higher faculty of the mind, and as it more fully occupies, and in occupying, exercises and exalts, the faculty by which it is received.' [20] Ruskin's way to achieve this is by a very close study of nature in all its details. But the important thing in this procedure is not the rendering of a particular subject in its smallest details—he fulminates again and again against the Dutch painters who are supposed to have done that ᶜ—but the great thing is the specific character of this natural datum, its structure and meaning, especially in connection with the greater whole of the work of art.[21] Not a thing in the work of art will be left to the 'imagination', except for the arrangement and the coherence of things—in which 'all so-called invention in landscape is nothing more than appropriate recollection' [22]—until the work of art has been completed in all its parts. For when this has been done, the artist may 'dash as much as he likes: throw, if he will, mist around it, darkness and confused light, whatever in fact, impetious feeling or vigorous imagination may dictate or desire'. For thus 'the imagination strengthened by discipline and fed with truth, will achieve the utmost of creation that is possible to finite mind.' [23]

To Ruskin also the 'imagination' is after all of supreme importance, notwithstanding his elaborate naturalism set forth with such great emphasis. 'The imaginative artist ... owns no laws. He defies all restraints, and cuts down all hedges. There is nothing within the limits of natural possibility that he dares not do, or that he allows the necessity of doing. The laws of nature he knows; these are to him no restraint. They are his own nature.' [24] In view of this there is doubtless some relationship with Delacroix and Baudelaire in their idea of nature as a dictionary. But there are also great differences. Ruskin much more strongly emphasizes the study of the structures of natural objects, of nature which has nothing problematic to him, perhaps also on account of his protestant origin.

Baudelaire and Delacroix, on the other hand, lay the stress on what is strictly personal and subjective, and assign to nature a less important rôle in a work of art. This is the reason why the passage quoted just now follows a direction for the construction of a work of art which is the exact opposite to that which Delacroix had sought, whose pronouncement Ruskin could never have subscribed to: 'L'homme a dans son âme des sentiments innés que les objets réels ne satisferont jamais, et c'est à ces sentiments que l'imagination du peintre et du poète sait donner une forme et une vie ... L'exécution la plus soignée dans les détails ne donnera pas cette unité qui résulte de ce je ne sais quelle puissance créatrice dont la source est indéfinissable.' [d] Such pronounced individualism, and such freedom with regard to the natural object would have deterred him.

There is no doubt that these things are also determined by the differences between English and French art as such. Ruskin and Baudelaire had something different in mind when they wrote or thought about art. For in spite of the mutual influence exercised by French and English art on each other in the course of the centuries they were of a quite different character, at bottom as different as a Frenchman is from an Englishman.[25]

Pre-Raphaelite movement

What kind of art are we to examine in connection with Ruskin's views? We shall not discuss Turner again, nor the other landscapists such as Constable, but the younger generation of painters making their debut about the middle of the century, viz. that of the Pre-Raphaelites. Among the three leading personalities it was undoubtedly *Holman Hunt* who followed Ruskin closest.[26] This Holman Hunt was an avowed naturalist, who was only satisfied when he had painted an exact copy of his subject in its smallest details on the spot. For this purpose he even made journeys to Palestine, and he was one of the first artists in Europe who painted out of doors.[27] Reading his autobiography—*Pre-Rafaelitism and the Pre-Rafaelite Brotherhood*—one cannot help getting the impression of something forced in his method, a stubbornness which is not quite justified by its results. He might be compared with Courbet, and certainly so when one studies a work like the 'Hireling Shepherd' of 1861,[28] a realistic representation of a shepherd with his girl. But in connection

57

with Courbet we had sooner think of Ford Madox Brown, who was a little older and very much akin to Hunt. His 'Work' (1852-1865) [29] gives a direct image of people working at the public road. If, e.g., we put Courbet's 'Stonebreakers' by its side, (1849, Mus. Dresden), the difference is also conspicuous. Madox Brown and Holman Hunt depict reality very accurately indeed, but in accordance with the requirements formulated by Ruskin their aim is to express a deeper thought.[30] A typically English trait is the moralistic tendency lending to the realistic vision a colour of its own. This shows also that there is a much stronger bond with the Christian (Puritan) tradition here than in the French artists who, after all, were sons of the French Revolution. Such a work as Hunt's 'The Awakening Conscience' [31] is in every respect almost the very opposite of Manet's 'Dejeuner sur l'herbe'.[e] The former picture represents a man with a dressed woman who is conscience-stricken, in the latter there are two dressed men and a naked woman who appears to consider this situation as quite normal.

Holman's art clearly reveals one of the aspects of Pre-Raphaelitism: the representation of universally human feelings and thoughts with a certain moralistic tendency by means of realistic subjects and in a very elaborate naturalistic technique. The fact that Hunt's art did not develop into something truly great was probably due to his lack of 'imagination'—which Ruskin also required after all from an artist after his own heart.

We shall not pay special attention here to *Millais,* who was originally closely related to Hunt, but rather soon chose the paths of the Salon artists, found in England just as well as in France. It is much more necessary to examine *Dante Gabriel Rossetti* more closely. For his influence was very great, and when the Pre-Raphaelites are mentioned his name is called to mind together with those of his imitators much sooner than Hunt and his followers, who perhaps during the first few years took the lead. Therefore Hunt may be right in saying that Rossetti had drifted apart from the original Pre-Raphaelitism. But we must bear in mind that the latter had as a matter of fact worked in a spirit akin to that of Hunt only for a short time—properly speaking only in his 'Found' of 1853.[32]

Rossetti's ideas of art at the time when he was without a doubt a faithful member of the Pre-Raphaelite Brotherhood, are found in his

essay at the end of 1849 written for *The Germ*. This essay showed
clearly that his art already then aimed at something quite different
from what Holman Hunt tried to achieve. It is a kind of art-historical study about an artist of the Trecento who existed only in
Rossetti's mind. He traced the development of this artist. At first
'Chiaro' tried to serve God by means of beauty, but very soon he
discovered that he worshipped beauty rather than God Himself. Then
he turned away from it and in the future he would produce only
those works that aim at 'The presentment of some moral greatness
that should impress the beholder: and in doing so he did not choose
for his medium the action and passion of human life, but cold
symbolism and abstract impersonation'.[33] So, we might say, he did
not do what the Pre-Raphaelites tried to do, namely, representing
'Moral greatness' by means of real 'human actions and passions'.
Thus every allegorical art is rejected, although Rossetti's own works
warrant the conclusion that he did not strive after the naturalism
of such men as Hunt. For he rarely represented contemporary reality
and visible nature as far as it can be painted. 'Chiaro', the trecento-
painter created by Rossetti, however, was not very successful in his
work, especially the people did not like it very much. Some incidents
revealed to him that this was not the way because thus he could not
come into touch with people. Then his own soul paid him a visit
in a vision—which by the side of Dante also reminds us of Blake
whose work Rossetti was well-acquainted with, as we shall see
presently—and tells him to give up those cold abstractions. 'How is it
that thou, a man, wouldst say coldly to the mind what God hath said
to the heart warmly?' Do you wish to serve your fellow-man? Then
you must 'work from thine own heart, simply; for his heart is as
thine, when thine is wise and humble; and he shall have understanding of thee ... Set thine hand and thy soul to serve man with
God.' [34] And then Chiaro sets about like Blake to paint his vision.
In short Rossetti's view boils down to this that an artist must express
his heart in his work and not only his intellect. His art should be
warm and true to life, and spring from the depths of his soul, and
give expression to its movements.

In the spring of 1847 Rossetti got acquainted with the art of Blake
after he had come upon a bundle of papers of the latter that have
since been known as 'The Rossetti Manuscript'. It also contained 'A

Vision of the Last Judgment', which was the treatise on art from which we have quoted when discussing Blake. There is no doubt that Rossetti was strongly influenced by Blake. The latter's idea about not working from nature and producing one's images from one's own mind was bound to appeal strongly to Rossetti.[35] For with his mind formed by the study of Dante and the medieval poets he preferred giving expression to the soul working with 'hand and soul', to adapting himself with difficulty to reality as understood by the naturalist. He lacked the interest in it that his contemporaries had— it is characteristic of him, e.g., that he did not take an interest in inventions and the discoveries made by natural science. He also had little interest in theories, as may appear from his judgment of the 'middle period' of 'Chiaro'. But there is no doubt that he was struck by Blake's idea of the different 'states' man had to go through, and by the doctrine of the 'correspondances'.[36] As is so often the case, it is hardly possible to decide whether the ideas made man or whether man chose the ideas in connection with his natural dispositions. For although Rossetti's mind, as we have observed already, had been prepared to appreciate such ideas as Blake's, it is certainly also true that his acquaintance with the latter carried him ever further away from that which people like Hunt were striving after.

He does not formulate his own typical art before he has detached himself from the ideas of Hunt and the latter's followers. Remarkable enough he is then all at once master of the technique which had given him a great deal of trouble before that time. His most important works of this period are his portraits of women, rarely if ever exact representations of their subjects, on the contrary, always stylized in accordance with the ideal type he had in view. He is in his true element only in his symbolical portraits of women, which were no cold intellectual products but warm-blooded expressions of his soul. He imparted to them a general meaning by embodying in them a 'state' and its corresponding emotions in a sensuous and spiritual sense. The lower part of the face then represents the lower element, directed to the senses, whereas the upper part with the eyes is related to the higher element, to the eternal.[37]

It is possible that Blake's influence assimilated by Rossetti in such a characteristic way only definitely asserted itself after 1861, the year when Gilchrist died who had been at work on a biography of Blake.

For then Rossetti was intensely occupied with Blake's ideas and art because he considerably contributed to preparing Gilchrist's manuscript for the press.[38] Although after 1861 his style is not materially different and he had already worked before that time in the same spirit as that of his later work in the treatment of subjects like 'Paolo and Francesca',[39] we find the first of these symbolical women's portraits after that date, especially the 'Beata Beatrix' of 1863.[40]

It is remarkable, or at least striking, that in his essay on Blake in Gilchrist's work he gave some critical notes with reference to Blake's use of colour. Obviously he had not understood its symbolical or expressive meaning, which cannot be measured with naturalistic criteria.[41] As a matter of fact such arbitrary use of colour is rarely if ever met with in Rossetti, but this does not detract from the fact that his art is really less naturalistic, at least further removed from the classicistic style than Blake's. It is certainly less graphic in character, although perhaps his book illustrations also show traces of the influence of Blake's style on their forms. In any case, he sticks to the method of representation determined by European tradition, which since the 15th century had started from the representation of actual reality. Thus his art no doubt has its mannerisms, although less than Blake's. In comparison with the work of his contemporaries it could not but appear to be very wilful, mysterious and manneristic.

Rossetti's influence was very great. In the first place he directly influenced a number of 'pupils', among whom Burne Jones and William Morris rank first, and also indirectly, or via the last named artists, a group of younger men who worked in a Pre-Raphaelite style during the last ten or fifteen years of the century. The term Pre-Raphaelite must then be interpreted in the spirit of Rossetti; for all this has little to do with Hunt and his circle. We are especially referring to Ricketts, Sturge Moore, and Reginald Savage, who a.o. published graphic works in 1893 in *The Dial*. But the style was much more generally accepted, especially by illustrators. For the influence of the Pre-Raphaelites was particularly strong in this division of art. For their original contributions to typography and to the illustrator's art, which up till then had been at a low ebb, started with the publication of Tennyson's work with illustrations by Hunt, Millais and Rossetti in 1857—the Moxon edition. In this department especially Morris, more than once in cooperation with

Burne Jones, created something quite original in his own editions of books which were at a very high level.[42] In this connection we must also mention the work of Walter Crane who was very nearly related to those we have mentioned. Especially his children's books published about 1880 have been very important for the spread of this new style, not only in England but also on the Continent of Europe, where there was a great interest in this new way of editing children's books.[43] It is also possible that even Gauguin made use of some reminiscences of this (illustrator's) art in the formation of his own style. But such influence will not have been very deep, and, if it existed at all, it concerned the method rather than the stylistic characteristics proper.[f]

The art of the Pre-Raphaelites had its social implications. A great deal of their work contained an implicit criticism or even rejection of the mental attitude in the life of their contemporaries.[44] In this respect also Ruskin no doubt showed the way, struck as he was by the avalanche of ugly products which resulted from the industrial revolution. A symptom of his interest in these things is the fact that he had part of his *Stones of Venice* printed separately under the title of 'The Nature of Gothic' to be distributed among the labourers. In it he praises earlier working-methods which he perhaps idealized a little in opposition to the work of the machine which was killing to the spirit and to beauty.[45] Characteristic of the attitude of the Pre-Raphaelites in this respect is also their joint cooperation in the 'Working Men's College' of F. D. Maurice, where it was attempted to teach labourers taste and artistic insight.[46] Thus we see that they have a growing interest in social questions, and an increasingly clearer awareness that in human society itself something ought to be changed if art and beauty were to flourish again as they had done in former times, in the middle ages, according to their view.[47] That is why Ruskin occupied himself for years at a stretch with more or less utopian projects in the economic field. But the most practical activity, perhaps, was the work of the firm of Morris, in which many of the artists cooperated who were associated with the Pre-Raphaelites. It was based on the principle of the self-activity of all the labourers without making them simple extension-pieces of the machine. This is not the place to examine the further development of these things,[48] but the important consequence was that in this way the style of Rossetti, Morris, Burne-Jones and Crane was transplanted into the field of the decorative arts.[49]

This is the origin of the style which under the name of Art Nouveau also conquered France about the year 1890. It was a decorative style with very strong linear qualities, supple curves, and no doubt often very imaginative, assimilating naturalistic elements. Especially what is herbaceous dominated in it.[50] In addition to Blake [51]—who had a considerable influence on the graphic artists, chiefly via the publication of Gilchrist—also the products of Japanese 'industrial art' had a stimulating effect. As far as France is concerned the publication of *Le Japon Artistique* (in 1888) was symptomatic in this respect. According to Bing's introduction this influence was explicitly intended.

In England all this created an atmosphere among the younger artists about 1890 which was not only revolutionary, socialistic but undoubtedly aestheticistic.[52] For the whole plan of Pre-Raphaelitism insofar as it was concerned with social problems, was aestheticistic in the sense that the artistic element was the starting-point and the aim of the entire movement. The art of Rossetti himself, of Burne-Jones and their comrades and followers, aimed at evoking a beautiful world. There was no realism to be found among them. It was really a dream-world, a beautiful day-dream, which sometimes assumed decadent traits because beauty was sought also in what is ugly and bad.

This movement was characterized by its opposition to what was generally accepted and bourgeois, of which the art of the Salon was considered to be typical; it was opposed also to the naturalistic character of the latter and its lack of imagination. It was a kind of revival of romanticism. 'At the bottom it was a revolt of the spirit against formal subservience to mere reason.' [53] Naturally the movement had a different colour from that in France where positivism and naturalism had been much more important in art and literature. It is, for instance, characteristic that in the nineties there was still a group of young artists who could turn to impressionism whose subjectivistic unconventionality was highly esteemed,[54] whereas in France this impressionism was considered as a dated view by the same generation.

With regard to ideas there was a strong French influence, that of

63

Baudelaire [55] and of writers like Huysmans. But it should not be forgotten that these theories were already known in their direct application from Rossetti's work, who not only in his pictures but also in his poetry adopted the ideas of Blake as his guiding line, which were in many respects related to those of the Frenchmen just mentioned. After all, the French theories could not have such a strange ring to those who knew Carlyle.

This Pre-Raphaelite art of the nineties especially aimed at what was poetic. Its subjects were, therefore, often derived from literature. There was a special predilection for what is strange, mysterious, horrible: 'Oedipus and the Sphinx' (Ricketts) [56], scenes from Coleridge's *Rime of the Ancient Mariner* (Sturge Moore), sentences from Poe's poems, such as 'But evil things in robes of sorrow assailed the monarch's high estate' or 'The night's Plutonian shore' (W. Heath Robinson). There were also subjects of their own invention: Reginald Savage's 'Behemoth' in which a monster inspired by Dürer's rhinoceros is seen to fly from a burning palace—on its walls there is a Cassandra wandering about, a two-headed Phoenix dives into the fire—or majestic mountains in human shapes (Sturge Moore). But what is lovely was not wholly absent. 'Daphnis and Chloe' (Ricketts), pleasant scenes of country life (Lucien Pissarro), or 'Centaurs, an experiment in line' (Reginald Savage). Elsewhere we find a kind of sublime mythical world with beautiful girls: Burne Jones' 'The Golden Stairs' and 'The Mirror of Venus', in which we see them admiring themselves in the water of a pond.[56] The atmosphere of the fairy-tale was not lacking—Crane's flower figures—, and are not Burne Jones' versions of Biblical stories really fairy-tales? The erotic element was present although it played a subordinate part; it was indirect rather than direct—the girlish female figures were rarely represented in a sensual way, on the contrary. The art of Beardsley, which was extreme in this respect, was an exception.[56]

Personifications, allegorical figures, symbolic forms, animals and things were very frequent in this tranquil pictorial poetry with its fancifully flowing play of lines and its evocative rather than clearly descriptive compositions. We call this art tranquil, because its figures rarely move passionately, they are never active, and in reality there is little happening—the primary thing is mood and narrative ranks second if it is at all there. The images are called up gently and, as it were, in a whisper.

This art can certainly not be called realistic and in a stylistic respect it displays strongly manneristic traits, e.g., in the excessive elongation and the linear elegance of the figures, whereas the play of its lines on the surface possesses strongly decorative qualities. But its means, viz. its images, are not new. In this respect it starts from the forms of the European art of the Renaissance. A considerable influence was exercised by Venetian book-illustrations of the late 15th century and by painters of the same period, such as Perugino and Botticelli. This is why we sometimes find surprisingly naturalistic details.

The world of these artists which Holbrook Jackson describes in such a masterly way in his *The Eighteen Nineties,* quoted already more than once, was certainly not a world of works of art and abstract discussions only. This view of life was put into practice, it determined the attitude of those who had been grasped by this spirit of the times. No wonder that dandy-ism was revived.[57] That is inevitable, for art is not something apart from reality and man cannot be divided into an artistic and a non-artistic part. For the very reason that this was a question of aestheticism, the influence of art (and of the theory of art) must have been stronger than ever: 'In our time we are agreed that we 'make our souls' out of someone of the great poets of ancient times, or out of Shelley, or Wordworth, or Goethe or Balzac, or Flaubert or Count Tolstoy... or out of Mr. Whistler's g pictures...'[57a] says Yeats, a typical exponent of this period. Well, the man of this time, this young symbolist, is caricaturized in a masterly way in the following lines from Gilbert and Sullivan's opera 'Patience' (of 1890):

'If you're anxious to shine in the high aesthetic line, as a man of culture rare,
you must get up all the germs of the transcendental terms and plant them everywhere.
You must lie on beds of daisies and discant us novel phrases of your complicated state of mind.
The reason does'nt matter if the subject only chatter of a transcendental kind.
And everyone will say, as you walk your mystic way,

If this young man can understand these things that are far too hard
for me,
Why, what a very cultivated, clever young man, this clever young
man must be.'

And elsewhere:

'Then a sentimental passion of a vegetable fashion must exite your
languid spleen.
An attachment à la Plato, to a blashful young potato or a not too
French French bean.
Though the Philistines may jostle you will rank as an apostle in
the high aesthetic band,
If you walk down Piccadilly with a poppy or a lily in your
mediaeval hand.' [58]

Rose†Croix

This English art, especially that of Rossetti and Burne-Jones, had a
great influence in France. There was a similar artistic climate there,
evoked by the symbolistic poets and by the 'Art Nouveau' movement.
There are many witnesses to this influence to be quoted. Thus, e.g.,
Mauclair writes later on, when giving a survey of this movement,
that there are artists who are indicated by the terms symbolists or
idealists, 'qui ont, jusqu'à une certain point, accompli en France une
oeuvre analogue à celle des préraphaelites anglais, ou du moins de
certains de ceux-ci, notamment Rossetti, Watts [h] et Burne-Jones. Ce
mouvement a été une protestation à la fois contre l'École et le
réalisme, et c'est en quoi il est curieux à étudier.' [i] Criticism of the
English artists that we are discussing was far from always favourable,
thus, e.g., that of G. Geffroy, who, on the occasion of three works by
Burne-Jones exhibited in the Salon, speaks of 'images mort-nées' [j]
and also includes Aman-Jean in his criticism.[59]

This Aman-Jean exhibited at the Rose†Croix exhibition of 1892.
In this group, assembled by the remarkable personality of Sar Péladan, a typical representative of this period, we find the painters that
we would call symbolists to distinguish them from the synthetists we
shall discuss later on as our principal subject. How very correct
Mauclair's characterization was may appear from what Péladan himself wrote in the introduction to the catalogue: 'Il nous serait donné
d'assister, simplement, à la concentration des forces idéalistes, au

66

renouveau de la mysticité définitivement victorieuse de la science, du matérialisme, de la Révolution, des temps modernes.' k This pronouncement at once shows the absence of a very characteristic trait in Baudelaire and his adherents, viz., their starting from contemporary reality in their art. On the contrary, it may be said here that 'L'art, c'est ni un torse, ni un tête, ni un corps, c'est l'âme, la foi, la passion, la douleur ... Tout art est idéografique.'l—in which the last term should not suggest to us what Baudelaire or Delacroix would have meant by it, but what we have quoted above from Péladan.[60]

At the exhibition of the Rose†Croix of 1892 there were works on view by Séon, C. Schwabe, Aman-Jean, Henry Martin, Pozieux, Dampft, artists who according to Germain really worked in accordance with these ideals.[61] Of course, there were also those among them who for some (perhaps more opportunistic) reason had joined them, but whose tendencies were different—we shall not investigate here whether or not Hodler, who also exhibited here, belonged to those we have mentioned. It is rather striking that several of these painters are said to be under English influence. It is even asserted that the Rose†Croix movement was characterized by it.[62]

However, this movement was not so very strongly represented in France. The reason was perhaps that here naturalism had created a brilliant art, also outside the world of the Salon, in that of the impressionists. The important painters worked in an entirely different climate. There were, therefore, no artists of a high order among these exhibitors. The movement was much stronger abroad where it had its centre in the XX in Belgium. For although there also the synthetists, and congenial painters, such as Seurat and his followers often exhibited their works, the attention was above all directed to such figures as Khnopff. The attention to the English was very marked here. It was said of Khnopff that he was losing his influence in proportion as the work of Burne-Jones, Rossetti and also Gustave Moreau became better known.[63] But also elsewhere, in the Netherlands, where the symbolists had very important representatives, a.o. in Toorop [64], in Norway in Munch, in Germany and Austria in the painters of the different 'Sezessionen', there are many works in this spirit to be found. Nearly always the English influence is very strong,[65] although more than once it worked indirectly via the circle at Paris.[66] This art was often the pictorial parallel to a

67

literary movement in their own country, which is very clear in the case, e.g., of Munch in Norway—in him, perhaps, English influence is the least marked.

That this art is entirely different from that of the artists we will call the synthetists, such as Gauguin and his followers, is at once obvious when we have a look in Dr. Bettine Polak's study devoted to the symbolist subjects.[67] Here the subjects mentioned as characteristic of the movement are the fatal woman, the sphinx, the snake, the Chimaere, the centaur, the bride, the lily, etc., subjects that are hardly if at all met with among the synthetists just mentioned. Symbolistic art often presented such subjects borrowed from literature, in an allegorical way, by means of metaphors and above all by means of personifications. They avoided almost scrupulously the use of the old generally accepted allegorical figures, for the important thing in this case was the objectification of strictly individual emotions and ideas in subjects which were often perfectly new to pictorial art. This art flourished for too short a time for the growth of a fixed system that was to a certain extent universally understandable. This is why their art is often obscure and their imagination sometimes far-fetched and bizarre in the eyes of the uninitiated. Entirely apart from their work, their theory sometimes suggests that of the synthetists, but the 'application' was so very different that we can hardly speak of a direct relationship. When, e.g., we read about Thorn Prikker that he does not want to represent 'de schijn der dingen, maar de mooie herinnering, die er van is bij gebleven', then this is a thought that we also find in Gauguin. But when he goes on to say that pondering on a flower he comes to view it quite differently from what it was ... 'bijvoorbeeld als een sterk omteekend stuk witte kleur ... met sterretjes eromheen, lijntjes die stil bewegen en zeggen hoe mooi zij was, hoe teer haar hele bestaan, dat zij zóó volmaakt was,'[m] then we can imagine that a man like Gauguin, e.g., on reading this, would have burst into scornful laughter at these 'travers symbolistes, autre genre de sentimentalisme.'[n]

As to style we may for the most part repeat what we wrote about the English style of this period. Its forms are still derived from those of the naturalistic style that had already existed for centuries, although they are now applied in a typically manneristic way and provided with graphic additions, formal exaggerations—e.g., the hairs in Toorop's female figures of this period.[68] This is character-istically expressed in Séon's method: 'Donc, MESURER figure et forme, enchâsser sa composition dans une ossature d'arabesques déco-ratives, élire luminosité et teintes en rapport avec le sujet à traiter... enclore sa fiction dans la vraisemblence...[o]

Although this art was entirely new and foreign to the ideals of the painters of the Salon, they still excercised their influence on it, more than Gauguin and his supporters. And this is plausible, for they do not break with the representational forms of the past, however man-neristic they may be, and their subject matter was as far removed from daily life. Thus mysticism could become a fashion.[69] But, of course, with regard to style they kept within the limits of what was generally accepted and shunned anything that might look too strange. Perhaps we may even recognise a faint echo of it in a 'Marguerite'—Goethe's Gretchen—by Dagnan Bouveret at the Salon of 1912,[70] really a very realistic painting of a half-nude figure with some vague phantom-like shapes in the background.

Symbolism and Synthetism

We have already indicated that the painters we group under the term synthetists do not think much of this symbolism. Did not Signac speak of the 'misérables déformations des Symbolistes?'[p] and did not Denis say emphatically that they were anything but 'peintres de l'âme' themselves.[q] In fact, the same Denis had said in his famous definition of the art of painting, just like Péladan, that the essence of art did not lie in a head, or a torso, or whatever subject of reality, but when Péladan spoke of passions, sorrow, etc., Denis on the other hand asserted that before anything a picture was a flat surface covered with colours and lines. As a matter of fact Denis empha-tically said that it was wrong 'à confondre les tendances mystiques et allégoriques, c'est-à-dire la recherche de l'expression par le sujet, et les tendances symbolistes, c'est-à-dire la recherche de l'expression par l'oeuvre d'art'—in which he called our synthetists symbolists.[r]

Indeed, the latter characteristic marks the most striking difference. We find a remarkable comparison mentioned by Bettina Polak, when she compares Toorop's 'De Anarchist' with that of Vallotton. The former is full of allegorical personifications, streaks of hair rising high up, whereas the latter represents an anarchist who is collared

69

by policemen in the street.[71] The analysis of the stylistic elements would show that Vallotton makes a much less direct use of the old representational system than Toorop, whose figures, although a little stylized, are after all more or less academic in their anatomy and plastic structure. Vallotton simplifies a great deal more and builds up his composition in very distinct black and white contrasts (without shadows) that cooperate in elucidating the subjects.

That the symbolistic artists were above all concerned with non-realistic subjects—and not so much with a new way of representation —is also implied in the criticism that Diepenbrock once made of this entire movement. We believe that its correctness may also appear from the fact that after all this movement did not develop into a truly general one. The pretentions were too little founded in reality and were not sufficiently proved by the works themselves. In 1893 Diepenbrock wrote about symbolic art as follows: 'Nu kan ik in de symbolieke schilderkunst niets anders zien dan het meest geoutreerde individualisme, dat in de waan bevangen is van algemeen meta-physische dingen uit te drukken dus het tegenovergestelde van in-dividuele dingen, en tot deze waan is gekomen door het element der reflexie, en door het werken met anti-naturalistische motieven.[s] Maar wat anti-naturalistisch is, is nog niet supra-naturalistisch, nog minder metaphysisch en naderend tot het absolute.'[t]

Symbolistic art

We have seen that about 1890 we can discover two sharply dis-tinguishable groups side by side. They are two entirely different spheres notwithstanding their mutual points of contact. We should like to distinguish a third tendency, if it did not seem a little strange to speak of a tendency in this case, as properly speaking we are referring to one or two artists only, namely Bresdin and Odilon Redon.

These three different movements are also found in literature. They run parallel to each other. For Michaud distinguishes three move-ments, rightly so in our opinion,[72] which all of them more or less clearly start from Baudelaire and are the continuation of tendencies that had already been found in romanticism.[73] One movement, that of the 'poésie affective' had Verlaine for its grandmaster, and may be called the movement of the 'décadents'. The third is that of the 'poésie fantastique' and centres in the figure of Rimbaud, whereas the second main stream is that of 'symbolisme', the 'poésie intellectuelle' with Mallarmé for its most important epoch-making artist.

In the years '85 and '86 the formation of their own art-theory is supposed to have started in the group mentioned last, no doubt also under the influence of Mallarmé's ideas. At that time Sarrazin draws the attention to the Pre-Raphaelites,[74] but their influence was slight in this circle. Much greater was the influence of Russian novels, on which, also in '85, Vogué published a book. It was precisely the interest in reality itself, but then inclusive of the spiritual forces working in it that struck them in these novels. Then Ghil is one of the first who gives a more detailed theory, entirely in the footsteps of Mallarmé, in which he clearly rejects 'les tristes vers', 'l'égoiste rêverie', in a word 'la poésie décadente'.[u] At the same time also Moréas published his well-known manifest of symbolism. These symbolists were doubtless important for the formation of the theory of art on the part of the painters, and this is why we shall discuss the personalities that are the most important for our subject later on when dealing with synthetist art-theory itself. The development of this literary movement need not be discussed here, as it has been elaborately treated in Michaud's work. In fact, the theories of the poets have always been given a great deal of attention to, so that they have been studied much more.

No more shall we enter into the movement of the 'decadents'. They shared the demand for freedom and the anti-naturalistic attitude with the symbolists.[v] From Michaud we shall borrow the following brief characterization of their strongly marked subjectivistic attitude: 'Tel est le contenu de la poésie décadente: le monde intérieur, mais réduit à ses couches les plus basses, aux émotions indéfinissables, aux sensations exacerbées, aux rêves que commandent les désirs refoulés et les exigences de la chair ... expression neuve: ... correspondances subjectives entre la musique des mots et la musique de l'âme, saisi en son courant mobile et fuyant.'[w] Indeed we find here what Kahn expressed in the following words 'The essential aim of our art is to objectify the subjective (the externalization of the Idea) instead of subjectifying the objective (nature seen through the eyes of a temperament). Thus we carry the analysis of the Self to the extreme, we let the multiplicity and intertwining of rhythme harmonize with the

71

measure of the Idea, we create literary enchantment by annulling the pattern of a forced and spiritual modernism.' [75] The last few words show where they deviate from Baudelaire's ideals, in contradistinction to the movement of Mallarmé and the synthetist painters, whereas in the use of the term 'idea' we may see them make a bow in the direction of Schopenhauer who had a great influence in this environment.

Negative attitude towards reality

This movement—and not only these 'decadents', but also the symbolists and, in a certain sense, the synthetists—is characterized by a very explicit aversion to reality. This is one of the reasons, if not the deepest cause, of their flight into what is subjective and detached from the outer world, modern or not. To understand the art of this period, at least some important aspects of it, it is almost indispensable to have an insight into the nature and the origin of this negative attitude towards reality.

This feeling of depression was characteristic for the romantics. Thus Sénancour wrote in his *Obermann*: 'Ainsi, voyant dans les choses des rapports qui n'y sont guère et cherchant ce que je n'obtiendrai jamais, étranger dans la nature réelle,[x] ridicule au milieu des hommes, je n'aurai que des affectations vaines: et soit que je vive selon moi-même, soit que je vive selon les hommes, je n'aurai dans l'oppression extérieure ou dans ma propre contrainte que l'éternel tourment d'une vie toujours reprimée et toujours misérable...' [y] This author has probed his mind very deeply, and he knows also that his estrangement from reality, his depression as such, is the consequence of the fact that he wants something more than this reality, more than is humanly possible in the creation.[76] It is the attempt to control everything, the wish to be limitless, lawless, which again and again causes him to come into conflict with that reality itself, because it cannot offer him *this* freedom. 'Je cherche ailleurs, un bien inconnu dont l'instinct me poursuit. Est-ce ma faute si je trouve partout des bornes, si tout ce qui est fini n'a pour moi aucune valeur'. [z]

The urge for freedom found here is of a religious [aa] character,[77] and implies man's wish to be self-determining, not subject to laws or norms he has not made or created himself. It is the old

72

humanistic freedom-motif that is again fervently and consciously avowed as the starting-point of all human (cultural) activity. Morice, in his influential book *La littérature de tout à l'heure* written in 1889, in which he enters into these things very elaborately, also sees this sharply when, writing on Byron as a typical romanticist, he says: 'Pour trouver et combiner les développements et les péripéties de son poème et de son drame, il n'a eu qu'à pousser à leurs extrêmes conséquences ses sentiments imaginaires, mais sincères, les sentiments qui lui ont bouleversé l'âme alors qu'il se demandait, exalté par la propre fumée de son génie et par l'électricité de l'air orageux: 'Si j'avais la toute-puissance, que ferais-je de mes ennemies, que ferais-je du monde?' [ab] And although it is important to know that about 1890 this profoundly spiritual urge was understood like this, it may plead in Morice's favour that in Carlyle there is a direct pronouncement to be found which confirms Morice's view of romanticism in this respect. It is even possible that what will follow was also in Morice's mind. Carlyle wonders how even a simple man like a shoeblack might be made happy. Nobody can do so, for 'the shoeblack also has a soul quite other than his stomach; and would require, if you consider it, for his permanent satisfaction and saturation, simply this allotment, no more, and no less: God's infinite Universe altogether to himself, therein to enjoy infinitely, and fill every wish as fast as it rose.' [78] Essentially, therefore, man demands no more, and no less, than being God's equal, the old wish-dream, always renewed, which Satan held out to man in Paradise.

Also in this respect it was Baudelaire who formulated the spirit of romanticism anew and thus carried it over to the generation working at the end of the century. In his Salon of 1855 he elaborately discusses the cultural situation in connection with the position of the artist. From the latter he demands that he shall be 'son roi, son prêtre et son Dieu',[ac] in short, a man who in the true sense of the word is driven on by the religious 'dynamis' [79] of the personality-ideal.[80],[ad] All this had been threatened with grave dangers by positivism, which had supposed it could bring freedom and the control of nature by means of the natural sciences, but had risked this foundational freedom by its very starting-point. For this positivism wished to formulate laws for everything according to natural science, and there was no certainty at all that it would stop at human free-

73

dom. On the contrary, the ideal of the domination of reality by the application of economic laws would drive man on along the road which would ultimately lead to the annihilation of this human freedom itself. Baudelaire saw this sharply when he asked himself: 'si, délicatement l'humanité en proportion des jouissances nouvelles qu'il —i.e. sciencialism—lui apporte, le progrès indéfini ne serait pas sa plus ingénieuse et sa plus cruelle torture; si, procédant par une opiniâtre négation de lui-même, il ne serait pas un mode de suicide incessament renouvelé, et si, enfermé dans le cercle de feu de la logique divine, il ne ressemblerait pas au scorpion qui se perce lui-même avec sa terrible queue, cet éternel desideratum qui fait son éternel désespoir?' ae

All this made the conflict with reality still sharper at the revival of the romantic attitude at the end of the century. For the nature with which they came into conflict was no longer nature in its self-evident existence, but a reality viewed through the glasses of the positivists, and as such it was loaded with a power which ran counter to the freedom intended in the personality-ideal. For reality in this sense consisted of a complex of fixed law-conformities without any subjective freedom under this law. Thus writing about de Goncourt, Morice says: 'Il a vu, dans le masque uniforme que la science jette sur la nature partout où elle est en relation directe avec l'homme, l'humanité s'en aller des choses, les choses reprendre, dans un silence menaçant leur vie personnelle, étrangère à l'humanité ainsi vaincu par sa victoire et impuissante à reconquérir ses ruines qui retournent à la nature.' af Viewed as a complex of fixed law-conformities, this reality turns into 'une robe de Nessos dont rien ne peut nous délivrer.' ag There would be an escape in the knowledge that everything is merely a dream, 'seulement celui qui nous rêve ferait bien de hâter le couvage de son opium.' ah

It was exactly this spiritual situation which was felt by this generation of 1885-1890 as one of the causes of their trouble in trying to achieve an art which was truly beautiful, i.e., really in accordance with their ideals. For, as Morice says, 'Notre vie étant cette chose affreuse, tant que l'art n'a pas eu les moyens d'une réalisation parfaite de nos rêves de bonheur, il devait en effet se maintenir dans le deuil des joies que la vie nous refuse et qu'il pouvait encore réaliser en rêve.'' ai Indeed they were even denied the beautiful dream of life

74

which art ought to be. This was (thus Valin in 1892) the 'impuissance dont souffrent surtout les artistes, incapables de réaliser pleinement leur rêve, c'est-à-dire de revêtir une pensée éternelle d'une forme véritablement réelle...' [aj] The question is whether it was really the ugliness of reality which incapacitated them to produce a good and sound art, just as we may ask ourselves whether their feeling of dis-comfort was not rather caused by their own attitude of life than by that reality as such. In truth, positivism was a danger to any human freedom, but this did not make it necessary by way of reaction to put every norm and every tradition out of action in the name of freedom, in the sense of romanticism. That is why we may speak of the 'perversité' with which they turned away 'volontairement de la norme'. They thus followed 'les conseils de la perversité qui veut toutes choses détournées de leurs limites et de leur équilibre naturels.' [ak]

They wanted to escape from the world as positivism had explained and disclosed it, the reality of the statistically observed facts and futilities.[81] They wanted to get free from the every day world, with its multitudes of things and events, this world, which oppressed a free man and forced the artist to live as common-place and super-ficial a life as 'everybody'. Positivism had dethroned every value and equallized everything according to its natural-scientific method. For if only individual visible, palpable and measurable events are meaningful, the insight into the difference between what from a human standpoint is meaningful and what is not will be lost. That is why there is a certain amount of truth in Radiot's assertion that 'l'esprit est devenu incapable de hiérarchie.' [al] It is characteristic of Western civilization, so very profoundly influenced by Greek thoughts, to seek the contrast again between soul and matter, or, at this time, coming after the 18th century sensualism, between the soul and the senses. 'Ce n'est plus le générale en chef âme qui a la parole, mais chacun de ses soldats mutinés, les nommés Sens.' [am] And so Aurier writes: 'Le présent n'est blessant et laid que par sa maté-rialité.' And what is the remedy? 'Ne faisons-nous autre chose, en croyant inventer les plus fabuleuses chimères, que d'évoquer les visions, inconsciemment ressouvenues, des temps où nos âmes pré-lassaient dans le merveilleux Eden des Idées pures?' [an] The human mind is mortal, 'losqu'elle se prélasse dans les douceurs ephémères

75

de la contingence; immortelle, lorsqu'elle sait s'élever jusqu'au paradis des absolus...' [ao]

Here we hear that the solution is sought in the spirit of Plato, as we have seen already more than once, also in the previous chapter. What may have induced them to take up these very old thoughts again? Perhaps the same cause that had so often made people advance them in former centuries, viz., in order to supply a firm basis to a non-naturalistic art. They were a justification which did not only exempt the artists from the necessity 'to copy' the reality given by the senses, but it even made him into a 'visionary' who was better able than any one else to render visible the Ideas behind reality which determine its meaning. Of course, Plato himself could not be appealed to directly, as he had declared art to be an inferior kind of activity, the imitation of natural objects.[82] But they turned to Plotinus who, simply stating that it was pre-eminently art which 'imitated' the Ideas, elevated art to one of the highest of human activities.[83] From this thought the aestheticists of the 15th century had started, and this had been the core of the theory of mannerism.[84] Later on, about 1800, these thoughts had been revived when a theory of art was wanted which would enable the artist to indulge in his own fantasy without lapsing into wild fancies without any sense of content. For also at that time the issue was how to secure a high rank for art.[85] These thoughts really make the artist free, and that which Aurier posited above—give your own imagination the reins, then we shall walk about in the Eden of the Ideas after all—is entirely in accordance with tradition.[86]

It is quite possible that Shestov is right in saying that Plotinus conceived these ideas because ultimately he thought the world too beautiful, preferred to enjoy it, and was not in the least minded to withdraw from it into asceticism. But it would have been consistent if he had arrived at conclusions similar to those of the gnostics who also affirmed that the creation, man's living-space as such, was evil and worthless.[87] The artists of this generation agreed with Plotinus that reality itself is something inferior. 'Le point de départ de la spéculation de Plotin ... est un sentiment de malaise, le sentiment que la vie humaine, sous la forme actuelle, est une vie arrêtée ou diminuée par des obstacles dus aux corps et aux passions.' [ap]

The generation of 1890 was not at all unacquainted with these old traditions. For not only did they always come across them when reading the works of their predecessors mentioned in the previous chapter, but at least those who were actively engaged in forming the new theory of art in their turn studied the old works of the Plotinian tradition.[88]

So Plotinism was a very useful way out of the difficulty of escaping from actual reality and of depreciating it as such while retaining all the joy that art can give us. This view was an answer to 'son besoin d'échapper à l'horrible réalité de l'existence, à franchir les confins de la pensée, à tâtonner sans jamais arriver à une certitude, dans les brumes du au delà de l'art',[aq] as it is put by des Esseintes, the principal character of Huysmans' book published in 1884, called *A Rebours*.

But having thus found a way of escape, they kept feeling that the kind of art they longed for was not to be achieved in the world of their time. We have already seen that Morice, while wishing to create an art that was to realize their beautiful dream, at the same time posits that such fulfilment is impossible in view of the miserable reality in which they find themselves (cf. page 75). For there is no real freedom although it is 'l'ordre naturel' so that 'si tout ce qui vit vit esclave, rien n'est selon les lois de la nature.' There is no freedom, as 'toute vie est enchaînée par une autre vie, ou par un vice, ou par de factices obligations que résume la Société telle qu'elle est.'[ar] And the consequences of the latter state of affairs were obvious. There was not only a crisis *within* art, but also a crisis *of* art, to use Redeker's distinction,[89] so that according to them it was necessary to change society itself in order to arrive at a truly good kind of art. And although a few idealists of Péladan's type will no doubt have fancied this change to be possible by means of art itself, it was nevertheless obvious that art qua talis is too weak or wholly unfit for such a task.[90] Thus it is not surprising that in such an artistic sphere the revolutionary sentiment ran high—in this respect they were the continuation of their naturalistic predecessors,[91] and they even preached anarchism, generally in words rather than in actions. But we shall not study this aspect of their activity any further.[92]

On the whole the ideas just mentioned did not have any considerable influence on their view of art as such. On the contrary, in

77

the years immediately before and after 1890 there was plenty of optimism so that Morice was able to say that the wish 'Anywhere out of the world' as even implied something positive with respect to art, for 'Cette plainte est de ce temps et c'est bien plus qu'une plainte: c'est la loi suprême de l'Art suprême.' at Yet their negative sense of reality was very important for the nature of their art. For man will seek after truth in his art, after that which seems to him to be meaningful and valuable. And as this was not 'ordinary' reality, the latter was something inferior also for art. Thus it was possible to say about 'decadent man' that 'il s'éloignait, de plus en plus, de la réalité et surtout du monde contemporain qu'il tenait en une croissante horreur; cette haine avait forcément agi sur ces goûts littéraires et artistiques, et il se détournait le plus possible des tableaux et des livres dont les sujets délimités se réléguaient dans la vie moderne.' au But this man will also somehow look upon one or other depiction of a glorious paradise as a lie. This was perhaps the real reason why at this time it seemed to be impossible to realize truly 'beautiful' art. Already in Baudelaire this is clear from the direct connection between the view of reality and the character of the works of art that were preferred: 'La nature est laide, et je préfère les montres de ma fantaisie à la trivialité positive.' av And even more explicit: 'J'ai trouvé la définition du Beau, de mon Beau. C'est quelque chose d'ardent et de triste, quelque chose d'un peu vague ... je ne conçois guère (mon cerveau serait-il un miroir ensorcelé) un type de Beauté où il n'y ait du Malheur. Appuyé sur—d'autres disent obsédé par—ces idées, on conçoit qu'il me serait difficile de ne pas conclure que le plus parfait type de Beauté virile est Satan—à la manière de Milton'.aw

Therefore the choice of subjects on the part of the symbolist painters is not so very surprising.[93] They were almost always 'fleurs du mal', beauty sought in what is ugly, in all that violates the norms and the tender relations. It is quite understandable that Salome should become one of the most important subjects of this period. Salome, who danced very beautifully in order to commit a horrible crime in a truly satanic mingling of over-refined beauty, sensuality, deeply rooted cruelty and purposeful cunning. She was the classical personification of decadence in whom almost all the motives were united that were dear to this mentality: aestheticism, the freedom of man (in a past which was far superior to the banality of the present), although not without the fatal subjection to the power of the passions, life on a different plane from the vulgarly commonplace, full of irrationality and mysteriousness, in which, after all, sin committed in a beautiful way is given its charming form.

Symbolistic art (continued)

This decadent sense of life had been given its first brilliant form in Huysmans' *A Rebours* written with the explicit purpose of getting out of the impasse of naturalism.[94] The book made quite a stir and had an immense influence both in France and abroad.[95] In it he portrays the decadent person as such, des Esseintes, and thus he is able to show what is relevant to his character. It was this work which brought a number of painters to the notice of a much wider circle of people, in the first place those belonging to that of the decadent authors and poets themselves. Huysmans was better acquainted with what was going on in the sphere of pictorial art than most of his colleagues as he had been an art critic for many years.[96] We first wish to pass in review these painters because it is they whose work runs parallel to that of the decadent literary artists. Their art is entirely different from that of the synthetists such as Gauguin, e.g., and consequently had hardly any influence on the latter. It is, however, conceivable that through the contact with this work, especially with that of Redon, these artists were encouraged to strike out their own paths consistently. Any possible influence of these painters on synthetism was due to their functioning as catalysts.

Gustave Moreau perfectly came up to the definition Baudelaire once gave of the artist after his own heart:

'Et peintre fier de mon génie
Je savourais dans mon tableau
L'énivrante monotonie
Du métal, du marbre et de l'eau
. . .
Et des cataractes pesantes
Comme des rideaux de cristal,
Se suspendent éblouissantes
À des murailles de cristal.' [ax]

79

The agreement with a particular aspect of Baudelaire, the Baudelaire of the *Fleurs du Mal,* was also sharply recognized by Huysmans
when he wrote about Moreau as follows: 'Il y avait dans ses oeuvres
désespérées et érudites un enchantement singulier, une incantation
vous remuant jusqu'au fond des entrailles, comme celle de certains
poèmes de Baudelaire...' [ay]

That Huysmans' words on Moreau were not merely the reading
of the former's dreams or wishes into Moreau's work, but the latter's
actual ideal and meaning, will appear when we consult the explanation or accompanying text that the painter wrote for some of
his paintings himself. What follows might, e.g., serve as a brief
summary of what we have written above—the subject is the painting
entitled 'Les Chimères'—: 'Décameron satanique. Cette île des rêves
fantastiques renferme toutes les formes de la passion, de la fantaisie,
du caprice chez la femme, la femme dans son essence première, l'être
inconscient, folle de l'inconnu, du mystère, éprise de mal sous forme
de séduction perverse et diabolique. Rêves d'enfants, rêves des sens,
rêves monstrueux, rêves mélancoliques, rêves transportant l'esprit et
l'âme dans le vague des espaces, dans le mystère de l'ombre, tout doit
ressentir l'influence des sept péchés capitaux, tout se trouve dans
cette enceinte satanique, dans ce cercle des vices et des ardeurs
coupables, depuis le germe encore innocente, jusqu'aux fleurs mon-
strueuses et fatales des abîmes... Au loin, la ville morte, aux passions
sommeillantes. Et cette ville, c'est la vie réelle, la vie vraie, ce qui est
caché, renfermé dans des murailles sombres, sous des toits surbaissés.
Mais les routes montueuses... se dressent et des figures... montent
toujours s'accrochant aux aspérités de cette roche aride et dure...
Peut-être arriveront-elles jusqu'à cette croix redemptrice qui se dresse
humblement dans l'Ether, dernière étape de la Vie, dernière épreuve
génératrice et bienfaisante, dernier refuge de l'Etre qui a pu éviter
ou vaincre après les épreuves cruelles le rêve chimérique, le rêve
terrible de ruine, de douleur et de mort.' [az] It may be called characteristic of this milieu that this cross is hardly visible in the picture
itself, and is certainly not victorious. It can only be reached after a
long and dangerous journey, 'peut-être'. The terrible though
beautiful day-dream of reality itself is predominant.

Moreau's views were characterized by a strong gnostic strain, as we
can read in his note on his 'Jupiter et Sémélé', in which the earth,

personified as Pan, 'courbe son front attristé, dans un regret d'escla-
vage et d'exil, tandis qu'à ses pieds s'entasse la sombre phalange des
monstres de l'Erèbe et la Nuit'... while there is also question of an
'ascension vers les sphères supérieures vers le Divin', by which 'Le
grand Mystère s'accomplit.' [ba]

There is a striking affinity with Blake, not in the subjects as such
but in their treatment. Here, too, mythological personifications are
used, the scenes are represented by means borrowed from the naturalistic tradition, which often gives rise to some marked mannerism.
Indeed there are even more than once direct borrowings from sixteenth century art reminding us of Bronzino or of the School of
Fontainebleau.[97]

Moreau's influence, inextricably connected with that of Huysmans'
A Rebours, was especially great in the case of the men of letters.
Fontainas says about it: 'Le Salomé de Gustave Moreau nous han-
tait' [bb] and then he quotes Huysmans, a brilliant description which
does not fail to impress, perhaps even more than the picture itself.
The interest in this kind of art was not at all restricted to France.
Jan Veth devotes an article to it in *De Nieuwe Gids* of 1890,[98] and
in England Moreau was discussed in *The Dial* of 1893,[99] and in
The Pageant of 1897.[100] Also at the first exhibition of the Gros-
venor Gallery in London (which specialized in the Pre-Raphaelites)
there was a work by Moreau on view.[101] These articles may prove the
fact that also painters were interested in him as all three had been
written by fellow-artists. In fact, two painters of the group of the
Rose†Croix, viz. Ary Renan and E. Aman-Jean had been his pupils—
the pupils that did not come to the fore until 1900, such as, e.g.,
Rouault, we shall leave out of account here. But we must observe
that the interest in Moreau was restricted to the group of those we
have called the decadents when discussing literature, or symbolists
when painters were concerned. Moreau on his part, finally, played
an important rôle in the spread of the knowledge of the Pre-
Raphaelites in France.[102]

The pictoral artists that may be considered as parallel to the third
group of authors distinguished by Michaud—Rimbaud, etc.—on the
whole do not try to represent a kind of gnostic Platonic truth with
the aid of some mythological allegory after the manner of Moreau,

81

for instance. They try to give direct expression to a negative sense of reality, a feeling of estrangement from reality, which is experienced as a hostile incomprehensible power. This was done either by a direct depiction of the products of an irrational phantasy, as Redon did, or by trying to represent reality in a way that laid special emphasis on that which seemed to them to be relevant in it. 'Le concret sans loi —tout ce qui reste à l'homme après le départ des dieux—la surnature civilisée, irrationnelle et psychique, engendre des fantômes qui peuplent le roman noir. Le fantôme n'exprime pas les mythes de la nature ou l'infini du réel, comme le dieu grec ou la fée. C'est un événement particulier qui se transforme en psychisme, une partie du réel transposée à l'intérieur de l'homme, et qui se réincarne—dans l'irréalité. Ces créations immaterielles expriment l'angoisse des hommes menacés par le mal extérieur devenu psychisme'.[bc] This is how some adherents characterized this art.

Meryon was one of the first to take this road, but *Bresdin* became better known. In his work he represents his view of reality, often rendering the latter in its smallest details. The concentration upon those details brings home to us the strangeness, the irrational, killing, mysterious, hostile, sinister character of reality—what the Germans call 'Unheimisch', i.e. where we do not feel at home (Heim). Only rarely—especially in his earlier work—he specifies his view by 'peopling' his reality with gnomes, skeletons proclaiming their triumph, etc., for instance in his 'Comédie de la mort' of 1854.[103] In most cases he suffices by representing some conceivable reality to express this horror and this estrangement. Thus the congenial Redon, who, although younger, had known Bresdin well, writes about him as follows: 'Ce qu'on retrouve partout, presque d'un bout à l'autre de son oeuvre, c'est l'homme épris de solitude, fuyant le monde, fuyant éperdument sous un ciel sans patrie, dans les angoisses d'un exil sans espoir et sans fin.'[bd] This work is like self-torture, an absorption in the minutest details of reality to discover in it the horror, the estrangement, that which is hostile to him as a human being without any contact with this reality. It stands to reason that he could not copy reality and gave free reign to his imagination, but it is characteristic of his vision to remain a conceivable reality, or rather, it is this reality itself viewed in one of its aspects.

The latter statement also applies to *Redon* to a certain extent,[be]

82

although in his case the products of the imagination are a great deal more spectral, irreal. But Redon, who is no doubt the most important artist of this group and—just as Moreau had been brought to the fore by Huysmans in *A Rebours*—was also highly esteemed by the symbolist writers,[104] himself always laid stress on the representation of his dream 'par ce simulacre du vrai' bf because he puts 'autant que possible, la logique du visible au service de l'invisible.' bg Whereas Bresdin concentrates on landscape transposed in order to give expression to the artist's sense of life, in Redon the figure is in the centre, a human being or some imaginary being.

Redon's art, too, is a direct concretizing of his 'mal de vie' bh, in relevent images, the evocation of an atmosphere described by Aurier as a 'frisson de peur dans l'infini de la nuit'.bi It is not necessary to argue this point elaborately as practically all the authors who wrote about Redon interpret his art in this sense,[105] while he himself more than once spoke about it in this spirit in his diary.[106]

The spiritual ancestors who inspired Redon and led him on his way are Goya and Poe—he devotes an album containing lithographs to both of them. More often than they do he creates phantastic beings that do not exist in reality, but apart from this there are parallels enough and to spare in their approach to the subject. This subject is detected by a close scrutiny of reality—it is all that is terrible, horrific, hideous, in a word, all that is relevant to their negative sense of reality. There remain differences between them: Redon is more subjective, more hallucinatory in his dreams, less exact than Poe, less directed to contemporary events than Goya.

Already Huysmans mentioned Baudelaire in 1883 in addition to Poe as one of the 'teachers' of Redon.[107] It is something remarkable that nearly all the tendencies existing at the end of the century, however much they might differ among themselves, were not only able to appeal to Baudelaire, but were also influenced by him and could start from his work. As a matter of fact Michaud had shown this already in his classificatory scheme.[108] Also Redon could appeal to Baudelaire, witness the latter's pronouncement in *Curiosités Esthétiques*: 'La nature est laide et je préfère les monstres de ma fantaisie à la trivialité positive.' bj In Baudelaire's work he could find subjects that suited him—1890, lithographs illustrating *Les Fleurs du mal*.

It is striking that Baudelaire's own critical work starts from entirely different premises, apart from an isolated sentence like the one just quoted. On the other hand the agreement is very clear when we consider Baudelaire's literary work. Perhaps we may put it like this: in his own (literary) art Baudelaire pointed the way to those whom we have discussed in the present chapter. But in his theory of art his attitude towards reality is different, a much more important place being assigned to it in the synthesis. This fact can only be explained really when we take into account the great admiration for and the great influence of the art and the ideas of Delacroix. This enabled him to point the way to the synthetist artists round Gauguin. The latter owed an immense debt to Baudelaire, but exactly on account of those elements in which he agreed with Delacroix.

None of the symbolist artists dealt with in this chapter broke with the old familiar method of representing their subjects. Their art is new with respect to its contents, often oriented to literature. They did not shrink from deformation or from fantastic beings, but in their forms they always followed the naturalistic way of representation with its perspective, shade, and plastic quality. As we have more than once indicated, the result was that their art often became mannerism. This symbolism was the last flowering of the art which had been born in Flanders and Italy in the fifteenth century.

The artists we wish to discuss in the following chapters are on the whole far different from these. 'Mais j'ai mille et mille fois horreur de ces mélancolies à la Meryon' van Gogh once wrote,[bk] and thus he became the spokesman of them all. In spite of the contacts and the points of agreement in their theory of art there was an immense difference in their approach to the artistic problems.

CONGENIAL CONTEMPORARIES

That which unites all the painters to be dealt with in this section, in contradistinction to those of the previous chapter, is the fact that they build on what the impressionists had brought. They share the admiration of the symbolist [a] painters for a few artists like Redon, but they consider as the great predecessors and pioneers Delacroix, the painters of Fontainebleau and Manet. They have a more or less pronounced aversion to the Pre-Raphaelites: 'Méfie-toi des préraphas...' [b] They also have in common their realism as regards their subjects. This shows in the clearest way perhaps, however sharply they may have expressed their critical views of impressionism, that, after all, they took their origin from the realistic-impressionistic tradition. Denis very clearly defines the difference between these artists and the symbolists when he says that we must sharply distinguish between 'les tendances mystiques et allégoriques, c'est-à-dire la recherche de l'expression par le sujet, et les tendances symbolistes [c], c'est-à-dire la recherche de l'expression par l'oeuvre d'art.' [d]

Impressionism

Impressionism had been realistic as far as the subjects were concerned. It clearly showed a disposition that was borne by a positivistic view of reality. 'Faith is by sight', this had been said already by the artists of the Renaissance. This is why they had sought to give expression in their art to truth as they understood it by trying to design a picture which showed some agreement with what the eye sees and observes. Only in the 18th century had the epistemological consequences been drawn from this viewpoint and had sensualism taught that the outer world can primarily be known by the 'sensations [1]—recall, e.g., Condillac's *Traité de sensations*. [e] And it is precisely this conception of our way of knowing reality and the truth about it which found expression not only in the subjects of the impressionists but also in their method of painting. 'Nature ... was the direct source of pure sensations, and these sensations could best be reproduced by the technique of small dots and strokes which ... retained the general impression in all its richness of color and life'.[2] —which at the same time may prove that 'sensations' and 'impression' were pretty well synonymous (in fact they had been synonyms already in 18th century sensualistic philosophy).[3]

It cannot be surprising that the impressionists took such a great interest in the problems of light and colour. For it was precisely in the years in which they were forming a style of their own that not only physics as such but also the theoretical problems concerned with light were in the centre of the general interest. The results of the investigations were followed also by the public at large with great attention.[4] This physical science was of course also based for the greater part on the 18th century philosophical conceptions, which were formulated and elaborated anew by positivism. This is why 'experimenting with effects of light and color'[5] is directly related with the attempt to register the direct sensation apart from any emotional interpretation. This view of reality had penetrated French thought in the 19th century so deeply that they did not even suspect that in reality they had to do with a theory. 'I have always had a horror of theories, ... I have only the merit of having painted directly from nature, trying to convey my impressions in the presence of the most fugitive effects ...'[6] this is a late pronouncement of Monet's. This simply makes it clear that the artist equalizes the representation of nature with the (unproblematic) notation of impressions or 'sensations'.

These things became clearer to the next generation who reacted strongly against the positivistic view of life. They began to understand that reality is more than the sum total of the impressions, but kept looking upon nature with the eyes of the positivists. This is why they were to blame the impressionists for having merely represented nature and thus forgetting what was truly human, such as emotions, thoughts, ideas. Mauclair said with reference to them: 'L'oeil et la main, ah! superbes, et ce fut assez: mais rien d'autre.'[f] All the same, the decadent authors, although they were akin to the symbolist painters whose art was a far cry to impressionism, defended this style. 'Au fond, ils n'avaient rien à voir ensemble, c'était la communauté de réaction contre les méchancetés de la presse qui les reliait', thus Mauclair.[g] This situation was due to the fact that impressionism (really the work of a very small group of artists), had been entirely hidden from the eyes of the official world of art. The prevailing tendency, that of the Salons, would have nothing to do with them, and deliberately closed its eyes to what was new and important in their achievements. Though impressionism especially flourished between 1870 and 1880,[7] the impressionists came to the fore only later, namely simultaneously with the symbolists—taking this latter term in a very wide sense. When they aroused the public interest it was at first no doubt in a spirit of rejection and condemnation.

As a matter of fact the original impressionism in the most literal sense of the word had already been a thing of the past in 1890. Nearly all the artists that might be called impressionists had searched for new ways after 1880 in order to get out of the dead lock to which the too exclusive interest in the 'sensations' of light and colour had reduced them. For this very reason it is important to inquire how it is that, e.g., in all kinds of handbooks on the history of music we again and again find the opinion defended that Debussy was pre-eminently an impressionist in music, which statement is based on 'La cathédrale engloutie' and similar compositions.[8] So this is considered to be the musical parallel to impressionism. But even apart from the real character of his art, it is well known that Debussy moved especially in a symbolistic environment,[9]—taking this term again in as wide a sense as possible. Did he not compose music to Maeterlinck's *Pelléas et Mélisande* and did he not write a tonal poem inspired by Mallarmé's *L'après-midi d'un faun*—in which, by the way, he hit off the atmosphere and the mood of this far from realistic work in a masterly way?

In its atmosphere, its conception, or in its starting-point there was hardly any connection between genuine impressionism and the 'symbolistic' music of Debussy. Yet there is some truth in the current opinion, but only if we consider the later development of *Monet*, who very consistently followed the road of sensualism. He had started as a realist and worked in the spirit of the painters of Fontainebleau —witness an early work of his of 1865: 'A small Street in Normandy' [10], note the way the structures of the houses, etc., are made clear in it. Afterwards he had come to emphasize the pure and exclusive representation of the sensations of colour and light, thus intensifying the subjective element at the same time. After 1875, his courage increasing, he drew more and more far-reaching conclusions from his viewpoint. In this way his art became exclusively a fixation of the effects of light and colour based on close observation in all kinds of weather—recall his well-known series, e.g., those of the cathedral of Rouen of the early eighteen-nineties—with the result that all matter seemed to have vanished, so that his reality consisted of a rarefied, vague totality composed of vibrations of colour and light. For the very reason that the matter and structure of things no longer seemed to exist in his eyes, his art became something ethereal and nebulous. For the spectator the work of art thereby loses its immediacy and the impression that a very particular moment has been fixed, as, e.g., we sometimes experience with Constable. But this vague indefiniteness is also characteristic of the literary art of the decadents and the symbolists.

This affinity might be more accurately described by paying attention to the meaning of the word 'rêverie', which term was rarely used at the end of the 19th century. It probably evoked too many associations with the past. But it was perhaps avoided even more on account of the fact that the word 'rêverie' implied a more passive attitude to nature. As we shall see, the symbolists and the synthetists strove much more after the 'rêve' (the dream), the active and creative day-dream. The word 'rêverie' in the sense intended here was connected with an attitude of life, with a very particular attitude towards reality, which had been embodied in a concrete artistic form for the first time by Jean Jacques Rousseau in his *Rêveries d'un promeneur solitaire*.[h] In it nature inspires man to indulge in a stream of thoughts and feelings which, as such, is entirely subjective and not really and immediately connected with the peculiar character, the structure and the nature of a particular natural phenomenon. Although neither this term, nor this thought as such, were of frequent occurrence among the generation of 1890, the character of their work was, nevertheless, more than once determined by this attitude towards reality. Both Verlaine and Mallarmé sometimes suggest a 'rêverie' rather than a 'rêve', at least, the line of demarcation between these two, theoretically speaking, clearly distinct conceptions of the relation between the artist and reality cannot be sharply indicated.[11]

Indeed, several of Monet's works of the series mentioned above, and his 'Nymphéas' even to a higher degree, might suggest a 'rêverie', just as some of Debussy's works like 'La Cathédrale engloutie' or 'L'après-midi d'un faun'. Viewed in this light the later lyrical Monet had remained an 'impressionist' and had many points of contact with the art of the 1890's and of Debussy. For then he was also strongly subjective and dreamy, evoking a mood rather than giving an exact description. How very much Monet thus kept pace with the times may also appear from a comparison of these later pictures with the great decorative works of the years 1894 to 1900 produced by Vuillard, who had after all come from the synthetist milieu.

Yet not only was Monet very far apart from the synthetists proper but also from the symbolistic literary men—much farther than he was from the decadents of the school of Verlaine. This becomes clear when Aurier makes the critical remark: '... il est permis ... de blâmer ce constant sacrifice des formes significatrices et ce parti-pris de plonger les êtres dans ces atmosphères si splendidement embrassées qu'ils semblent s'y vaporiser; sans doute, aussi est-il légitime de souhaiter un art moins immédiat, moins directement sensationnel, un art de rêve plus lointain et d'idée...'[i] This is a criticism of the 'rêverie' from the standpoint of the 'rêve'.

Seurat

A painter who will probably have satisfied the wish implied in the words just quoted is Seurat, although Aurier is not likely to have had him in mind. Seurat and his friend and kindred spirit Signac aimed at 'reflection' and 'permanence' in contradistinction to the method 'd'instinct et d'instantanéité'.[k] He had been subject to various influences, among which we must not underestimate that of Delacroix, whose work he had closely studied already at the time when he was forming his own conceptions,[l] whereas Signac repeatedly cited Delacroix when elaborately discussing neo-impressionism (as their art was soon called). He especially quoted Delacroix's pronouncement that nature is nothing but a dictionary for the artist in which to look up the words required to frame his own sentences.[12]

Their own pronouncements and the treatises written by their supporters (such as Fénéon) who had known them personally make it clear indeed that instead of what is momentaneous and transient, 'le fugace', they sought for what is permanent and durable, in order to 'conférer à la nature, que laissait à la fin sa réalité précaire, une authentique réalité'. (Signac) [m] This meant that they attempted to capture the permanent character of things, the meaning and structure of their subject, in opposition to the momentaneous impression which is perhaps not representative at all: 'synthétiser le paysage dans un aspect définitif qui en perpétue la sensation.' (Fénéon) [n]

In their works we again find Baudelaire's aim to create an art in which chance does not play a part, and in their way of realization everything is under their control to the minutest details. Only with this difference that Baudelaire demands at the same time that the method be easy and fluent, without constraint, direct, and look spontaneous, which is made possible by the previous thoroughly considered conception. The latter requirement is maintained by neo-impressionists, but their technique with its necessary planning of even the smallest details is the opposite of spontaneous and direct.

They want to render their vision of the subject in its permanent character and meaning by different means of expression which are purely aesthetic and can certainly not be understood in a naturalistic way. This is at once clear when we study their conception of colour. For at first sight the pointillist's technique, founded in the theories of light propounded by Chevreuil and others, has all the appearance of being purely impressionistic, but only according to a method that has been thought out in a more scientific way. Their method had arisen indeed under the influence of the Impressionists, but the colours were chosen with a view to their aesthetic effect on the eye of their mutual contrast, optical mingling, etc., owing to which they can become the bearers of the expression,[13] and of the artistic meaning. The very first lines of Seurat's own summary of his aesthetics clearly show this. 'L'art, c'est l'harmonie. L'harmonie, c'est l'analogie des contraires, l'analogie des semblables de ton, de teinte, de ligne, considérés par la dominante et sous l'influence d'un éclairage en combinaisons gaies, calmes ou tristes.' [o] In this theory we do not find a statement to the effect that thus the natural effects of light are rendered in a better way, but on the contrary, that by

90

this method the work of art can be realized in a much better way aesthetically.

Also with regard to tonal values and to the lines on the surface of the canvas these artists searched for aesthetical laws. The direction of the lines, e.g., was said to represent different emotions. Their aim was by no means the detection of psychological laws, but aesthetical regularities, fixed rules to be observed for a composition to be truly harmonious. They supposed that it was possible to formulate these laws in the same way as was done in the natural sciences.[p] The (mathematical-natural) science ideal dominated their thought and their action. At the same time, however, they rightly pre-supposed the existence of a close mutual coherence of purely aesthetical values —harmony—and iconic meaning [q]—'calme, triste' and such like.

The primacy of the science ideal in Seurat's artistic attitude is also evident from the fact that he consulted all kinds of scientific treatises on light—those by Chevreuil, Helmholtz [14] etc.—and consequently in this respect he was much more consistently positivistic than the impressionists proper. But at this point the great difference between them is revealed, as he did not at all strive after the fixation of 'sensations' in their direct momentaneousness, but tried to render what is more general and permanent. His art was summarizing and human in its interpretation.

At first sight this statement might suggest an anti-positivistic attitude, because human freedom seems to be given greater emphasis. This element is really there—it has never been absent in Western humanism—but it remains of subordinate importance. We find it in Signac's pronouncement that 'soumettant la couleur et la ligne à l'émotion qu'il a ressentie et qu'il veut traduire, le peintre fera oeuvre de poète, de créateur.'[r] But for a correct idea of what is said here it will be useful to read the following words of Sutter's: 'Les règles ne gênent pas la spontanéité de l'invention ni de l'exécution malgré leur caractère absolu ... La science délivre de toutes les incertitudes, permet de se mouvoir en toute liberté et dans un cercle très étendu ... Toutes les règles étant puisées dans les lois mêmes de la nature, rien n'est plus facile à connaître par principe, ni plus indispensable. Dans les arts, tout doit être voulu.'[s] So the wish to give human freedom free scope is there, but it is entirely bound to following the laws of nature. The motif of freedom was very weak

91

indeed in the idea that 'il faut voir la nature avec les yeux de l'esprit et non uniquement avec les yeux du corps, comme un être dépourvu de raison...' t For although this writer argues against naturalism, which wished to render only that which the eye saw, this seeing 'avec les yeux de l'esprit' means nothing but the application of the aesthetic laws conceived of as laws of nature.

The above quotations are from David Sutter, who had explained his ideas in a series of articles in 1880 entitled 'Les phénomènes de la vision', which are concluded with his positing 167 rules for art. Consequently this constituted an aesthetics in the scientific sense of the word, akin to the somewhat later work by Henry as to composition and method. The titles of some articles of Henry's are telling enough: 'Une esthétique scientifique',ᵘ 'L'esthétique des formes',ᵛ and the article which was so important to Seurat and his followers 'Cercle chromatique et sensation de couleur.'ʷ They were in direct contact with Henry; Seurat made a very thorough study of Sutter's article. This is one of the very rare cases in the 19th century that aesthetics in the proper sense directly influenced artists—if, at least, we keep the academic art of the Salons out of the picture.

The idea of art being bound to fixed rules as to its purpose and execution is closely related to classicism. This relationship is very profound, so that R. Rey could rightly speak of *La renaissance du sentiment classique* (1921) in the title of his book, also with a view to Seurat and his adherents. Later artists, too, have been occupied with the search for artistic rules, although their art could by no means be called classical of expression. But if we look at, e.g., Seurat's 'Baignade' in the Tate-Gallery, London, done in 1884 before he had arrived at pointillism also through his contact with Signac, then the total impression is really classicistic, or if you will, classical: a quiet surveyable composition, a harmonious reality in which the figures suggest perfect calmness and ease of movement, without any vehement emotions, in a clearly defined space. These are qualities that are also found in Raphael.

As a matter of fact, the first words in Seurat's 'manifest' quoted above were: 'l'art c'est l'harmonie'. In view of his 'origin',[15] as a pupil of Lehmann's, who himself was an adept of Ingres so much admired by Seurat, we need not think this strange. It is rather much more remarkable that he was never a classicist with respect to his subjects, but immediately took the side of the realism of his time. Already his first chief work, the 'Baignade' just mentioned, is about a contemporary subject far from sublime. Not only in his subjects, but also in the forms he chooses, Seurat keeps entirely clear of any reminiscence of the art of antiquity or of that of classicist tradition. This once more clearly proves that classicism (in a traditional sense) had lost its hold on this generation. It had too much committed itself by the academic works of the painters of the 'Salon' like Bouguereau. Daumier's criticism contained in his lithographs which ridiculed classical subjects had really been deadly.

Seurat seems to have thought this so much a matter of course that he hardly mentions it. Fénéon accounts for it, though, when writing on the neo-impressionists in 1887. Then he said that, in contra-distinction to the impressionists who wished to fixate very evanescent effects, they strove to 'synthesize landscapes in a definite aspect which will preserve the sensation implicit in them ... Objective reality is to them a simple theme for the creation of a higher and sublimated reality.' [16] Also Verhaeren was occupied with this facet when writing about Seurat's work at the exhibition of the XX: 'What the masters did to express their time, he attempts for his, and with equal care for exactness, concentration and sincerity ... The gestures of the promenaders (in Seurats 'Grand Jatte'), the groups they form, their goings and comings, are essential.' [17] These pronouncements even more clearly illustrated the classicist tendency in Seurat's work. Thus a classicist of the academic tradition was likely to have spoken about his subjects and the relation to reality, although Seurat's classicist contemporaries (and their 19th century predecessors) only wished to restrict themselves to so-called sublime subjects.

The great difference from the realists of his own time, however, was especially to be found in his giving up naturalism, and his regaining the insight that a work of art represents reality in an iconic way. Goldwater has rightly pointed out that in building up his compositions Seurat sometimes worked from different visual points,[18] and thus succeeded in rendering reality distinctly and clearly—even though in this way he came into conflict with the naturalistic laws of perspective. Seurat might also have been influenced indirectly, via the work of his contemporaries, by Japanese woodcuts. We are thinking, e.g., of the dark figure at the bottom of the 'Chahut'.

93

So Seurat's art was determined by two directly related elements: the strong, rigorously balanced composition, entirely directed to the creation of aesthetic harmony, and the lucid and surveyable rendering of the permanent, essential meaning of the subject, in a configuration of the representational forms that could only be understood iconically and not in a naturalistic way.

Finally, when Denis writes of Seurat, saying: 'Il eut le mérite de tenter la réglementation de l'impressionisme—ce premier effort contre la liberté',[x] we understand at the same time why Seurat was not held in such high esteem by the synthetists. For they wanted to maintain their freedom, however much their art and their art-theory were akin to Seurat's in many respects.

Puvis de Chavannes

Puvis de Chavannes was held in high esteem by the artists who are the subject of our investigation.[19] If we pay exclusive attention to composition he was very much related to Seurat. But apart from technique, the greatest difference is to be sought in the subjects dealt with. For Puvis de Chavannes was certainly no realist. All the same, he is not an academician either, no more in his subjects, as he generally avoided traditional allegories and tried to bring home to the spectator a particular idea or atmosphere, to express the latter, as it were, poetically in his pictorial compositions of figures elevated above time. In themselves these figures appear to be very naturalistic at bottom, i.e., his nudes are free from the classicistic idealizing stylization. In this respect his work sometimes bore a strong resemblance to Corot's figure paintings. But at the same time there was a strong tendency to simplification: he omitted all that was superfluous, all (photographic) details. He made efforts to compose genuine mural paintings which filled larger areas decoratively and were clear and surveyable, and, therefore did not make the impression of enlarged easel-pictures.

His compositions were very carefully done, and also by this means, in the play of line and colour, in the rhythmical arrangement of the groups and figures, he wanted to elucidate and to underline the poetic idea.[20] It is exactly on this point that the younger generation must have felt its relationship to him, and must have been prepared to be taught by him. The structure of reality as we see it remains intact—as has been observed already, there was a distinctly naturalistic strain in his work in spite of his subjects and his simplifications. Did not Fontainas rightly observe with reference to his figures: 'ils ne sont point par un vain caprice désincarnés mais strictement figurés selon les nécessités essentielles de la matière.' y?

That which Puvis really had in common with the synthetists—and in this respect he may be called a predecessor—was the fact that he did not at all elaborate his poetic ideas as if they were (photographic) illustrations of a poem. And as far as historical pictures are concerned (e.g., in his series in the Pantheon devoted to St. Geneviève), they were not, as it were, a photographic reconstruction of the events. But he represented his subjects in a purely pictorial manner, elucidating the meaning and contents in a telling way by means of the structure of the composition and the arrangement of the colours. That he was thoroughly conscious of this procedure may appear from his pronouncement that 'pour toutes les idées claires il existe une pensée plastique qui les traduit.' z This idea must be made clear in an iconic way; 'je cherche un spectacle qui la (idée) traduise avec exactitude' aa—and then he added that this kind of art might be called symbolism.

Cézanne

The brilliant artist Cézanne played an important part in the formation of synthetism, not personally so—for he had not only retired to Aix, but in addition he had broken off every contact with Gauguin—but by means of the works of his which, e.g., were on view at Tanguy's,[21] or those that were in the possession of Gauguin. We must, however, also take into account that Gauguin (together with Pissarro) had co-operated with him for some time,[22] and that Cézanne's ideas may certainly have influenced Gauguin already at that time, in 1881. The question that must be asked, therefore, is what were Cézanne's theories in those days?

Looking through Cézanne's correspondence, it appears that hardly any theories of art occur in his earlier letters. In 1866 he wrote about the use of working in the open air,[23] and in 1878 he said something about the art of painting as a 'moyen d'expression de sensation'.ab This observation made at the time when Cézanne was an impressionist in the full sense of the word is only remarkable on account of the use of the term 'expression' instead of 'notation'. Perhaps we might detect here the first symptoms of a growing consciousness of what he expected from art. But then we have to wait till the end of the century before there is again any distinct utterance on the nature of his art and his views. He himself placed his work before anything, and in this respect he wished to be put in the right only 'sur nature',[ac] though he also felt the need to give his art a more or less theoretical foundation.[24]

Our impression is that there is a great deal of truth in Mauclair's statement, written down in 1922: 'Toutes les théories sur le génie pictural de Cézanne, tous les boniments sur son art de synthèse, ont été faits après coup, je les ai vu naître.' [ad] In the synthetist milieu the first efforts may have been made under the lead of Gauguin and Bernard to formulate the peculiar character of Cézanne's art also theoretically. And thus, together with the growing interest in his art, also a considerable dose of their own interpretation may have become common property in the milieu of the symbolists and synthetists after 1890. Later on he repeatedly came into contact with younger artists who plied him with their questions about his art. In answer to their sympathetic questions he started formulating his ideas more adequately, the result of which we find in his letters written since 1900 or thereabouts and also in some books in which we are told about contacts with the old Cézanne.[25]

Owing to the negative reactions to their compositions and the scantiness of the interest in their work the impressionists landed in a crisis about 1880 [ae]—that is why in the years that followed they all started to reflect thoroughly on their art and their method.[26] It is quite possible that precisely in these years Cézanne began to strive deliberately after 'faire de l'impressionnisme quelque chose de solide et de durable comme l'art des musées.' [af] And by the reflections and discussions that took place in this sense Gauguin as an artist who had only started about 1881 may have been deeply impressed. This might appear from a letter he wrote to Pissarro: 'Has M. Cézanne found the exact formula for a work acceptable to everyone? If he discovers the prescription for compressing the intense expression of all his sensations into a single and unique procedure, try to make him talk in his sleep...' [27] We may possibly find a precipitation of what was then discussed in a letter written by Gauguin in 1885 to Schuffenecker, and in which he enters into details about the meaning of colours and lines as means of expression for what inspired the artist. And then he immediately goes on to say: 'Voyez Cézanne, l'incompris, la nature essentiellement mystique de l'Orient... il affectionne dans la forme un mystère et une tranquillité lourde de l'homme couché pour rêver, sa couleur est grave comme le caractère des orientaux ...', and he continues saying: 'plus je vais plus j'aborde dans ce sens de traductions de la pensée par tout autre chose qu'une littérature...' ᵃᵍ

Even if we should have to assume that, in his view of the symbolic meaning of lines and colours, and in his wish thus to give more than is perceived by the eye, he was inspired by the ideas advanced at that period by literary men, or, possibly, even by Seurat, the fact remains that he cites Cézanne as evidence. It may be that via Cézanne Gauguin had got into touch with the first start of the new ideas that were taking shape in authors such as Huysmans—for Cézanne followed their work closely.[28] For the rest, both Cézanne and Gauguin had got acquainted with Baudelaire's and Balzac's thought, and, of course, with the art of Delacroix (perhaps also with the latter artist's writings published shortly after his death). Although, therefore, the part that Cézanne played with respect to the formation of the new theories of art is by no means clear, it is certain that Gauguin considered his own art with an eye on this. And that he thought he was working in accordance with Cézanne's ideas may appear from the fact that later on, about 1890, when preparing to make a picture, he often used to say: 'Let's make a Cézanne'.[29] And yet Gauguin's work had hardly anything in common with Cézanne's as far as style is concerned—which all the more proves that this was in the first place a matter of conception and approach.

Considering Cézanne's art-theoretical contemplations as he formulated them later on when synthetism had fully developed, we may say that he wished to combine two elements in his art. He wanted to produce an art which should be an interpretation of nature, giving a human vision of what is permanent and meaningful, but which is at the same time the result of observation directly obtained after the manner of the impressionists. This is expressed most clearly and concisely in the demand: 'ce qu'il faut, c'est refaire le Poussin sur nature.' ᵃʰ What he meant by it will become clear when we read:

97

'Dans le peintre, il y a deux choses: l'oeuil et le cerveau, tous deux doivent s'entr'aider; il faut travailler à leur développement mutuel, mais en peintre: à l'oeil par la vision sur nature, au cerveau par la logique des sensations organisées qui donnent les moyens d'expression.' ai That in this we are confronted with the striving to retain that which impressionism had brought and at the same time to give human freedom its due, thus bringing about a synthesis of nature and freedom, may appear from the following: 'On n'est ni trop scrupuleux, ni trop sincère, ni trop soumis à la nature; mais on est plus ou moins maître de son modèle, et surtout de ses moyens d'expression. Pénetrer ce qu'on a devant soi, et persévérer à s'exprimer le plus logiquement possible.' ak

Cézanne did not in the first place seek to render what is transitory and momentaneous in the impressions of nature, but much rather to elucidate this nature in its structure and meaning for thinking and feeling man: 'la nature est toujours la même, mais rien demeure d'elle de ce qui nous apparaît. Notre art doit, lui, donner la frisson de sa durée avec les éléments, les apparences, de tous ces changements.' al We get the impression that Cézanne in his work as well as in his ideas found great difficulty in accomplishing something that previous generations, e.g., Jan van Goyen, could only consider as a matter of course. Just as in the case of Delacroix we are aware of the consequences attendant upon the increasing influence of the epistemological theories that had occupied the minds of people since the 18th century. Did he not say that 'le peintre concrète, au moyen du dessin et de la couleur, ses sensations, ses perceptions'.am

It stands to reason that in this attempt Cézanne was obliged to occupy himself thoroughly with the pictorial means as such. This is clear from the previous quotations, and it is especially obvious in his frequently occurring pronouncement that intensive observation was at least as indispensable as 'la connaissance des moyens d'exprimer notre émotion.' an And while working and thinking in this direction, he again came upon the insight that a work of art can never catch hold of reality as such, i.e., that which is given by our observation; but that such reality must be represented in a different, that is to say, in an iconic way. 'J'ai voulu copier la nature—je n'y arrivais pas. J'ai été content de moi lorsque j'ai découvert que le soleil par exemple (les objects ensoleillés) ne se pouvait pas reproduire mais qu'il faillait

le représenter par autre chose que ce que je voyais—par la couleur . . .' [ao]

No doubt Cézanne's toilsome striving testifies to a high degree of
originality. With respect to his art this is incontestable. But it is
possible indeed to hesitate with respect to his art-theoretical ideas.
For to what extent had he been influenced by what was going on in
symbolistic-synthetistic circles? Even if he rarely came into contact
with them, he is sure to have read about them, and to have made
acquaintance with their (literary) work in whatever measure this may
have been. And, besides, in what sense were the younger artists who
came to him about the turn of the century contributors to his ideas?
For already by the questions they asked they influenced his thoughts.
Although we cannot ignore the influence of synthetism without more
ado, Cézanne's formulations are certainly his own and original. They
were bound to be so, for his own art, which had by no means arisen
'spontaneously' but owed its existence to careful consideration was
totally different in style and partly also in its subjects from that of
the synthetists.

In summary of the above, and as an attempt to define Cézanne's
position in relation to Gauguin and his followers, we might submit
the following quotation, which probably contains more truth than
would be supposed at first sight: 'La reconstruction d'art que
Cézanne avait commencé avec les matériaux de l'impressionisme,
Gauguin l'a continué avec moins de sensibilité et d'ampleur, mais
avec plus de rigueur théorique. Il a rendu plus explicite la pensée
de Cézanne.' [ap]

Van Gogh

Although Van Gogh was a Dutchman, his art can scarcely be said to
have its origin exclusively in the Dutch artistic traditions or to be
directly connected with what was produced in the Netherlands at
that time. He may have studied with Mauve for a short time, he may
have had a good look at the work of his contemporaries, already from
the beginning he was very well posted up in what was achieved in
the realm of the art of painting abroad especially in England and in
France. He got to know this art as an employee in an art business,
and, therefore especially the more or less 'current' art. Only
during his stay at Paris after 1885 did he come into direct contact

with the impressionists and with others, who were outside the official art-life.

Both from his choice of books—Michelet, for instance,[30]—and from his predilection for particular artists—Lhermitte, Millet, e.g.,[31] —it is clear that at any rate from the moment he began to devote himself to the art of painting, he was a whole-hearted adherent of realism. And so he remained all his life. This becomes clear from his controversy with Bernard treating biblical subjects: 'Ah, il est sans doute sage, juste, d'être ému par la Bible; mais la réalité moderne a tellement pris sur nous que même en cherchant abstraitement à reconstruire les jours anciens dans notre pensée, les petits événements de notre vie nous arrachent à ce même moment à ces méditations et nos aventures propres nous rejettent de force dans les sensations personnelles—joie, ennui, souffrance, colère, ou sourire.'[aq]

This preference for realism was, doubtless, very deeply rooted, namely in a view of life and the world in which the humanistic motif of nature was given the main stress. Did not his brother Theo—who knew him out and out—write saying that Vincent considered living beings as tightly bound to nature?[32] That is why he objected to working from a dream—the creative day-dream as the synthetists understood it. He much rather started from thought which is much more bound to natural reality.[33] This also shows, nevertheless, that he did not want to fixate the fugitive impressions of nature as the impressionists tried to do, but wished to express the human view of it, inclusive of the subjective feelings aroused by the subject. With a view to this he is sure to be much more arbitrary in his use of colours,[34] which also shows his urge for freedom.

Van Gogh's mind may also be understood when we study the names of the artists he appeared to admire most when he had later on made a thorough acquaintance with French art in its different facets, also outside the Salon. They are Daumier, Ziem, Millet, Théodore Rousseau,[35] Monticelli, and, of course, Delacroix.[36] He cannot stand Ingres, Raphael, Degas.[35] It is quite possible that his being a Dutchman played some part in his reaction to the latter artists. For in the Northern Dutch mentality the calvinistic protestant tradition is a strong co-determinant for which ultimately the world of beautiful harmonious forms created by the classicist masters with refined aestheticism implies a lie. The Roman-Catholic-Humanistic dream of

100

the harmonious man is foreign to it, while in building up the ideal reality in the pictorial image too little account is taken of the fact of our living on a cursed earth. All this was certainly true in Van Gogh's case, as he came from a minister's family, however much modernist they were, and however much he was estranged from them. For the formative influence of a view of life, continued for many centuries, cannot be turned into an entirely different direction at a moment's notice, and certainly not in these deeper strata of our being where judgments are more or less 'instinctive' [ar] and taste and commitment to a position are more or less unreasoning.

On the other hand his predilection proves that he apprehended the realists all right, as well as those who manifested a profoundly romantic sympathy with nature. Surely he wished to keep within the limits of what is possible: 'Personally I love things that are real, that are possible.' [37] The atmosphere Baudelaire or Meryon evoked in their works was uncongenial to him, not only on account of their estrangement from reality which he certainly felt to be present in them—did not he speak about the 'mélancolie à la Meryon'? [as]—but also because of their search for what was irrational, strange, and unreal—did he not oppose 'the Baudelaire aspect of Paris' to 'the possible, the logical, the real'? [37]

Although later on he became mentally deranged, it appears that— apart from the periods in which he had an attack which made every kind of orderly thinking or working impossible—he was not at all open to a 'morbid' mental attitude that was capable of being entirely wrapped up in the 'fleurs du mal'. It is perhaps possible to explain his extreme sensitiveness, his inconceivable fast and fiercely concentrated way of working like one possessed in his Arles period, by referring to the approach of a fit of mental derangement. But the opposite interpretation is also possible! We consider it to be rather risky to explain his artistic ideas as the effects of a diseased mind. When, e.g., Jaspers supposes that Van Gogh's striving after the symbolic use of colours is connected with this [38], it would amount to declaring that the whole of this group of artists inclusive of Delacroix and Baudelaire were mentally diseased!

But the fact that he was such a pronounced realist does not at all imply that he was a naturalist. On the contrary! Already at the time when he was at Antwerp he rejected the academic naturalistic

101

method. 'Sans le savoir is die academie eene maîtresse, die verhindert dat er een meer serieuze meer warme meer vruchtbare liefde in u wakker wordt—Laat die maîtresse loopen en word tot over de ooren verliefd op uwe eigentlijke beminde dame nature of réalite.' [at] He seeks for a method that will be better suitable to do justice to reality than the naturalistic manner: 'Welnu, dat algemeene mooi doen tegen elkaar van de tonen in de natuur, men verliest het door pijnlijk letterlijke nabootsing, men behoudt het door herschepping in een kleurengamma evenwijdig, maar desnoods niet precies of lang niet eender aan 't gegevene.' [au]—thus he wrote when still living in Brabant.

In this direction his thought developed later on, especially owing to the stimulating influence of people like Gauguin and to Japanese art. And this is why he was not only very proud—with a pride born of modesty—when in 1890 at St. Remy he read Aurier's article on him, but he also thought that the latter had written how he ought to paint.[39] For Aurier wrote saying: 'Sans doute comme tous les peintres de sa race, il est très conscient de la matière, de son importance et de sa beauté, mais aussi, le plus souvent, cette enchanteresse matière, il ne la considère que comme une sorte de merveilleux langage destiné à traduire l'Idée. Il est presque toujours un symboliste... sentant la continuelle nécessité de revêtir ses idées de formes précises, pondérables, tangibles, d'enveloppes intensément charnelles et matérielles.' [av] As a matter of fact he himself more than once wrote in the same spirit. A very frank instance is the following: 'J'ai toujours l'espoir de trouver quelque chose là dedans. Exprimer l'amour de deux amoureux par un mariage de deux complémentaires, leur mélange et leur oppositions, les vibrations mystérieuses de tons rapprochés. Exprimer la pensée d'un front par le rayonnement d'un ton clair sur un fond sombre...'[40], [aw] That he expressed himself rather modestly and metaphorically when speaking of his hope to discover something, may appear when we read what he wrote about the painting representing his bed room. He then explained how he expressed quiet and peace precisely in the colours and the manner in which he had treated the subject.[41]

In such a way he tried to find the synthesis, i.e., the expression of the human vision of a very realistically conceived subject as such. Thus a thought will be expressed by means of an image which does not violate reality. In connection with his controversy with Bernard about the latter's 'Christ in the Olive Garden' he wrote to Theo, that Bernard was wrong in omitting to try and make a clear image of the reality of things 'et ce n'est pas le moyen de synthétiser.' [ax] But in order thus to make the representation of (visual) reality into an expression of a thought it is of course necessary to lay some particular emphasis on colour and line which deviate from what is perceived with the eye. He then called such use of colour 'arbitrary'.[42] This shows that naturalism had had such a profound influence on the minds of people that a deviation from strict naturalism was felt to be something arbitrary, even by him who practised it with full conviction. It was, therefore, only possible for a man who had a strong disposition to enable his own personality and his own subjectivity to express themselves. In the synthesis meant here there is the search for more than only a new method; for there was also a striving after a kind of equilibrium allowing both the motif of nature and that of freedom to be given their due.

As a direct consequence of this striving also Van Gogh made the re-discovery of what is iconic, i.e. he became conscious of the fact that artist's painting is intended to express a human vision by the use of the means of pictorial art, without copying reality in a naturalistic-photographic way. He appeared to be thoroughly aware of this state of affairs: 'Je ne peux pas travailler sans modèle. Je ne dis pas que je ne tourne carrément le dos à la nature pour transformer une étude en tableau, en arrangeant la couleur, en agrandissant, en simplifiant.' [ay] He also saw sharply the difference between this method and that of earlier artists who had expressed their thoughts primarily by means of their subjects, while their way of painting itself had remained naturalistic.[az] This is why he said: 'ce n'est pas un retour au romantique ou à des idées religieuses, non. Cependant en passant par le Delacroix davantage que cela paraîsse, par la couleur et un dessin plus volontaire que l'exactitude trompe-l'oeuil, on exprimerait une nature de campagne...' [ba] That this quotation is really concerned with the subjects (so not with romanticism or christianity in the sense of a view of life) may very clearly appear from what he wrote to Bernard half a year later: '...pour te rappeler que pour donner une impression d'angoisse, on peut chercher à la faire sans viser droit au jardin de Gethsemane historique; que pour donner un motif consolant et doux il n'est pas nécessaire de représenter les personnages du sermon sur la montagne.' bb

Van Gogh no doubt arrived at these conceptions on his own account—the fact that he had to teach a lesson on these views to Bernard who later on asserted to have been the inventor of synthetism, is very remarkable—although we should not exclude the influence of such contemporaries as Gauguin, Seurat, and possibly a few others. But Delacroix was certainly very important for Van Gogh, and this pretty well without the former's literary writings or the explanations of Baudelaire. This appears from the brief summary of the above given by Van Gogh himself: 'Je reviens plutôt à ce que je cherchais avant de venir à Paris, et je ne sais si quelqu'un avant moi ait parlé de couleur suggestive, mais Delacroix et Monticelli tout en n'en ayant parlé, l'ont faite.' bc So he seemed to have forgotten that at one time he had sent Theo cuttings from a paper on Delacroix's use of colour, in which there occurred various quotations from the latter's literary work. For the rest, it is quite conceivable that also Carlyle's *Sartor Resartus* had exercised some influence on the formation of these ideas in those days at Nuenen.[43]

But, though at the time when the theories of the Synthetists were elaborated Van Gogh is not likely to have had a direct influence on them,—for he was far removed from them at that time, in the South of France,—it is possible that he had fructified the thoughts of these Frenchmen, perhaps twice: the first time when, having just arrived at Paris from the North, he came into contact with Gauguin and Bernard there. On the whole, however, we think that Van Gogh was then rather receptive than suggestive, and is sure to have abandoned this theory (recall the above quotation) rather than passed it on to others. And the second time when Gauguin stayed with him at Arles for some time in 1888.[44] Although the importance of a few letters should not be entirely passed over in silence, we do not believe that they were of decisive significance in this respect. If we were to give a short summary of the rôle of Van Gogh with regard to the Synthetists, we might say that he was a parallel figure who exercised some influence on them.

'Rive Droite'

In addition to the view of life and the world and the conceptions of art founded in it, the formation of the individual character of a particular art is also influenced by the style of living, the social environment that is sought, and the way one behaves in it. If anywhere, this is especially clear in the case of the artists of the 'Rive Droite'. As soon as we make a closer investigation of their work, we hear about clubs, cabarets, and so on, and we are obliged to get acquainted with the motley night-life of Montmartre as it was spent at the end of the century at the 'Chat-Noir' of Rodolphe Salis [45] and among such ephemeral groups as that of the 'Hydropathes', 'Hirsutes', 'Zutistes' and 'Jemenfoutistes', whose very names can already enlighten us about the 'blague' and 'esprit' cultivated there.

One of the first typical artists in this milieu was Félicien Rops, originally a realist who was in close contact with what was going on in this field in Belgium in the nineteen sixties. Later on, however, he was entirely taken up with the production of prints, drawings, and illustrations which were not quite free from pornography. 'Rops n'a rien du mystique ni du névrosé. C'est un esprit sain dans un corps sain, dédaigneux de toutes les faiblettes pudeurs, heureux d'exalter sa virilité...' [bd], this is what was written by one of his admirers. 'Je tâche tout bêtement et tout simplement de rendre ce que je sens avec mes nerfs et ce que je vois avec mes yeux: c'est là toute ma théorie artistique.' [be], he wrote himself. But, of course, then the question is what he felt and saw. And this is very concisely described by the words: 'Personne jusqu'àlors n'a touché aussi profondement la notion catholique de la luxure, le plaisir démoniaque de la perversité, l'au-delà du mal.' [bf] He had wanted to be a great painter, and might have become one under the influence of Baudelaire, whom he knew very well, but ultimately he occupied himself exclusively with illustrating the works of such writers as the Goncourts, Huysmans, Verlaine, etc.—between 1880 and 1890 he was the illustrator that was most sought after.[46]

After 1890 or thereabouts Rops' rôle was at an end, but the painters of Montmartre like Villette, Léandre, Forain and Steinlen (whose work strongly influenced by socialistic ideas we shall leave out of account at present), continued working in Rops' spirit. Their work may perhaps best be characterized by the 'Programme' that Forain inserted in his paper *Le Fifre*: 'Conter la vie de tous les; jours, montrer le ridicule de certaines douleurs, la tristesse de bien des joies, et constater rudement quelquefois par quelle hypocrite façon le Vice tend à ce manifester en nous: c'est mon projet. Chercheur fantaisiste, j'irai partout, m'efforçant de rendre d'un trait net et immédiat, aussi sincèrement que possible, les impressions et les émotions ressenties...' [bg] It is exactly this term 'fantaisiste' which denotes the wide difference from the synthetists proper with whom they had a great deal in common, but from whom they were separated by the wide and deep Seine. For the synthetists lived and worked on the 'Rive Gauche': 'Les symbolistes dédaignaient le Chat Noir et les artistes de Montmartre: ils étaient rive-gauchers, hermétiques, assez pontifiant, et s'ils admettaient l'humour ils eussent trouvé indigne d'eux le rire de la blague.' [bh] This is what Mauclair wrote, who was a faithful paladin of Mallarmé's. He lived at that time, and is a dependable informant.

At the moment it is not necessary to discuss the greatest artist in this milieu in which there obtained a lighter tone, and which strove after a kind of 'Degas-realism' in an easy style appreciating the strictly subjective 'handwriting', viz., Toulouse Lautrec. His art, too, was in the first place graphic, and he was also influenced by Japanese art—via Gauguin, via the 'Art Nouveau' and also directly. All this did not mark him off from his contemporaries mentioned, however. He differed from them rather by his sharper observation, his more telling characterization, his faultless composition and his controlled delicate style of drawing.

Trying to define the greatest common denominator of the artists dealt with in this chapter, and to find what united them, we may point out that they all started from realism or impressionism, with the exception of Puvis de Chavannes, who had, after all, greater affinity with Ingres. They were contemporaries of the symbolist painters such as Moreau, but there was hardly any relationship. No more did they play a part in, or belonged to the Art Nouveau movement. Although they wished to conquer the world of the Salon, they remained faithful to realism with respect to their subjects. And at least two of them, viz. Cézanne and Van Gogh, gained the insight

106

into the characteristic element peculiar to the art of painting, viz. the iconic element, of which Van Gogh once said: 'Ce n'est pas là du trompe-l'oeuil réaliste [bi] mais n'est-ce pas une chose réellement existente?' [bk] Indeed, the issue in art is always: what is expressed, and what does reality ultimately mean to the artist?

V

THE ARTISTIC IDEALS
OF THE SYNTHETISTS

Anti-naturalism

The generation that came to the fore in the nineteen eighties was
not only mature enough but also anxious to adopt new ideas, to help
building up a new art. Thus Denis wrote that a number of younger
men working in the studios of Cormon and Julian were favourably
disposed to all that was new and attacked all that was old: 'Nous
allions à ceux-là qui faisaient table rase non seulement de l'enseigne-
ment académique mais encore et surtout du naturalisme, romantique
ou photografique, alors universellement admis comme la seule
théorie digne d'une époque de science et de démocratie.' [a] So they
felt the artistic and the cultural situation connected with it to be very
unsatisfactory. And especially the circumstance that the art with
which they came into contact in no way presented an elevated aspect
will have induced them to search for something else. Another factor
that led to this was no doubt also the presence of a strong movement
among the young men of letters who wanted to strike out new paths,
at any rate to find an art which was different from that of the
prevailing naturalism in Zola's sense. They discussed a great deal
about it.[1] The climate of their thoughts will be found reflected in
Aurier's works of a somewhat later date, in which all this had been
given a better formulated form: 'Les sciences naturelles, ou sciences inexactes, par opposition aux sciences rationnelles ou exactes,
étant, par définition, insusceptibles de solutions absolues, conduisent
fatalement au scepticisme et à la peur de la pensée. Il faut donc les
accuser, elles, de nous avoir fait cette société sans foi, terre à terre,
incapable de ces mille manifestations intellectuelle ou sentimentales
qu'on pourrait classer sous le nom de dévouement. Elles sont donc

108

responsables ... de la pauvreté de notre art, auquel elles ont fixé pour unique domaine l'imitation, seul but constatable par les procédés expérimentaux.' Thus we have arrived at 'l'animalité pure et simple' and that is why a reaction is needed. 'Il faut recultiver les qualités supérieures de l'âme.' [b]

But not only the literary groups of their time with their numerous periodicals will have caused them to react against the prevailing mentality with its faith in the sciences. Also Delacroix and Baudelaire had already pointed out how much art was impoverished by the predominance of positivistic naturalism. The latter wrote: 'Chez nous le peintre naturel ... est presque un monstre. Le goût exclusif du Vrai [c] ... opprime ici et étouffe le goût du Beau ... Il (l'artiste) sent ou plutôt il juge successivement, analytique.'[d] Baudelaire's *Curiosités Esthétiques* from which we quoted had been published at this very time, 1884! Also Delacroix had more than once expressed himself in the same spirit,[2] and they may have been acquainted with it by means of G. Dargenty's book: *E. Delacroix par lui-même,* of 1885. No doubt Delacroix's own work was also important in this respect.

Also Gauguin, of course, frequently fulminated against every naturalism: 'Nous (this refers to Western civilization) sommes tombés dans l'abominable erreur du naturalisme' [e] This pronouncement leaves nothing to be desired as regards clarity. He, too, seeks the cause of the error in the science ideal: 'Ils cherchèrent autour de l'oeil et non au centre mystérieux de la pensée, et de là tombèrent dans les raisons scientifiques.' [f] And even at the end of his life he deems it necessary to explain to Morice that the past period was so much influenced by physics, chemistry and the study of nature that the artists had lost 'la force de créer'.[g]

This is how matters looked to the milieu to which we are directing our attention at the moment, in which 'la copie myope des anecdotes sociales, l'imitation imbécile des verrues de la nature, la plate observation, le trompe-l'oeil, la gloire d'être aussi fidèlement, aussi banalement exact que le daguerréotype, ne contente plus aucun peintre ... digne de ce nom.' [h] But we shall have to resist the temptation to give more quotations that illustrate what Denis summarized in one short sentence: 'Ils ont propagé la haine du naturalisme.' [i]

It is clear that these artists could not develop or approve of a view

109

of art with a scientific tinge. This is no doubt the basis of their rejection of Seurat's theories—Seurat, it is true, was quite new and original, and in some respects he showed some affinity with these artists, but his theory was too much determined by this hateful physics. With reference to the creation of his own work Gauguin, therefore, says explicitly: 'Où commence l'exécution d'un tableau, où finit-elle? Au moment où des sentiments extrêmes sont en fusion au plus profond de l'être, au moment où ils éclatent et que toute la pensée sort comme la lave d'un vulcan, n'y a-t-il pas une éclosion de l'oeuvre soudainement créée . . .? Les froids calculs de la raison n'ont pas présédé à cette éclosion . . .' k

Subjectivism

We cannot be surprised to find them demanding an art that was subjective, in which, consequently, the maker's personality expressed itself. 'Au lieu de travailler autour de l'oeil nous cherchions au centre mystérieux de la pensée, comme disait Gauguin. L'imagination redevient ainsi, selon le voeu de Baudelaire, la reine des facultés. Ainsi nous libérions notre sensibilité; et l'art, au lieu d'être la copie devenait la déformation subjective de la nature.' (Denis) [1]

It is, of course, true that also impressionism, and even the positivistic philosophy and aesthetics—e.g., that of Taine—were already subjectivistic. This has been pointed out by Aurier in his article on the 'peintres symbolistes', in which he said that also naturalism represented reality 'vu à travers d'un tempérament.' But he is not satisfied with that which Zola (who is not mentioned here) meant. For the work of art as such must be a 'signe visible de ce tempérament', or, better still, a symbol of this personality, 'le Symbole de l'ensemble idéique et sensitif de l'ouvrier.' [m]

Individualism

Without a doubt there is a strongly individualistic trait in all this. 'Nous aspirions à la joie de s'exprimer soi-même' que réclamaient les jeunes écrivains d'alors,' [n] thus Denis. But then he immediately goes on to say that the theory of the equivalents provides him with the means to accomplish this, so that, as we shall see, the bond with reality is retained. We should not think this

110

individualism to be of the extreme philosophical kind approaching solipsism, but rather to be the artist's freedom to express in a strictly personal way what he considers to be meaningful in reality —which, therefore, has a claim to being truthful.[3]

Synthesis

One of the remarkable things in the world of thought of those days was that there was a striving to clarify in the work of art the artist's personal vision, that which impresses him in a strictly individual sense, but at the same time to represent and elucidate reality itself in its deepest essence. The fundamental idea of the 'synthèse' has been developed precisely to solve this contradiction. Thus Aurier says: 'Qu'est-ce-que le Poème? Une synthèse de toutes les idées générales perçues par un moi donné.'[o] Which satisfies Baudelaire's demand made upon 'l'art pur suivant la conception moderne', viz., 'créer une magie suggestive contenant à la fois l'objet et le sujet, le monde extérieur à l'artiste et l'artiste lui-même'.[p] The same Baudelaire who also wrote: 'L'artiste ne revèle que lui-même... Il a été son roi, son prêtre et son dieu.'[q] This proves that this contradiction had existed already earlier.

We might characterize the factual state of affairs best as follows: these artists wanted to claim freedom for man again, also as an individual person. For this purpose man had to be freed from the grasp of nature as it had become predominant by positivistic science. But they themselves, too, were still tied down very tightly to this reality, so that a complete realization of their freedom in the work of art was not yet possible to them. What they sought was in fact to get free from the making of a photographical record of reality as seen in a positivistic view, hence the freedom of naturalism. There was as yet no question of getting loose from nature in its concrete real structure. They did not yet think of abstract (non-figurative) art, such as was to arise some twenty years later. At any rate they never wrote about it. And the individualistic realization of their own freedom apart from any reality outside of man, as is found among experimentalists, tachists and similar groups, was still entirely outside of their horizon. But the urge for such absolute freedom was alive in their hearts and drove them on in their search for a new art not bound by nature.

111

Freedom

In what has so far been said we have already come upon the motif of freedom which assumed the form of the personality-ideal,[4] man's wish to express himself, to note down and objectify his own internal vision and motives. This freedom motif [r] also manifested itself in the wish to dominate nature. The difference between the primacy of the motif of nature in the science ideal and in artistic naturalism and his own attitude is very clearly indicated by Gauguin's words: 'L'art primitif procède de l'esprit et emploie la nature. L'art soi-disant raffiné procède de la sensualité et sert la nature. La nature est la servante du premier et la maîtresse du second. Mais la servante ne peut oublier son origine, elle avilit l'esprit en se laissant adorer par lui. C'est ainsi que nous sommes tombés dans l'abominable erreur du naturalisme.[8]

Thus they aimed at an art in which man could use nature at will to express his own ideas. Hence their frequent demand not to paint from the model, but from memory. Their ideals of that time found splendid expression in Denis' (later) summary of the development of their art in those years: 'A Paris, chaque année, aux Indépendents . . . il [t] voit quel travail s'opère, en apparence vers plus de liberté, en réalité vers plus de raison et d'ordre, un ordre nouveau, paradoxal, un ordre issu de la tourmente symboliste et dont le succès marque le triomph de l'esprit de synthèse sur l'esprit de l'analyse, de l'imagination sur la sensation, de l'homme sur la nature.'[u]

As has been observed above, about the year 1890 the extreme profession of freedom in its ultimate consequences was not yet found. Also the letters of that period that have come down to us are really silent about it. It was especially Gauguin whose thought turned in this direction consistently in later years, and who posited that by realizing the artist's freedom over against nature his work made absolute freedom possible for later generations. This is also the reason why he also posits that the artists rather than the public will have to be grateful to him.[5] This new conception of freedom which urged them on implicitly in all their efforts to create a new style in the years between 1885 and 1890 had not yet become explicitly conscious. It became so in Gauguin's words in 1902: 'Il était donc nécessaire, tout en tenant compte des efforts faits et de toutes les recherches, même scientifiques, de songer à une libération complète, briser les vitres, au risque de se couper les doigts, quitter à la génération suivante, désormais indépendante, dégagée de toute entrave, à résoudre généralement le problème. Je ne dis pas définitivement, car c'est justement un art sans fin dont il est question, riche en techniques de toutes sortes, apte à traduire toutes les émotions de la nature et de l'homme. Il fallait pour cela se livrer corps et âme à la lutte contre toutes les Écoles, toutes sans distinction, non point en les dénigrant, mais par autre chose, affronter non seulement les officiels mais encore les Impressionnistes, les Néo-Impressionnistes, l'ancien et le nouveau public... En tant que travail, une méthode de contradiction, si l'on veut, s'attaquer aux plus fortes abstractions ᵛ faire tout ce qui était défendu, et reconstruire plus ou moins heureusement, sans crainte d'exagération, avec exagération même. Apprendre à nouveau, puis, une fois su, apprendre encore. Vaincre toutes les timidités, quelque soit le ridicule qui en réjaillit. Devant son chevalet, le peintre n'est esclave, ni du passé, ni du présent, ni de la nature, ni de son voisin. Lui, encore lui, toujours lui. Cet effort, dont je parle, fut fait, il y a une vingtaine d'années, sourdement, en état d'ignorance, puis il alla s'affirmissant...'ʷ Rarely has an artistic ideal been formulated so lucidly and exactly—Gauguin himself has hardly realized this program. That was to be the work of the twentieth century.

Realism

Summarizing the requirements made by the synthetists, we can say that they aimed at a subjective kind of art trying to clarify what is strictly personal, also in the reaction to the outer world in a way that was not naturalistic. It would be possible to say the same thing about Delacroix's work, so that it is not surprising that they admired it very much. But they were not trying to revive romanticism. They attempted to express this mental attitude in an entirely new way.

In 1892 somebody wrote: 'Leur idéal, sans doute, n'est pas le même que le romantique, ils ne se plaisent pas à la fougueuse expression des passions ni des sentiments du coeur... ils couvrent une vérité abstraite d'un vêtement d'eblouissantes réalités.' ˣ Indeed, in their opinion romanticism did not penetrate deep enough and remained too superficial. For what was romanticism? According to Morice: 'Ce n'est

pas le fond des passions, c'est leur gesticulation extérieure, leur manifestation active' ʸ, or in other words, it remained too much only human
passion as such, and did not give an insight into full reality. And above
all they wanted to grasp this full reality in their art. In connection
with this we should never forget that all these artists originated from
the school of the realists—in Courbet's sense—and from the impressionists,⁶ and that in this respect they were separated by a large
gulf from the painters we have called symbolists and who are
characterized by Denis as 'peintres de l'âme.' ᶻ They were very
keenly aware of the shortcomings of the positivistic ideal of art, but
wanted to keep hold of nature in their art. Their objection is exactly
the fact that some part of reality is not sufficiently done justice to in
naturalism, ᵃᵃ whereas we have seen that romanticism took too little
account of nature and rendered the outside of the passions only. They
might be said to have aimed at correcting both romanticism and
positivism by not only uniting them but by digging deeper than was
possible for each of them in virtue of his starting point. Thus Denis
writes about his fellows: 'C'étaient des esprits passionnés de vérité,
vivant en communion avec la nature ... S'ils furent amenés à 'dé-
former', à composer,—things that had not been done by their
immediate precursors— ... c'est aussi pour apporter plus de sincérité
dans le rendu de leurs sensations—i.e., their predecessors had failed
somewhere in the realization of their own starting-point—.ᵃᵇ Thus
the painter expressed himself. The literary artist who was closely
related to them, Morice, expressed all this in a little more involved
and poetical manner, but it boiled down to the same thing. He spoke
of 'cet intense et contemporain désir de l'esprit humain de faire
confluer en un seul large et vivant fleuve de Beauté réuni à la Vérité
dans la Joie le courant mystique et le courant scientifique.' ᵃᶜ Then
there will be 'L'art integral.' ᵃᵈ

They did not give up realism in their subjects. For there was
another valid reason why in giving up naturalism they did not resort
again to expressing their vision allegorically (as, e.g., the symbolists
had done). This reason was expressed tersely and concisely by
Delacroix in a note dating as far back as the year 1820. How much
more it must have been applicable to the situation at the end of the
century when academism had become increasingly more superficial.
Delacroix, then, observed the following in his note: 'Je prétends que

114

celui qui se jette dans l'allégorie, s'impose la nécessité de trouver des idées si fortes, si neuves, si sublimes, que sans cette ressource, avec Pallas, Minerve, les Gràces, l'Amour, la Discorde, etc. rétournés de cent façons diverses, on est froid, obscur, plat, commun.' [ae] And however paradoxical it may seem to be, the avoidance of such vulgarity and obscurity was the very reason (for these were also their grievances against the art of their time) why they stuck to realism in their subjects. In rendering 'ordinary reality' they tried to express its meaning rather than what was seen with the eye. For this, too, they could appeal to Baudelaire, and from this point of view it is easily understood why they admired such works as Balzac's *Séraphita* [7] — seemingly so naturalistic (in Zola's sense) but in reality giving so much more.

In art they tried to enable man's freedom to express itself, even to rule, it is true, but in such a way as to embrace everything that escaped the positivistic analysis of reality, and to incorporate all this into the whole that they designed. Again Gauguin and Morice [af] gave clear expression to these things, in the following words —which should be understood as an artistic ideal rather than as an instance of overestimation of themselves—: '(L'artiste) est le maître de la vérité, de la vie. Il t'apporte la nature vivante. L'invention que tu lui reprochais, dont tu te défiais, c'est précisément l'âme de son oeuvre, le souffle qui la vivifie, c'est la chaleur et c'est l'eau qui manqueraient aux fleurs coupées, tôt desséchées—this is a reference to the science-ideal and its shortcomings—. C'est invention qui fait la vie de l'esprit comme elle fait la vie des oeuvres, l'invention qui circule comme un sang dans les éléments empruntés par l'imitation à la Nature...' For the highest thing will be if 'un grand artiste a couronné de son génie quelqu'une des innombrables figures belles de la NATURE, quand l'artiste, enfant lui-même de la NATURE,[ah] nourri par elle, vivant d'elle, se lève pour dire la beauté de sa mère: quand la Nature laisse un des aspects changeants de son mystérieux visage éterniser le mot de son énigme dans l'oeuvre d'art.' [ag]

Art and Nature

Less poetically Denis put this ideal in words when he wrote: 'Peut-être un jour arriveront-ils à la Nature: c'est-à-dire que leur conception des choses pourra devenir assez complète, assez profonde, pour que l'oeuvre d'art réalisée par eux conserve tous les rapports logiques qui sont le caractère essentiel de la Nature vivante, et qu'ainsi il y ait plus d'analogie entre l'objet et le sujet, entre la création [ai] et l'image qu' ils en auront reconstituée...' [ak] What this meant to him appears from what he says about Gauguin's 'Calvaire' and kindred works: 'De la toile elle-même, surface plane enduite de couleurs, jaillit l'émotion amère ou consolante, 'littéraire' comme disent les peintres, sans qu'il soit besoin d'interposer le souvenir d'une autre sensation ancienne (comme celle du motif de nature utilisée).' The latter statement constitutes the great difference from the symbolistic painters we have discussed in our third chapter. 'Dans l'un c'est la forme qui est expressive, dans l'autre c'est la nature qui veut l'être.' [al]

Indeed they aimed at elucidating the meaning of nature, and at expressing their idea of it with the aid of purely artistic means, without expressing this idea in an explicitly figurative way by means of allegory and the like. And for this purpose they sought for the expressive power implied in particular lines and colours. 'Observez dans l'immense création de la nature et vous verrez s'il n'y pas des lois pour créer avec des aspects tout differents et cependant semblables dans leur effet, tous les sentiments humains' [am]—thus Gauguin in 1885 in a letter we shall revert to later.

'Au lieu d'évoquer nos états d'âme au moyen du sujet répresenté c'est l'oeuvre elle-même qui devait transmettre la sensation initiale, en perpétuer l'émotion' [am]—this they strove after. This idea was to have a great influence later on especially in expressionism. This was the new element separating them from the symbolistic painters. But this was not their sole aim. This arrangement of colours in lines had to be beautiful, too.

Much more than the symbolistic milieu these artists were always occupied with purely painter's questions. From a reaction against academic art they again clearly realized that after all a picture is a two-dimensional area. This idea was given a very extreme form of expression in Denis' too famous utterance—too famous, because it denoted a facet of their striving, it is true, but not the essence of their art: 'Se rappeler qu'un tableau—avant d'être un cheval de bataille, une femme nue, ou une quelconque anecdote—est essentiellement une surface plane recouverte de couleurs en un certain ordre assemblées.[ao]

116

THE ORIGIN AND DEVELOPMENT OF THE
SYNTHETIST THEORY OF ART 1885-1890

Gauguin and the artists of his circle were no doubt revolutionaries striving after a complete break with existing state of affairs. But they did not look down on the achievements of the past. On the contrary, they often felt they were merely winning back what had been lost in the course of time—especially during the previous hundred years. Gauguin often explicitly confessed to his admiration for Rafael and Ingres, [1] and Denis calls this movement (in 1890) Neo-traditionalism. They always admired Delacroix and Cézanne whom they even considered as an older master and precursor.

Reflection and contemplation always accompanied their artistic work proper. This is almost a matter of course. If an artist does not just paint according to the 'fashion', the 'times', and the 'current' method, but fiercely reacts against contemporary and current things, it is, of course necessary for him to realize clearly what he wishes and not to adopt a merely negative attitude. What former generations had considered as only a matter of course had to be recovered by reflection and ratiocination. The synthetists sometimes felt their own non-naturalistic method to be something 'arbitrary'.[a] This proves that they were so much imbued with the naturalistic way of thought that any deviation from it seemed to them to be a deviation from the norm. This is the reason why the revolutionary character of their work is less obvious to us now than it was then. We look back on this development and we have witnessed the realization of the freedom of the twentieth century. They were still very close to naturalism and impressionism, and when they simply gave their figures an outline or slightly stylized them, this process was experienced as an extreme conquest of their own freedom.

In view of this situation it is to be understood that the first work

117

that was seen made the spectator ask after the 'why' and the 'wherefore'—just as is the case at present with abstract art or another kind of modernistic work—so that the artists were compelled to give an account of their own activities and aims. For, as Aurier says, 'il faillait justifier (l'art idéiste)[b] par d'abstraites et compliquées argumentations, tant il semble paradoxal à nos civilisations décadentes et oublieuses de toute initiale révélation ...' [c] Besides, the introductory word was also worth while to convince fellow artists of the rightness of their starting-point. For this purpose it was necessary to show that thus the impasse into which art had landed could be overcome. It is, therefore, not surprising to hear Denis say: 'En outre, Sérusier nous prouvait par Hegel, et les lourdes articles d'Albert Aurier insistaient sur ce fait que logiquement, philosophiquement, c'était Gauguin qui avait raison.' [d] Very often, no doubt, the words and thoughts of the predecessors rather than their works as such will have induced young painters to prefer the new movement.

It should not be supposed that the theories were made afterwards only to justify the works of the artists. On the contrary, when examining the development in this circle we shall more than once find that theory and reflection preceded its realization or concretizing in a work of art. As a matter of fact, with them action and thought, painting and talking always accompanied each other, and were indissolubly interwoven in the totality of their evolution. For their art was not an 'applied theory' however much reflection influenced their method. This is why in our expositions of the development of their theories we shall often have to include the pictures themselves and the stylistic evolution.

Gauguin's early development

We have already seen Cézanne's probable fructifying influence on the first formation of a trend of thought in Gauguin which deviated from strict impressionism. But this cannot possibly explain the ideas that Gauguin expounded in his famous letter from Kopenhagen to Schuffenecker in the year 1885. We must, doubtless, remember that Gauguin was acquainted with what was going on at Paris.[e] Although in those years Gauguin was not actively or thoroughly occupied with the development in the literary milieu, the chief points will not have escaped him, even if only through what he had

118

probably read in the Figaro. [f] He will no doubt have read Baudelaire's *Curiosités Esthétiques* published in 1884—even if only on
account of his great interest in Delacroix, some of whose work he
had seen at Arosa's already at an early age and whom he held in
high esteem all his life. It is possible that in those years he also read
in one of the editions of Delacroix's writings that were then in
existence.

What particular ideas may have influenced Gauguin in those
years? We need not be under the illusion that Gauguin should have
studied Baudelaire's and Delacroix's works in the same way as we
tried to do in our second chapter. On the other hand, however, it is
not necessary to suppose that he was content to be influenced by a
few slogans without grasping the basic thoughts. Not only was he
near to them as to time and environment, but he also knew Delacroix's paintings very well. Therefore Baudelaire's expositions and
Delacroix's observations that reached him [g] could be immediately
related to things seen and to his experiences of them, so that they
were far removed from being a drab theory.

In addition to Baudelaire's introductions to translations of Poe Gauguin will have acquainted himself with Baudelaire's *Curiosités Esthétiques*. The primacy of the personality ideal found in that work, the
vindication of the artist's freedom without any violence done to
reality, are as many motifs that will no doubt also have influenced
Gauguin in realizing his own attitude with respect to such problems.
We shall insert a few quotations that may have had a strong appeal
to Gauguin. Although in the literal sense of the word they are not
actually found in Gauguin's writings, the thoughts embodied in
them are there all the more unmistakably. 'C'est un bonheur de
rêver, et c'était une gloire d'exprimer ce qu'on rêvait.' [h] Then there
is the idea of the musicality of painting, also found in Delacroix's
writings, to which we shall revert later on, and on the same page:
'Il y a des tons gais et folâtres, folâtres et tristes, riches et gais, riches
et tristes, de communs et d'originaux.' [i]

As for Delacroix we will suffice with a quotation from a work published in 1885. It is not a quotation from the great artist himself,
it is true, but the thought will no doubt have had a strong appeal to
Gauguin in connection with the artistic ideal formulated in it:
'L'oeuvre de Eugène Delacroix contient la sensation, l'émotion

119

constante, l'emotion aiguë qui conduit en un instant le spectateur par toutes les phases de l'activité intellectuelle surexcitée. L'idée fixe du maître, si je ne me trompe pas, a été de rendre pour ainsi dire palpables, visibles au moyen des couleurs et des formes, les combats qui s'agitent au secrèt des âmes.' [j] Gauguin speaks in a similar way in his letter to Schuffenecker from Kopenhagen on the 24th of May 1885. He asks for a photo of the 'Barque de Don Juan' [k] and a.o. he says: 'De même chez Delacroix les bras et les épaules se retournent toujours d'une façon insensée et impossible au raisonnement, mais cependant expriment le réel dans la passion.' And further on: 'Rien que la peinture, pas de trompe-l'oeil.' And: 'le trait chez lui (est) un moyen d'accentuer une idée.' [l]

But already before this, on the 14th of January, he had written the famous and often quoted letter to the same gentleman. In it he starts with thoughts that are closely akin to those quoted above with respect to Delacroix: 'Pour moi le grand artiste est la formule de la plus grande intelligence, à lui arrivent les sentiments, les traductions les plus délicates et par suite les plus invisibles du cerveau. Observez dans l'immense création de la nature et vous verrez s'il n'y a pas des lois pour créer avec des aspects tout différents et cependant semblables dans leur effet,[m] tous les sentiments humains.' [n] In this couple of short sentences we have the quintessence of the whole programme of Gauguin's later art. We especially point to his search for a different kind of representation which should tell us more of the subject than was possible to the naturalistic artist, but maintains the latter's reality. 'J'en conclus qu'il y a des lignes nobles, menteuses, etc.' [n] is his not quite logical or convincing conclusion from a short exposition to the effect that a particular object, e.g., a spider, arouses a multitude of feelings in us which contain more than only the visible aspect as such. This idea of lines that express something in an iconic way is found in hardly any of the precursors or contemporaries [o] discussed by us. But we do find the idea that colours may express something, as appears from our above quotation from Baudelaire. Gauguin has assimilated the latter thought entirely, so that he had no need to use the same examples as Baudelaire. He writes: 'Les couleurs sont encore plus explicatives quoique moins multiples que les lignes par suite de leur puissance sur l'oeil. Il y a des tons nobles, d'autres communs, des harmonies tranquilles, consolantes, d'autres qui vous excitent par

120

leur hardiesse.' q And what follows suggests that which we have already quoted concerning Delacroix: 'les lignes et les couleurs ne nous donneraient-t-ils aussi le caractère plus ou moins grandiose de l'artiste.' q But instead of going on with Delacroix he speaks of Cézanne. It remains possible that Cézanne had spoken of these things—although he hardly makes use of it himself or speaks of it later on. But Gauguin does not say here that Cézanne tried to find it in this direction. He rather quotes him as an evidence of his thesis quoted here. And then he formulates the thought that actually contains the whole theory of synthetist art in a nutshell: 'Plus je vais, plus j'aborde p dans ce sens de traductions de la pensée par p tout autre chose qu'une littérature.' And finally he summarizes his ideal clearly in the words: 'travaillez librement et follement... un grand sentiment peut être traduit immédiatement, rêvez dessus et cherchez en la forme la plus simple.' q Here the term 'rêver' is used exactly in the way Baudelaire did in the quotation given above.

It is true that his work of this period and of the following years hardly does justice to these words. Theory is many years ahead of its realization. Yet in his work he seems to have been occupied with it. Did not he often speak in 1886 about the 'synthesis' he is aiming at? r The sole use of the term shows that he is entirely ahead of or at least abreast with his time.

Yet also his work of the time immediately after this makes it clear that his art is gradually changing, that he was searching for a method of giving a more summarizing vision by a new way of approach. We do not find a genuine break with the past, s but we do find strong influences of Cézanne and Degas.

We are referring particularly to some landscapes from Martinique. 2 In this we see how the choice of a high visual point (suggesting Degas' Japanizing manner) enables the whole painted surface to play a part in the realization of the subject and breaks through naturalism in landscape painting, also because the interplay of the lines of the composition assumes a more independent meaning in this way. This is further underlined by the network of the treetrunks on the surface in a manner reminiscent of Cézanne 3, although we cannot say for certain that Gauguin knew the latter's works of the eighties—he may have seen them at Tanguy's. The new aspect of those landscapes is also due to the absence of any perspective of the sky. This feature

121

had been suggested by Cézanne's work made about 1880.[4] But in contradistinction to Cézanne and Degas, Gauguin used these means to impart to colour and line an artistically expressive value of their own.

These statements make it clear that in his letter of 1885 Gauguin was not concerned with a kind of symbolism, but with that which Baudelaire called 'musicality' and which we have discussed before,[5] viz., that the atmosphere of a picture as a composition, as the artistic interplay of lines and colours, is the bearer of the expression of the subject. And at this time already Gauguin broke with impressionism in this respect that in the conception of his composition is included the human evaluation of the meaning of things. This appears from the rôle assigned to the human figures in his pictures. It is true, the manner of painting itself was still impressionistic; viz., little touches side by side; and the manner in which he described the forms in their plastic quality and in their own colours was in principle similar to what he had learnt from Pissarro. But the vision embodied in the picture was by no means derived from what is visible only—and this is, in fact, what was new in it. So Gauguin very carefully tried to extend the possibilities of the art of painting. His development was certainly not rectilinear. In 1886 he painted the portrait of Laval, a work which anticipated the future in many respects,[6] but two years later, after his return from Martinique, he still made a view of Pont-Aven,[7] which was almost purely impressionistic and in his 'Three dancing Breton girls'[t] in the same year he very nearly approached a more academic kind of art after the manner of Cottet.

Living at such a long distance from these events we have a difficulty in estimating the renovations of those times at their true value because later on the artists broke with the past in a much more violent, more consistent and more extreme way. It is clear, however, that in his art Gauguin tried to find ways to represent more than what is strictly visual. We do not think it correct to say that in his art he did not strive after that which he knew how to express in comparatively clear language, so that he may be said to have remained an ordinary impressionist. Indeed, also his own words about the work he made, contradict this supposition. From Martinique he wrote: 'je n'ai jamais eu une peinture aussi claire, aussi lucide (par exemple beaucoup de fantaisie).'[u] Especially the words 'lucide' and 'fantaisie' point in the direction of his new conception of art.

The early development of Bernard

In many respects it is difficult to form a clear idea of what
Bernard thought about art in those years before 1888. We do not
possess direct pronouncements made by him, but we have all the more
at our disposal of what he noted down himself later on, or of what
others wrote down of his utterances. But in view of the controversy
with reference to these after-considerations, we should not attach too
much value to them in our opinion. And certainly not if accurate
definitions are required.

There is no doubt that before 1888 Bernard had achieved a few
things that might be called new. His art is an effort to strike out new
paths. In this he was strongly influenced by Cézanne—he saw the
latter's work at Tanguy's [8] —although this influence is not easy [v] to
point out in his own style. It seems to us that the Japanese influence
was more important, which does not only appear from the choice of
a high view point in the landscape,[9] but especially from the composition. He aims at a well-considered 'decorative' [w] composition, built
up of large areas of colour. The forms are sometimes as surprising as
with the Japanese: although in the whole it is a fascinating and
striking blot of colour, its exact meaning is not immediately clear
at first sight. Later on we discover that this particular form certainly
has an iconic meaning. [x] The interplay of forms thus has a twofold
function: on the one hand it has a fascinating decorative function,
and on the other it has a very accurately defined iconic sense.

As has been said, it is difficult to say what conceptions of art Bernard had in those years. It is, of course, clear that he rejected naturalism, and also classicism was not particularly congenial to him then.
This latter fact was perhaps chiefly due to the influence of his milieu,
for later on he comes into his own when he changes over to a kind
of classicism. In 1886 he often came into contact with Vincent van
Gogh; but it is not easy to say if the latter had any influence on his
thoughts on art. In view of the fact that van Gogh often discussed
art with him, we think it probable that Bernard learnt a few things
from him. It is striking e.g., that in 1885 Bernard started making
biblical pictures, but since 1886 with one exception he devoted himself entirely to painting landscapes, farmer's wives from Bretagne, and
a portrait,[10] whereas later on, in 1889, so when van Gogh's direct in-

123

fluence had expanded itself, he again reverts to biblical subjects. To this Van Gogh reacts with slashing criticism.[11] Van Gogh may have explained to him that art should represent the peculiar individual character of persons and things. These thoughts had already been expressed by him before with reference to the 'Potato-eaters'. However, he did not mean it in a naturalistic sense, but in a realistic sense, not excluding deformations, if necessary. Thus Van Gogh's views might be characterized.[12]

Already at the beginning of his career Bernard had come into contact with impressionism and had sympathized with it in some measure. But very soon he tried to overcome this impressionism. His contacts with men like Van Gogh, Gauguin (his contact with Gauguin was slight, but all the same it was sufficient for him to know what Gauguin was doing), Signac, and Cézanne's work,[13] but perhaps more important his knowledge of what was going on in literary circles, opened his eyes to the deficiencies of impressionism. So after a very short impressionistic period he is immediately in the centre of the movement of 1885. He even made poems in the symbolistic spirit.[14]

In 1888 his views would have been something like the following y: 'Puisque l'idée est la forme des choses recueillies par l'imagination, il fallait peindre non plus devant la chose, mais en la reprenant dans l'imagination, qui l'avait recueillie, qui en conservait l'idée, ainsi l'idée de la chose apportait la forme convenable au sujet du tableau ou plutôt à son idéal (somme des idées) la simplification que l'essentiel des choses perçues et par conséquent en rejette le détail...' z These thoughts are closely related to those advanced by the literary artists about 1885. And instead of referring vaguely to the generation of 1885 we can be more precise and like Michaud speak of the symbolists who are clearly distinguished by him from the 'decadents' and the people of the 'poésie fantastique.' aa If we consider the opinion expressed by Ghil, e.g., in 1885, a member of Mallarmé's school, who was also strongly opposed to the 'decadents',[15] this relationship is very clear. This is why it is no accident that in spite of his admiration for Redon, e.g., Bernard himself never dared to make such works of (pictorial) art as we have called symbolistic. As a matter of fact the entire social milieu in which he moved was averse to it.

To circumscribe the influence exercised by the men of letters on

Bernard's thought we may e.g. quote Moréas' famous manifesto, which Bernard will no doubt have known: 'Symbolic poetry endeavors to clothe the Idea in a sensitive form which, nevertheless, could not be an end in itself, but would be subordinate to the Idea while serving to express it... art can derive from objectivity only a simple and extremely succinct point of departure.'[16]

But no doubt, other influences, too, determined his ideas of pictorial art. The use of the word 'imagination' immediately calls up reminiscences of Baudelaire's *Curiosités Esthétiques,* a work that Bernard is sure to have known. Besides there are many points of resemblance between the way in which in the above quotation he defines the relation between the idea and the reality perceived and that which Delacroix had written in his diary. [ab] It is true, this diary had not yet been published, but the passage referred to by us occurs as a quotation in Dargenty's book on Delacroix published in 1885, and there Bernard may have found it.[17]

For our examination of Bernard's view of art in the years before he met Gauguin in Pont Aven in the summer of 1888, Van Gogh's letters to Bernard are very valuable. In these we read that Bernard is busy studying old Italian and German art in order to discover 'la signification symbolique que peut contenir le dessin abstrait et mystique...', and a little further on he again mentions 'tes recherches relatives aux propriétés des lignes à mouvements opposés'. [ac] So Van Gogh here points out certain ideas in Bernard concerning the manner of composition, and the meaning the latter attaches to the language of lines and colours in a composition. This is a purely synthetist thought that we have already come upon in Gauguin, and which we shall find again in a more elaborate form later on. And the fact that Van Gogh cautiously warns him against the danger of 'stériles méditations métaphysiques' at any rate suggests that at that time Bernard was occupied by art-theoretical problems—problems in which Van Gogh took little interest when they were thus posited and thought out.

Finally we wish to mention another possible source of Bernard's thought. We are referring to the 'Art Nouveau' movement which precisely in those years began to assume more distinct features. In the rise of this kind of art in France there were two decisive factors at work; viz., the example of the English—the work of William

125

Morris and his followers, e.g., Crane with his illustrations of Children's books—and Japanese art. This Art Nouveau was in the first place a revival of decorative art. And it is remarkable in this connection that Bernard himself so strongly emphasizes this decorative element. Thus, later on, he wrote that in those days he had asserted: 'Painting, being decorative, should above all please the eye and the mind: and for this there were but two means; color on one hand, invention of the picture on the other . . .' [18]. When in an essay by Gonse published in March 1888 we read about this Art Nouveau milieu, we are struck by his emphatic statement that it seems necessary to some people for a work of art also to contain 'un contingent d'idées psychologiques et quasi-littéraires' and that the Japanese may perhaps lack this element, but that on the other hand they have something else, namely 'cette prédominance absolue du principe décoratif dans toutes les branches de l'art.' And this is why he wishes to honour them as the greatest ornamental painters of the world. The Japanese, he says, possesses 'le goût naturel de la synthèse', 'un instinct merveilleux des ressources de la couleur', 'une connaissance approfondie des lois de leur harmonie', 'une délicatesse infinie à varier leur emploi.' [ad]

The English influence is even harder to establish from the source-material; this is certainly so with respect to art-theories. Yet the artists in question are sure to have known English art, both from the pictures they saw at Bing's in Paris and from books. Gauguin appears to have possessed a book of illustrations by Caldecott and to praise it highly. [19] But it is really almost unthinkable that Bernard should have been ignorant of English art in the spirit of Morris etc.,[ae] not only because he took such a great interest in everything that presented it-self as something new, but especially because the carved wooden cabinet doors he made at Pont Aven in 1888 [20] would else be almost inexplicable in their style and construction. The same thing applies to the stained glass windows of this period. [20]

The events of the summer of 1888

We have arrived now at the events of the summer of 1888, to which there has always been given such a lot of attention.[af] For then Gauguin and Bernard entertained a close contact with each other at Pont Aven for a somewhat longer period of time. The younger man is supposed to have induced the older one to produce an entirely new kind of art. There is no doubt that Bernard was ahead of Gauguin as to style, and the latter will have borrowed the former's use of flat colours, 'cloisonné' [ag] at least temporarily. For even in those cases in which before his meeting Bernard, Gauguin explicitly mentioned his working in the spirit of the Japanese, he still sticks to a loose and shaded way of painting in small strokes.[21] When, however, we examine the compositions concerned, it is clear to us that Gauguin had developed a new art and was by no means any longer a mere impressionist. In fact he realized this himself, for in the letter in question he explicitly adds these words: 'Ce n'est pas du tout des Degas'.[ah]

But the most important thing for us is what was thought and said in the field of the theory of art. Here it is quite plausible that Bernard had a great deal to say to Gauguin, for the former knew what was going on at Paris. Gauguin was, indeed, not entirely ignorant of these things, but Bernard's mental disposition and his greater literary interest naturally enabled him to be better informed of art-theoretical matters than Gauguin.

It is not unlikely for Bernard to have rendered the same service to Gauguin that he did to Cézanne later on. He compelled Gauguin to realize and to define his own ideas more precisely, for Bernard asked him questions and was very much intent upon theoretical clarity. He wanted to realize discursively what a painter really does when he is painting. At the same time Bernard may have brought Gauguin's terminology up to date. So we do not believe that Gauguin was now, as it were, confronted by an entirely new trend of thought, but we think that their conversations carried both Gauguin and Bernard further. If it were really true that Gauguin took over everything from Bernard after the true manner of a pupil, it is not quite understandable why exactly at this time Bernard conceived such a great admiration for him.[22] As a matter of fact, although these two men now came into closer contact with each other for the first time, they had had an indirect contact through Theo and Vincent van Gogh and many mutual friends and acquaintances among the Parisian vanguard. The almost immediate agreement that arose between these men at Pont Aven in the summer of 1888 exactly with respect to their conceptions of pictorial art is, therefore, in no way a miracle.

Indeed, it remains to be seen whether Bernard really wanted to say that he had shown Gauguin the way to a new art theory. For it is true that Bernard says that Gauguin 'vit en vérité dans mon travail et éprouva par l'exposé de mes idées tout ce que l'on pouvait tirer de Cézanne',[ai] but this does not mean that he transferred entirely new ideas of art to Gauguin. It is possible that only some theories on colours and their effect were concerned of which Gauguin admitted their correctness. Perhaps Bernard's contribution was connected with purely technical matters, viz. the fact that colours which have been applied unmixed and flat have a much greater effect, which may be intensified by means of black-blue contours.[23] Bernard's influence on account of which he considered himself to be the real 'father' of synthetism is, therefore, less a question of theories than one of a new style which was based on Bernard's manner of composition described above.

Nevertheless we really think that in the summer of 1888 an important step was taken in the direction of a new art-theory, that of synthetism. And although we do not seem to be warranted to say that Gauguin only now started thinking things out and breaking with the pre-suppositions of the older impressionism, it is not possible to entirely rule out the stimulating influence exercised by Bernard in this respect.[ak] This also appears, e.g. in a later letter of Gauguin's from Arles, in which Bernard and Laval asked him what part is played by the shade in a picture. If Bernard had formed the new ideas on art on his own such a question would have been foolish, and Gauguin would rather have asked Bernard about it. But in our opinion Bernard's contribution to the new development consists exactly in his asking such questions. For without this Gauguin would probably never have found such a definite answer to this problem, which was certainly not unimportant with respect to the representation of reality.[24]

We have passed by an important remark in silence, viz., Bernard's assertion that his expositions had induced Gauguin to derive his inspiration from Cézanne more intensely than he had done up till then. This assertion is rather remarkable, for a comparison of Gauguin's work before this time and that after it will have to arrive at the conclusion that Gauguin had got further away from Cézanne rather than nearer to him. What did Bernard consider to be essential to Cézanne's work? In one of the pictures he had taken along with him from St. Briac to Pont Aven, which is given so much praise by Gauguin, [25] Cézanne's influence is very clear.[26] In this landscape, a somewhat

128

accidented terrain without trees, the depth has been built up after the manner of Cézanne, so without the use of aerial perspective. Owing to this method the surface of the picture retained its brightness of colour and the light aspect was not disturbed. Just as in the case of Cézanne the structure of the subject of this work was made clear by a lucid composition. But it is precisely this painting that shows little resemblance to synthetism which was to arise only a short time afterwards. Properly speaking the much older 'Railway bridge at Asnières' (1885) [27] is much nearer to it. The problem is, therefore, far from easy to solve. Perhaps Bernard saw that in Cézanne's work impressionism had been broken through exactly at the point where a transparent composition was concerned in which the whole surface is of a bright colour. But in synthetist works in the proper sense of the term—e.g. 'Breton women in a meadow' and 'Vision après le sermon'—this thought has been realized entirely apart from Cézanne's stylistic characteristics.[al] For now that art arose of which Cézanne said that it proved that Gauguin had never understood anything of him and that such Chinese art seemed to him to be a mockery.[28]

But to revert to the art-theoretical considerations proper: what kind of thoughts were formulated in the summer of 1888? In the first place, then, that the artist is free with respect to nature as given in its visual appearance. The issue is about what is essential and meaningful to man in what has been observed and spiritually experienced. And this can be best painted from the memory which acts like a sieve, selecting and retaining from the object only that which the artist thinks important as a human person. He chooses the essential thing from the multitude of his visual impressions.[am] Similar ideas—how very much they are akin to Baudelaire's—are found in Gauguin as well as in Bernard, although the latter wrote them down from memory only later on. [29] According to Morice Gauguin is reported to have said [an]: 'Mieux est de peindre de mémoire, ainsi votre oeuvre sera vôtre; votre sensation, votre intelligence et votre âme survivront alors à l'oeuil de l'amateur . . . Cherchez l'harmonie.' [ao] And also in a letter to Schuffenecker, shortly after Bernard's arrival, he wrote: 'Un conseil, ne peignez pas trop d'après nature. L'art est une abstraction,[ap] tirez-la de nature en rêvant devant et pensez plus à la création qui résultera.' [aq]

What could be meant by the word 'abstraction' he mentioned just now? We think that it clearly expresses the idea that a work of art has a structure of its own which may be widely different from nature perceived naturalistically, although there is an invariable intention to represent the subject according to its structure and meaning. This is clear from the advice about the shadows referred to above. In it he says that the Japanese, it is true, do not make use of the shadows, and yet 'Ne se servant de la couleur que comme une combinaison de tons, harmonies diverses, donn(e)nt l'impression de la chaleur etc.' [ar] Thus the artist may use shadow when he wants it for his composition, but he may also leave it out: 'C'est en quelque sorte elle (the shadow) qui est à votre service.' [as] A similar thought must be read in the letter he wrote a short time before in which he gave a brief summary of his own work: 'synthèse d'une forme et d'une couleur en ne considérant la dominante.' [at]

We may also refer in this connection to a letter to Schuffenecker at this time with the remarkable pronouncement: 'Que me parlez vous de mon mysticisme terrible. Soyez impressioniste jusqu'au bout et ne vous effrayez de rien.' [au] In the first place it shows that Gauguin had written him a few things about his ideas,[av] and that in this Schuffenecker had recognized such a great deal of similarity to the thoughts of the 'Décadents' or to the (pictorial) symbolists that Schuffenecker thought he should warn him. 'No,' Gauguin said 'soyez impressionniste', in spite of the fact that he rejected impressionism. Just like Van Gogh [30] Gauguin sticks to this term, because it clearly denoted the distance from the academic art of the Salons, whereas he did not think it necessary at this time to lay too much emphasis on the difference from the impressionists proper. Exactly in this context it is all the more clear that this term also means something else, viz., a non-academic art which is realistic—for he distinguishes impressionism from a mystic kind of symbolism (after the manner of Moreau, for instance).

The most important works of this period are Bernard's 'Breton women in the meadow' and Gauguin's 'Vision après le sermon'. Both lay strong stress on composition, the artistic form. Yet in both the subject remains important, although to a lesser degree in Bernard's case. His work is more like a decoration, and is much nearer to what may be called 'Art Nouveau' than Gauguin's work whose content is much more telling and important, and this is not some-

130

thing accidental for this content is fully borne by the artistic configuration. This was Gauguin's deliberate aim.[31] This work is really the explicit and very clear pictorial expression of the thoughts found in the famous letter of 1885. But we must emphatically state that this does not mean that it happened for the first time. Only,—and this was the part played by Bernard—this ideal again presented itself very clearly to his mind and he began to see better how to realize it. Bernard's method connected with Japanese art and with the 'Art Nouveau' suggested the means to him.[aw] But never would Gauguin allow the work of art to merge into mere decoration, and he always wanted to go further and dig deeper. This is not only the difference between Gauguin's art and that of Bernard, but also between their theories.

Gauguin with van Gogh in Arles

Shortly after Gauguin went to Vincent van Gogh at Arles. Their discussions there no doubt made Gauguin even more conscious of his own ideas and induced him to put them in words even more clearly. From the debate about the different artists it appears that Gauguin considered a finely balanced composition as an essential requirement, and not only life caught in an image: 'je vois du Puvis à faire mélangé de japon.'[ax] Even before Gauguin's arrival Van Gogh had stated that he wanted to express something of the object by means of colours.[32] He was thinking of a direct iconization and not of aesthetic effects for their own sake—the poetry was to be in the subject of the painting, in the artistic expression of it.[33] Gauguin, however, laid the accent on the aesthetic aspect, on the beautiful composition of the work which was to be poetic in itself apart from the subject.[33] This composition, however, was to be related to the subject. Thus an aesthetic configuration should be created, which, although meaningful itself, was an accompaniment to the subject of the work and underlined that subject while accompanying it.

It was characteristic of Gauguin that at Arles he found 'une source de beau style moderne.'[ay] He indeed made some pictures here which were stylistically strongly akin to the Japanism and Anglicism of the Art Nouveau.[34] These pictures exhibited that element more clearly than all the other works by Gauguin. Van Gogh followed his example,[35] in a composition which (obviously after Gauguin's manner) was explicitly made from motifs of remembrance—'un souvenir de notre jardin à Etten.' [az] The idea of painting from memory and not direct from nature here found its extreme application. Owing to this we are at any rate sure that Gauguin advanced this conception at that time. This 'garden at Etten' [36] is pretty well the only picture Van Gogh did in this manner.

When very early in 1889, shortly after Gauguin had left, he set about doing the famous picture 'La Berceuse' in the synthetist spirit, he certainly painted from the model and he did not perform a stroke of the brush, not even when making a replica, without having her, Madame Roulin, before him. He tried to arrange the colours in this work in such a telling way that it was significant even on that score alone. 'Heb ik met de kleur al een wiegeliedje gezongen laat ik aan de critici over...' [ba] 'Peut-être dans la Berceuse il y a un essai de petite musique de couleur d'ici...' [bb] It is remarkable that in these two pronouncements the iconic sense of the harmony of colours was related to something different. Later on this method, the method of 'abstraction', was considered as a blind alley by Van Gogh, at least as far as he himself was concerned.[37] But precisely owing to this course of events the characteristic element in the synthetism of Gauguin (and Bernard) has become clear to us. But for these data we should perhaps have been unable to reconstruct their theory in the way we did, namely, that the effect of the colours and the play of the lines in themselves should in the first place make for harmony, and in addition relate to the subject. The above statements made by Van Gogh even suggest that as early as 1888 the term 'musicalité' (following Baudelaire) was used in this connection. It is true, already before Gauguin's sojourn at Arles Van Gogh had also repeatedly spoken of an iconic, non-naturalistic use of colours,[38] but then the question was how to render the typical trait of the object which, as it were, was thus pictorially described in a direct way. It was not meant to be an aesthetic whole working parallel to the subject, without coalescing with it qua talis. The contrast pointed out by Gauguin between Van Gogh and himself: 'du Daumier à faire', or 'du Puvis coloré mélangé de japon' is clear enough in this respect.

Sérusier

Finally we wish to call special attention to another event which may be conducive to getting an insight into the ideas that were formed in the circle of Gauguin in 1888. We are referring to the meeting with *Sérusier*. This young artist was the enthusiastic leader of a small group of pupils of the Académie Julian. Under his influence their interest was much more comprehensive than was mostly the case in such company. It was especially he who called their attention to all that was new in what occupied the minds of his contemporaries, to Wagner, to the 'littérature décadente',[bc] while Sérusier, in connection with the anti-positivism that was in the air, also displayed a great interest in Plotinus.[bd]

In the summer of 1888 Sérusier stayed at Pont-Aven for some time, where he established a hesitant contact with the people round Gauguin, Bernard, Filiger, and others. Shortly before his definite departure he at last ventured to approach Gauguin himself. In connection with the controversy about the question who was the 'initiator' of the new movement it is a remarkable and instructive fact that Bernard referred Sérusier to Gauguin for further information.[39] Although we do not possess direct contemporary reports of al this, we may trust Denis' later writings providing us with all the data, especially in connection with their general agreement with each other. The more so as later on Sérusier never repudiated or corrected Denis' opinions, not even in his private correspondence. Denis relates how after returning from Pont-Aven to the Academie Julian Sérusier showed the lid of a cigar box on which he had made a painting under Gauguin's guidance, 'un paysage informe, à force d'être synthétiquement formulé, en violet, vermillon, vert veronèse et autres couleurs pures, telles qu'elles sortent du tube, presque sans mélange de blanc.' 'Comment voyez-vous cet arbre, avait dit Gauguin devant un coin du Bois d' Amour: il est vert? Mettez donc du vert, le plus beau vert de votre palette;—et cette ombre, plutôt bleu? Ne craignez pas de la peindre aussi bleu que possible.' [be]

It is striking that here Gauguin did not tell Sérusier to work from memory, but exactly with his eyes on nature, although the pupil was advised to maintain a great measure of freedom with respect to it. Again we are aware of the idea that in its aesthetic composition as

133

such the work should be beautiful and telling—for 'take the finest green of your palette' means: on the pictorial surface there must be a beautiful patch of green, and it does not matter whether this green is exactly in agreement with the green of the tree in question.

It is difficult to decide whether the passage given below means that in his exposition of Gauguin's ideas, Sérusier said all this, or that we are here dealing with the result of later contemplation embodying the fruits of more prolonged discussions on this new view. But even if this is so, the essential part of the new ideas on art transmitted by Sérusier has been preserved.

By the way, in this case we would point out the fructifying influence of the spoken word and of art theory together with the direct example of the painting. Denis continues: 'Ainsi nous fût présenté pour la première fois, sous une forme paradoxale, inoubliable, le fertile concept de la 'surface plane recouverte de couleurs en un certain ordre assemblées.'bf (We shall revert to the last sentence when discussing Denis' manifesto of 1890). The final conclusion drawn from this confrontation with a new method is at once that here reality was not rendered naturalistically, but that in an iconic sense 'tout oeuvre d'art était une transportation, une caricature, l'équivalent passionné d'une sensation reçue.' bg

It is a remarkable fact that at the very outset the young artists were engaged in the formation of the new art although they hardly knew impressionism as yet. They will indeed have felt that here was something that (in its anti-naturalism) was akin to the new movement in literature of which they knew something. The synthetists of Pont Aven had apparently initiated Sérusier also in the recent events in French art and had shown him the way how to know about it. For, as Denis tells us, since that day they frequented the gallery of Theo van Gogh and Tanguy's shop to get acquainted with the work of Vincent, Monet, Degas, and Cézanne.40

The fact that here Gauguin handled the matter quite differently from his method when he was with Van Gogh some time later shows that he was by no means a dogmatist with regard to his manner of working. He was especially concerned with an art that should leave the artist a larger measure of freedom than naturalism and impressionism did, so that the work of art might give something that was peculiar to the artist. This ideal inspired Gauguin and directed

134

his development and consequently also the guidance he gave to the younger men. This is also made clear by Denis' observation: 'Gauguin n'était pas professeur . . . C'était au contraire un intuitif. Dans sa conversation comme dans ses récits, il y avait des aphorismes heureux, des aperçues profondes, enfin des affirmations d'une logique pour nous stupéfiante.' [bh]

Gauguin in Paris in 1889

In the early part of 1889, after the tragical events at Arles, Gauguin was again at Paris. He does not seem to have met Sérusier there,[41] but to have cooperated with Bernard. At this time he will also have made acquaintance with Meyer de Haan, and will have met some other pupils such as, e.g., Filiger. His old friend Schuffenecker again entertained him. All this, however, is of minor importance for the history of art-theory, as we do not know what was discussed at that time. Also the fact that Gauguin exhibited with the XX at Brussels may be important for the history of the appreciation of Gauguin, but does not carry us a step further.

Sérusier and some others of his group of the Académie Julian no doubt met Gauguin a little later in the year, namely in the latter part of the summer, when after a short stay in Brittany (where Sérusier looked him up) [bi] he was again at Paris in connection with the exhibition at Volpini's.[bj]

It remains questionable whether or not he had already met the 'avant-garde' of the literary men that year—the source material almost exclusively speaks of the year 1890 in this connection. But if perhaps he did not make any contacts in the winter of that year, he certainly made them in the summer at—or in connection with—the exhibition organized by him and his followers, because various young critics of the symbolist circle wrote about the show.[42] It is almost certain that he then met Aurier, who knew Bernard to whose paper 'Le Moderniste' Gauguin shortly after contributed some articles. [43]. However this may be, it is pretty well inconceivable for him not to have got acquainted with the work of the 'avant-garde' of authors and poets and of their ideas, in view of Bernard's and Sérusier's interest in these things. We think we can discover his reaction. For in this year he made a number of works whose conception was akin to the symbolistic poetry. They are the exception among Gauguin's works,

135

but for this reason they are all the more important, as indicators of a new and alien influence. We are especially referring to his large wooden relief: 'Soyez amoureuse, vous serez heureuse'.[bk] Stylistically this work again testifies to a strongly Japanese influence assimilated more or less after the manner of the 'Art Nouveau', but with a stronger literary element in the painting: 'Le renard symbole indien de la perversité.'[bl] This introduced a new element into Gauguin's art. The composition itself with its peculiar configuration was new and different from the old naturalism. This new manner had already been found in his 'Vision après le sermon'. But in addition to it the composition as such could only be understood 'symbolistically', i.e., the different figures were a rendering of a poetic thought in their iconic relation, and any bond with a visual entity had vanished. But in the details there are enough realistic elements—e.g., in the female nude—showing that Gauguin did not at all renounce his realistic impressionistic past and was absolutely disinclined to adopt the idealizing method characteristic of the symbolistic art after the manner of Moreau.

Gauguin and his friends at Le Pouldu

It would be conceivable that Gauguin had arrived at such a method without any personal contact with the 'avant-garde' of the men of letters or with their work, but directly under the influence of Baudelaire's *Fleurs du Mal*. But it is certain that in this relief we may also recognise a reflex of what occupied him and his circle in Le Pouldu. Notwithstanding the almost total absence of exact data, we may be sure that there was no end of the discussions on art theory, at which Sérusier's and de Haan's real knowledge of philosophy is sure to have contributed to deepening their theories. From the portrait of de Haan made by Gauguin, with both Carlyle's *Sartor Resartus* and Milton's *Paradise Lost* [44] on a table, we know a little about what kind of works appealed to them. Carlyle, by the side of Baudelaire, may have imprinted the idea of 'musicality' deeper into their minds. Baudelaire's work was no doubt also read and discussed, and together with Milton's poem it will have inspired Gauguin to make his 'satanic' self-portrait. [45]

It is difficult to say exactly what theories were elaborated there or in what way. Apart from the source material mentioned there are few documents to inform us of these things. In any case Gauguin still appears to be searching for the synthesis. This cannot only be gathered from the title of the exhibition held in the summer of 1889, 'Groupe impressionniste et synthétiste', or from the drawing representing Bernard, Schuffenecker, and Gauguin against a background inscribed with the word 'Synthétisme',[46] or from the cry 'Vive la sintaise' proving that Gauguin is capable of ridiculing that which he takes very much to heart,[47] but above all from an exposition given by him in a letter to Bernard. In it he says he can appreciate work done from observation—la sensation—as well as work constructed according to strict rules of composition. And he continues to say that this is why 'il y a à faire dans les deux Sens.'[bm] It is clear that we should not read any eclecticism in these words, but that this shows the way to supply the deficiency that Gauguin felt in the works of 'sensation', viz., 'le manque du au-delà'.[bn]

There is another source of information on this period in Le Pouldu in 1890 which deserves our attention, viz. two letters written from there by Sérusier to Denis. He started writing the first when he had just arrived—Gauguin had disappointed him. In this letter written 'Jour de Vénus'[bo] he immediately started with a problem which occupied him and for which he had apparently not yet received a solution from Gauguin, viz. 'Ce qui m'a surtout embarassé, le voilà: quelle part la nature doit-elle avoir dans l'oeuvre? Où s'arrêter? Enfin, au point de vue matériel de l'exécution, faut il travailler d'après nature, ou seulement regarder et se souvenir?'[bp] It seems possible that he hit upon this specific question, which was not without some importance with regard to the working method, on account of a contradiction in Gauguin which he could not explain. For in the year before, Gauguin had taught him to work with his eye on nature and to seek for the synthesis from there, and now he had probably been told to work from memory. It was the same contradiction in Gauguin's views that we have referred to above and then ascribed to the fact that this point was of minor importance to Gauguin.

A few days later Sérusier wrote a second letter which he opens with the remark: 'Je me repens de ce que je t'ai dit sur Gauguin, il n'a rien d'un fumiste, du moins à l'égard de ceux qu'il sait pouvoir le comprendre.'[bq] This quotation fortifies us in the opinion that Sérusier had at first thought that Gauguin had been poking fun at

137

him and had only assumed an air of having a conception of his own. The rest of the letter will claim our attention in a later context.

Although all the source-material proves that Gauguin and his friends were occupied with art-theoretical problems, we should not think that they tried to build up an abstract kind of aesthetics. On the contrary, aesthetics as a branch of philosophy, which is concerned with beauty as a given phenomenon, did not interest them. Their discussions on art, although touching its very foundations, were certainly not abstract but immediately directed to their own work, to their manner of approach and to their working method. And connected with these things there were all kinds of strictly technical problems, from the use of special brushes and colours to questions of composition and the harmony of colours. This is why it is not contrary to what has been said when in a letter written later in the year Sérusier says: 'De toutes mes théories br cherchées cet hiver, cette loi simple me reste: éviter de rapprocher deux tons trop écartés comme valeur, à moins qu'ils n'aient entre eux une parenté de couleur . . .' bs

Gauguin in 1890

In 1890 Gauguin often came into contact with authors and poets of the new movement. Morice tells us how he started oracling on the new art in the midst of those literary men (with an air he had at times also adopted before his pupils). This manner did not seem to meet with such a very favourable reception at that moment, 48 but it proves that after all Gauguin no doubt had definite ideas on art —on this and on other occasions, he will have realized that where theories were concerned he still had a lot to learn.

The quintessence of his exposition on that evening in the Café La Côte d'Or has been summarized by Morice as follows: 'L'art primitif procède de l'esprit et emploie la nature. L'art soi-disant raffiné procède de la sensualité et sert la nature. La nature est la servante du premier et la maîtresse du second. Mais la servante ne peut oublier son origine; elle avilit l'esprit en se laissant adorer par lui. C'est ainsi que nous sommes tombés dans l'abominable erreur du naturalisme . . .' bt It is as clear as daylight that he rejects naturalism. But this is not saying that he considered the kind of (literary) symbolism that we have indicated above as 'decadent' as parallel to what he sought himself.

138

It is not at all certain that he made a sharp distinction between the different tendencies after the manner of Michaud; but we think it very likely that he had his likes and dislikes with regard to the one or the other. This might appear from the people with whom he had a closer contact, Morice and Aurier, and less intensively, also with Moréas—who changed over to a kind of neoclassicism at that time —while we should not underestimate the importance of his contact with Mallarmé—in the sense that Mallarmé, with his erudition now also admitted a Gauguin to his Tuesday-evenings, although the artist would probably not understand much of what was said.

At first sight we should, therefore, be inclined to consider as a foolish tale unworthy of any belief the myth that Gauguin with Sérusier had heard the theory from a set of men of letters and had not understood much of it—especially because Sérusier was present who was himself an erudite theorist to the backbone. But the circumstances indicated above make us suspect that there might be some foundation for this story,[48a] namely, that Gauguin will have responded to the ideas and ideals of the decadents in a strongly negative and disapproving way. In this light we shall, therefore, have to read a (later) pronouncement—in a letter from Sérusier to Verkade in 1893—: 'Gauguin va revenir, j'ai reçu de ses nouvelles. Il a, me dit-il, étudié sans chercher du symbolisme. OH! tant mieux. Il a surgi des gens qui me font détester même ce mot,' [bu] whereas later on Gauguin himself said that he had liberated art from the 'entraves du symbolisme'.[bv] That such pronouncement cannot have been meant to deny his earlier art and to imply that he had started developing new ideas is clear from his own development as an artist and from his letters which every now and again explain his work.

There is, indeed, an other indication that we may interpret Gauguin's attitude in this way, viz., in his attack on Huysmans the 'decadent'. He rejected the latter's interpretation of Redon's work,[49] and found in it something far more profound and essential than a mere 'decadent' play with what is lugubrious and monstrous, an exaltation of what is a-normal and morbid. It appears that Gauguin no doubt understood this art and highly appreciated it. It was a kind of proto-surrealism parallel to the poetical movement characterized by the name of Rimbaud, the movement of the 'poètes maudits' in the narrow sense of the word.[50] Gauguin himself, however, did not take this road, and kept free from any influence exercised by it. The fact that in the portrait of Moréas [51] he quite clearly worked in Redon's manner is an isolated case implying nothing, as Gauguin made more or less a caricature.

But his attack on Huysmans' preference for Gustave Moreau is sharper and even stronger. At the same time it becomes clear why he was never guilty of this pictorial kind of symbolism: he looked upon it as an art which did not really render 'literary' ideas in a pictorial way, but was much rather content with illustrating old stories (which, therefore, roused the realist Gauguin to opposition) in the naturalistic manner. He also sharply rejected the typically decadent preference for all kinds of jewelry: 'His impulsive moment is very far from the heart and he loves the richness of material wealth.' In short, what he found lacking in Huysmans and Moreau was 'simplicity, nobility'. [52]

All this may show that Gauguin's power of judgment was no doubt sharp enough at times. Nor should we think that Gauguin was an illiterate man who did not know about anything. On the contrary, he was a great reader. Rotonchamps relates an anecdote showing that as early as about 1880 Gauguin had read Poe, [53] while also at the time we are now discussing he had certainly read a great deal. From a later letter to Morice it plainly follows that he knew the latter's *Littérature de tout à l'heure* quite well, and was also acquainted with Renan's work.[54] And further, we have Morice's witness in his Gauguin biography of a much later date, which, however, we need not distrust on this point, namely that Balzac and Poe were his favourite authors, and especially Balzac with his *Études philosophiques*, like *Séraphita*.[55]

Finally, the fact that he was in intensive contact not only with the men of letters personally but also with their works is proved by Gauguin's own writings. There was a clear change in style in those years, not so much when factual information or questions were concerned, nor in his perennial complaints about money, etc., but in the description of his own works. In these descriptions he sometimes appeared to have developed a style that is truly literary and of a peculiar kind of beauty. Its abruptness, its telegraphic character sometimes suggests Mallarmé. He himself pointed to Mauclair. [56]

Also at this time Gauguin rarely took the path of (pictorial)

140

symbolism in his paintings and notwithstanding many renewals his
work remained realistic. Only in a few cases did he make something
that revealed a stronger influence of literature in a symbolistic spirit.
The most striking example of this kind was no doubt his 'Perte du
Pucelage'. [57] The choice of the subject as well as the way in which
the symbols are used are not realistic. With regard to the composition,
so to the way in which the subject is treated, we might point to influences exercised by Puvis de Chavannes, however much the colours
deviated from the latter's art. It is a debatable question as to whether
or not this work has the 'nobility' of which he spoke at this time
himself, but the 'simplicity' that he failed to find in Moreau is there.
Although in this Gauguin comes nearest to a conception akin to
Moreau, the real distance between them remains immense, especially
owing to the fundamental difference in their use of pictorial means.
For Moreau derived them from naturalism and Gauguin developed
new means.

VII

THE DEFINITIVE FORMULATIONS

Morice

In 1890 and later Gauguin had a rather intensive contact with Morice, whose ideas will certainly not have failed to influence him. Although it is difficult to decide exactly what are formulations and ideas advanced by Morice himself and what Gauguin actually said in the summing up of his thoughts given by Morice in his Gauguin-book of 1919, these summaries will no doubt represent the artist's views expressed in these conversations, at least as to their purport. Morice tells us that Gauguin was in his own way interested in philosophy: 'Il 'philosophe' quand il manifeste sa manière de comprendre les idées générales... (saying): 'La philosophie est lourde, si d'instinct elle n'est pas en moi. Douce au sommeil avec le rêve qui lui donne parure—ce n'est pas science... elle n'est une conséquence comme de graves personnages voudraient nous l'enseigner, mais bien une arme qu'en sauvages nous seuls fabriquons par nous-mêmes. Elle ne se manifeste comme une réalité, mais comme une image: tel un tableau, admirable si le tableau est un chef-d'oeuvre.' [a] The style of this quotation strongly suggests Morice himself, but the thoughts and images employed may very likely be Gauguin's— they nowhere contradict later pronouncements in the latter's writings. These quotations show at any rate that Gauguin will have been very much interested in Morice's theoretical explanations (whose book as we saw he had thoroughly read) if only to convince younger men of the correctness of his own views.

In this respect Morice was the right man to turn to. For Morice was one of the prominent men of letters of the younger generation who are grouped together under the name of 'Symbolists'. He owed this position to his book: *La littérature de tout à l'heure* [1] published in 1889, a work in which by his closed and well-considered exposition he once for all gave symbolism its fixed form—we are using the term in the narrower sense of the word for the literary group related to pictorial synthetism. In lucid language and without any wavering or doubt he explained his own conceptions of the function of art in the human world, of the meaning and the purpose of every artistic activity, of the high respect that was due to it and of the corrupt state in which it was found in many respects. If anywhere it is in this book that the fundamental meaning of synthesis was elaborated and proclaimed to be the essential thing of any art that understands its time and its task.

Indeed the search of synthesis was not something new,—we have already met with it rather often. But let us not forget that by men like Baudelaire and Poe and others with whom we have found it before, it was indeed presented as something new. They tried to retain romanticism and to connect it with contemporary scientialistic positivism, or, considered from the other point of view, it was an effort to compensate for the one-sidedness and the shortcomings of positivism with its sociological-naturalistic tendencies by clinging to the passion for freedom of the romantic personality-ideal. The seekers for this synthesis—among whom Baudelaire took the lead and was one of the determining factors that framed the future of France owing to his enormous influence—, had been isolated figures, to such an extent even that more than twenty years after Baudelaire's death the viewpoint of the 'synthesis' was still something new in French cultural life. We should not forget that at the time when Baudelaire wrote his articles that were to bring him such fame later on, Comte had finished his most important work only a short time ago,—in 1842 appeared the last volume of his *Cours de philosophie positive*—whereas only two years before the death of Baudelaire Taine published his *Philosophie de L'Art* (1865), a work in which the positivist way of thought was also elaborated for art-history and art-theory.

It is true, in 1889 Morice was justified in saying that Baudelaire and Poe 'érigent en dogmes qui n'auront plus d'hérétiques parmi les vrais poètes' [b] the fundamental conceptions of the viewpoint of the synthesis. But he also appeared to think it necessary to open his book with an attack on the science-ideal, 'la vulgarisation des sciences' [c] resulting in 'Mediocreté. Produit fatal de la 'diffusion de lumières' —cette énorme plaisanterie, cette monstrueuse extase moderne,' [d] in which the battle-axe lifted already by Baudelaire was taken over and handled in almost the same way. Morice is still able to state that 'ils ne veulent plus que des formules, 2 et 2 font 4, il n'y a que cela au fond de tout'.[e]

But however this may be, he said, even though the poets no longer have an audience, they must write all the same. This is their fate. And then he continued with a theory of art based on an ontology which follows Plotinus very closely [f]: 'Émanations de Dieu, étincelles echappées du Foyer de la Toute—Lumière, ils—the poets—y retournent.' [g] This is 'l'universelle loi de la vie', 'des âmes'. These souls 'sont les manifestations extérieures de Dieu qui les émet avec la mission à coopérer, toutes diversement, à la lumineuse harmonie mondiale.' [h] And it is art which can bring this about best. For, Morice said, 'Le livre, l'objet d'art, la phrase musicale, la pure pensée elle-même ... sont des éternisations du Moi. C'est que nous en faisons autant de moyens de dégager notre Moi des contingences et c'est qu'aussi, par là même et dès qu'il échappe aux contingences, le Moi humain recourt ... au foyer de l'absolu, au lieu metaphysique des Idées, à Dieu'.[i] So it appears that for Morice the activity of the subject in its creative work consisted in liberating himself to freedom (in the humanistic sense of the word), which at the same time enabled him to the intellectual mystical merging into the Plotinian god.

According to Morice, a true work of art is directed to the totality of man, not only to his mind nor only to his senses. It will be perfect in form precisely to please the senses, for 'la forme, dans l'oeuvre ainsi parfaite et idéale, n'est que l'appât offert à la séduction sensuelle pour qu'ils soient apaisés, endormis dans une ivresse délicieuse et laissent l'esprit libre, les sens enchantés de reconnaître les lignes et les sons primitifs, les formes non trahies par l'artifice et que trouve le génie dans sa communion avec la Nature.' [k] Thus a genuine work of art will have a strong and living bond with natural reality exactly because then the meaning of the work of art will get its due. For in this case 'l'apparition vague et charmante d'une entité divine de l'Infini' [l] will be left to the liberated spirit. And this is decisive for the high value of art, for, 'ainsi entendu, l'Art n'est que le révélateur de l'Infini: il est le moyen même d'y pénétrer. Il y va plus profond qu'aucune Philosophie, il y prolongue et répercute la révélation d'un Évangile . . .' [m]

And then he emerges with his creative principle as with a triumphant manifesto: 'C'est là le grand, le principal et premier signe de la Littérature nouvelle, c'est là, dans cette ardeur d'unir la Vérité et la Beauté, dans cette unité désirée de la Foi et de la Joie, de la Science et de l'Art'—'l'Art Intégral'. [n] How does this connection between art and (philosophical or religious) truth arise? By means of the idea of the symbol: 'Nous cherchons la Vérité dans les lois harmonieuses de la Beauté, déduisant de celle-ci toute métaphysique —car l'harmonie des nuances et des sons symbolise l'harmonie des âmes et des mondes—et toute morale . . .' [o] He then enlarges upon the history of 19th century art with its romanticism and its naturalism, to point out that there were predecessors who strove after an 'idéal esthétique plus complet', mentioning the names of Chateaubriand and Goethe. [2] They and Stendhal, de Vigny, Sénancour, Gérard de Nerval wrote for the generations that were to read them, about 1890, announcing the desire 'de faire confluer en un seul large et vivant fleuve de Beauté réuni à la Vérité dans la Joie le courant mystique et le courant scientifique.' [p] A synthesis, therefore, of the personality-ideal and that of science, of (human) freedom and nature, as we have characterized these basic motives of humanism above—but we should remember of course that in the humanism of these people coming of a (however much secularized) Roman-Catholic milieu there are strong influences of Plotinus and of Christianity at work, of motives that had become manifest in the first few centuries of our era in the attempt to combine Greek philosophy and Christian doctrine. [3] Of this art, says Morice, Balzac and Wagner are the great forerunners and builders, and Baudelaire and Poe the dogmatic theorists. [4]

But although Morice enthusiastically proclaims that he wants a synthesis in which also science is given a place and is taken full account of in the work of art, as well as mysticism and human freedom, there remains an important restriction with respect to science. First we read the accusation that art asked the advice of science, but that the latter took advantage of it in order to dominate over art. He is no doubt referring to naturalism in literature. And it is still more

145

clear that by this science he certainly does not merely mean positivistic science when we read: 'En attendant que la Science ait décidément conclu au Mysticisme, les intuitions du rêve y devancent la Science, y célèbrent cette encore future et déjà definitive alliance du Sens réligieux et du Sens scientifique dans une fête esthétique où s'exalte le désir très humain d'une réunion de toutes les puissances humaines par un retour à l'originelle simplicité.' q

We have already found the word 'simplicité' used in this way in Gauguin—in his letters in which he speaks of Redon, Huysmans, and Moreau 5—and we have no doubt that this may be interpreted as evidence of Morice's influence on Gauguin's thought (and the way of formulating his thought). r

A little further on in his book he comes back to the subject of synthesis, and thus clearly shows that in his opinion—as in that of Gauguin and his followers—nature does play a certain part in art and that they do not at all seek for a 'non-figurative' art which in its exaltation of the freedom motive cuts through any bond with (observable) reality. The real issue was how to find an art which should realize the demand 'de suggérer tout l'homme par tout l'art.' s All the elements that were essential for the creation of a work of art in Romanticism and Naturalism will have to cooperate together. For: 'la synthèse ne peut se localiser ni dans la pure psychologie passionnelle, ni dans la pure dramatisation sentimentale, ni dans la pure observation du monde tel que nous le voyons dans l'immédiat, puisqu'elle risquerait de cesser d'être la Synthèse et de redevenir l'Analyse.' t A little further on he even more clearly states the real issue —leaving out all plotinian philosophizing he had used to give his art-theory a firm ontological basis—, 'L'oeuvre d'art est une transaction entre le tempérament de l'artiste et la nature.' u

This plotinian thought is evidence of the working of old motives of the christian world.v We need certainly not suspect Morice of pulling our leg in a somewhat erudite way, but we should thoroughly realize that at bottom this synthesis is a matter that should be understood from the dialectic of humanism,6 in which the religious dynamis of the freedom motive is the determining impulse. This is very clear when we read point one of his programme drawn up to arrive at the realization of the new art: 'L'art est une reprise par l'âme de ses propres profondeurs, que (in order that!) l'âme s'y libère de toutes entraves pour la joie et l'intelligence du monde et d'elle-même.'ᵂ And then he starts with an exposition ⁷ which shows that the freedom he is after is something characteristically humanistic, and of an entirely different nature from the biblical freedom. 'Toute vie est enchaînée par une autre vie', he says to prove that the freedom he desires does not yet exist in this world, so that there is 'le désordre du monde'.ˣ But already the second great commandment given by Christ Jesus shows that our human task and our glory is to be sought in this very bond with the other human persons—thou shalt love thy neighbour as thyself! For Christian freedom implies the love of all men (II Peter 1 : 7) in a very concrete sense and not at all that loneliness of man which is the result, according to Morice, of the attainment of or even the search for freedom—'cette reprise de soi dans la liberté—.'ʸ And the thesis that this freedom gives man 'un sentiment d'illimitée puissance' ᶻ throws an even clearer light on the radical difference between this humanistic striving of man to be a god—compare what we have quoted from Carlyle in an earlier chapter—⁸ and the Biblical Christian striving after being a good and faithful servant who expects everything from his Lord whose Kingdom is sure to come.

This humanistic ideal of freedom is always connected dialectically with the nature motive, as absolute freedom is necessarily unrealizable and man will always have to capitulate to reality itself if the latter is felt to be the non-I and is identified with nature. Thus Morice may land in an antinomy, although he is no apostate from humanistic tradition, when after the quotations given above he continues saying 'la gloire de l'homme dans le monde est de se reduire à n'être, au lieu de l'élu contestable d'un chimérique titre royal—a clear allusion to the Biblical-Christian idea with regard to this subject—que le réel ministre de la Nature (with a capital letter!) et son confident. Ici, la Science naturelle intervient pour conclure avec la Métaphysique le pacte d'une alliance féconde...' ᵃᵃ But we shall no longer follow his trend of thought closely. We have only entered into this matter to show that what we have said above about the synthesis that was sought at this time is not some construction of ours. On the contrary, in the history of humanism this synthesis is an element in which the attempt was made to connect the two basic motives of nature and freedom; and the more profound thinkers in this artistic milieu were

147

aware of the fact and understood it in this sense.

The second point of Morice's programme: 'Synthèse dans l'idée; Fiction' again shows clearly that this group of artists did not at all shun contemporary reality as a subject to start from in the work of art. According to them a poet is concerned with 'de symboliser sa pensée', but for this purpose he may very well start with 'l'instant contemporain'. For, 'le Rêve s'échappant de lui-même peut atteindre aux apparences des réalités quotidiens.' [ab]

The third and last point of Morice's programme is 'Synthèse dans l'expression; Suggestion'. Of this he says: 'La suggestion peut ce que ne pourrait l'expression (i.e. the explicit description). La suggestion est le langage des correspondances et des affinités de l'âme et de la nature.' And this makes it possible for 'la suggestion seule peut rendre par quelques lignes l'entre-croisement perpétuel et la mêlée des détails auquels l'expression consacrerait des pages', a thought that is further elucidated by what follows: 'elle est remontée aux sources même de tout langage: aux lois de l'appropriation des sons et des coulours des mots aux idées.' [ac] Here Morice falls back on a well-known pronouncement made by Baudelaire in the opening passage of his article on Wagner, viz., that colour and sound may suggest each other mutually, and that each of them may 'translate' the ideas in their own way, a thought he found in the theory of the 'correspondences'. Both Baudelaire and Delacroix expressed similar views also elsewhere, viz., when they spoke of the 'musicality' of a picture.

Gauguin

As in a strongly personal way Gauguin assimilated the influences exercised on him with regard to theories and ideas, and as there was a great deal more that was important for him in addition to Morice, it is not easy to point out the latter's direct influence. To our mind it is most obvious in the remarkable 'Paragone' that Gauguin wrote. It is not easy to determine the exact date of this article that was published posthumously. But considering the style in which it is written, it is almost inconceivable that he wrote it before the Parisian time of 1890. In this article we read: 'Le poète est l'intermédiaire nécessaire entre l'humanité et, non pas seulement la nature, mais aussi la pensée. Les arts se hiécharchisent selon le plus ou moins de moyens qu'ils fournissent au poète pour accomplir sa fonction intermédiaire.' [ad]

This thought shows a strong resemblance to the idea developed in the first few pages of Morice's book.

For the rest Gauguin's ideas with respect to the question as to which of the arts is best are interesting enough, and are certainly his own. Not any man of letters would have dreamed of assigning the highest place to painting. It is typical of Gauguin's world of thought that the element of remembrance plays such an important part in it— the meaning of the 'Imagination' is strongly suggestive of Baudelaire, but has been worked out in a very personal way. About pictorial art he writes: 'La peinture est le plus beau de tous les arts; en lui se résument toutes les sensations, à son aspect chacun peut, au gré de son imagination, créer le roman, d'un seul coup avoir l'âme envahie par les plus profonds souvenirs; point d'efforts de mémoire, tout résumé en un seul instant.—Art complet qui résume tous les autres et les complète—' [ab] And indeed, here again nature—'toutes les sensations' —as well as freedom—in the 'Imagination'—play an important part, and the synthesis has been realized in a way that is entirely his own, although these two motives have not really been united and they remain opposites. For Gauguin may say that 'la science du coloriste' is a rich means 'pour entrer en relation intime avec nature', [af] but only a moment before he detached the spectator from nature, for he was able to project the image he wanted in his own freedom and in connection with his own remembrances. This even constituted one of the most important gains of pictorial art—'vous pouvez rêver librement en entendant la musique comme en regardant un tableau'—[ag] whereas when reading a book one would be a slave of the thoughts of the author.

Mallarmé

Through Morice Gauguin also came into contact in 1890/1891 with Stéphane Mallarmé, the poet and theorist who was in very high esteem with the poets and writers of the generation of 1885, who was even considered to be their leader and predecessor. Gauguin attended some of his famous Tuesday-evenings, and etched a portrait of Mallarmé, showing that their contact must have been of a less temporary character.

Mallarmé had a philosophical view which was peculiarly his own,[9] and which was by no means identical with that of the younger men referred to a moment ago, although his thought moved in a similar climate. The influences of Plotinus, and more directly those of such English philosophers as Berkeley—who will no doubt have interested him in connection with the Englishman's views of language and word [10]—certainly played an important part, and his reaction to the positivistic-naturalistic method [11] was very sharp and vehement. This also appears clearly from the following quotation which is very characteristic of Mallarmé and, as it were, embodies a summary of his art-theory. His strong urge for freedom is clearly revealed in it, although he keeps starting from reality as given in our experience—as he once said: 'la divine transposition, pour l'accomplissement de quoi existe l'homme, va du fait à l'idéal' [ah] so that he certainly does not want art to be exclusively occupied with the creation of a world of the imagination, nor does he want to call up phantoms in the spirit of Redon notwithstanding his inner relatedness to and appreciation of the latter. He wrote: 'Abolie, la prétension, esthétiquement une erreur, quoiqu'elle régit les chefs-d'oeuvre, d'inclure au papier subtil du volume autre chose que par exemple l'horreur de la forêt, ou le tonnerre muet épars au feuillage: non le bois intrinsèque et dense des arbres . . . Les monuments, la mer, la face humaine, dans leur plénitude, natifs, conservant une vertu autrement attrayante que ne les voilera une description, évocation dites, *allusion* je sais, *suggestion:* cette terminologie quelque peu de hasard atteste la tendance, une très décisive, peut-être, qu'ait subit l'art littéraire, elle le borne et l'exempte. Son sortilège, à lui, si ce n'est libérer, hors d'une poignée de poussière ou réalité sans l'enclore, au livre, même comme texte, la dispersion volatile soit l'esprit, qui n'a que faire de rien outre la musicalité de tout.'[ai]

We may wonder what Gauguin can have learnt from Mallarmé. The latter's view of art, though showing differences, was internally related to Gauguin's aims in the sense that there was a striving after freedom, and, giving up any naturalistic description, both made the attempt to represent the object in its fullness. It is not impossible that Mallarmé's strong emphasis on the freedom of the artist, loose from the material (in a literal sense) made a deep impression on Gauguin. As we shall see further on, he spoke much clearer about artistic freedom in his later years than ever before. To him this freedom was the essential thing in the new art of painting of which he considered himself as one of the leaders and builders, by which it

150

was distuinguished from what had been done formerly. But we think we can find evidence of a direct influence exercised by Mallarmé in the sense of the quotation given just now, viz., in the letter in which he comments upon his 'D'où venons-nous? Que sommes-nous? Où allons-nous'. In this letter Gauguin made reply to a critic who had posited the thesis 'rien ne nous révélerait le sens de l'allegorie'.[ak] The artist answered: 'mon rêve ne se laisse pas saisir, ne comporte aucune allégorie; poème musical, il se passe de libretto. Citation Mallarmé.[al] Par conséquent immatèriel et supérieur, l'essentiel dans une oeuvre consiste précisément dans 'ce qui n'est pas exprimé': il en résulte implicitement des lignes, sans couleurs ou paroles, il n'en est pas matériellement constitué.' [am]

To say nothing of the reference to Mallarmé, the latter's influence is discernible even in the style of Gauguin's writing: but there is certainly a very strong agreement with Mallarmé in the use of the idea of the 'musicality' of a work of art. And, in addition, this agreement appears also from the idea that the artist should use suggestion rather than description, an idea that is not found thus anywhere else in Gauguin's writings.[12]

Mallarmé did not give an art-theory adapted to pictorial art, although he was a lover of this art, witness his own collection. [13] This is why he could not lead painters like Gauguin any further. He restricted himself to the transmission of some general thoughts and new ideals. But this was important enough.

Gauguin's escape from France

It is not easy to say in how far Mallarmé contributed anything of decisive importance to Gauguin's ideas and plans to go to the tropics and to escape from France. [14] Morice once showed him a poem by Mallarmé which made a deep impression on him:

> 'Fuir! Là-bas, fuir! Je sens que des oiseaux sont ivres
> D'être parmi l'écume inconnue et les cieux
> ....
> Je partirai! Steamer balançant ta mature,
> Lève l'ancre pour une exotique nature!'.[an]

This is really in the spirit in which Gauguin will have felt these things. And it is certainly not impossible that on one of the Tuesday-evenings at Mallarmé's such a subject was discussed. However this may be,—there is nothing to prove here—if Mallarmé should have influenced Gauguin in some measure with respect to this subject, he really did nothing but intensify an existing tendency. He merely urged Gauguin on to realize plans and ideas that the latter had already been entertaining for some time. As is so often the case, this influence, also, was only an intensification of existing inclinations.

For there is no proof needed that Gauguin had been entertaining such plans for a long time already. Had he not actually carried out a similar plan many years ago, when he set out for Martinique? And had he not more than once expressed himself in such a sense? [15] But only in 1890 did these ideas assume a more definite form, as appears from his correspondence with Bernard. [16] He will no doubt have wished to escape from his eternal financial worries and from the continuous struggle and obloquy—the result of misconception or jealousy—while he will also have been attracted by the prospect that he would not need to exercise any restraint in sexual matters. 'Libre enfin, sans souci d'argent et pourra aimer, chanter et mourrir.' [ao]

But this was certainly not the only reason. A deeper motive was his wish to have an opportunity to renew his art by tearing loose from the influence of his Western environment: 'L'Occident est pourri en ce moment et tout ce qui est Hercule peut comme Antée prendre des forces nouvelles en touchant le sol là-bas'.[ap] Also in a letter to his wife he lays emphasis on his wish to find his own way, and he points out to her that it is a gain rather than a loss to be far away from the artistic life: 'Mon centre artistique est dans mon cerveau et pas ailleurs et je suis fort parce que je ne suis jamais dérouté par les autres et que je fais ce qui est en moi'.[aq] And then he continues to refer on the one hand to the deaf Beethoven and on the other to Pissarro, who always followed the tendency of the times.[17]

Baudelaire may have suggested to him already at an early date that a journey to a distant country might be conducive to the renewal of his art. For Baudelaire wrote saying: 'Si . . . je prends . . . un (homme) intelligent et je le transporte dans une contrée lointaine, je suis sûr que . . . elle créera en lui un monde nouveau d'idées . . . toute cette vitalité inconnue sera ajoutée à sa vitalité propre; quelque milliers d'idées et de sensations enrichiront son dictionnaire de mortel . . .' [ar]

And indeed, this was what Gauguin tried to achieve; he wanted to receive new impressions in order to enrich and to deepen his art. At this time, while he still hesitated whether he would go to Madagascar or to Tahiti, he wrote: 'En outre Madagascar offre plus de ressources comme types, religion, mysticisme, symbolisme'. [as]

Aurier

The literary writer and critic who contributed most to the elaboration of the synthetist art-theory was no doubt Aurier. He was of course most intimately connected with the literary movement and knew all about what was being written. He had studied philosophy and had been in direct contact with Bernard—who had met him in Brittany for the first time in 1888— [18] and with Gauguin. [19] And what was most important of all, he was thoroughly acquainted with the work of these young painters. [20] Unlike Morice's theories (which no doubt had a great influence on Aurier) Aurier's reflections on painting were written with a clear idea of the kind of art he was actually talking about.

There are two articles written by him that are worth considering a little more closely, viz., one of the year 1891 on synthetist art and Gauguin,[at] and one of 1892 explaining the theory of this art again, a little more elaborately this time, with a survey of the young artists who worked in this direction.

The latter article opens with the quotation with which we started this book, a splendid piece of rhetoric with a profound background. In it nineteenth century positivism is accused of having chased poetry away in its naive optimism of being able to solve all mysteries, whereas actually man walks about more than ever in 'ce formidable inconnu'.[au] But this state of affairs can be changed if the poets (here he uses this term in the broad sense of artists in general) are called back into the world of the formers of culture, for they are the 'dépositaires de l'eternel savoir.' [av]

Materialistic art, 'expérimental et immédiat' will have to go—that naturalist art starting from this 'antinomie de tout art: la vérité con-crète, l'illusionnisme, le trompe-l'oeil,' [aw] an art that leaves no room for any further suggestion and thus kills the insight into the idea, the true reality. This art can no longer satisfy anybody, this art with its 'copie myope des anecdotes sociales, l'imitation imbécile des verrues

153

de la nature, la plate observation.' [ax] He is clearly referring to the naturalist art at the Salon. But as clearly he rejects the thought that the academic art, the older 'idealistic' art of classicism might be a solution. For, he says, the latter may produce 'objets beaux', but here, too, the artist is 'pauvre stupide prisonnier de l'allégorique caverne (de Platon).' [ay]

No, 'de toutes parts on revendique le droit au rêve, le droit au pâturages de l'azur, [az] le droit de l'envolement vers les étoiles niées de l'absolute vérité.' [ba]

This new, 'symbolist', art was not called into existence out of nothing by the new generation, for it already existed with men like Puvis de Chavannes, Moreau, Henner, Carrière, Rodin, the Pre-Raphaelites, although they did not yet possess a lucid doctrine of art.[21] What did they search for that was also striven after by the new generation? 'Ils se sont efforcés de comprendre la mystérieuse signification des lignes, des lumières et des ombres, afin d'employer ces éléments, pour ainsi dire, alphabétiques, à écrire le beau poème de leurs rêves et de leurs idées.' [bb] This thought is exactly like the one that Gauguin had already advanced in 1885. Here he immediately points out the peculiar characteristic of the new art, viz., that the object in nature is not rendered in a merely naturalistic way. Neither is its essential character sought in the subject as such, but in the way in which the artist's thought concerning the object, the idea of things, is represented. It is remarkable that he connects this theory—heard perhaps either from Gauguin or from Bernard—with the thought advanced by Baudelaire (and Delacroix), viz., that reality is a dictionary for the artist. But the emphasis has been shifted: for he does not compare the natural object as seen by the artist to a word in a dictionary—such a word is given its meaning only by its position in a context with other words—but here the artist exclusively uses the aesthetic elements as line and colour of whose expressive value he is aware for the writing of his 'poem'. In comparison with Delacroix and Baudelaire this means a further remove from the objects of nature and a stronger emphasis on the elements by means of which the work of art is composed iconically. This shift is also made clear in the metaphor as such: Aurier no longer speaks of words but of letters. The artist is entitled to exaggerate, to weaken, to deform 'ces caractères directement significateurs (formes, lignes, couleurs, etc.)' [bo]

154

that he derives from reality not only in connection with his individual vision but also in order to give a clearer expression to the
idea. For in two ways a work of art will show deviations from the
strict imitation of nature given by a daguerréotype, [22] viz., on
account of 'un tempérament'—here he implicitly refers to Zola's
well-known definition—and secondly because a work of art should
represent the idea of a natural object.

And then he tries to give the latter thesis a philisophical foundation and elaboration, although, just like Baudelaire in his article
on Wagner, he first posits a priori that it is impossible to imagine
that 'l'art, mode suprême d'expression, ne puisse exprimer l'universa-
lité des psychies.' [bd] After this he sets forth a clearly Plotinian
theory saying that every 'objet'—this word is best rendered by
'being' or 'entity' in view of the fact that he also refers to man as
to an 'objet'—has self-consciousness (conscience de son être), viz.,
'la Pensée'—which will become clear if we look upon the word
'pensée' as a translation of the Greek Plotinian word 'Nous' [be]—
and a form which is also the 'objet' itself. This form must, therefore,
be in direct relation to that 'pensée' by which assertion the theory
of the 'equivalences' is there: 'la forme,... le corps de tout...
objet est... la tangible modalité de son être, c'est-à-dire la signification visible d'une pensée'. [bf] Thus he arrives 'à travers tout ce
rébarbatif jargon et toute cette hirsute scolastique' [bg] to this definition: 'Dans la nature, tout objet n'est, en somme, qu'une Idée
signifiée' in which he again identifies 'pensée' with 'Idea' [bh]
without giving any further account of this fact. Thus, according to
Aurier, here the possibility is given of a more profound symbolism
than that which the naturalists accepted implicitly—for they said that
a work of art reflects something of its maker's temperament. [23]

But the average man does not know the 'réalité idéique'—only 'les
intelligences supérieures de notre pauvre aveugle humanité', the true
artists should know it.[bi] The artist is 'l'exprimeur des Êtres absolus',
because as 'homme supérieur', 'dompteur du monstre illusion', 'sait
se promener en maître dans ce temple fantastique

> où de vivant piliers
> laissent parfois sortir de confuses paroles...

alors que l'imbécile troupeau humain, dupé par les apparences qui lui feront nier les idées essentielles, passera éternellement aveugle

> à travers les forêts de symboles
> qui l'observent avec des regards familiers.' bk

This quotation proves that he has combined these Plotinian thoughts with metaphors directly borrowed from Baudelaire.

Then he reverts to the idea that 'les diverses combinaisons de lignes, de plans, d'ombres, de couleurs, constituent le vocabulaire d'une langue mystérieuse, mais miraculeusement expressive' bl which every true artist ought to know. This thought is not clearly connected with the symbol-theory or founded in the latter with the concept of equivalence associated with it. For to say that the form of a thing is the symbol of the idea of a thing—which is a purely philosophical theory—is something different from saying that in a work of art lines and colours, etc. can express something about a thing—which is an art-theoretical assertion, or rather, an experience gained from looking at works of art.

The elaboration of this theory of expression is something new, viz., that 'cette langue, comme toutes les langues, a son écriture, son orthographe, sa grammaire, sa syntaxe, sa rhétorique même, qui est: le style.' bm Later on Gauguin made an observation on style which suggests to us that he had taken over this thought. He writes: 'Beaucoup de personnages disent que je ne sais pas dessiner parce que je fais des formes spéciales. Quand donc comprendra-t-on que l'exécution, le dessin et la couleur (le Style) doivent accorder avec le poème?' bn This is especially clear if we consider this pronouncement in the light of Gauguin's explanation of his manner of working: 'j'agis un peu comme la Bible dont la doctrine ... s'énonce sous une forme symbolique présentant un double aspect; une forme qui d'abord matérialise l'Idée pure pour la rendre plus sensible ... c'est le sens littéral, superficiel, figuratif, mystérieux d'une parabole; et puis le second aspect donnant l'Esprit de celle-ci. C'est le sens non plus figuratif; mais figuré, explicite de cette parabole.' bo This exposition shows that Gauguin had a similar art-theory—derived from Balzac, Baudelaire, and especially Morice—so that he did not meet with any difficulties in taking over Aurier's theory on style.

According to Aurier, therefore, a work of art symbolizes a spiritual datum in the first place by reflecting the artist's mind—this is unavoidable—and secondly because the artist has expressed in it the Idea of things. Thus the art-object is 'comme minimum un fragment de la spiritualité de l'artiste, comme maximum cette entière spiritualité de l'artiste plus la spiritualité essentielle des divers êtres objectifs'. [bp] Then the object of art is a new being with a life of its own owing to a soul 'qui est la synthèse de deux âmes, l'âme de l'artiste et l'âme de la nature.' [bq] In proportion to the depth of this soul of the work of art it is able to convey to the spectator emotions, ideas and feelings. 'C'est cette influx, ce rayonnement sympatique ressentie à la vue d'un chef-d'oeuvre, que l'on nomme le sentiment du beau, l'émotion esthétique.' [br]

Being, plastic autonomy

There are two remarks to be made here. In the first place, that this art-theory is perfectly subjectivistic: for beauty is considered to be only a particular state of mind evoked by the work of art in the spectator. And further, this theory makes the beauty of a work of art dependent on the degree to which it expresses spiritual truths, and not on the presence or absence of its agreement with particular aesthetical norms, nor on its having certain qualities inherent in the structure of the work of art as such. The correctness and the force with which a work of art expresses something about the artist and the object in nature with which it is concerned are decisive for its beauty. Consequently it must be judged according to some criterion of truth (however subjective this may be) rather than according to abstract-aesthetical norms. This remarkable trait in the theory of art is found in exactly the same way in Plotinus: 'L'esthétique de Plotin est en effet impregnée de cette idée que la beauté ne s'ajoute pas aux choses comme un accident extérieur, mais en constitue véritablement l'essence *(Ennéades* I, 2) . . . il faut donc que la beauté . . . soit le reflet d'une Idée, qui fait de cette être ce qu'il est. Valeur esthétique et valeur intellectuelle coincident.' [bs]

This aesthetic feeling arising from the contact between the work of art as an (active) agent and the spectator as a (passive) receptor is very much analogous to Love—a purer love than human love which is always impaired by 'quelque boueuse sexualité', thus Aurier continues. This is a very important point to him. For according to him on account of positivism we have landed in 'l'animalité pure et simple', and 'il faut réapprendre l'amour, source de toute compréhension'. [bt] However owing to sensualism we cannot discover anything

Art as "love"

in a woman but flesh to gratify material desires; and through scepticism God himself has become a mere nominalistic abstraction so that this love of Him has also become impossible.[bu] 'Un seul amour nous est encore loisible, celui des oeuvres d'art. Jetons-nous donc sur cette ultime planche de salut.' [bv]

Art as religion

These kinds of ideas, founded in Plotinian Swedenborgian theories about the 'correspondences', making art to take the place of the Divine Revelation and thus elevating it to religion, were of rather frequent occurrence in the circles with which we are now concerned. Already Baudelaire expressed himself in this spirit,[24] and—even more explicitly—Morice, whose *Littérature de tout à l'heure* Aurier will, of course, have known thoroughly, and whose art-theoretical views must have had a great influence on him. For Morice wrote: 'Ainsi entendu l'art n'est que le révélateur de l'Infini . . . De nature donc, d'essence, l'art est réligieux'.[bw]

Continuing his discourse, Aurier says that this art is the true and absolute art—and it is only because our positivistic society has obliterated any fundamental revelation that such a complicated theoretical argumentation has become necessary. It is true and absolute because it is legitimate theoretically, but also because it 'se trouve, de plus, au fond, identique à l'art primitif, à l'art tel qu'il fut deviné par les génies instinctifs des premiers temps de l'humanité.' [bx] This is a thought he may have derived from Gauguin—recall the latter's discourse when he met men of letters at Paris for the first time [25] —or he may have read it in Denis' expositions, or he owed it to both sources. Denis even called the new art 'neo-traditionaliste' in his article of 1890 which we shall consider in more detail below.

All this is brilliantly summarized in Aurier's rhetorical passage on Gauguin that this artist was the leader and the most important exponent of the art that Aurier was referring to here: 'C'est, on pourrait presque dire, du Platon plastiquement interpreté par un sauvage de génie.' [by] The latter additional observation was certainly not superfluous. Aurier was too well informed of the art of his time not to know that the mere adherence to some correct theory does not yet produce master-pieces—as a matter of fact we have already pointed out that he looked upon great artists as exceptions, as men who can see and are thus able to reveal what others cannot understand. But, at least in his first article, he also points to the necessity of 'le don d'émotivité', which, if translated into a more sober idiom than Aurier's terminology, only means the artist's talent. [26]

Finally we wish to consider what Aurier really meant by his slogan-like summary of his artistic ideals at the end of his article on Gauguin. His summary is more rhetorical than clear. He says that the new art is to be [27]:

1. 'Idéiste, puisque son idéal unique sera l'expression de l'Idée' [bz] This may be clear after what we have discussed so far.

2. 'Symboliste, puisqu'elle exprimera cette Idée par des formes'.[ca] With this he refers to his expressivistic theories.

3. 'Synthétique, puisqu'elle écrira ces formes, ces signes, selon un mode de compréhension générale.' [cb] This is far from clear. Aurier rarely mentions synthesis—we have come upon the term only once, viz., in the second article, in which he uses this term in the same sense as Morice. [28] Here, in this important passage, this notion is put in the foreground for the first time. It is as if Aurier suddenly realizes that he has not yet used this term which was so often employed by Gauguin and his fellow-artists in particular, and therefore Aurier just jots it down here. His short digression probably means that this art speaks clearly and is not esoterically strange and only intelligible to the initiated.

4. 'Subjective, puisque l'objet n'y sera jamais considéré en tant qu' objet, mais en tant que signe d'idée perçue par le sujet.' [cc] This thought, too, was not plainly expressed in his expositions although it was given eo ipso in the view that only a genius can 'read' the signs of the Idea that are represented by the objects.[29]

5. '(C'est en conséquence) décorative—car la peinture décorative proprement dite, telle que l'ont comprise les Egyptiens, très pro-bable les Grècs et les Primitifs, n'est rien autre chose qu'une manifestation d'art à la fois subjective, synthétique, symboliste et idéiste.' [ed]

Again he introduces a new thought into his 'summary'. He possibly wants somehow to do justice to an idea of Bernard's. If we take this digression seriously, this decorative character is the centre of this entire theory of art, for the decorative quality implies all the positive qualities he has ascribed to the new art. His reference to the Egyptians might be considered to be reminiscent of ideas that Gauguin took very much to heart, [30] or perhaps this passage is only

159

a free rendering of a passage in Maurice Denis' article of 1890, viz.,
of point XXIV of that 'manifesto'.

Indeed in surveying these articles we cannot but grant to Denis that
he was right when he observed that **Gauguin** must have been
astonished when, on his arrival at Paris in 1890, he saw what proportions the new art-theory had assumed that had started from his
up till then only fragmentary thoughts about the new art. [31] All this
was very important to the young artist, for 'Sérusier nous prouvait
par Hégel, et les lourds articles d'Albert Aurier insistaient sur ce fait,
que logiquement, philosophiquement, c'était **Gauguin** qui avait
raison.' [ce]

Maurice Denis

We shall now have to consider the theories developed in this circle
to which we referred a moment ago, the group of Denis and Sérusier,
young artists that knew each other intimately from the time they had
spent together at the Académie Julian. Denis does not leave us in
doubt of the fact that Sérusier was the motive power; this appears
from the quotation given above. [32] Yet Denis was the first to publish
an article which was all the more important as it was the result of
discussions and conversations carried on among the artists themselves
—unlike the articles dealt with above, which were all of them by
literary men, although Aurier had been in rather close contact with
the painters. But Denis' article shows us what the painters themselves thought of these things about the year 1890.

The article opens with a thesis which has later on been quoted
again and again and which became a kind of slogan at the time of
the rise of non-figurative art: 'Se rappeler qu'un tableau—avant
d'être un cheval de bataille, une femme nue, ou quelconque anecdote
—est essentiellement une surface plane recouverte de couleurs en un
certain ordre assemblées.' [cf] It may be doubted whether the appeal
made to this pronouncement later on was justified. Denis in the first
place turns on the art of the Salon of his time. This polemical element
cannot be ignored. It also appears from the theses immediately following this pronouncement, which relate to Bouguereau, Meisonnier,
Dagnan-Bouveret. For this Salon art was naturalistic in the extreme
and sought to represent the natural object in the picture as exactly

160

(i.e. as much like a photograph) as possible. In this procedure it was too much overlooked that a work of art is an iconic representation, an artistic achievement which is not identical with what is given in reality. And it is the renewed insight into this truth—viz., that a work of art is an artistic object representing reality iconically—which was posited in this first thesis. It is true, a year later Denis said: 'I think that above everything else a painting should be an ornament. The choice of subjects or scenes means nothing. It is through its coloured surface, through the value of tones, through the harmony of lines that I attempt to reach the mind, arouse the emotion.' [33] But from his memoirs of a slightly later date it appears that this thesis was certainly not intended in an abstract-expressionistic sense. In his memoirs of the time spent at the Académie Julian he tells how from Brittany Sérusier brought the 'talisman' embodying the result of an afternoon's lesson given by Gauguin. His comment is as follows: 'Ainsi nous fut présenté, pour la première fois, sous une forme paradoxale, inoubliable, le future concept de la 'surface plane recouverte de couleurs en un certain orde assemblées.' [eg] When reading on we see more clearly that this is concerned with what we have called 'the iconic aspect': 'Ainsi nous connûmes que tout oeuvre d'art était une transposition, une caricature, l'équivalent passionné d'une sensation reçue.' [ch]

After quoting Gauguin in his XV thesis: 'L'art, c'est quand ça tourne', [ci] exposing again the defects of the entire art of the Salons with its 'trompe-l'oeil, modelé en ronde bosse', in short its quasi classicistic hyper-naturalism, he continues in XX with a discussion of Gauguin's 'Calvaire Breton': 'De la toile elle-même, surface plane enduite de couleurs, jaillit l'émotion amère ou consolante, 'littéraire' comme disent les peintres, sans qu'il soit besoin d'interposer le souvenir d'une autre sensation ancienne (comme celle du motif de nature utilisé)'.[ck] We notice how much Denis is struggling with the difficulty of putting these new thoughts in words. For his use of the term 'littéraire' is, properly speaking, incorrect—in the quotation that will presently be given below this word is used in a different and more correct way. If, however, we should not yet be convinced of the fact that Denis is not engaged in drawing up a theory of non-figurative art—which in itself would be an anachronism, as a tendency in this direction was as yet out of the question in 1890, at least certainly

161

not in such a deliberate and conscious form,—the clarifying passage immediately after this one is no doubt convincing enough: 'Un Christ byzantin est symbole; le Jésus des peintres modernes, fût-il coiffé du plus exact kiffyed, n'est que littéraire. Dans l'un c'est la forme qui est expressive, dans l'autre c'est la nature imitée qui veut l'être'.[cl] Here the term 'literary' is used in its proper sense [cm] of 'descriptive, rendering something elaborately and literally.'

Once more we wish to emphasize the fact that Denis was no symbolist. Thus in 1892 he wrote: 'Nous nous étonnons que des critiques renseignés ... se soient plu à confondre les tendances mystiques et allégoriques, c'est-à-dire la recherche de l'expression par le sujet, et les tendances symbolistes [cn], c'est-à-dire la recherche de l'expression par l'oeuvre d'art.' [co] Later on he explains that the predecessor of synthetism is not to be found in academic art, nor in an art that was akin to Pre-Raphaelitism, or in one that was entirely determined by symbolic poetry, but much rather in the realism of the previous period: 'Ceux qui l' (what we call synthetism) ont inauguré étaient des paysagistes, des nature-mortistes, pas du tout des 'peintres de l'âme.' [cp]

plastic painters or constructive painters

When studying the history of art there are always three elements to be distinguished. Each of them must be examined apart if we are to gain an insight into the nature and character of a particular group. There is first the class of subjects that are treated—they will always be relevant, i.e., related to the artists' view of life and the world and connected with the function a work of art is to have—; the style— i.e. the way in which the different motifs (figures or things) are rendered, 'peinture' and (idealizing or not) 'deformation',[cq]—and finally the purely aesthetic peculiarity—the composition, the play of lines and colours on the painted surface. Of course, these elements will have to be adapted to each other as, properly speaking, they presuppose each other, in order that they may together elucidate the content of the work of art.[cr] In a true work of art of high standing they will, therefore, form an indissoluble unity, in such a way that it will not be possible to speak of one of them without saying something about the other at the same time, and vice versa. This insight was not consciously realized in this way by Maurice Denis or by any of the other art-theorists, although it is remarkable that Denis showed these elements in their close mutual relation. As an artist

162

he starts from this interrelatedness as it were as from a matter of course. This fact was already clear to us when we discussed the first of his theses in his article of 1890, of which thesis XXIV is also important in this connection.

There he wrote: 'L'art est la sanctification de la nature, de cette nature de tout le monde, qui se contente de vivre. Le grand art qu'on appelle décoratif, des Indous, des Assyriens, des Egyptiens, des Grecs, l'art du Moyen-Age et de la Renaissance (that is to say all art that was really important) et les oeuvres décidément supérieures de l'art moderne (referring to Gauguin and Cézanne), qu'est-ce? sinon le travestissement des sensations vulgaires—des objets naturels—en icones sacrées, hermétiques, cs imposante.' ct He clearly reveals a realistic attitude with regard to his subjects, or at least with regard to his motifs cu which are derived from every day reality and experience. But they are treated in such a way that a picture elucidates those objects as it were in their permanent meaning, we would almost say the picture *reveals* their permanent sense. Thus arises beauty— our third element, already referred to by the term 'decoratif'. 'Triomphe universal de l'imagination des esthètes sur les efforts de bête imitation, triomphe de l'émotion du Beau sur le mensonge naturaliste.' cv The coherence of the elements mentioned by us is even clearer expressed by the following quotation derived from an article of a somewhat later date: 'Ils (the first generation of the new art) voulurent se soumettre aux lois d'harmonie qui régissent les rapports des couleurs, les agencements des lignes (recherches de Seurat, Bernard, C. Pissarro); mais c'est aussi pour apporter plus de sincérité dans le rendu de leurs sensations.' After this he gives in one single sentence the following brief summary containing the essential thing of the synthetist theory of art: 'Il y avait donc étroite correspondance entre des formes et des sensations.' cw

The latter, i.e., the correspondence is the pre-requisite for the artistic unity in the work of art. It enables the artist's activity to make also the (purely aesthetic) composition into something of an expression which at the least runs parallel to the object represented. We purposely use the word 'parallel', for neither Denis, nor Gauguin, Aurier, etc., succeeded in arriving at a conception which really explained the unity of the aesthetic qualities and the expressive rendering of the object in the work of art. For on the one hand we re-

163

peatedly find in their views the demand to deform the given object
in order to elucidate it in accordance with the artist's vision; on the
other hand there is the demand to realize the 'decorative' beauty in
the work of art. It is as if, notwithstanding their expositions, there
is to them something static, something abstract in this beauty, an
obedience to universal laws apart from any expressiveness. This appears clearly from Denis' distinction (in a later article) of objective
and subjective deformation. The former is related to the universal
laws of beauty, the latter to the artist's subjective vision of his object: 'Au point de vue objectif, la composition décorative, esthétique
et rationnelle . . . devenait le contre-partie, le correctif nécessaire de
la théorie des équivalents. Celle-ci autorisait en vue de l'expression
toutes les transpositions même caricaturales, tous les excès de caractère:
la déformation objective obligeait à son tour l'artiste à tout transposer
en Beauté. En résumé: la synthèse expressive, le symbole d'une sensation, devait en être une transcription éloquente, et en même temps
un objet composé pour le plaisir des yeux.' cx

This emphasis on the purely aesthetic element is hardly found in the
authors we have discussed above. However much they tried to explain the peculiar character of pictorial art and to give an account
of its relation to nature on the one hand and that to the creative artist
on the other, their art-theory was defective. It was rather a kind of
epistemology than a formulation giving an answer to the question
what constituted the beauty of a work of art. We may be glad that
they laid such a great emphasis on the demand for truth and concentration on what is meaningful. Yet their views were often hardly
an answer to the question what after all is essential in a picture as
a work of art, and how together with the 'idéique' it also embodies
beauty proper. It is possible that Denis being a painter himself was
conducive to laying a stronger emphasis on the purely aesthetic elements. But perhaps Sérusier's influence was more important in this
connection. Denis repeatedly referred to him at that time (c. 1890) as
the man whose influence and guidance were so decisive precisely with
respect to his views of art.

Passing the whole of Denis' conceptions of art in review again, we
shall find them to be in a great measure free of any philosophizing.
What Denis wrote about the movement of 1890 much later is hardly
applicable to his own article of that period: 'Nous faisions un singu-

Sérusier

lier mélange de Plotin, d'Edgar Poe, de Baudelaire et de Schopenhauer.' ^{cy}

No doubt *Sérusier* was very important with respect to the more exact
formulation of the synthetic art-theory. Denis said Sérusier was
really his teacher in this matter [34]—so that we may suppose that
Denis' article of 1890 contained a great deal of Sérusier's thought,
and at the same time we must not overlook the possibility that as
early as 1889 he influenced Gauguin and his circle at Le Pouldu. He
was certainly co-responsable for the further formulation and extension
of the theory. It is not possible to say in how far he influenced
Aurier directly. However this may be, Aurier is sure to have learnt
a great deal from Morice's book of the year 1889; but as the latter's
theories and those of Sérusier—also on account of the fact that they
drew their inspiration from the same sources—were very much akin
they could be easily worked into a whole. Sérusier, too, fell back
on Plotinus; he, too, admired Balzac's *Seraphita* and *Louis Lambert*,[35]
and he also had had a direct contact with old mystic traditions via
Schuré's book: *Les grands Initiés*.^{cz} We have already pointed out
that Aurier may have learnt one thing and the other from Denis'
article.

Theory of Correspondences

Before examining the way in which Sérusier practically gave the
synthetist art-theory its definitive formulation and final content we
wish to see how the theory of the correspondences (or of the
equivalences) had developed.

   Its first clear exposition in connection with contemporary art is
found in *Baudelaire,* who, as a matter of fact, had derived it from all
kinds of older sources. [36] Baudelaire actually points out how colours
may have a particular meaning and effect, [37] and in connection with
Delacroix he shows that the latter's colours are in perfect harmony
with the subject of the picture. [38] He does not explicitly found this
thought in his 'Salons' on the theory of the 'correspondences', perhaps to avoid deminishing the intelligibility of these articles, although
the discussion 'in extenso' in the Salon of 1859 is really based on this
theory. In this article he concentrates the attention on the 'imagina-

tion' which does not work in an arbitrary way but is based on 'une collection de règles réclamées par l'organisation de l'être spirituel.' [da] Only in his article on Wagner he gives a very concise and dogmatic exposition of his view—colours and sounds can express ideas on account of the analogies or correspondences. [39]

Yet we can hardly maintain that Baudelaire bases his theory on the thought that colours (and lines) can represent ideas—such representation is rather a means, like others, for the artist to arrive at a grand conception. Delacroix achieved his impressive results, according to Baudelaire, 'par l'ensemble, par l'accord profond, complet, entre sa couleur, son sujet, son dessin, et par la dramatique gesticulation de ses figures.' [db] And although he did not say so literally, we may suspect that when Baudelaire spoke of reality as a dictionary to the artist, [40] he did not exclusively, not even in the first place, refer to colours (and lines), but to figures, human beings, things observed in reality. In fact, on reading carefully what Delacroix observed in this connection, [41] we shall see that also to him colour and composition play an important part in the work of art as co-determinant elements, but he certainly did not mean to say that it is not necessary to select real data from reality for the artist to realize his conception. Finally, however much Baudelaire's views were concerned with the art of painting, things literary played a great part in it; and recalling his poem 'Correspondances' we shall have to think of some symbolical language, some kind of metaphor, to understand it correctly, rather than of abstract-aesthetical means like colour and rhythm, etc. As a matter of fact he himself said so clearly elsewhere.[42]

Directing our attention to *Morice*, we see that the state of affairs has really remained what it was. Morice mentions 'suggestion' as one of the chief points of his programme. In explanation he appears to mean that line, colour and sound can elucidate a particular situation better than a possibly much more elaborate description. This thought is based on the theory of correspondences, it is true, but remains only one of the building bricks of the work of art, and the theory of art as such is not restricted to it.[43]

Aurier goes a step further. The elements with which the pictorial artists write their 'poème de leurs rêves' are, indeed, the purely pictorial means of lines, colours, etc. But strictly speaking the art-theory proper that he bases on Plotinus, is not the foundation of this

166

thought. For he does not say how it is that lines and colours can represent the idea. Yet his meaning is clear, viz. that lines, colours, etc. are the means by which the forms can be made to speak—i.e. to reveal the idea.

It is as if in Aurier we come upon two theories, derived from two different sources, viz. the literary Plotinian source of the correspondences, and the other one of the expressive force of lines and colours, which he had taken over from the synthetic painters. But he does not succeed in composing a (theoretical) closely-reasoned whole of them.

In his articles developing his ideas *Denis* speaks typically as a painter. For he says: 'Il y avait donc étroite correspondance entre des formes et des sensations',[dc] but he does not enter any further into the theoretical implications of the theory of the correspondences. The impression is made that he has borrowed the term from usage current in his circle, it is true, but that he uses it as it were naively, as founded in an experience of the iconic aspect by looking at art. And, what is very characteristic, he does not at all mention ideas that must be represented, but 'sensations' (visual experiences). The laws determining the coherence of lines and colours are properly speaking always related by him to a purely aesthetic harmony, as such side by side (and so by no means identical) with the expressive deformation applied by the artist to elucidate his vision. Summing up Denis' various articles we cannot avoid having the impression that in his first article perhaps directly influenced by Sérusier the immediate connection between the iconic representation and the purely aesthetic composition of the work (called the 'decorative element') is posited clearest of all, but that later on these two elements are more and more considered apart from each other, while the philosophical foundation is omitted.

Sérusier (continued)

And thus we come to *Sérusier* himself, who immediately continues the work of the great forerunners Delacroix, Gauguin and Baudelaire in building up an expressivistic theory, but who is also the sole author who tries to explain what constitutes the pure beauty of a work of art in this connection. For this purpose he connects the theory of the correspondences with the ideas obtaining in the circle of Seurat, and later on also with the closely related ideas of the Beuroner school.

167

In this way that which used to be merely one of the means at the disposal of the artist was made the basis of a total theory of art. For the theory of the correspondences was almost invariably one of the chief motifs of the art-theory of the authors we have reviewed so far, but this theory in most cases provided rather the foundation of something like a metaphor than explicitly concerned itself with pictorial means as such.

We have more or less to reconstruct Sérusier's thought of the nineteen-nineties from the scanty data at our disposal in letters and other source-material. Thus in a letter of 1892 addressed to his pupil Verkade we read: 'Je veux un dessin ferme et simple, fini. J'entends par là non pas que tous les détails y soient, mais que toute ligne soit voulue et ait son rôle, expressif et décoratif, dans l'ensemble; je veux que toute ligne soit nécessaire ... Mais pour arriver à ce but il faut bien connaître son sujet.' [dd] This latter observation at any rate clearly shows that we need not at all look for a striving after a non-figurative art in Sérusier. His formulation is a very concise and brilliant summary of the world of thought of Gauguin and his circle. Here the synthesis so eagerly sought for at that time has been found in an almost irreproachable form. Human freedom is implied, no doubt, in the concept 'expressif'—although this is not entirely separated from nature or from the world in which we live. For the expression is directed to the explication of the meaning of the object (as it is understood by the artist)—while nature plays a rôle in the work of art in an entirely different way, viz., in the 'natural laws' of aesthetic harmony. This was perhaps implicitly intended in Gauguin's views but it had never been clearly expressed. Here the idea of the decorative element,—still to be considered as a more or less secondary matter in Bernard and Gauguin, a motif derived from an art which is essentially foreign to them, viz., the Art Nouveau— has become an intrinsic element of art-theory.

If it should be thought that we are really inferring too much from this short quotation, we would refer to the data we possess of 1896. Mellerio then in a small book summarizes briefly what are essentially the ideas of different artists of the new generation among whom also Sérusier. He says that the latter thought the following about the origin of a picture: 'Le spectacle direct de la nature, suscitant les sensations—la mémoire, qui les rapelle—l'imagination, qui les crée

par combinaisons—nous mettent dans un état d'âme involontaire.
Puis l'Idée se forme dans l'esprit, supérieure aux limbes génératrices
par sa logique et son harmonie, elle apparaît à l'artiste. Il s'efforce de
l'exprimer dans son intégrale intensité, résultat qu'il obtiendra
d'autant mieux que, négligeant les détails, il ne retiendra que les
seules caractéristiques. Alors l'artiste place ainsi le spectateur dans
l'état d'âme où lui-même s'est trouvé—ce qui est le but d'art.' [de] This
shows clearly that Sérusier very closely follows what Gauguin had
taught him. But we wish especially to point out how strong is the
voice of the freedom-motive—both in apprehending what is given
and in representing it, man is free and far transcends reality, which
is meaningless in itself and only functions as a stimulant. By the side
of this in a letter from Verkade to Sérusier of this same year we
see how very much the latter was constantly occupied in submitting
the pictorial means themselves to closer examination and how he
concentrated the expressivistic theory on this: 'Nous avons suivi de
bonnes voies, cherchant l'Idée exprimée par les formes décoratives,
expliquée par les couleurs simples...' [df] We know that Sérusier was
also busy with a 'cercle chromatique' and with other investigations
in the field of the purely aesthetic laws, in a way which no doubt
evidences the influence of Henri (and Seurat). [44] We may also note
that, by the side of the expressivistic idea based on the theory of the
correspondences applied by Sérusier in the purest and most consistent
way, the scientific element is not lacking in this synthesis.

So we are confronted here with an almost seamless texture of two
interwoven motifs, viz., that of the primacy of human personality (in
his freedom) and that of the primacy of science motif (in its search
for laws of nature). We have found the former in the first quotation
of 1896—which as such did not posit absolute freedom but allowed
nature to play a rôle, although a subordinate one. The second motif
was implied in the second quotation, although by the side of pure
law-conformity the human freedom of choice was not lacking (in the
conception of the Idea—the purport of which was given in the first
quotation—although subordinated to the aesthetic norms conceived
of as laws of nature.)

Only in this light can it become clear how it was that in the
following years Sérusier gave up the splendid unity of his theory.
Then we hear him promulgate very contradictory opinions—which

169

alternately lay the main stress now on the one motif, now on the other. After all, the synthesis is not really possible and the two motifs remain mutually contradictory in their ultimate consequences.[dg] Thus in a letter of the year 1905 to Willibrord Verkade we read: 'Je crois que notre époque est plutôt moins avancée comme Art crétien qu'aux premières époques du christianisme. Je crois donc qu'on peut appliquer à notre époque ce qu'il (P. Didier) dit de ces temps: que la recherche de la beauté empêcherait l'expression directe et naturelle des idées, exprimons-nous n'importe comment, et soyons surtout sincères avec nous-mêmes: c'est en cela que consiste l'esprit des primitifs; la correction viendra peu à peu, elle ne peut précéder les idées sans leur barrer la route. Du reste, nous ne nous entendons pas sur le sens du mot Beauté ... Je crois que tu prends ce mot dans le sens objectif, tandis que je le prends dans le sens subjectif. C'est cette différence qui sépare les Écoles de ce siècle, qui ont abouti à Cabanel et Bouguereau, de celle que j'ai embrassées ...' [dh]. The latter statement clearly shows that he rejected any academic art, whereas his own ideals pointed in the direction of intuitive and free expression. A year afterwards however, his words were very emphatically in favour of the opposite tendency—here he himself demanded what he had condemned a year ago because it would put obstacles in the way of the artist's self-expression: 'Je crois actuellement que la seule chose que puisse faire un artiste est d'établir une harmonie en formes et en couleurs. L'harmonie est le seul moyen, comme la prière, de nous mettre en communion avec Dieu. Tout le reste, dans l'Art, n'est qu'illustration, sentiment personnel, individualisme, poésie humaine. Quant à la copie d'objets naturels, surtout de modèles, qui ne sont même pas naturels, elle me fait horreur.' [di] In this case this one element in his view of art had ousted nearly all the others, to such an extent even that he drew conclusions in a direction that very nearly approached a theory of abstract art.—At that time he was indeed the life and soul of a group of young artists of whom Delaunay was to be the first to realize literally the thought expressed in this quotation.[dk]

Sérusier's activity was completed with his booklet *A.B.C. de la peinture* of 1921, a summary of all that he had thought out and sought in former years. The work opens with a sharp rejection of any naturalism and any idea of imitation and then it continues with a discourse about the way our knowledge and understanding of things is determined by experience, remembrance, the relative situation with respect to other facts, and our own situation and condition at the moment at which we observe all these things.[45] As the given facts apprehended thus personally are translated by us in the work of art by means of pictorial signs (with iconic means, we should say) and as we can do so only in a personal way—because absolute beauty is impossible for us to reach on account of our human limitations— this gives rise to style.[dl]

But, he says, in and behind this style, which is peculiar to a personality, a period or a nation, there is 'une qualité supérieure, langage commun à toute intelligence humaine. Sans quelque trace de ce langage universel, il n'existe pas d'oeuvre d'art . . . Ses élements sont inhérents à notre constitution, donc innés . . .' [dm] Owing to the present low standard of education and breeding, however, we are compelled to rediscover these elements 'par l'abstraction et la généralisation'. And then he goes on to give a treatise on these general laws of art based on the numerical laws and especially on geometry —here he refers to the golden section, etc. [dn] But this aesthetics is only a means, the alphabet [do] with the aid of which the artist expresses himself—here we notice that in this well thought-out treatise he reverts back to the well-balanced synthesis of the eighteen-nineties —'Or, les pensées et les qualités morales ne peuvent être représentées que par des équivalents formels. C'est la faculté de percevoir ces correspondances qui fait l'artiste.' [dp] This may be achieved if the artist studies 'le monde extérieur dans ses lois et non dans ses accidents.' [dq]

This shows clearly that Sérusier is aware of the fact that art is an iconic representation clothed in the idiom of a pictorial language of what is given in human experience, an expression of what man has grasped and understood of some given reality. It is striking that although he appeals to the theory of the correspondences he did not think it necessary to elaborate it or to give it a philisophical basis. This is all the more striking as—apart from what others have said about him—he himself relates that in the period about 1890, when all this had been formulated, they were absorbed in the study of Plato, Aristotle, and the Neo-platonics.[46] It is as if that philosophical background is taken for granted. Men like Morice and Aurier, not

171

to mention Balzac and Baudelaire, had already laid the foundation. He was now concerned with the elaboration of a genuine theory of art which was really directed to art itself and to artistic methods and did not lose itself in philosophic speculation. This constitutes Sérusier's great merit, and the transparency of his views makes him the strongest exponent of the synthetist art theory.

Nevertheless it must be admitted that there is also some rigidity in his theory, as it really systematized Gauguin's conceptions in too rigorous a framework,[47] so that the fulness and liveliness, the richness in ideas found in Gauguin crumpled up and was lost in more than one respect. We might draw a direct parallel to the relation between the art of both men. Sérusier's art is inferior as to warmth, richness and variation in comparison with Gauguin's—so much so that if Sérusier happened to take over some motif from Gauguin, this motif was deprived of its staggering impact, of the surprise it was to the spectator and which it still is even now long after it has lost its revolutionary meaning and become history and a tradition.[dr]

Bernard

Now there is only one more figure to be considered, viz., Bernard, in his later development. We shall not go into the controversy—or should we say the quarrel and breach—between Gauguin and Bernard. Let us only examine in what sense he himself elaborated the theories advanced before 1890. Entering more deeply again into these views of art, we discover a remarkable complication in the typically Roman Catholic personality that Bernard was. We might have pointed it out elsewhere and in an earlier context, but nowhere does it come out so clearly as here. For we have already found more than once that the ideas (as well as the concrete activities) of the formers of culture and the artists dealt with were determined by the basic motif of Humanism with its internal duality of nature and freedom. In order to solve this tension, or at least to reduce it to a kind of balance, they had recourse already very early (e.g. Baudelaire) to theories whose origin was to be sought in an entirely different world from that of Humanism, in this case to late antique Neo-platonism. But the latter itself was dependent on a wholly different basic motif, viz., that of form and matter.[ds] This form-matter motif always raises the question of the relation of a permanent, self-supporting 'eternal' form to an always 'flowing', changing matter which composes and decomposes itself perpetually, and in which that form manifests itself in some way or another.[dt] We might say that in the synthesis between Greek and Humanistic thought the 'nature' of Humanism is as such conceived after the manner of the Greek form-matter duality—in which the latter is deprived of its intrinsically religious sens. [du] There is a further complication in the case of Bernard who was a very well-informed Roman Catholic believer, and whose thought was determined in all kinds of ways by the motif of nature and grace which had been given its more elaborate formulation and determination in the Middle-Ages—a motif which in itself was already the result of a synthesis between Christian-Biblical and classical thought starting from the form-matter polarity.[dv]

Let us now consider how these things were concretely formulated by Bernard in his views of art. In an article written in 1895 we read: 'Car, si les choses sont la figure des choses invisibles'—this is a Greek way of thinking, or to be more exact it is Neo-platonic—'l'essence de l'homme, tenant du divin et douée d'harmonie, coordonne et transforme la nature selon sa suprematie pour lui faire exprimer son origine propre et surnaturelle.' [dw] The latter part of this quotation is clearly the expression of the primacy of the personality embodying the freedom motif. It is hardly christianized by its references to the 'divine'. Especially the expression 'supremacy' is significant. The same state of affairs is found a little further on and expressed in the following way: 'Il y a donc en l'homme—de par Dieu—une création latente et supérieure au monde visible.' [dx]

Next he dwells on the symbol, appealing (with elaborate quotations) to Pseudo-Dionysius Areopagite, [48] presenting us a pure Neo-platonism only slightly christianized.[dy] Finally he fits all this into a framework which is strongly suggestive of the scholastic doctrine of the 'donum super additum'. For he writes: 'Le Beau qui est le résultat d'une illumination particulière et qui est le don du Saint-Esprit.' [dz]

Meanwhile it appears that in all this Bernard also implicitly understood that a work of art is of an iconic nature—this is the real discovery of this generation. And a great part of their philosophizing was intended to justify and to found this thought which they felt to be something perfectly new. Thus he can give an elaborate and

173

no doubt adequate defence of the meaning and the composition of the (Greek-Catholic) icons leading to the thesis: 'Les lignes ont leurs accords plus ou moins significatifs, les couleurs sont des caractères, leurs unions des phrases ... Les formules jeunes ou vieilles sont donc une manière d'écrire que nous devons toujours entendre, toujours connaître et ne point nier.' [ea]

That the significance of the theories developed by the synthetists really far transcended the style of their own group—which they wanted to defend with it against naturalism with all its implications —may appear from the fact that even after Bernard had turned his back upon synthetism as such he continued to defend this theory and to adhere to it. He did so, e.g., in a short exposition in 1926 (his polemical afterthought, viz., to defend his own authorship is left out of the account here), in which he wrote as follows: 'Dans la nature, il n'est pas une forme qui ne soit un signe pour l'esprit (viz. the Greek 'nous' or Aurier's 'pensée'), la nature toute entière est donc elle-même symbole'. [eb] This purely Plotinian thought is elaborated in an exposition of the method by which an artist can achieve the desired result working from memory, because thus the image will be 'purified' (which idea we have come upon more than once before this), with his conclusion: 'Un travail intérieur s'est fait inconsciemment; tout ce qui est inaliable à mon tempérament s'est effacé de moi; ce qui reste est réellement propre à lui.' [ec] It is remarkable how, after all, this theory results in a purely humanistic and even purely individualistic view of art with its ideal of giving expression to the strictly personal.

Speaking about Gauguin Bernard then continues with a striking thought: 'grandes directions des lignes, simplification de la couleur, devenant plutôt significative du sujet que réprésentative de la lumière ou du ton propre...'' [ed] Here we see him trying to attain to a direct result of the insight into the iconic character of a work of art, viz., that of the 'Indifferenzlicht', the true meaning of which had no longer been recognised owing to the 'natürliches Naturlicht' of nineteenth century art. [ee] It is a really striking thing that in the work of Gauguin and his circle the 'Beleuchtungslicht' had vanished. This 'Beleuchtungslicht' belonged to post-Renaissance art which always started from the observer standing on the same spot. It was replaced by the iconic representation of persons and things in a

174

painting by means of the 'Indifferenzlicht'. As a matter of fact, Gauguin had been aware of this to a certain extent when in answer to a question asked by Bernard and Laval about the shadows he said that the latter as such are by no means indispensable.[49]

To come back upon the remarkably complicated synthesis, which is so obviously manifest in Bernard we would in summary quote his pronouncement that in his art he sought 'd'unir la vérité visible du monde et le divin de la vie intérieure.'[ef] The former agrees with the symbol theory founded in the Greek basic motif and is used here to give 'nature' (in the sense of the Humanistic polarity) its due, whereas the latter clearly expresses the personality ideal. We see that on closer examination the synthesis that was aimed at in those days was even more complicated than it appeared to be at first sight, whereas, remarkably enough, the Roman-Catholic basic motif did not have any profound influence on art-theoretical thought in general, although it is noticeable in men like Bernard.

VIII

SOME TERMS AND CONCEPTS

In the synthetist movement at the end of the century a definitive
reaction against positivism forces its way through, against naturalism,
against the primacy of the ideal of natural science. The exact opposite
is sought of what at one time Darwin wrote in the preface to his:
The Botanic Garden (1789): 'The general design of the following sheets is to inlist the Imagination under the banner of
Science.' [1] Gauguin formulates the contrast sharply in his exposition
(quoted by Morice): 'L'art soi-disant raffiné procède de la sensualité
et sert la nature', whereas the art that was to come was to proceed
quite differently, for it 'procède de l'esprit et emploie la nature.' [a]

'Synthèse'

In this connection the term 'synthèse' was often used in those days,
—so often, indeed, that it occurs almost on every page then written
or printed. For this reason it is impossible and meaningless to
enumerate all the passages where it is found. But it is important to
examine how the term was used.

It is certainly unnecessary to enter into all kinds of cases where
the word is used carelessly or only more or less rhetorically, so that
it is difficult to discover any real sense in it. Such usage, however,
evidences the popularity of the term. Its meaning in these instances
will no doubt be remotely related to the one that we are trying to
discover in this section. To give an example of what we mean we will
quote Maurice Denis: 'Ainsi se forme chez l'artiste moderne, par
choix et synthèse, une certaine habitude éclectique et exclusive d'inter-
preter les sensations optiques.' [b] Here he discusses the Salon artists
with their naturalism and in the term 'synthesis' we cannot detect

176

anything more than the assertion that the artists worked from a particular artistic point of view.

More than once we can translate 'synthèse' by artistic unity, harmonious composition, internal unity of conception, the understanding and the coherence of forms and colours. Thus Aurier says in a review of the Salons of 1891 about the art exhibited there: 'C'est ... surtout l'oubli complet du style, du vrai style, qui au fond n'est que la compréhension de l'intellectualité des formes, et qui est devenu impossible, d'abord par l'oubli de toute synthèse en art...' c The same Aurier wrote about Sérusier: ' ... ses dernières toiles, d'un symbolisme poétique, d'une belle et savante synthèse de lignes et de couleurs, font présager un artiste de premier ordre.' d The term 'synthesis' is really used here in a way that does justice to Sérusier's own conception. For he himself writes: 'La synthèse consiste à faire rentrer toutes les formes dans le petit nombre de formes que nous sommes capable de penser, lignes droites, quelque angles, arcs de cercle et d'ellipse; sortis de là nous nous perdons dans l'océan des variétés.' e And perhaps we find the term used most correctly in this sense by Denis, when speaking of the classics and the classicists he says: 'Ce qui domine, c'est l'idée de synthèse. Pas de classique qui ne soit économe de ses moyens, qui ne subordonne toutes les grâces de détails à la beauté de l'ensemble, qui n'atteigne la grandeur par la concision.'f

But (apart from the last quotation) it is difficult to abide by the translation given. In this term we feel a connotation which has a wider meaning than merely 'a consciously balanced composition'—it also denotes something of the relation between a work of art and reality.g This becomes clearer when in connection with the new art we read: 'Le triomphe de l'esprit de synthèse sur l'esprit d'analyse, de l'imagination sur la sensation, de l'homme sur la nature.' h At the same time this shows the origin of the term.

For originally 'synthesis' is a scientific term meaning 'combination', considering things in their interrelation. As such it is mostly used in opposition to analysis, setting apart, a sharp distinction between the separate parts viewed in themselves. In French 'synthétique' often means something that we could translate by 'inductive'.[2] Also in Baudelaire we come across this original meaning when, e.g., he writes about the (naturalistic-academic) artist of his day: 'Il sent,

177

ou plutôt il juge successivement, analytiquement', opposing to them others who 'sentent tout de suite, tout à la fois synthétiquement.'[i]

Baudelaire here uses the term already in connection with artistic questions, and we can understand that thus it gradually gained ground in the world of the artists. Thus in a dictionary we find sub voce 'langue synthétique': 'qui exprime des rapports complexes par un seul mot, et qui groupe les idées accessoires autour de l'idée principale dans des phrases périodiques.'[k] And although we have never found in any dictionary that the men of letters indicated in this way a particular technique or attitude with respect to the artistic use of language[l], we may assume that it certainly existed. How else to explain the sudden rise and popularity of the term after 1885? Also the painters no doubt used the term in a similar way—this will be examined in a later context.[m]

The artists of this generation opposed naturalism blaming it for its (positivistic) analytical attitude. They themselves strove after a new art which was to represent reality in a new synthetic way. It is, therefore, understandable that the term was very suitable to express their ideal, especially on account of its scientific connotations, and also in connection with the linguistic (and artistico-technical)[n] sense given to it in their own circle. And as these artists were so busily occupied with all kinds of theories to give their own point of view its foundation and to defend it, quite naturally the term was burdened still more, and that with a very specific sense connected with their art-theoretical considerations which in their turn were connected with their starting-point based in their view of life. The more so as in philosophy proper the term had been used in this sense at a much earlier time, as we shall see in what follows.

We have already explained more than once that in those years they were sharply aware of their own position as to their view of life: they wanted to wrench themselves free from the primacy of the science-ideal and to vindicate man's freedom again without giving up what the 19th century had yielded as to the domination of nature. They sought to find a way of doing equal justice to the two basic tendencies in the humanistic motif of nature and freedom.

'Au fond de leur pensée il y a le désir de TOUT. La synthèse esthétique, voilà ce qu'ils cherchent,'[o] thus Morice briefly summarizes the main thought. The attempt was made to recapture human freedom—after the period of slavery in the service of nature—without, however, giving up nature. Thus it was hoped they would grasp the fulness of being—while there was a deep-rooted feeling that only in art such a synthesis could be fully realized. Morice even more amply formulates this 'artistic synthesis' in his sensational book of 1889 *La Littérature de tout à l'heure*: 'C'est là, dans cette ardeur d'unir la Vérité et la Beauté, dans cette unité désirée de la Foi et de la Joie, de la Science et de l'Art, ᵖ in which we clearly see truth and natural-scientific insight and even faith placed on one level and opposed to beauty, joy, and art. And if this pronouncement is to be taken seriously, it entails remarkable consequences. For, if the new art aims at a synthesis of the elements mentioned, but nevertheless truth and beauty, science and art remain clearly opposed to each other, how can art ever reach a synthesis. For art is only one of the elements to be synthetized and is as such of a different kind from the element of truth found in natural science.

In fact we are confronted with an internal contradiction here showing how they stuck to the view of reality based on the primacy of the ideal of science, and how on the other hand they wanted to oppose to it and at the same time to connect with it art and beauty —which in the sense intended by them (cf. p. 115 ff.) are connected with the personality-ideal.�q. It is understandable that not long after this at the turn of the century both elements contained in the synthesis tear themselves loose from each other: painting then becomes the direct expression of human freedom and is not to be related to truth in any way in the sense of conformation with reality as such, whereas there is also a tendency toward a kind of super-naturalism with a more-dimensional colour-film for its ideal (evoking an image which does not in any way deviate from the natural visual objects).

Also in Aurier we meet with the term and the concept 'synthesis' in a very elaborate form. Especially in his plan for his 'Oeuvre' as a totality consisting of poems: 'Qu-est-ce que le Poème? Une synthèse de toutes les idées générales perçues par un moi donné. La synthèse des sensations constitue: les sciences. La synthèse des sciences constitue: les philosophies. La synthèse des philosophies constitue: les dogmes. La synthèse des dogmes: 1e poème. Le poème est donc, par excellence, la conclusion intellectuelle, le poème est l'essentielle

179

synthèse du moi.' [r] In the parts he understands by synthesis what is understood by it in science generally—summary, total view—but on examining the final conclusion we notice that thus in art a synthesis is achieved (and now the term is used as in the passage from Morice mentioned above, i.e., as the combination of the two polar tendencies within the humanistic view of life and the world) between the given (natural) reality and human personality. Somewhere else Aurier expresses himself more clearly and more simply when he says of the work of art that it is 'un être nouveau ... puisqu'il a pour l'animer une âme, qui est la synthèse de deux âmes, l'âme de l'artiste et l'âme de la nature ...' [s]

The demand for such a synthesis gives rise to a special problem for art, a problem which was not new as a matter of fact, but had already been seen by men like Baudelaire. It had even presented itself before, namely in the first attempts of the romantics to assign a place to nature too, so before they abandoned themselves entirely to positivism. At that time the artists sought the new art in what was natural but would not relinquish the peculiar character of romanticism. This was the very opposite to what was seen at the end of the century. Van Tieghem has very sharply formulated the problem: 'Vouloir ... faire entrer la vie contemporaine dans la littérature constituait une des tendances les plus nouvelles, les plus hardies ... du mouvement romantique; le plus difficile aussi à réaliser, si l'on tenait à maintenir et à développer les droits de l'imagination, de la sensibilité, de l'idéal, à garder la divine robe de la poèsie pure de toute souillure au contact de la réalité terre à terre, à éviter le prosaïsme de la forme et la vulgarité du fond.' [t]

How it was thought possible to solve such a problem has been explained by Paul Adam writing in 1886 as follows: 'La vie moderne ne nous demeure point interdite ... Mais il sera permis de transfigurer dans une synthèse [u] autre que celle donnée jusqu'à ce jour par l'impressionnisme du roman. Nous ne la peindrons pas telle qu'elle se subjective dans la cervelle du palefrenier ou du peintre d'enseignes, mais telle que nous la fera notre rétine individuelle, notre vision plus largement embrassante. Nous y introduirons les fantômes du rêve, de l'hallucination, du souvenir, les évocations imaginaires, parce que cela se trouve dans la vie et le fait.' [v] But we now know that this effort failed: the movement defended here ultimately landed in an art that we have called 'decadent' in an earlier context. In this art the natural and contemporary datum has practically disappeared to give room to a kind of traditionalistic or allegorical-symbolistic subject-matter—such as is found in pictorial art with the Rose † Croix group which had even the following formulation in their rules: 'Voici les sujets repoussés . . .: Toute représentation de la vie contemporaine ou privée ou publique' and recommended as subject-matter a.o.: 'L'inter-prétation de théogonies orientales, sauf celles des races jaunes' and 'l'allégorie soit expressive comme 'modestie et vanité', soit décora-tive comme l'oeuvre de Puvis de Chavannes.' [w]

The best solution of the artistic problem posited was affected by those who broke with naturalism not only as a starting-point but also as a style. For thus it was possible to maintain realism in the subjects fairly well without any proviso—without introducing queer phantoms and hallucinatory subjects—and yet to avoid 'le prosaïsme de la forme et la vulgarité du fond'.[3] This is what we find in the group we have called the synthetists. But here, too, the synthesis has proved to be of a transitory character: for the anti-naturalistic element has overgrown everything to such an extent that in the end the natural-ness was lost, notwithstanding the ostensible realistic subject matter (e.g. in Picasso's still-lifes about 1910 or with the Fauves).

In the above we always came upon the tension between the ten-dency to abide by realism which at that time implied the risk of relapsing into naturalism with its copying of nature as in photography, and the pushing forward of the artist's personality in the realization of his vision in his own freedom. The tension between the science ideal and the personality ideal with its striving for freedom may manifest itself also in another way. We have already discussed this point in the preceding chapter when dealing with Sérusier. Denis again sharply formulates the antinomy we have in mind when writing down his reminiscences of the 'great' time of 1890: 'L'art, au lieu d'être la copie, devenait la déformation subjective de la nature. Au point de vue objectif, la composition décorative, esthétique et rationelle à laquelle les impressionnistes n'avaient pensé [x] parce qu'elle contrariait leur goût de l'improvisation, devenait la contre-partie, le correctif né-cessaire de la théorie des équivalents. Celle-ci autorisait en vue de l'expression toutes les transpositions même caricaturales, tous les

181

excès de caractère: la déformation objective obligeait à son tour l'artiste à tout transporter en Beauté. En resumé: la synthèse expressive, la symbole d'une sensation, devait en être une transcription éloquente, et en même temps un objet composé pour le plaisir des yeux.' ᵞ By objective deformation Denis no doubt means working in accordance with fixed laws such as, e.g., Sérusier had formulated (in the line of Henry, and others), viz. the rational mathematically exact laws alleged to determine the aesthetical. And of course these laws are in sharp contrast with the freedom sought and found in the expression of the strictly personal vision—'la déformation subjective' legalized by means of the theory of the 'equivalences.' [4]

The antinomy has certainly been posited more correctly here. For here we are concerned with a conflict within the artistic creation itself, with the question about the artistic means and the way to use them. Before that time the antinomy was really found in the artist's attitude towards reality, while the question of the artistic realization was not raised, or, if raised at all, was not formulated in such a sharp way. The latter case was especially found in the symbolistic circle e.g.,—leaving literature aside in the Rose † Croix movement. We have already seen how it was realized there, whereas the antinomy formulated by Denis can only be found in circles that have radically broken with the academic-naturalistic method.

It stands to reason that also the attempt to effect a synthesis in the sense so correctly formulated by Denis could not last. When consistently thought out in one direction this effort leads to work created in the spirit of Delaunay after 1914. The aim was to evoke a pure kind of beauty by confirming the aesthetic laws with circles and contrasting colours, while any meaning or any expression had disappeared. The other direction led to the Expressionists and the Fauves, to the art that was, e.g., made by Kandinsky in his 'Blaue Reiter' period lacking any 'rational' composition.

'Entre tous autres, la peinture est l'art qui préparera les voies en résolvant l'antinomie du monde sensible et de l'intellectuel' ᶻ , thus Delaroche in an article on Gauguin quoted by the latter with approval. The general opinion of those days was indeed that the synthesis sought for could be brought about especially in and through art.

This thought was certainly not new. We find it, e.g., strongly represented in romanticism. At that time, too, a synthesis was striven after similar to that at the end of the century. The most striking example is that of Krug, whose philosophy is called a 'transcendental Synthetism' in which the fundamental idea is that 'Reales und Ideales als gleich ursprünglich im Bewusztsein gesetzt und aufeinander bezogen sind.' [aa] Art was in a position to concretise this synthesis. Thus in Kant: 'Im Bereiche menschlicher Vernufttätigkeit wird also die gesuchte Synthesis von Freiheit und Natur, von Zweckmäszigkeit und Notwendigkeit, von praktischer und theoretischer Funktion durch das Genie repräsentiert, das in absichtsloser Zweckmäszigkeit das Werk der schönen Kunst erzeugt.' [ab] These thoughts were carried through in the circle of the Jena idealists in the aesthetic idealism, [5] in which we must especially refer to Schiller [ac] and Schelling.[ad]

No doubt the German idealistic philosophy influenced thought in France at the end of the century.[6] But generally speaking we shall not have to think of the two men just mentioned but of Schopenhauer (and Eduard von Hartmann). We have already spoken about this in the second chapter, where we have also pointed out that above all Carlyle must be looked upon as an important link between the German philosophy of the early part of the 19th century and French thought—especially in artistic circles. For the painters in whom we are in the first place interested Carlyle was no doubt very important. The influence of German idealistic philosophy was only indirect as may appear from, e.g., Morice's book repeatedly quoted by us (and to the talks we know he had with Gauguin and possibly also with others). Whatever may have been the state of affairs among the literary artists and the painters, we must always consider that there was only question of a purely philosophical interest on their part in so far as it enabled them to elucidate or to promote their own new ideals. And in any case we should guard against the thought that the new tendency arose under the influence of the idealistic philosophy from Kant up to and including Schelling and Hegel. And we need not suppose that there was any contact or any acquaintance with German neo-Kantianism, which came very markedly to the fore in those very same years.

Here we are concerned with the use of the term 'synthesis'. This term was indeed current in the German thought referred to in a sense similar to that which we found with the French of the latter part of the 19th century. But is was less frequent than might have been expected. Even in Kant's 'Kritik der Urteilskraft' it occurs rarely, and never explicitly in the sense obtaining among the French. [ae] At any rate in the specific sense in which the latter used it so often (at least at that time and in that milieu) the term occurs too seldom in the German philosophers for us to seek the origin of the frequency of the term in these thinkers—also considering their rather indirect and far from important influence.

In 1915 Sérusier wrote: 'Le mouvement auquel nous appartenons était antérieur aux influences allemandes. En philosophie nous parlions de Platon, d'Aristote, des néo-platoniciens et jamais de Kant.' [af] This shows that at least with regard to the painters any question of a direct and conscious influence on the part of the German idealistic philosophy is precluded—a conclusion we dare to risk because especially Sérusier was the most philosophically-minded and philosophically grounded figure among them.

It seems to be meaningful however, in connection with our present inquiry, to try and find out what Neo-platonism may have contributed both as regards the ideas and as regards the term used. The short summary of some of its principal thoughts given by Windelband will immediately make things clear: '... in ihr erscheint der Geist als die synthetische Funktion, welche aus ihrer höheren Einheit die Vielheit erzeugt. Von diesem allgemeinen Gesichtspunkt aus haben die Neuplatoniker die Psychologie des Erkennens unter dem Prinzip der Aktivität des Bewusztseins durchgeführt. Denn die 'höhere Seele' kann hiernach nicht mehr als leidend, sondern ihrem Wesen nach auch in allen ihren Funktionen nur als tätig angesehen werden. All ihre Einsicht beruht auf der Zusammenfassung (συνθεσις) verschiedener Momente; selbst da, wo die Erkenntnis sich auf das sinnlich Gegebene bezieht, leidet nur der Körper, während die Seele in dem Bewusztwerden sich aktiv verhält: und dasselbe gilt von den sinnlichen Gefühlen und Affekten.' [ag]

Calling to mind the theories advanced by Gauguin and his followers about 1890 we are at once aware of being in a kindred climate. The question what this is due to, whether such ideas appealed to the artists of that period as a more exact foundation of their artistic aims, or whether such ideas became common property via Swedenborg, Balzac, Baudelaire, etc. in such a way that this kinship is only a matter of course, cannot be answered univocally. And yet it is striking that these ideas were not found in other movements of this period or of the time shortly before it. Perhaps we had best conceive of the situation as follows. When once the search was made for ways of realizing the primacy of the human mind over nature, the Neo-platonism contained in the tradition mentioned directed thought as it were automatically and determined the formulations.

Finally, however, we shall not extensively elaborate this theme,— also in the Plotinian world of thought, art was the ideal way in which man could free himself from materiality and concretise his view of the ideas. Perhaps Plotinus himself only casually referred to something that we should call art—e.g., in this connection he speaks of hieroglyphs—[ah]. At any rate he gave these thoughts in principle, but they were elaborated in that direction by the latter Neo-platonics. Thus, e.g., by Ficino—a typical Renaissance man in his emphasis on the freedom of the human will, who considered the freedom of the human mind to be man's supremacy. This may also explain the great similarity to the synthetist art-theories. Ficino posits that 'art does not copy nature: it has its own laws. The supremacy of human art is rooted in man's power of self-determination. Thus Zeuxis' bunch of grapes, Appelles' horses and dogs, Praxiteles' Venus are superior to what nature could do: for they are evidence of the triumph of the human mind over matter.'[7] But although it is clear that this Neo-platonism might be a source of the idea of the synthesis or at least might have further determined it in its concrete formation, and although the term synthesis actually occurs in this movement, as we have seen, it does not seem plausible that we have found its origin here. For this philosophy and the literature in which it was discussed lay too far outside of the interests of these artists and literary men. But we must not ignore this Neo-platonism as a co-determinant of the popularity of the term.

Barre thus summarizes Moréas' ideas (a.o.): 'Le rapport synthéti-que de l'Idée avec ses apparences ne peut être fixé que par un style archétype et complexe.' [ai] This is a good example showing how the word is directly borrowed from the Plotinian sphere of thought and applied as an art-theoretical term indicating one of the principal elements of the new art.

Especially in the circle of the painters the term 'synthesis' seems to have been very popular. This may appear from the fact that one day Gauguin, supreme scoffer as he is, makes a pot on which he writes 'Vive la sintaize',[8] and still more undeniable from the fact that the first exhibition at which the group of artists round Gauguin made their collective début in 1889 during the World exposition, was entitled 'Groupe impressionniste et synthétiste'.[9]

Would it be possible to trace how the painters used this term in actual practice, i.e., what it implied for them with respect to their manner of working? In 1888 Gauguin wrote about his own work that it contained 'synthèse d'une forme et d'une couleur en ne considérant la dominante.'[ak] This clearly means the composition, the combining organization, a meaning that is a very near approach to the one we quoted in connection with language.[10] It is, however, evident that summarizing and subordinating to one facet is immediately connected with the question about what and how the artist is to select —and certainly so at that time when they were so sensitive to the problems concerning the relation between nature and art. This explains that in this term the art-theoretical and the philosophical opinions as well as their view of life were always implicitly comprehended. Perhaps we might explain these things best with the aid of the following short survey of Gauguin's theories, given by Dom Eduard Verkade in 1926: 'The impression of nature must be wedded to the aesthetic sentiment which chooses, arranges, simplifies and synthesizes. The painter ought not to rest until he has given birth to the child of his imagination ... begotten by the union of his mind with reality ... Gauguin insisted on a logical construction of composition, on a harmonious apportionment of light and dark colors, the simplification of forms and proportions, so as to endow the outlines of forms with a powerful and eloquent expression.'[al]

On quietly reading the first sentence we realize that there and in all other cases in the world of artists, the terms 'choose', 'arrange', and 'simplify' are more or less synonymous with 'synthesize'. In this use the primacy of (artistic) man over nature given in the impression is concretized. This thought is further qualified by the following sentences of the quotation. The synthesis implied, therefore, meant in concreto that which we read in the last sentence: great attention paid to the individual peculiar character of the artistic realization so that it may forcefully express that which reality meant to the artist.

186

When we have become aware of this state of affairs with regard to this term we also see how it is possible for the term to have so many apparently diverging acceptations, and how it is that the same writer uses it now in this, now in that sense. For at one time the same fundamental thought or 'Leitmotiv' is viewed according to its philosophical aspect, then again to its practical-artistic meaning, or it is considered in a more close relation with the artist's view of life, or according to the artistic form in which it has been concretized.

Imagination

In the quotation we have just been studying we left one sentence out of account, viz. the statement that a work of art is supposed to be 'a child of (the artist's) imagination'. It is clear that in this way the element of the freely-creating human personality is emphasized, one of the elements in the synthesis, that is to say one of the two poles of the basic motif (which is to be brought into a relation of equilibrium, or at least into some coherence with the other one).

We can hardly be surprised to find this term frequently used in this period. As we have already seen, it plays an important rôle also with those whom we have called precursors, especially with Baudelaire. It was not only in current use among the artists outside of the Salon, but even in the latter circle. Thus some Ph. Gauckler devotes a whole section to it in his book *Le Beau et son histoire* (Paris 1873). This Gauckler is perhaps best characterized by his definition of 'le beau': 'la manifestation vraie de l'Unité de l'Être par des phénomènes finis.' [am] After an elaborate explanation of all kinds of concepts like 'le sublime', 'le joli', and 'le goût', remaining within the world of thought of the Academicians although not without some originality, he discusses 'l'imagination'. He starts from the statement that even if in our work we have followed all the correct precepts and methods—things he had treated elaborately before—it is still possible that the result is dead and meaningless. This is due to the lack of the imagination: 'Bafouée par les modernes [an] qui ne la comprenaient pas et dédaignent de la comprendre, elle a été appréciée des Anciens, qui sous le nom d'inspiration lui attribuaient une origine divine.' [ao]

The synthetists and their nearest adherents nearly always use the

187

term in direct opposition to the servile copying method of naturalism, to the soulless art of the Salon. In this, too, precursors, had shown them the way. Thus Baudelaire writes, more or less repeating Delacroix according to his own words, that 'la nature n'est qu'un dictionnaire': 'Ceux qui n'ont pas d'imagination, copient le dictionnaire. Il en résulte un très-grand vice, le vice de la banalité.' [ap] For Delacroix said: 'le vrai peinture est celui chez lequel l'imagination parle avant tout.' [aq] and more exactly he observes elsewhere: 'L'imagination chez l'artiste ne se représente pas seulement tels ou tels objects, elle les combine pour la fin qu'il veut obtenir; elle fait des tableaux, des images qu'il compose à son gré.' [ar]

It needs no further argument that the latter statement was bound to appeal to the generation of 1890. Thus Denis calls to mind his reminiscences of that period and says: 'Au lieu de travailler autour de l'oeil, nous cherchions 'au centre mysterieux de la pensée' comme disait Gauguin. L'imagination redevient ainsi, selon le voeu de Baudelaire, la reine des facultés.' [as]

'Imagination', therefore, besides inspiration, means above all creative artistic power using the given object as material to arrive at a very personal free expression in the work of art.

'*Rêve*'

As we have seen these precursors also rendered the concept 'imagination' by the term 'rêve', dream. And this, too, is found at that time. It is certainly true that more than once the term loses its sharply defined meaning through its frequent use, and becomes a slogan with very little sense—more as the indication of an atmosphere, in any case implying the connotation 'non-naturalistic'.[11] For the term was extremely frequent in oral and written use among this young generation. This may be proved by the publication of 'Les Deliquescences d'Adoré Floupette, poèmes décadents' in 1885, a book containing a mocking caricature of the circle of literary artists. For in this booklet we find the sentence which is so significant in the present context: 'Le rêve! le rêve! mes amis, embarquons-nous pour le rêve...' [at]

The original 'dream'—but we should not think of a dream in the sense of what happens to us when we sleep—still plays a rôle—, i.e. the 'rêve', the day-dream, the ideal, something we aspire after, something

188

we hope will happen or that we wish to attain to. This is the meaning of the word in a sentence like the following: 'Son rêve d'art commençait à prendre corps.. ' [au] For also this dream is something made by man himself, a projection. As soon as this projection in the future is directed to the work of art that one intends to produce, thus concentrating it on a very particular piece of work one very nearly approaches the meaning attached to the word especially by the artists of the 19th century we are discussing. Extending this meaning a little we arrive at the acceptation of style, artistic ideal, vision or conception. In view of the use of the term by artists like Baudelaire and the attitude which was so strongly opposed to naturalism, it is not surprising that 'rêve' also came to mean the free self-projected vision of the artist. Besides the term was naturally adaptable to such use: is not a dream the opposite of the common place everyday reality? This explains such a pronouncement as was made by Bernard (even without the art-theoretical connotations proper to the term as we shall see): 'Ce qui trompe-l'oeil c'est l'identité. Ce qui rejouit l'esprit et l'élève—car un tableau est avant tout un rêve écrit, et, à un certain point de vue, pour l'esprit lui-même une sorte d'illusoire tremplin—c'est l'harmonie, le senti.' [av]

'Le rêve' is consequently the day-dream, and for our understanding of their ideas of art it is very instructive to recall Gauguin's pronouncement: 'Rêver réveillé, c'est à peu près la même chose que rêver endormi. Le rêve endormi est souvent plus hardi, quelquefois un peu plus logique.' [aw] Thus the 'rêve' is less concerned with the style, the artistic realization, than with the subject-matter, this being a difference of nuance we should always bear in mind when we come upon the term. This will be clear when we read what Gauguin wrote about his picture 'Te Rerioa' (Le rêve) of 1897: 'Tout est rêve [ax] dans cette toile; est-ce l'enfant, est-ce la mère, est-ce le cavalier dans le sentier ou bien est-ce le rêve du peintre! Tout cela est à côté de la peinture, dira-t-on. Qui sait? Peut-être non.' [ay]

In the theory of art in the circle of Poe, Baudelaire, Mallarmé, Morice, the men of letters who precisely as thinkers had such a great influence on the painters round Gauguin, the word 'rêve' had an even wider implication. Baudelaire directly influenced by Poe writes about 'the dream' as follows: 'Mais le rêve est aussi moyen de connaissance, mode de perception du réel, ou plutôt d'une surréalité 'dont notre

189

univers stable n'est que la simplication et, pour ainsi parler, la caricature.' az

But it was Mallarmé whose view had been thought out sharpest and most consistently. Wyzewa summarizes this view concisely in the following words: 'Il admit la réalité du monde, mais il l'admit comme une réalité de fiction. La nature, avec ses chatoyantes féeries, le spectacle rapide et coloré de nuages, et les sociétés humains effarées, ils sont rêves de l'âme; réels: mais tous rêves ne sont-ils point réels?' ba Mallarmé's application of these thoughts to literature in his 'poème en prose', 'Un spectacle interrompu' is very characteristic. He describes his ideal of a paper 'qui remarque les événements sous le jour propre au rêve.' For, he continues, 'Artifice que la réalité, bon à fixer l'intellect moyen entre les mirages d'un fait; mais elle repose par cela même sur quelque universelle entente: voyons donc s'il n'est pas, dans l'idéal, un aspect nécessaire, évident, simple, qui serve de type.' bb

In what might be called a typically artistic-aristocratic attitude, this is a view of reality and of our knowledge about it which is strongly oriented to Berkeley. The latter denies the existence of any matter and says that all reality consists in 'ideas' that persons possess. He distinguishes 'ideas of sense' from 'ideas of imagination'; the latter are the product of our activity, the former are created in us by God—by means of which Berkeley tries to escape the scepticistic consequences of his conception. The unity of our experience of reality—which to Berkeley can only consist in the combination of 'ideas' which when considered in themselves are always individual—is not an original datum, but is the product of the combination of activities in man, and as such really arbitrary, although experience always works regularly and constantly in this combining activity. This shows that here an important step is taken in the direction of subjectivizing knowledge, in the sense, that is, that the contribution to knowledge made by what is knowable exclusively consists in its being knowable. Later on, in Kant, both thought about what is given and our experience of it in time and space became apriori, i.e., they became categories, qualities of human understanding, thus changing epistemology into 'transcendental logic'. Then there is no longer question of a reality apart from human logic.bc

When we call to mind what Plotinus said in this connection—see

190

above under synthesis—the agreement with this conception is obvious. Thus discovering a tradition, a line via Plotinus and Berkeley to Mallarmé, we at the same time understand why Mallarmé, who at first sight does not seem to be quite in keeping with the rest of the circle we are discussing, fits in with them perfectly. He is only less directly influenced by Plotinus, he handles the same conception (philosophically speaking) in a modern way, so that also on this account the connection between him and Neo-platonic tradition in art-theory is less obvious and less marked.

But the term 'rêve' is very heavily burdened with him: it denotes Berkeley's 'ideas of imagination' and at the same time it emphasizes his scepsis with regard to the knowledge of reality. Everyday knowledge is only based on a 'universelle entente', and as a matter of fact everything is only 'rêve', the product of man's creative imagination—although, as we have seen in the previous chapter, Mallarmé does not entirely cut through the bond with given reality, certainly not in (artistic) practice. This term 'rêve' is consequently something new in comparison with the old tradition, it is the contribution of the 19th century giving a positive sense to this 'rêve', which first had a negative content—e.g., in Kant's *Träume eines Geistessehers*. Its origin in the literary sphere seems to be an established fact, although it had been introduced into the world of the painters at an early period already, viz., in Goya.[12]

Morice (as well as Aurier) used the term in a similar sense and applied it to art-theory in a characteristic way. Thus Morice writes: 'Beauté ... le Rêve du Vrai. Mais qu'est-ce que cette jouissance des 'sens spiritualisés' sinon le rayonnement de la Vérité en des symboles qui la dépouillent des sécheresses de l'Abstraction et l'achèvent dans les joies du Rêve?'[bd] Thus it becomes clear for what purpose these thoughts were used, viz., to get free from the primacy of analysis as used in natural-science.

We may ask whether the painters were aware of all this. They were certainly not aware of the philosophic meaning we have tried to define in the above. Still less did they realize the historical background—in which they probably took no interest. On reading again the quotatious from the painters given above in this connection, it appears that there was always a certain apprehension of this connotation, some understanding of the deeper meaning expressed

191

by this term and put in words by the men of letters.[bc] But even then it is almost identical with 'imagination'—recall that Berkeley did not speak of 'rêve' but of 'ideas of imagination'. So 'rêve' is generally speaking (and certainly in the case of the painters) distinguished from 'imagination' only by some vague connotations, by a certain feeling tone—the word strongly emphasizes the free, self-creating aspect of the imagination, it is still more markedly subjective and individual. We might find a further confirmation of this statement in the way Gauguin uses the term 'rêve' in his letter to Fontainas in 1899. There we might translate it by 'imagination', but then we would fail to express a shade of meaning that we might retain if we translated 'rêve' by 'artistic day-dream', artistic conception of a strictly individualistic and in any case obviously subjectivistic view of reality: 'L'idole ... faisant corps dans mon rêve ...'; 'Et tout cela chante douloureusement en mon âme et mon décor, en peignant et rêvant tout à fois ...'; 'mes yeux se ferment pour voir sans comprendre le rêve dans l'espace infini qui fuit devant moi ...' [bf]

Symbol

The typically synthetistic standpoint has been sharply expressed by Bernard in a short summary: 'Il n'y a de symbolisme qu'à ce prix: le symbole n'étant autre chose que l'esprit présenté sous la forme, l'idéal sous le sensible.' [bg] This shows how the idea of the symbol is used in order to effect the synthesis we are discussing. Less kind but very clear and no doubt with some foundation is Poizat's description—it is true he speaks of the decadents in this case (their pictorial equivalent we have called the symbolists), but in this matter the theories of both tendencies are pretty well alike [bh]: 'Les décadents s'étant ralliés au subjectivisme ... ne regardaient plus les choses qu'à travers le miroir déformateur qu'était leur âme rêveuse. Et comme, d' autre part, ils étaient en même temps très raisonneurs, ils en vinrent assez vite à ne plus voir dans les choses ainsi réfléchies et immatérialisées en eux que des emblèmes et des symboles.' [bi]

As a fact the art-theoretical notion of the symbol is no novelty. We come upon it already in the time of the romantics. Even such a man as Heine—the connecting link between German romanticism and French literature—makes use of it—his exposition even excels in clarity and lucidity. 'Töne und Worte, Farben und Formen, das

Erscheinende überhaupt, sind jedoch nur Symbole der Idee, Symbole, die in dem Gemüthe des Künstlers aufsteigen, wenn es der heilige Weltgeist bewegt, seine Kunstwerke sind nur Symbole, wodurch er andern Gemütern seine eigenen Ideen mittheilt... Ist der Künstler so ganz willensfrei bei der Wahl und Verbindung seiner geheimnissvollen Blumen? [bk] Oder wählt und verbindet er nur, was er muss? Ich bejahe diese Frage einer mystischen Unfreiheit... In der Kunst bin ich Supernaturalist. Ich glaube, dass der Künstler nicht alle seine Typen in der Natur auffinden kann, sondern dass ihm die bedeutendsten Typen, als eingeborene Symbolik eingeborner Ideen, gleichsam in der Seele geoffenbart werden.' [bl]

This thought is also clearly found in Baudelaire: [bm] 'Chez les excellents poètes, il n'y a pas de métaphore, de comparaison, ou d'épithète qui ne soit d'une adaption mathématiquement exacte dans la circonstance actuelle, parce que des comparaisons, ces métaphores et ces épithètes sont puisées dans l'inépuisable fonds de l'universelle analogie et qu'elles ne peuvent être puisées ailleurs.' [bn] After all that has been said we need not argue any longer that such a pronouncement will certainly have influenced the artists of the generation of 1885/90. Also Mallarmé's similar theory will have strengthened this thought and made it almost inevitable. Ghil's *Traité du verbe* of 1885, the influental publication that explained and distributed Mallarmé's ideas will have contributed a great deal too. Among other things he writes in it as follows: '(Pour le poète à composer) la vision seul digne: le réel et suggestif Symbole d'où, palpitante, pour le rêve, en son intégrité nue se lèvera l'Idée prime et dernière, ou vérité.' [bo]

But if it is so clear where these artists got their ideas from, the question remains where is the origin of this thought. After what we have written especially about Aurier and Morice the answer is not difficult to find. Without doubt we are dealing here with a Neoplatonic tradition. As a matter of fact they were well aware of this state of affairs. Thus Bernard has an elaborate quotation from Pseudo-Dionysius Areopagita, [13] a.o. this passage: 'Aussi avons-nous généralement peine à croire les paroles relatives aux divins mystères que nous ne contemplons qu'à travers l'enveloppe de sensibles symboles... les diverses formes dont un symbolisme sacré revêt la divinité, car, au dehors, ne sont-elles pas remplies d'une inadmissible et imaginaire monstruosité.' [bp] Is it not as if we hear a direct echo of

193

such thoughts when in Remy de Gourmont we read: 'il doit chercher l'éternel dans la diversité momentanée des formes, la Vérité qui demeure dans le Faux qui passe, la logique pérennelle dans l'Illogisme instantané'? [bq] But we need not look for ideas like these in the works of the literary men who had hardly any contact with the painters treated by us. Aurier expresses pretty well the same thoughts,[14] and that while appealing to Swedenborg—who himself also derived his thoughts from similar Plotinian sources. From this he concludes: 'Or ceci admis, c'est concéder la possibilité et la légimité pour l'artiste d'être préoccupé, en son oeuvre, par ce substratum idéiste qui est partout dans l'univers et qui, selon Platon, est la seule vraie réalité.' [br]

Indeed, when we go more deeply into the literature handled by these artists and men of letters we again and again come upon the same considerations. We are referring to Carlyle, for instance, who in his turn started from the German idealistic philosophy, romantic literature and art-theory: 'In the symbol proper . . . the Infinite is made to blend itself with the finite, to stand visible, and as it were attainable thereby . . .' [15] Of this we find, as it were, the direct flowery translation in Morice: 'Celle (l'oeuvre d'art) qui révèle, celle dont la perfection de la forme consiste surtout à effacer cette forme pour ne laisser persister à l'ébranlement de la Pensée que l'apparition vague et charmante, charmante et dominatrice, dominatrice et féconde d'une entité divine de l'Infini.' [bs]

It is to be understood that they were so strongly convinced of the truth of these ideas that art was considered to be impossible without them: 'une simple imitation des matérialités ne signifiant point une quelconque spiritualité n'est jamais de l'Art, en d'autres termes, qu'il n'y a pas, qu'il n'y a jamais d'Art sans symbolisme' (Aurier).[bt]

Art as revelation

If we allow the thoughts concisely summarized in the above to be impressed in our mind, the conclusion is unavoidable that art reveals a higher reality to us, 'L'Infini', the ideas found behind reality according to the theory of Plato. And in fact the view that art is the pre-eminent instrument of divine revelation is found especially with the literary men, and is repeatedly placed in the foreground.

This thought was already old and was found implicitly at least in Plotinus. But we meet with it explicitly in Ficino, for whom it was connected with the typical religious basic motive of modern times, which assumes such a clear form especially with these men, viz. the theme of the freedom and independence of the human mind.[16] Thus it becomes explicable that he can say that art has its own laws and does not copy nature. For the exalted character of human art is rooted in man's power of self-determination. Thus the grapes of Zeuxis, the horses and dogs of Apelles and Praxiteles' Venus are works that are superior to those of nature, for they testify to the triumph of the human mind over matter.[17]

Via all kinds of mysticistic and occultistic movements which were so strong during romanticism,—in what precedes here we have more than once pointed out the importance of Swedenborg—this kind of thought also penetrated to the world of the artists. V.E. Michelet makes this clear in the following passage of his writing in 1891: 'Qu-est-ce que le Poète? C'est une des incarnations sous lesquelles se manifeste le Révélateur, le Héros, l'homme que Carlyle appelle 'un messager envoyé de l'impénétrable Infini avec des nouvelles pour nous.' Cette conception du Héros, exprimé par un visionnaire de génie, est la directe conséquence d'une autre conception universelle-ment admise par les occultistes et les mystiques, et formulé ainsi par Novalis: 'Tout être créé est une révélation...' [bu]

In *Noa Noa* Morice elaborates these ideas in connection with Gau-guin in his own poetical way: 'Quelque part hors du monde, dans le ciel de la joie et de la beauté, c'est jour de suprême épiphanie quand un grand artiste a couronné de son génie quelqu'une des inombrables figures belles de la NATURE; quand l'artiste, enfant lui-même de la NATURE, nourri par elle, vivant d'elle, se lève pour dire la beauté de sa mère: quand la Nature laisse un des aspects changeants de son mystérieux visage éterniser le mot de son énigme dans l'oeuvre d'Art.'[bv] But already some years before Morice had preached this gospel of beauty very clearly in his important book: 'L'art n'est que le révélateur de l'Infini: il est au Poète un moyen même d'y pénétrer. Il y va plus profond qu'aucune Philosophie, il y prolongue et répercute la Révélation d'un Evangile, il est une lumière qui appelle la lumière...' [bw] How is the truth found in a work of art? 'Nous cherchions la Vérité dans les lois harmonieuses de la Beauté, déduisant de celle-ci toute métaphysique—car l'harmonie des nuances et des

195

sons symbolise l'harmonie des âmes et des mondes—et toute morale ...' bx

Reading the quotations just given, which sometimes border on profanation, and knowing that kindred thoughts did not only remain restricted to the world of the artists, but also penetrated the ecclesiastical milieu, we cannot but consider it understandable, and even a matter of course, that criticism was inevitable. And thus it is perhaps not so surprising that it was precisely Dr. Abraham *Kuyper* who in 1898 subjected symbolism to a penetrating criticism. We will study the contents of his paper here.by

Kuyper starts with a survey of the symptoms of the new movement as it manifested itself in the churches; a growing interest in liturgy, especially as regards its artistic aspect,bz a great interest in symbolism; a lower estimate of the importance of the preaching of the Word, in particular in the sermon; the ignoring of the differences between the various ecclesiastical groups,ca a depreciation of the values of the confession of faith and of dogmatic clarity. Then he says: 'childish it would be not to realize at once the inner connection between the general increase of love of the symbolical in literature, in painting, in sculpture, in service of worship outside our own churches,cb and the clearly distinguishable change of religious appreciation by which no keen observer can keep from being impressed in our own circles.' [18]

He rightly continues: 'It is not art but symbolism ... that took hold of the mind ... a new religion has set in.' [19] We may also speak of a 'predilection for mystical piety ... (but) it is devoid of any personal and definite character ... no demand at all for deliverance from sin; no desire for a conscious personal reunion with the living God... Their watchword is the merging of the soul in the ocean of the Infinite; the afterthrilling of the soul of the Cosmos in the vibrations of their own heart: the perception of an all-pervading power, inspiring them and the coveting of an unattainable ideal.' [20]

How true the latter statement is may appear from the plan for a novel found among the papers of Aurier and published in his *Oeuvres posthumes*. After all kinds of blasphemous incidents have happened, which have greatly depressed the mistress of the principal character (Aurier's mouthpiece), he observes: 'Pauvre enfant! Ne

196

te désole point . . . Il existe une rédemption.—Où la trouverais-je?—
En toi . . . Descends en ton âme! . . .—Ai-je donc en moi, sans le
savoir, pareille puissance? Porte-je donc en ma chair tout un univers?
—Un univers, enfant, plus grand et plus beau que l'univers! Un
univers dont tu es le Dieu . . . Ne faisons-nous autre chose, en croyant
inventer les plus fabuleuses chimères, que d'évoquer les visions, inconsciemment ressouvenues, des temps où nos âmes se prélassaient
dans le merveilleux Eden des Idées Pures?' cc At this point it is not
necessary to point out the clearly Platonic inspiration, nor to enter
into the connection with mysticism which advances such thoughts
usually in a christianized way—still less are we in a position here to
examine whether such a combination of the Christian tradition with
Platonic thoughts can really be attained without cutting through the
bond with Holy Scripture as the Divine Revelation in a more or less
evident way (although we think this question must certainly be
answered in the negative).

After discussing the further characteristics of such mysticism
Kuyper draws the conclusion that 'their constant endeavour is not
to fear, to serve and to love the living God . . . but to enjoy fully
the mystical titillations of a delightful religious feeling.' What are
the sources of the movement, rightly called a purely aristocratic
one, according to Kuyper? He mentions three of them: the new
German philosophy, the historical school, and the revival of the Arts.
The first of the three and the second are to be conceived of as a
reaction to the disintegration of life and thought brought about by
the French Revolution, and the too superficial and reckless cutting
through of all historical bonds. The question may be asked if German
philosophy itself had been so far removed from the ideas of the
French Revolution. After all the young Hegel, Schelling and many
others had danced round the tree of liberty and had sung revolutionary
songs.[21] No doubt Kuyper knew Groen van Prinsterer's book on the
French Revolution [22] too well to think that the Restoration in Europe
had really attacked the basic principles of the French Revolution and
had liberated itself from it. For it is probable that for the sake of
brevity Kuyper formulates his thought thus, and that he wanted to set
in the light that positivism which in its essence as well as in its tradition of thought was developed by the spirit that had borne the French
Revolution, was combated most in Germany in the 19th century.

197

However this may be, there was certainly a connection between German idealism with its romantic art-theory [23] and the movement of the nineteen-nineties in France—as we have pointed out more than once.

We are more concerned with what Kuyper says about art there. As one of the origins of the symbolic movement he mentions the 'revival of art life, under the all permeating influence of Lessing and Goethe, in its adoration for the classical beauty [cd] of the Greek world, must feel scandalized by the ridiculous extolling of uncultured nature, as was to the French revolutionists the real point of depart for their system.' [24] No doubt he is referring to German classicism, while it is not so easy to guess what he is thinking of with respect to French art. Zola's naturalism, or that of the art of the Salons? We shall have to seek in this direction probably. Or are we to go further back and to think of Rousseau?

'About the middle of the century France sank, Germany rose.' [24] It is certainly not easy to say what Kuyper had in view with respect to the pictorial arts. Hildebrand, Böcklin, Feuerbach? Or did he not at all think of painting and sculpture *in concreto*, and was it rather Wagner he had in mind, or was he especially concerned with German literature of the latter half of the 19th century? However this may be, there will at present be few people who would take over Kuyper's words.

Next Kuyper points out Plato's importance and that of Phidias for the forms and ideas of the German movement mentioned above. 'In this abstract form, however, this new leading thought could not radiate from the German to the Anglo-Saxon mind ... until Darwin gave it its material basis ... The Idea of the Infinite becoming phenomenal in the finite, by means of a material process, adapted itself to the Anglo-Saxon mind.' [25] A very remarkable utterance showing at any rate how little Kuyper was familiar with English and American thought —we only mention the names of those who contradict the former hypothesis: Coleridge, Emerson, Carlyle, Poe, Rossetti and his school, although we must admit that also in England the positivistic ideal of natural science dominated the minds of people, whose most spectacular representative was no doubt Charles Darwin. [ce]

Kuyper is clearer and less easily refutable when in the following pages, coming to his own sphere of interest, he is occupied with the

198

nature and character of Revelation and of symbolism. 'Everyone who, moving in the finite, becomes aware of the existence of something Infinite, has to form a conception of the relation that exists between both. Either the Infinite reveals itself to man, and by this revelation unveils the really existing relation, or the Infinite remains mute and silent and man himself has to guess, to conjecture and to represent to himself this relation by means of the imagination; that is, in an artificial way. The first is the christian one... Paganism... wants the symbol and creates it in its idols. Symbol means a fictitious link between the invisible Infinite and the visible finite. Derived from symballein, i.e. bringing two different spheres together, Symbolism is the grasping of something outward and material upon which the imagination may put the stamp of the unseen and unspeakable. The symbol is the middle link, being related from one side to what you can see and grasp, and to the other side to what you feel, fancy and imagine... what she (symbolism) is longing after is a comprehensive impression of the Infinite in its totality, in its all-pervading and all-permeating action... such an infinite sensation only Symbolism can produce...' This exposition is to the point, sober-minded and transparent, and explains a great deal of what we have been discussing.

The conclusion is obvious: 'Revelation and Symbolism are opposed one to the other by principle.' In the one case the acceptance of Revelation by faith will be the way to gain fundamental knowledge of the basic principles of reality, in the other case art will be the medium: 'art, by the wonderful power of its imaginative gifts, creating the corresponding symbols.' [26] It is a confirmation of the correctness of his view that here Kuyper uses exactly those terms that we have found in the symbolistic or in the synthetistic theories of art. Recall only what Baudelaire said about the 'imagination'. [cf]

Also his next statement can immediately be corroborated by a quotation from Morice. Kuyper said: 'Accomodation to existing religion has always been in leading thought, and this accomodation is achieved at once by taking as poetry what the church confesses as the highest reality',[27] and in Morice we read: 'La critique moderne ne permet plus qu'on croie à des choses incroyables, et pourtant l'esprit moderne comme l'esprit ancien, reste avide de beaux mystères: comment n'a-t-il pas compris, Wagner, que, puisque la religion ne peut vivre pour l'art qu'autant qu'elle voile son élément de vérité sous un entassement toujours croissant de choses incroyables, cg et puisque, cependant, les hommes ne veulent plus que ces belles chimères soient proposées à leur raison, c'est à leur imagination SEULEMENT qu'il faut les offrir!' ch

After the quotation from Kuyper given above he continues saying that 'all actions of worship' are interpreted as 'mere symbolical utterances'—thus humanizing and subjectivizing them. According to Kuyper, who refers back to a thought expressed already in the beginning of his paper, this explains the great interest in Roman-Catholicism, which is so much better adaptable in this mentality than protestantism. And then he points to the many conversions to Roman-Catholicism already during the romantic period. No doubt this also holds in many respects for the circle of men who are the subject of the present study: we are referring to Huysmans, and in our country to Toorop, while Maurice Denis, Emile Bernard and the entire group of kindred minds were strong representatives of symbolistic thought although they were fervent Roman-Catholics —apparently they were unaware of the contradiction between the faith in Revelation and Symbolism.

Symbol (continued)

But what we have written above on the symbol was pretty well exclusively concerned with theory. It remains to be examined what these artists meant by their symbolism in a concrete and practical sense, what it meant for their view of a work of art in its concrete shape.

Exclusively occupying himself with the men of letters Lehmann has tried to answer this question by examining carefully in what meanings the term was used. He recapitulates his findings as follows:[28]
'1. Any isolateable member of the external world or any quality, which bears witness (to the mystic) of the supranatural unity and 'universal analogy' in the world (Baudelaire).'
—This is the meaning that we, too, have found, and which no doubt may be called the ordinary sense. It is nearest to the generally accepted meaning attached to this concept.—
'2. Any sensible thing or any word in so far it suggests to the Mallarmean poet the Platonic idea immanent in it (Mauclair).'

—Properly speaking this is not a new meaning of the word, but only a particular explanation of the origin and the meaning of the symbol, as we have seen in an earlier context. It is only a further definition of what has been said sub one, as also Baudelaire and his followers tried to found their theory of the symbol in a similar climate.—

'3. Any representation serving as a sign or a general attitude which either tradition or supernatural decree has invested with powerful emotional resources (Yeats)'.

—This, too, is merely a further determination of what has been given subone. We have not dealt with Yeats in further detail, as he was not in any way important for the (French) painters, nor did he write during the first few years of the new movement (his work belongs to the end of the nineteen-nineties). On the other hand his occult magical symbolism is interesting enough.[29]—

'4. An allegory, provided always that the art possesses, or tended to possess, a high degree or artistic integration. Hense, also, all myth, and by extension, pseudo-myth (Wyzewa, etc.)'

—Here we are in the climate of Wagner and of the art-theory influenced by him, which for the rest is in all kinds of ways closely related to that of the ideas of the group we have called the 'decadents'. And this conception is, therefore, most conspicuous in the typical symbolistic painters (those of the Rose† Croix and people like Toorop) with respect to their choice of subjects and their manner.—

'5. A single representation abstracted from a complex of experience involving many associated representations, which intended to do duty for its fellows as the most characteristic (Kahn).'

—Here we are nearer to the practical application of the theory, and so nearer to the answer to the question raised above.—

'6. Any work of art, not being an allegory or myth, whose evident purpose is to express the artist's attitude (Verhaeren).'

—Here the term is used to denote the typical subjectivism in its own colour, in its artistic concrete form. Properly speaking this view is perfectly inherent in the views of Baudelaire e.g., although the latter would perhaps not use the term in this particular application.—

'7. A formal construct or poetic image of great force which

201

constantly recurs in the poet's work as his mind circles around
a certain predominant attitude (Valéry etc.)'.

—This conception is a near approach to the one mentioned
under the previous number, it is, as it were, its practical
consequence.—

'8. Any work of art at all, considered as a formal unity, or
embodying an aspiration to formal unity (Gide).'

—Here we are not at all far removed from the theories explained
in the previous numbers, but this is a particular application. We
have, however, found that this thought was especially expressed
by the term 'synthesis'.—

Lehmann now tries to reduce all these meanings to one common
denominator and that is the concept language. 'Language ... em-
braces everything and anything which an artist appropriates to himself
from tradition and uses as a vehicle for expression,' [30] and a little
further: 'symbol' is the form—and of course the content—of a book or
other piece of writing. And the formal construction of a work of art
is simply the way in which its creator expresses an attitude—is an
attitude— ...' [31]

We cannot agree with Lehmann's words, at least not without some
qualifications. For when we pay attention to the way in which he
explains his thesis that this generation was concerned especially
with 'Language', we see that he is formulating the structure
of a work of art. Before giving the summary we have quoted in
great detail, he himself says that these artists are urged on by the
desire for 'a revival of the claims of art against not-art.' [32] Yet this
confusion of language and (literary) art is quite understandable. For
the issue in this case was not language as such, nor a theory of
language, but the recovery of the insight into the essential character
of a work of art precisely also in its use of language.

In this circle the attempt was made to give a new formulation of
the peculiar character of a work of art, of its peculiar way of expression and representation of reality. And as this was done in a
strong spirit of reaction to naturalism, which for all kinds of reason
had become unacceptable in its view of life, this generation was
bound to fall a victim to all manner of mysticistic theories, which
as it were, were readily available in a strong tradition. Naturalism

had degraded art to a kind of copy of every day life, owing to which also the artistic use of language had got lost. Metaphors, poetically exact but not therefore scientific ways of expression, an artistic manner of giving expression to what is relevant by means of language, all this and a great deal more was implied in their endeavours, because in the tradition based on the (natural-)science ideal the peculiar character of art, its structure and meaning, had been lost for the greater part.

All this is really much more apparent in pictorial art. Here the naturalistic art of the Salon was all-powerful, which as a matter of fact meant a vulgar photographical naturalism, an art which did nothing but copy what the eye saw. It made even the most sublime subject vulgar and (or) theatrical without the least trace of an interpretation of its meaning. Here the peculiar nature of a work of art had been completely lost sight of. The pictorial means had become so much a matter of course, they were so much determined by a tradition which started from the idea that a picture should 'imitate' the reality that we know by means of our senses, that in consequence it was forgotten that every pictorial artistic achievement makes use of iconic means which (in their own way but similar to language) are not identical with the given object represented by them. [ci] Indeed, for pictorial art the important thing was to regain an insight into the peculiar character of the pictorial manner of expression by means of an image. This was even more obvious and urgent in pictorial art than in literature. [ck]

In two ways the artists tried to rehabilitate the artistic and peculiar character of a work of art over against the Salon tradition. The one tendency sought to renew the subject-matter, more or less mythologizing in an extensive use of allegorical and metaphorical ways of representation, a method which was closely akin to that of literature—the way of the symbolists. The other tendency applied itself rather to the structure of the work of art as such, and kept faith with realism as it had been formulated in the line of Fontainebleau - Courbet - Manet - Impressionism. In the former case the way of depiction remained in the line of art since the Renaissance, as we have already tried to show in an earlier context. The latter found an entirely new way of artistic expression, a manner that shows its relationship with all pictorial art except that of the classical and the

203

modern period. But the latter remark should not blind us to the fact that also Rafael, Rubens and Rembrandt—to mention only a couple of names—were certainly alive to the peculiar character of pictorial 'language'. In this section we do not speak of the background of the view of life, but we try to define what was the real discovery made by the artists of this period, in which, therefore, they have recovered something that had been lost in the naturalism of especially the art of the Salons.

The Iconic—the real achievement of synthetist art-theory

We are referring to the Iconic [cl], a term which we have used a few times more already, but which we shall have to explain further. By the word Iconic we want to express something that might be indicated by the Dutch word 'beeld-spraak' (= speaking in images) if this term were not a little confusing as it means metaphor. For the important fact is that iconically we can express something by means of lines, colours, and three-dimensional forms—in a way similar to what happens in language by means of sounds. Language does not express something by means of sounds alone, because it requires 'organised (i.e. speech) sounds'—an organisation that will have to be brought about according to the norms of language. In the same way the icon operates. Both belong to the same modality: [cm] the relation between the word table and the concrete thing denoted by this word is in principle identical with the relation of a drawing or painting of a table to a real table. In naturalism there is sometimes—not always— question of a mimetic relation *(Abbildrelation)*—which is comparable to the onomatopae in language—, but this is by no means necessary for an iconic image. Surveying the great number of ways in which in the course of history the objects of the reality round us—both the realia and the invisible things—have been represented, we see that there are many image-languages possible. But if the typical norm of the iconic is to be observed, viz. that of clarity, (as it should also be in language), the structure of things must be represented. Take, e.g., the way a child represents a human being. This may be clumsy of expression, in its image he may have rendered only the most elementary state of affairs, and it may not contain any nuance or complication, but we recognise a human being in this thumbnail sketch because he has been clearly indicated iconically by it.

204

It needs no comment that by means of the iconic quite different things may be expressed, represented, from what is denoted by language. There are states of affairs that can hardly be made clear in an iconic way—e.g. a philosophical theory, an adjunct of place or time, etc.—but there are also many cases in which language fails us, whereas the iconic means may be very clear and unambiguous. We are referring, e.g. to geographical maps, to portraits, topographical drawings, etc. The iconic 'language'—which is generally speaking international but may certainly change with the times to such an extent that to a later generation the iconic representation is not at all clear [cn] —has its own norms again and again requiring further positivizing, a further concrete formulation.

We might call the latter 'style' if there were no objections to be raised against this term. For the iconic element qua talis is not artistic —no more is language as such. The example of the geographical map just mentioned—we might also refer to picture statistics—makes this clear. Yet it is understandable that our thoughts are immediately turned to style. For this positivizing of iconic norms is nearly always done by artists in their works—in which they sometimes look for new iconic means to express particular new visions. Here, too, appears the profound and non-metaphorical but real agreement with language. For exactly by literary artists language and linguistic usage are often given (a new) form in prose and poetry. But in the pictorial arts as well as in literature the iconic and the linguistic expression respectively are turned in an artistic direction, they are aesthetically disclosed or expanded. The latter statement will be explained after we have seen how the generation of 1885/90 had regained a clear insight into this aspect of a work of art, (although they had not always found a lucid formulation for it). It is precisely the extreme denial of this state of affairs by the Salon artists which held it under their very noses so to say and which made them aware of something that had really been a matter of course before their time (before the 19th century), at least it had implied nothing problematical.

Delacroix is without doubt one of the first to posit the question at issue in a clear way. Thus we read in his *Journal:* 'Il n'y a plus de contours qu'il n'y a de touches dans la nature. Il faut toujours en revenir à des moyens convenus dans chaque art, qui sont le langage de cet art.' [co]

We shall not again investigate the difficult problem of the way in which Delacroix's ideas had found their way to Gauguin and his followers. It is striking, however, that as soon as Gauguin liberated himself from the Impressionists and started seeking for new ways he posited the problem very lucidly: 'Plus je vais plus j'aborde dans ce sens de traduction de la pensée par tout autre chose qu'une littérature . . .' cp And some time later his answer to Bernard and Laval's question concerning the shadows in his pictures shows that in his entire 'instruction' it was exactly the question of the iconic representation that came to the fore again and again. It is characteristic that here he rightly points to the Japanese who, indeed, handled a totally different manner of positivizing the *iconic* element, a manner which could certainly not be explained on the basis of some representational relation. 'Vous discutez avec Laval sur les ombres et me demandez si je m'en fous. En tant que quant à l'explication de la lumière, oui. Examinez les Japonais qui dessinent pourtant admirablement et vous verrez la vie en plein air et au soleil sans ombres. Ne se servant de la couleur que comme une combinaison de tons, harmonies diverses, donnant l'impression de la chaleur, etc. . . .' cq Much later, in Tahiti he still appeared to realize this state of affairs thoroughly and clearly, almost more sharply than formerly. He discusses the Tahitian world and his artistic picture of it: ' . . . toutes ces couleurs fabuleuses, cet air embrasé mais tamisé, silencieux. Mais tout cela n'existe pas! (this is the critic's objection; Gauguin replies:) Oui, cela existe comme équivalent de cette grandeur, profondeur de ce mystère de Tahiti, quand il faut l'exprimer dans une toile d'un mètre carré.' cr

If Lehmann is right, the men of letters in their field were again clearly conscious of this circumstance—although in their case, in view of the character of literature which makes use of language whose proper nature can never be misinterpreted, its direct concentration on its artistic use is much more explicit than in the case of the painters. For the latter had still to reconquer the conception of the iconic element as such after a long period in which this element had been ignored. It is understandable that Aurier had a keen insight into this question, although we should certainly not underestimate the direct influence of Gauguin and his followers on Aurier in this respect. In opposition to the idea of the mimetic relation in a naturalistic sense, he writes: 'Le strict devoir du peintre idéiste est, par conséquent,

206

d'effectuer une sélection raisonnée parmi les multiples éléments combinés en l'objectivité, de n'utiliser en son oeuvre que les lignes, les formes, les couleurs générales et distinctives servant à écrire nettement la signification idéique de l'objet...' cs The latter statement, freed from the Neo-platonic scheme of interpretation, really means that the structure of what has been represented should be rendered in an iconic way.

In another passage Aurier is very explicit and concentrates on what occupies us here: 'Cela revient à constater que les objets, c'est-à-dire, abstraitement, les diverses combinaisons de lignes, de plans, d'ombres, de couleurs, constituent le vocabulaire d'une langue mystérieuse, mais miraculeusement expressive, qu'il faut savoir pour être artiste. Cette langue, comme toutes les langues, a son écriture, son orthographe, sa grammaire, sa syntaxe, sa rhétorique même, qui est: le style'. ct If many present-day art-historians and aestheticians can unreservedly agree with Aurier in this case, cu it is because the fundamental discovery made in this respect has become more and more clear and evident via the synthetist art-theory and the works of art in which this discovery was made use of.

It need not cause any surprise that this insight is also found in Gauguin's pupils, especially in Sérusier and Denis. cv It is remarkable that together with Gauguin himself and his example also Cézanne has played an important part for them. Cézanne's opinion (published only later on) on this is again and again quoted in the short slogan: 'Méditons ce mot de Cézanne: 'J'ai voulu copier la nature... je n'arrivais pas. J'ai été content de moi lorsque j'ai découvert que le soleil par example (les objets ensoleillés) ne se pouvait pas réproduire mais qu'il fallait le représenter par autre chose que ce que je voyais— par la couleur ...' cw Elsewhere the phrase 'autre chose' is still further explained thus: 'par des équivalents plastiques.' 33

It is certainly not inconceivable that Gauguin had also learnt something from Cézanne precisely on this point,—the latter being indebted to Delacroix etc., although the creative and personal element in this cannot be denied to either Cézanne or Gauguin. This thought urges itself all the more strongly upon our minds as Gauguin used the same word 'équivalent' more than once in this connection (whereas this synonym of 'correspondant' is rare in the case of the men of letters). We have already come across the term in one of the quotations from Gauguin made a moment ago. But this passage is by no means the only one.[34]

That people were aware of the fact that they had done with the naturalistic theory of imitation may appear from the following quotation from Denis: 'Nous avons substitué à l'idée de la ‘Nature vue à travers un tempérament' la théorie de l'équivalence ou du symbole: nous affirmions que les émotions ou états d'âme provoqués par un spectacle quelconque, comportaient dans l'imagination de l'artiste des signes ou équivalents plastiques capables de reproduire ces émotions ou états d'âme sans qu'il soit besoin de fournir la copie du spectacle initial; qu'à chaque état de notre sensibilité devait correspondre une harmonie objective capable de le traduire.' [cx] And Sérusier—from whom we might quote extensively—observes that this method of working is really the ordinary one: 'Or, les pensées et qualités morales ne peuvent être représentées que par des équivalents formels. (It is, of course, not accidental that Sérusier and the others so often talked of the invisible human experiences that must be depicted, for in this respect the extreme form of naturalism was deficient in the clearest and most serious way). C'est la faculté de percevoir ces correspondances qui fait l'artiste. Tout homme, en naissant, a cette faculté en puissance; son travail personnel la développe; une mauvaise éducation peut l'annihiler' [cy]—the latter statement certainly refers to the 'Academie'.

It is quite understandable that the art of other periods, especially the non-naturalistic kind, was an aid to making these artists aware of the meaning and the character of the iconic element, especially also in their confrontation with the art of the Salons. We have already mentioned the Japanese in this connection. Bernard writes about the Byzantine artists as follows: '...enfin je compris encore que dans l'icône ... tout doit etre empreint d'un caractère simple, explicatif, exact et symbolique, que chaque acteur doit avoir une dimension proportionnée à l' importance de son rôle...' [cz] And Denis says quite rightly and sharply: 'Un Christ byzantin est symbole. Le Jésus [da] des peintres modernes, fût-il coiffé du plus exact kiffyed, n'est que littéraire. Dans l'un c'est la forme qui est expressive, dans l'autre c'est la nature imitée qui veut l'être.' [db] And, finally, also Gauguin owed a great deal to his study of the art of Giotto,[dc] Cambodja (even though this was in reality the Burubudur on Java), [dd] the Egyptians, etc. [35]

Naturally, these artists were not concerned with a theory of the iconic element as such, a theory of the image and imaging. No more were the men of letters concerned with language and linguistic theory apart from the works of art, or the painters with the iconic element apart from the artistic aspect. On the contrary: their view of language and of the iconic aspect are always directly connected with the use of these means in a work of art: the issue is the literary language, the artistic icon. The aesthetic aspect is a modality [de] which is realiter of a different nature than the iconic element and qualifies a work of art. And this is why the iconic elements in a work of art will be arranged in such a way that they help to build up a composition [df] which is aesthetically justified. But in the aesthetic modality itself the iconic, (or the linguistic) moment will be reflected as an analogous element, [dg] i.e., the aesthetic form as such will be adapted to the iconic (linguistic) aspect in a work of art. This state of affairs makes it possible for a work of art to be a unity—as an artistic object its unity consists in the close coherence of the aesthetic and the iconic (linguistic) factors. In poetry, e.g., this appears in the 'plastic' quality of a poem. In its 'aesthetic symbolism' we find rhythm, hiatus, assonances and consonances used to underline the meaning of the poetic subject (comparable to madrigalism in music).[dh] By way of an example we shall quote a line from Coleridge's 'Rime of the Ancient Mariner':

'Down dropt the breeze, the sails dropt down'.

in which in a typical aesthetic way the first word 'dropt' underlines the sudden falling away of the wind mentioned in the (linguistic) text. [di]

But although the artists of the generation of 1890 were not in the least intent upon the theoretical analysis of such questions, they were certainly aware of them. When they speak of the iconic element, they often do so in the immediate connection with the aesthetic organisation of the image—the quotations given above have been chosen with some care, so that this aspect would not come to the fore too much in order not to make the discussion too complicated—while they denoted this 'aesthetic symbolism' [dk] by the term 'musicality', as we shall try to show in what follows.

So these artists were in the first place aware not only of the iconic character of the image, but especially of the requirement that the work of art as such should represent the meaning of the object, and that a narrative, or, as the case may be, the imitative depiction of the given visible things in itself does not imply anything artistic. That is why Denis wrote: 'Au lieu d'évoquer nos états d'âme au moyen du sujet representé, c'est l'oeuvre elle-même qui devait transmettre la sensation initiale, en perpétuer l'émotion.' [dl] In this circle the expression by means of the subject was simply called 'literary'—because it ignored the expansion of the iconic by the aesthetic modality qualifying a work of art. This is what Gauguin was referring to when he wrote: 'Qu'il me suffise d'avertir le visiteur que Gauguin est un cérébral—je ne dis pas, certes, 'un littéraire'—, qu'il exprime non ce qu'il voit mais ce qu'il pense par une originale harmonie de lignes, par un dessin curieusement compris dans l'arabesque.' [dm]

Writing in connection with Gauguin's art Morice elucidates this situation very clearly saying: 'Il était naturel que la synthèse conduisit l'artiste au symbole. Des sacrifices et un ordre dans la composition qui avaient pour but de rendre intelligible la pensée de l'auteur, un affranchissement des sujétions immédiates de l'observation directe, devaient inspirer à l'artiste le désir de retenir de la nature des aspects seulement où il lisait une allusion significative à cette pensée et de réunir ces aspects en quelque grande image, à la fois libérée de toute vraisemblance (scl. naturalistic mimesis instead of iconic representation) et profondement, c'est-à-dire vitalement et artistiquement, vraie.' [dn] And then he adds: 'Cette image, c'est le symbole'. This is the meaning of the word 'symbol' given by Lehmann under the points 5 and 8, which was every way a sufficient reason to consider the fundamental meaning of the symbol as an 'aesthetically expanded language.' [36]

Musicality

We shall now examine the meaning and the use of the term 'musicality' more closely. No doubt it was Delacroix who was the first to use this term with great emphasis—he is at least the first writer in a tradition that led to synthetism. He wrote: 'Il y a un genre d'émotion qui est tout particulière à la peinture ... Il y a une impression qui résulte de tel arrangement de couleurs, de lumières et d'ombres etc. . . . C'est ce qu'on appelle la musique du tableau. [do] Avant

210

même de savoir ce que le tableau représente, vous entrez dans une cathédrale et vous vous trouvez placé à une distance trop grande du tableau pour savoir ce qu'il représente, et souvent vous êtes pris, par cet accord magique: les lignes seules ont quelquefois ce pouvoir... C'est ici qu'est la vraie supériorité de la peinture sur l'autre art, car cette émotion s'adresse à la partie la plus intime de l'âme... Elle ajoute à ce que serait le spectacle de la nature cet élément qui vérifie et choisit, l'âme du peintre, son style particulier.' dp

Inquiring after the exact meaning of Delacroix' utterance, we are induced to studying Baudelaire's elaboration of this thought—which he had almost certainly heard from this artist. Such a study will no doubt explain things: 'Un tableau de Delacroix, placé à une trop grande distance pour que vous puissiez juger l'agrément des contours ou la qualité plus ou moins dramatique du sujet, vous pénètre déjà d'une volupté surnaturelle... Et l'analyse du sujet, quand vous vous approchez, n'enlèvera rien et n'ajoutera rien à ce plaisir primitif, dont la source est ailleurs et loin de toute pensée secrète. Je puis inverser l'exemple. Une figure bien dessinée vous pénètre d'un plaisir tout à fait étranger au sujet. Voluptueuse ou terrible, cette figure ne doit son charme qu'à l'arabesque qu'elle découpe dans l'espace.' dq This quotation should be supplemented with the following pronouncement: 'La bonne manière de savoir si un tableau est mélodieux est de le regarder d'assez loin pour n'en comprendre ni le sujet ni les lignes. S'il est mélodieux, il a déjà un sens, et il a déjà pris sa place dans le répertoire des souvenirs.' dr

In the quotations given here we see that factually Baudelaire says that colours and lines are already brimful of meaning in themselves, even apart from the motif represented, or rather: their expressiveness is due to a quality which is not identical with their representational function as such. When reading that the metaphorical term 'melody' —whose meaning is identical with that of the term 'musicality'—is intended to describe this state of affairs, we may perhaps infer from these quotations from Baudelaire in connection with the one from Delacroix that here he refers to the purely aesthetic moment. As, however, these colours (and lines) are also expressive—'Il y a des tons gais et fôlatres, fôlatres et tristes, riches et gais, riches et tristes', ds as he observes two lines further on after our last quotation —we must not think of aesthetic meaning entirely apart from the thing

211

represented. The qualities of the colours and the lines giving the motif or subject represented iconically its artistic sense (which thus has such a strong appeal to man) will have to be in accordance with the character of the object. This is also clear from the entire discussion of the colourists in the Salon of 1846, of which the passage just quoted was a detail. And as we are here concerned with a purely aesthetic quality having a certain expressive value, although it is not iconic *qua talis*, we think we are justified in taking the term 'musicality' to refer to the iconic analogy in the aesthetic aspect of the work of art, (the 'aesthetic symbolism'), as we have already established above without giving a more detailed explanation.

The predilection for music appearing from the use of the term 'musicality' to indicate the aesthetic element was not something new. Already in the eighteenth century there was a shift in terminology noticeable: the earlier invariable comparison of poetry with painting —ut pictura poesis—disappears almost entirely from the art-theoretical discussions. Especially by the prae-romantics poetry was compared with music, for the very reason that the latter did not contain any imitative element. Music was considered as the art which gave the most direct expression to emotion and to mental qualities. This is stated very explicitly by Wackenroder: 'Die Musik... (malt) menschliche Gefühle auf eine übermenschliche Art, weil sie uns alle Bewegungen unsers Gemüts unkörperlich, in goldne Wolken lustiger Harmonien eingekleidet, über unserm Haupte zeigt...' [dt] A little further on he writes: 'Und ebenso ist es mit dem geheimnisvollen Strome in den Tiefen des menschlichen Gemütes beschaffen, die Sprache zählt und nennt und beschreibt seine Verwandlungen, in fremden Stoff;—die Tonkunst strömt ihn uns selber vor... In dem Spiegel der Töne lernt das menschliche Herz sich selber kennen; sie sind es, wodurch wir das Gefühl fühlen lernen...' [du]

The idea that music may be a direct expression of human feelings, etc., is not at all new: it was found as early as in Aristotle in his *Poetica*—also with respect to music he calmly speaks of mimesis,[37] especially referring to human feelings and emotions. Via the classicistic-humanistic art-theoretical literature such ideas had naturally penetrated deeply into Western thought. Although in Romanticism the term 'expression' was preferred to the word 'mimesis', practically speaking they come to the same thing. Adam Smith made a characteristic pronouncement—which may represent the average opinion on this matter in the 18th and the early part of the 19th century—: 'The effect of instrumental music upon the mind has been called its expression. Whatever effect it produces is the immediate effect of the melody and harmony, and not of something else which is signified and suggested by them: they in fact signify and suggest nothing.' [38]

At the same time it was said that consequently music was meaning-less and that it was the direct expression of the human mind itself, of the promptings of the human heart. We may observe that this state of affairs is best explained by remembering that while speaking of the aesthetic element people referred in particular to 'aesthetic symbolism', as we have already tried to explain above. There is, therefore, a striking agreement between the (German) Prae-Roman-tics and the (French) painters with respect to the direction of their attention.

We are pointing out this state of affairs because it may explain why we come upon these ideas so often in the 19th century. We need not assume that Delacroix was entirely original as to his views of these things. On the contrary, even though we do not have any inclination to belittle the importance and also the originality of his observations.

A very remarkable utterance is that of Carlyle's—who assigns a very high place to this musicality. We quote here the passage found in the chapter 'The Hero as a Poet' in his *On Heroes, Hero-worship, and the Heroic in History,* because in Taine's book *L'idéalisme anglais* we find it translated. This book introduced Carlyle's ideas into France, and it will no doubt have been well-known in the circle of artists we are discussing. Carlyle then writes: 'Poetry being metrical, having music in it, being a song... If your delineation be authentically musical, musical not in word only, but in heart and substance, in all the thought and utterances of it, in the whole conception of it, then it will be poetical; if not, not.—Musical: how much lies in that! A musical thought is one spoken by a mind that has penetrated into the inmost heart of the thing, detected the inmost mystery of it, the in-ward harmony or coherence which is its soul, whereby it exists, and has a right to be, here in this world. All inmost things, we may say, are melodious; naturally utter themselves in Song. The meaning of Song

213

goes deep. Who is there that, in logical words, can express the effect music has on us? A kind of inarticulate, unfathomable speech, which leads us to the edge of the Infinite, and lets us for a moment gaze into that! ... All deep things are Song. It seems somehow the very central essence of us; of us, and of all things ... See deep enough, and you see musically; the heart of Nature being everywhere music, if you can only reach it.' [39]

This passage shows that such a thought as e.g. Wackenroder formulated has been carried to its extreme, we would almost say, to absurdity. The essence of a poem is its musicality—for in its musical quality the human soul, man's inner being will express itself most directly and without any inhibitions, without logical precision, without the need of describing reality in a metaphorical or any other way. But in a characteristically subjectivistic manner,—i.e. locating the knowable in the (absolutized) subject [40]—, in the line of German idealism this direct expression of the soul is equalized with the revelation of the essential 'inner nature' of reality as such. This is a remarkable utterance on the part of Carlyle, but this was all the more a reason for the generation about 1890 to lay emphasis on this 'musicality': for it was not only beauty that could thus be achieved, not merely expression, but reality itself could be caught in its essence and embodied artistically in a work of art.

Bearing this development of the idea of the musical element in mind we shall also better understand a passage of Aurier's which might at the first glance seem a little too flowery. He writes: 'Une oeuvre d'art n'est réellement oeuvre d'art qu'à condition de refléter, ainsi qu'un miroir [dv], l'émotion psychologique éprouvée par l'artiste devant la nature ou devant son Rêve. Cette émotion peut, à la derniere limite, n'être qu'une sensation pure: sensation d'un accord particulier de lignes, d'une symphonie déterminée de couleurs.' [dw] So the metaphors in this passage derived from music have a much more profound sense than might appear at first sight. Here, too, music is mentioned in connection with strictly subjective emotions: for this 'sensation pure' can only be an emotion apart from observation or experience, so a perfectly internalized experience. It is, indeed, evoked by observation, but it does not constitute the observational 'content'.

If thought out, matters are as follows: in the image—Aurier speaks about pictorial art—reality is represented iconically, whereas in the strictly aesthetical 'musicality' the deepest and innermost feelings (in accordance with the given object) are expressed. If we again turn to our quotation from Baudelaire and study it in this light, viz. the passage about the picture seen from a distance, etc., the quotation will be even clearer. We think we are justified in assuming that the synthetists read Baudelaire in this way, whereas he himself will presumably not have been so sharply aware of this state of affairs—or of this supposed state of affairs.[dx]

Especially in his later years Gauguin more than once spoke about 'musicality'. In *Diverses Choses* he closely follows the quotation from Delacroix that we, too, have given,[41] without, however, mentioning the latter's name. Perhaps when he was back in Paris in the years 1893-1895 he had read Delacroix's article again. Possibly we should consider that pronouncement as the direct source of the great value Gauguin assigned to this notion in his later writings.

In a letter to Fontainas he wrote: 'Pensez aussi à la part musicale que prendra désormais la couleur dans la peinture moderne. La couleur qui est vibration de même que la musique est à même d'atteindre ce qu'il y a de plus général et partant de plus vague dans la nature: sa force intérieure'. [dy] The meaning of this pronouncement may become clear when we think of what Carlyle had written in this connection, who only went a little further than the immediate leaders of the Synthetists Delacroix and Baudelaire.

The idea we have characterized by the term 'musicality' occurs again and again with Gauguin's 'pupils'. We only quote one utterance (of Sérusier): ... les sons, les couleurs, les mots ont une valeur miraculeusement expressive, en dehors de toute représentation, en dehors même du sens littéral des mots.' [dz] In this passage—and we have seen that there are more such in Sérusier—a thought given implicitly by Gauguin and other leaders is made explicit by means of a very clear and short summary, however devoid of any poetry.

After our elaborate discussion of Denis' views in a previous chapter especially in connection with the question if he strove after non-figurative art, we think there is now no need to explain again that none of the painters or men of letters we have quoted directed his efforts to something like that. But we can certainly indicate some factors that might have led them in that direction—we shall revert to this point

215

later on. They had too high an opinion of art to go that way. To put the issue clearly we shall quote Ruskin and Raymond with approval. Both in their own way explained what obvious misconception might follow from carrying through the idea of musicality and why it should be avoided.

Ruskin has more than once been accused of it that his insistence on truth in art was in reality in favour of a kind of super-naturalism, and that he did not attach any significance to the purely aesthetical element proper. Yet, though he should never have said anything about it, even a cursory look through his work will show that we have to do with a man who took an intense delight in art. Although he was not without marked prejudice and passion in his rejection and his approval, he was certainly capable of appreciating beauty of colour, line and composition at its true value. Perhaps we should say that the very fact of his wholehearted engagement in his positive as well as in his negative criticism, in short, that all his very prejudices are the conclusive evidence of his love of beauty and his full appreciation of its importance. For only a man who is not really moved by the image before him can talk about it in an 'objective' and unprejudiced way.

But there are indeed pronouncements made by Ruskin—and, remarkably enough, he also avails himself of the metaphor of music—: 'These abstract relations and inherent pleasantnesses, whether in space, number or time, and whether of colours or sounds, from what we may properly term the musical or harmonic element in every art; and the study of them is an entirely separate science. It is the branch of art-philosophy to which the word 'aesthetics' should be strictly limited, being the inquiry into the nature of things that in themselves are pleasant to the human senses or instincts, though they represent nothing, and serve for nothing, their only service being their pleasant-ness.' [42] And elsewhere, too, as Dougherty has pointed out,[43] Ruskin spoke of the significance of the purely aesthetic qualities of art with great emphasis. For the very reason that he valued them highly and did not like to be unjust to them, he refrained from talking a great deal about them.

But Ruskin would never have been able to accept non-figurative art. He, too, had too high an opinion of the human significance of art. As the result of the creative activity of man a work of art will have to appeal to man as a totality, it will have to possess a fulness and riches

216

exactly consisting in the close relation between the iconic element re-presenting reality and the aesthetic element constituting the beauty of the work of art. Dougherty rightly says in a brief summary: 'Rodin's famous remark: 'A woman, a mountain, a horse—they are all the same thing; they are made on the same principles' would have brought the retort from Ruskin that a man who thinks so has little knowledge of or love for women, mountains or horses. They are not the same thing, and they are not made on the same principles.' [44]

Marcel Raymond's words are more directly related to the question we have considered, and therefore his observations are of more imme-diate importance for our discussion. He points out that even the most 'musical' poem in the sense of the symbolists or synthetists does not leave a musical emotion as such in us. This is true, for who can remember Verlaine's 'Les sanglots long/Des violons/De l'automne/ Blessent mon coeur—etc.' apart from the words, purely as a melody? The poem cannot be explained from the relations between the sounds— the writers we have quoted so far have never asserted such a thing, on the contrary—, but here we have to do with the associations evoked in us. 'The 'musical' poet must be capable of feeling the affinities existing between the world of sound and the world of thought. Here again, the problem is to bring out mysterious 'correspondances'; cer-tain syllables, thanks to an infinitely subtle accord with the meaning of the words which they compose, by virtue of the confused memories evoked by this word even more than by its sonorous charm, actually 'move' the mind, magnetize it in a specific direction. But in no case can the psychological value of the word and its virtual treasury of images and associations be considered independently of its sonorous qualities. Consequently, the 'music' of words can be distinguished on-ly arbitrarily from their meaning—in the broadest sense—and a cer-tain 'inner music' must always be placed above a quasi-material har-mony, which is pleasing only to the ear.' [45]

We have quoted Raymond extensively as he has given an excellent analysis of the state of affairs with respect to poetry. In pictorial art matters become even more complicated: words have sounds, but neither colours nor lines possess something like them in reality. Yet Raymond's exposition is valid for colours and lines as well if only we bear in mind that aesthetic symbolism as such cannot be explained psychologically, but is a purely aesthetical quality having only an

217

aesthetic meaning, although this is a case of an analogon of the iconic aspect. This does not detract from the fact that some specific associations connected with colours and lines can find their basis in purely psychic reactions. But the fact remains that those colours and lines reveal their 'musical' meaning only when viewed in connection with the iconic representation—which, sometimes literally, has been 'coloured' by it in a particular way. Would not the content of one of Van Gogh's last paintings, the ravens above the field, be changed entirely if the birds were not black but white or blue, or whatever other colour?

Let us now again consider Sérusier's pronouncement given a moment ago on the expressive meaning of colour and line, etc. It strikes us that—as he does so often—he posits matters as if there is only question of purely artistic laws, and that he manages to camouflage the instigation issuing from the artist's view of life which led to a particular formulation. It is quite possible that to him this seemed to be the real state of affairs, and sometimes we have to admit that he really discovered how matters stood. But even in the latter case we cannot at all consider the views of these painters and poets apart from that which prompted them in the depth of their hearts. It is far too obvious for us to prove that in their case we have by no means to do with a kind of scholars intent upon the discovery of factual truths that are really non-committal to themselves. As a matter of fact such scholars as we are referring to by way of example are rarely if ever mere machines for registering laws, but they are men of flesh and blood driven by a particular idea which is ultimately based in a view of life and the world as the expression of a religious choice of position. Even though the latter will not be clearly put in the foreground, let alone be professed consciously by the persons in question, already what they think relevant—and almost even more important, what they judge to be irrelevant—will reveal this state of things on closer analysis.

This generation of artists between 1885 and 1890 is certainly not a set of dry-as-dust aestheticians examining states of things without any inner participation in them. On the contrary, the problems we have analysed and whose origins had to be sought in a remote past, were very near to their hearts. And the new discoveries they made were due to their devoting all their efforts to the realization of a very particular artistic ideal. Their search was concerned with an art (a style) that should satisfy them because it consciously or unconsciously reflected their spiritual attitude.

We once more state this view in order to prevent misconceptions. For we have deliberately eliminated these latter questions when dealing with the iconic element and 'musicality' in order to be able to arrive at a clearer definition of the concepts concerned. But now that we want to say something about Mallarmé, we see that this is made almost impossible to us by the author himself.

For Mallarmé also mentioned 'musicality'. And this in a passage which is characteristic of his style, his way of thought and his attitude. 'Les monuments, la mer, la face humaine, dans leur plénitude, natifs, conservant une vertu autrement attrayante que ne les voilera une description, évocation dites, allusion je sais, suggestion: cette terminologie quelque peu de hasard atteste la tendance, une très décisive, peut-être, qu'ait subie l'art littéraire, elle le borne et l'exempte. Son sortilège, à lui, si ce n'est libérer, hors d'une poignée de poussière ou réalité sans l'enclore, au livre, même comme texte, la dispersion volatile soit l'esprit, qui n'a que faire de rien outre la musicalité de tout.' [ea]

To understand an utterance like this we shall have to ask what Mallarmé is really saying in it: in a work of art the spirit should get free of matter, of commonplace reality, and be concerned with what is implied in the facts of reality—the sea, the human face, etc.—and can be suggested by them, viz., the 'musicalité de tout'. For a correct understanding of this latter phrase it is necessary to examine Mallarmé's world of thought somewhat closer. Things will perhaps be clearer when (in a letter of the year 1866) we read: 'Oui, je le sais, nous ne sommes que de vaines formes de la matière—mais bien sublimes pour avoir inventé Dieu et notre âme. Si sublimes, mon ami! que je veux me donner ce spectacle de la matière, ayant conscience d'être, et, cependant, s'elançant forcenément dans ce Rêve qu'elle sait n'être pas, chantant l'âme et toutes les divines impressions pareilles qui se sont amassées en nous depuis les premiers âges, et proclamant devant le Rien qui est la vérité, ces glorieux mensonges! Tel est le plan de mon volume, lyrique et tel sera peut-être son titre, la Gloire du Mensonge ou le Glorieux Mensonge. Je chanterai en désespéré...' [eb] We see that here the real meaning, the basic idea and the essence of reality, the highest truth is Nothing or Nothingness—the matter he had already mentioned in the first quotation given a moment ago. He

219

is indeed willing to sing (in a Carlylian sense) in praise of this reality given in matter because he cannot help it—it is his profoundly felt experience of Heidegger's 'Geworfen-sein' ('Thrownness'), [ec] which is expressed in it—but he sings 'en désespéré'. Yet in this way he can also try to show the truth, this Nothingness, this essential fact 'behind every concreteness also in description', this 'musicality'. Thus he will attempt to abstract all the non-essential elements from the objects in the no longer descriptive 'allusion' and 'suggestion'— compare also his famous pronouncement in Hurot's enquiry [46]—knowing he will never reach the essential element as this is Nothingness itself: as soon as we make use of the word, we have passed from essence to existence, even though this realization is the manifestation of the spirit. [47] Thus Mallarmé's musicality hovers on the borders of Nothing —it is not nothingness in the full sense of the word, for that absolute stage ('le moi projeté absolu') would entail the disappearance of the I itself—and material reality, which, however, must be free from every concrete determinatedness in order to approach that absolute kernel in it, its essence, as nearly as possible. For this purpose the term 'musicality' is excellently suited as it hits off the heart of the matter (recall what Delacroix and Baudelaire said about it) without its visible defining concretizing.[48]

In 'musicality', consequently, Mallarmé seeks to find not only the abstract aesthetical element, but in and together with the latter also what is permanent in the temporal, the Idea in the object. We may ask what it was that drove him—and less explicitly also the other art-theoreticians (and artists) of 1885-1890—in this direction. Why, after all, was that 'materiality', i.e., the concrete object, so lustreless, such a 'Mensonge'?

We hope we shall be able to find an answer to this question in the analysis of the term 'mystère' and 'mystic' so often used by all these poet-writers and these writing painters.

'Mystère'

In 1886 the result of an inquiry was published in *Vogue* by a certain L. d'Orfu—the question was what was poetry. Mallarmé's answer (it had already been given in 1884) was: 'La poésie est l'expression, par le langage humain ramené à son rhythme essentiel, du sens mystérieux des aspects de l'existence: elle doue ainsi d'authenticité notre séjour et constitue la seule tâche spirituelle.' ed So Mallarmé wants to represent especially the mystery of reality in art—and this is not in conflict with what we have found above—for to his mind this mystery is the essential thing.

In this opinion he is certainly not alone. Aurier—possibly influenced by him—even goes so far as to say: 'C'est le mysticisme qu'il faut aujourd'hui, et c'est le mysticisme qui seul peut sauver notre société de l'abrutissement, du sensualisme et de l'utilitarisme. Les facultés les plus nobles de notre âme sont en train de s'atrophier ... nous serons revenus, par la science positive, à l'animalité pure et simple. Il faut réagir. Il faut recultiver les qualités supérieures de l'âme. Il faut redevenir mystiques. Il faut rapprendre l'amour, source de tout compréhension.' ee

Such a quotation clearly shows that these writers sought for mysticism in their reaction to positivism; they made an effort to free themselves from naturalism and natural science in their approach to reality—age-old traditions surviving especially in the Roman-Catholic world were to help them. Their immediate predecessors in this respect are found in Romanticism, which in its own way had reacted to the positivism of the Encyclopaedists and sensualists of the 18th century. What those romanticists had preached in their period had become known and passed on to them through the intermediary of such men as Balzac, Baudelaire, etc. as we have pointed out more than once. Thus it becomes clear that to them it is applicable what had once been said about the romantic mystics: 'Leurs définitions reposent sur la théorie de l'inspiration directe. Dégager, par l'initiation, ce 'moi intérieur', cette 'étincelle divine' existant dans la personalité humaine, jouir de cette 'intuition', de cette 'Intelligence' profonde des choses qui repose sur 'une illumination spirituelle', de 'ces relations d'un genre exceptionnel avec les habitants du monde invisible', posséder la 'vision intime du principe de la réalité du monde', telles sont bien les espérances des adeptes.' ef Both at the time of romanticism and now at the end of the century it was an effort to get hold of a certainty behind or above that of commonplace reality in a naturalistic sense, however while retaining their purely individualistic subjectivism. Therefore Viatte is right when he says: 'Bien des âmes, dédaigneux des chemins battus, s'enquièrent de voies nouvelles ou ignorées. Née sous l'ombre

221

tutélaire d'une Église, ou dans l'absence de toute croyance, le doute se combine chez elles avec l'anxiété réligieuse.' [eg]

For two reasons their mysticism was eminently suited for their purpose. In the first place mysticism had always been something esoteric in Western Civilization, something that was not precisely the privilege of everybody—mysticism dated from very early times, it is true, but to their minds it was by no means a trodden path—while, secondly, mysticism had always pretended (under the strong influence of Neoplatonism or that of Plotinus) that it opened up a source of knowledge revealing the deep essence of reality without the intermediary of the senses which make us only acquainted with the 'exterior aspect' of things. For mysticism just like the life-and-world view of this generation of 1885-1890 was fed by a strongly negative sense of reality.

Mysticism with its fusion of Neo-platonic thoughts with Christian traditions had, indeed, always given form to a particular religious attitude. Mystics like Saint Teresa have always directed their efforts to attain to a unio mystica with the divine, although the latter often had very few traits in common with the Lord, the Father in heaven, given in the Biblical revelation. In such christian mysticism there was often a strongly individualistic and subjectivistic tendency, and also in this the revelation of the Scriptures had been depreciated to a lower kind of revelational source at the most.[49]

But there also existed a mysticism outside the Christian world and detached from the direction to a personal God. And the mysticism of the synthetists and symbolists showed a much stronger affinity with the intellectualistic mysticism of a man like Plotinus than with that of Saint Theresa, e.g. For their first concern was a new source of knowledge. For their mysticism was an effort to gain a new certainty apart from the dogmas of the Church—although of course dogmas do play a part with some of these artists, the fervent Roman-Catholic ones like Denis, Sérusier and Bernard—a source of knowledge which because it is not concerned with the 'exterior' of things, considered to be contingent and accidental, accessory and superficial, might reveal the absolute to them.

The way of this mysticism is that of art—thus it was hoped that via the purely subjective they might reach something transcending all (human) limitations, something permanent, and therefore something that should make the contingent in the cosmos meaningful. They hoped they would get free from reality in its actual form which in their opinion had been moulded too much after the positivistic pattern and was consequently an obstacle to the free personality and kept them caught in too tight a strait jacket.

Thus Morice wrote: 'Le livre, l'objet d'art, la phrase musicale, la pure pensée elle-même ... sont des éternisations du Moi. C'est que nous en faisons autant de moyens de dégager notre Moi des contingen-ces et c'est qu'aussi, par là même et dès qu'il échappe aux contingences, le Moi recourt ... au foyer de l'absolu, au lieu métaphysique des Idées, à Dieu.' [eh] In a similar context Aurier writes that in this way the fetters are shattered and we get away 'loin du cruel cachot naif' which is reality itself.[50]

This is also the meaning of the search for symbols which are related to reality only via the 'correspondences', or, to put it in another way, in which reality is deprived of its proper character and remains merely as a metaphor of the authentic absolute 'reality'—in which the term 'reality' is meant in a Platonic (so in a Greek) sense.[ei] Michaud truth-fully summarizes Mallarmé's ideas as follows: 'Puisqu'il s'agit d' atteindre l'absolu, le langage poétique ne doit-il pas rechercher des symboles nécessaires, qui échappent à toute relativé?' [ek]

Behind and in all this they were driven on by their religious attitude as a strong 'dunamis', the urge for freedom in a humanistic sense, in which man is free from any commandment, any rule, any limitation, to be a god himself, to be self-determining, free from all that is the non-I, which is considered as an irksome counter-instance forever re-minding man of the fact that he is really only a human being, only a creature. Thus in connection with the creation of a work of art we read in Morice: 'Et en effet, de ces trois vertus fondamentales, Liber-té, Ordre, Solitude, résulte aussitôt un sentiment d'illimitée puissance, qui est le conseil-même de l'Infini; aussitôt, l'âme acquiert la certitude de sa propre éternité dans cette solitude d'exception, et qu'il n'y a pas de mort comme il n'y a pas de naissance, et que la vie véritable est d'être un des centres conscients de la vibration infinie.' [el]

The humanistic personality ideal with its free self-determination was the motive power also of these artists. And the whole of this eso-teric theory, this entire mysticism was to serve this purpose. Do we not read in Bernard: 'Car, si les choses visibles sont la figure des choses invisibles, l'essence de l'homme, tenant du divin et douée d'

223

harmonie, coordonne et transforme la nature selon sa suprématie pour lui faire exprimer son origine propre et surnaturelle.' em

In the next chapter we will examine how Gauguin elaborated such thoughts in the last years of his life. He still sticks to a figurative art like all the other artists of this group. Only later on were these tendencies towards freedom and towards the representation of the absolute free from the world known to us through the senses, to urge the artists on towards a non-figurative art. Then 'musicality' will be the essence of the work of art and the latter will then become 'geistig'—we are referring to Kandinski, to Mondriaan. On paper at least such thoughts have been expressed in the nineteen-nineties by some figures who started from the development outlined above: we mean Bahr and Endell, who were Germans, which might be no accident.[51]

GAUGUIN'S LAST YEARS

Gauguin went to Tahiti in 1891. He did so for several reasons which we have tried to analyse in an earlier context. Thus he followed in the path that had already been found by Bougainville and Cook [1] in the 18th century, the path to an earthly paradise. In the 18th century, and even as late as the year 1890 [2] the natives reminded men of Greek gods; they were 'noble savages' and as it were the living evidence of Rousseau's theories and those of his followers with respect to the glorious state of nature. Kunstler has compared Gauguin to Rousseau, [3] and not entirely without reason. He, too, holds a rather idealized view of the Tahitians. 'Et on les appelle des sauvages? Ils chantent, ne volent jamais . . . n'assassinent pas. Deux mots tahitiens les désignent: Iorama (bonjour, adieu, merci, etc.) . . . et Onatu (je m'en fiche, qu'importe, etc. . . .) et on les appelle sauvages?' [a] It is a remarkable fact that, unlike pretty well all other Westerners, he immediately joins the natives without any previous reasoning, and that he proves to be free of any colonial attitude in which one puts oneself above these people, at least as regards social standing. This attitude gave rise to difficulties with government officials later on, at the time he was in the Marquises islands.

Also a comparison with La Fargue [2] who visited Tahiti only a very short time before him is instructive. It appears that this American displayed a typically 19th century attitude, not so much in that he, too, idealized these people, but in his great interest in the ethnological aspect of the matter, in the folklore and the tradition of the natives. Gauguin, however, nowhere adopts such a (semi-)scientific attitude, and as a matter of fact his paintings are no dependable sources to learn anything about the life and thought of the Tahitians, however intimate he may have been with the population. For, it is true, that he seems

to be engrossed in the study of their religion to which then *Noa Noa*
would testify, but in actual fact he is listening to Moerenhout as
Huyghe has established conclusively,[4]—and his would-be absorption in
that religion is properly speaking merely apparent, as the whole of
this mythology had for a great part disappeared from the world of
thought of the Tahitians. At any rate he had learnt and heard little
about it from his Tahitian friends. His treatise on it is after all more
of a 'rêve' than a genuine study, more of the interesting make-up
of a local colour than ethnology or the result of investigations in the
line of the science of religion.

Ultimately Gauguin's stay in the Pacific islands was determined for
a small part only by these idealizing motives. In addition to the eco-
nomis motive it were no doubt in the first place artistic motives that
led him. He always remained the artist who did not at all aim at
identifying himself with the population, at living their life in order
thus to turn his back upon Western culture. He had his 'centre
artistique' [5] really with him, kept pace with what happened in France
and finally boasted that he had conquered new possibilities for the
rising generation of artists, as we shall see at the end of this chapter.
All this may also appear from his observation in a letter of 1892: 'J ai
bien des tracas et si ce n'était nécessaire à mon art (j'en suis sûr), je re-
partirai de suite.' [b]

Gauguin's Realism

In his book on Gauguin Morice writes that this artist had always been
occupied with reality, even in the remote parts of the world to which
he had retired. He made notes, in the form of drawings and written
annotations, and from these documents he started: 'son imagination a
dans le réel son point de départ et ses références.' [c] There are two
negative pronouncements of Bernard's proving that this opinion is
correct. In a publication of the letters that Gauguin had sent him Bernard makes the slightly sour remark: 'Paul Gauguin, en vérité, fut
plutôt un peintre décorateur qu'un peintre symboliste; car jamais dans
aucun de ses tableau une idée quelconque n'apparaît.' [d] We hope to
prove that the latter remark is wrong, but in any case this utterance
proves that in the eyes of Bernard Gauguin stuck too much to reality.
For we can understand this remark better when we bear in mind
what he wrote about Anquetin later on. After the account of the latter's

development till about 1896 when Anquetin still adhered to a kind of art which was related to that of Daumier and Courbet Bernard saw a fundamental change: 'Son imagination, prisonnière jusqu'alors dans le réel, s'était éveillée, désireuse de s'exprimer par les images dont se sont servis les grands maîtres. Il reconnut tout à coup combien il était vain de s'attacher aux aspects passagers de son temps.' He now sought something else: 'au savoir sommaire de la palette et des pratiques courantes, il opposait la grande science de l'art; aux faux styles, la forme; à l'anémie des methodes, la force; aux sujets immédiates, les grands lieux communs de l'humanité... ne plus une belle Parisienne à la toilette, mais une nymphe guetté par un satyr...' [e] On the Academic standpoint there is hardly a sharper kind of criticism conceivable of the theory and the work of Gauguin, but this very circumstance makes it all the more clear what Gauguin aimed at.

In a positive way Morice states that Gauguin made use of his observation and experience of reality, of his notes written and drawn for his search for 'des équivalents plastiques de la nature' [6], or in other words, to represent this reality in an iconic and non-naturalistic way. For Gauguin remained a realist as to his subjects and he did not break with the tradition that had radically cut the bond with the 'grands lieux communs' by means of the work of Daumier, Courbet, Manet and the impressionists and had ended in a strongly pronounced realism with Degas, Lautrec and Van Gogh.

We will try to explain this fact with the aid of two principal works of art.

Manao Tupapau

Manao Tupapau is the title of a picture of the year 1892 which Gauguin calls: 'le plus raide et... celui que je tiens à garder ou vendre cher', [f] so a picture he valued very highly himself, and the only one of this period that he dwells upon elaborately. He also tells us on what occasion he had made it—how one day he came home very late and then he saw his mistress lying in bed in great fear [7]—this experience is a 'documentation' of the kind Morice mentions. But Gauguin is not merely content painting this situation, in it he summarizes an aspect of the life of the Maori. We will first quote in full his explanation of the picture:

227

'Une jeune fille canaque est couchée sur le ventre, montrant une partie de son visage effrayée. Elle repose sur un lit garni d'un paréo bleu et d'un drap jeune de chrome clair. Un fond violet pourpre, semé de fleurs semblables à des étincelles électriques: une figure un peu étrange se tient à côté du lit. Séduit par une forme, un mouvement, je les peins sans aucune autre pré-occupation que de faire un morceau de nu. Tel quel, c'est une étude de nu un peu indécente, et cependant j'en veux faire un tableau chaste en donnant l'esprit canaque, son caractère, sa tradition. Le paréo lié intimement à l'existence d'un canaque, je m'en sers comme dessus de lit. Le drap d'une étoffe écorce d'arbre doit être jaune, parce que de cette couleur il suscite pour le spectateur quelque chose d'inattendu; parce qu'il suggère l'éclairage d'une lampe, ce qui m'évite de faire un effet de lampe. Il me faut un fond un peu terrible. Le violet est tout indiqué. Voilà la partie musicale du tableau tout échafaudée.

Dans cette position un peu hardie, que peut faire une jeune fille canaque toute nue sur un lit? Se préparer à l'amour? Cela est bien dans son caractère, mais c'est indécent, et je ne veux pas. Dormir? L'action amoureuse serait terminée, ce qui est encore indécent. Je ne vois que la peur. Quel genre de peur? Certainement pas la peur d'une Suzanne surprise par des vieillards. Cela n'existe pas en Océanie.

'Le Tupapaou (Esprit des Morts) est tout indiqué. Pour les canaques, c'est la peur constante. La nuit, une lampe est toujours allumée. Personne ne circule sur les routes, à moins d'avoir un fanal, et encore il vont plusieurs ensemble. Une fois, mon Tupapaou trouvé, je m'y attache complètement et j'en fais le motif de mon tableau. Le nu passe au deuxième plan.

'Que peut bien être, pour une canaque, un revenant? Elle ne connaît pas le théatre, la lecture des romans, et, lorsqu'elle pense à un mort, elle pense nécessairement à quelqu'un déjà vu. Mon revenant ne peut être qu'une petite bonne femme quelconque. Le sens décoratif m' amène à parsemer le fond de fleurs. Ces fleurs sont des fleurs de Tupapaou, des phosphorescences signe que le revenant s'occupe de vous. Croyances Tahitiennes.

'Le titre, Manao Tupapaou, a deux sens: ou elle pense au revenant, ou le revenant pense à elle.

'Recapitulons. Partie musicale: lignes horizontales ondulantes, accords d'orange et de bleu, reliés par des jaunes et des violets, leurs

228

dérivés, éclairés par étincelles verdâtres; partie littéraire: l'Esprit d'une vivante lié à l'Esprit des morts. La nuit et le Jour.

'Cette génèse est écrite pour ceux qui veulent toujours savoir les pourquoi, les parce que. Sinon, c'est simplement une étude de nu océanien.' g

We are really grateful to Gauguin for his explanation—for after all we are among those people who always want to know the how and the why, as a matter of fact this is the origin of all science. Gauguin's last utterance should not be taken to mean that he did not consider his expositions to be of any importance. He rather wanted to point out that even without his explanation the contents of his painting were clear even if we did not know in every detail why the painter had done his work thus and what his considerations had been. Had not he once written about similar observations with respect to another picture saying: 'Tout cela est à côté de la peinture, dira-t-on. Qui sait. Peut-être non.' h

These reflections clearly show his manner of working which was really in accordance with what we have found concerning his art-theoretical views. Reality was the starting point but more was expressed about it than was visible to the eye. As a matter of fact he preferred making an impression by means of purely iconic means to painting an exact imitation of the visual object i— this is seen in the passage where he speaks of avoiding the effect of the lamp, whereas he did want to suggest such a fall of light by means of the colour of the sheet.

We also note how in such a painting various experiences and observations are summarized. What he says about the paréo on the bed shows that we must never use Gauguin's pictures as a a source of exact information on the customs of the Tahitians. Yet this paréo is certainly in its place, it is like an indication of place—in this respect the work is comparable to the nude of Anna the Javanese painted in Paris a few years later, which by the mere presence of the chair makes it clear that we are not in the tropics. His remarks concerning the reason why he represents the figure of death or of the ghost as a somewhat mysterious old woman are very striking. This old woman has been deliberately made entirely different from the traditional figure of a ghost in Western art, (and rightly so).

The subject—'partie littéraire'—has not only been represented icon-

229

ically, it has been underlined by the whole aesthetic structure in line and colour—'partie musicale'—. It is clear in this case that the harmony of colours and lines, although as such of a purely aesthetic nature and representing nothing, are an accompaniment to the iconic aspect, an intensification made in tune with it and clarifying it. Thus an artistic whole is achieved embracing a great deal more than a mere naturalistic depiction of visual things. In this work Gauguin is realistic, and any symbolism trying to clarify the atmosphere and the object by means of allegorical figures or metaphorical indications [k] is alien to him.

Actually more than one layer of reality is embraced by this picture —as was also the case with paintings of former times [8]—: first of all we see only the back of a nude with a woman beside it (a variation of the subject of Manet's Olympia). But in and by means of this representation a great deal more is told, viz., about the world of thought of the Tahitians with their fears and their belief in ghosts. The realistic trait in all this is the fact that the artist derives his inspiration immediately from ordinary reality so that we cannot at all speak in this case of a 'lieu commun d l'humanité', the expression of a profound thought in the allegorical and personifying way of humanism. [l] True, it is more than a nude, one that evokes a whole world of thought.

Gauguin's work proves to be in perfect agreement with the views of art he had advanced when still at Paris. The supposition that he had then been a symbolist but had turned his back upon this tendency later on is clearly refuted by this work.

D'où venons-nous? Que sommes-nous? Où allons-nous?

At the time when Gauguin painted his principal work 'D'où venons-nous? Que sommes-nous? Où allons-nous?' (1897-1898) there was hardly any longer question of a synthetistic movement.

Bernard had gone in a different direction, which was much more traditional and academic, even though he continued to adhere to some of the chief tenets of the theory propounded between 1888 and 1890. In his own way Denis had developed what he had then achieved more and more deriving his inspiration from the Florentine quattrocento. Theoretically speaking Sérusier was still purely synthetistic, but in his art he had not the courage to deviate very strongly from the traditional style, and the famous 'Talisman'—the cigar box painted on according to the suggestions made by Gauguin—was to remain his most advanced work. And many of the artists who had been influenced by Gauguin and his followers only indirectly, such as Bonnard, Vuillard, Lautrec, Maillol, had built on what they had learnt then now more, now less clearly, and had found their own way.

Yet this great work of Gauguin's which is now in the Museum of Fine Arts at Boston, may be considered as the principal work of the whole movement. For this was after all the mature fruit of Gauguin's development and a summary of the aims and the works of this whole group. In it their artistic ideals were given a very adequate form. And even if it were true that some of Gauguin's smaller works were aesthetically as strong or even stronger, we think that after all Ruskin's definition still holds when he said that 'the art is greatest which conveys to the mind of the spectator, by what means whatsoever, the greatest number of the greatest ideas,' if we bear in mind that also in Ruskin's view the stress is not laid on 'number' but rather on the quality of the 'ideas'.[9] And there is no doubt that 'D'où venons-nous? Que sommes-nous? Où allons-nous?' is a work with a very complex content in which many motifs and thoughts have been embodied.[m]

In February 1898 he wrote about this work for the first time, viz. to his faithful friend Daniel de Monfreid. He also relates his futile effort at suicide after he had completed his great picture. One gets the impression that he had as it were staged this scene: committing suicide and leaving behind as a testament a striking canvas which is at the same time the summary of all that he had always striven for. A theatrical death, thus leaving not only a perfect oeuvre ending in a summarizing master-piece, but also a death that finishes his self-determined course of life in setting a future biographer the great task of elaborating a grand theme, which could end on a more triumphant note, a different and more glorious one, than the life of the master of Balzac's *Un chef d'oeuvre inconnu*— a death resembling the suicide of de Nerval.[10]

In that letter Gauguin continues with an exact description of the canvas measuring 4.50 by 1.70 metres, which he compares to a fresco—probably having in mind Puvis de Chavannes (whose name he mentions in connection with this work later on). He also speaks of a white goat which is not white in the picture now, and of a squatting figure near an idol which is lacking—it is possible that he

made some alterations later on. A little further on he briefly indicates the principal contents, 'le poème' of the work, after which he
triumphantly concludes: 'J'ai terminé un ouvrage philosophique sur ce
thème comparé à l'Évangile ... je crois que c'est bien.' [n]

The subject of this picture was neither new nor uncommon. Yet we
do not believe that he had been inspired by the German publications
quoted by Bettina Polak in connection with the Dutch Symbolists,
nor by writers belonging to Maeterlink's circle,[11] people with whom
Gauguin had not had any contact and whose writings he almost
certainly had not read.

We get a great deal nearer to Gauguin's world when we refer to Balzac's *Séraphita*, a work he no doubt knew and appreciated highly. When
Wilfred has fallen into a hypnotic sleep—and will not Gauguin have
dreamt that his picture would do the same thing to the spectator as
was done by Séraphita's words to Wilfred?—Séraphita says: 'Que mes
paroles revêtent les brillantes formes de rêves, qu'elles se parent d'
images, flamboient et descendent sur toi ... Comprends-tu par cette
pensée visible la destinée de l'humanité? d'où elle vient, où elle va? ...
Comprends-tu ... de tels spectacles emporteraient et déchiraient ton
intelligence ... comprends-tu ...?' [o] We are for a moment reminded
of these words—if, after all, the whole work does not speak of this—
when reading the description of his work quoted above where he says:
'Une figure ... lève les bras en l'air et regarde, étonnée, ces deux
personnages qui osent penser à leur destinée.' [p]

But there were also other sources of inspiration for Gauguin with
respect to this work. We are especially referring to Carlyle's *Sartor
Resartus*.[q]

In this book Carlyle penetrates very deep, also in consequence of the
remarkable form in which he clothed his thoughts. He speaks of the
spiritual crisis into which Teufelsdröckh gets involved when he had
lost his (Christian) faith, and when for this reason he had lost all hope
because to him the whole of this world seemed to be one great
meaningless process: 'Thus must the bewildered Wanderer stand, as
so many have done, shouting question after question into the Sibyl-
cave of Destiny, and receive no answer but an Echo ... no Pillar of
Cloud by day, and no Pillar of Fire by night, any longer guides the
Pilgrim.[r] To such length has the spirit of Inquiry carried him.' [12]

These fundamental questions occur again and again in this book:

'Who am I? what is me? A Voice, a Motion, an Appearance;—some embodied, visualized Idea in the Eternal Mind? 'Cogito, ergo sum'. Alas, poor Cogitator, this takes us but a little way. Sure enough, I am; and lately was not: but Whence? How? Whereto?' s And this question remained even after Teufelsdröckh had reached a turning-point and had recognized his place and accepted it, 'a revelation to Sense of the mystic god-given Force that is in him; a 'Gospel of Freedom', which he, the 'Messiah of Nature', preaches, as he can, by act and word.' 13 For—and this trend of thought is very similar to that of Balzac's *Séraphita* t—we read: 'On the hardest adamant some footprint of us is stamped in; the last Rear of the host will read traces of the earliest Man. But whence?—O, Heaven, whither? . . .' 14

It might be asked whether Gauguin had also read all this. There is no certainty about this. Yet, at Le Pouldu it has been investigated— in the portrait of Meyer de Haan of this period there lies a copy of *Sartor Resartus* on the table,15 and we may assume that this work had been discussed by them, and that Gauguin was acquainted with its contents. It is possible that de Haan had read out some characteristic parts, such as the one we have quoted. For the possibility that Gauguin had also read it himself depends on the question whether Gauguin could read English, and if so, whether he read it so well as to be able to understand this by no means simple kind of English. u

But there is still another way in which Gauguin might have come into contact with Carlyle's work. For Taine wrote a book on this philosopher in which there are all kinds of quotations.v Also the forever recurring question in Carlyle's book: 'O Whence—Oh Heaven, Whither?' is found in Taine in French. He translates these words, 16 not quite accurately, although correctly according to the meaning as follows: 'Mais d'où venons-nous? O Dieu, où allons-nous?' w In view of the importance of this book for the symbolistic authors—about which we have spoken in our second chapter—it is not at all impossible that Gauguin was acquainted with it, even if only indirectly by means of a talk with Morice, e.g.

Gauguin did not embody these thoughts in his work in an allegorical way, he did not have them 'staged' by metaphorical figures. On the contrary we are confronted with a work which at first sight does not give more than a (realistic) view of daily life in Tahiti—even if immediately in a particular summary. But if we saturate ourselves with the whole of it, even the spectator who has not read Gauguin's reflections will understand that in and with these figures and these motifs more has been given than the daily life of the Tahitians, that a particular vision has been given, that this painted world is metaphorically related to a deeper layer of reality, the nature of the life of man and woman there, and in this nature, we would almost say, the structure of human life in general. In this the question about the meaning of life has also been posited. The colours and the composition are by no means unimportant in this connection, on the contrary, precisely by their means it becomes clear that we do not have before us some folkloristic-ethnological study of life there, such as was, e.g., given by La Fargue. Its title is an aid to the spectator's meditations, which is not exclusively 'literary' in the sense that here thoughts are concerned which are really unconnected with the picture and its own artistic qualities—on the contrary, the work will reveal its meaning, its 'great number of ideas' in various layers of reality when we study the work thoroughly. Thus also that meaning in its most profound sense, in its relatedness to that which lies nearest to the painter's heart, his view of life and the world, will become poetically visible. For the relevancy, the relation of the work to this view imparts to every colour and every line, to every figure and every stroke with the brush its profound artistic sense, iconically, 'musically', and aesthetically.

Gauguin himself also speaks about these questions, when in connection with this work he compares his own manner of working with that of Puvis de Chavannes. 'Puvis explique son idée, oui, mais il ne la peint pas. Il est grec'—i.e. he joins the classicistic-academic tradition —'tandis que moi je suis un sauvage'—i.e., its opposite—. 'Puvis intitulera un tableau Pureté et pour l'expliquer peindra une jeune vierge avec un lys à la main—Symbole connu, donc on le comprend. Gauguin au titre Pureté peindra un paysage aux eaux limpides; aucune souillure de l'homme civilisé, peut-être un personnage. Sans rentrer dans des détails il y a tout un monde entre Puvis et moi. Puvis comme peintre est un lettré tandis que moi je ne suis pas un lettré mais peut-être un homme de lettres'. [x] The latter pronouncement means probably that he is certainly not a naturalist, telling his thoughts merely by the figures represented.

According to the art-theory of the synthetists the work of art was a child of the 'imagination'— a free creation in which the artist embodies and summarizes what he has observed and thought out in an artistically justifiable and meaningful image, representing it not allegorically but metaphorically with iconic means. In this case Gauguin has explained the way in which his 'imagination' worked—although his 'rêve' was noted down a long time afterwards, we do not believe that his description is a mere fiction, but really a short, poetic analysis of the atmosphere in which the work of art came into existence. He wrote to Fontainas in 1889: 'Ici, près de ma case, en plein silence, je rêve à des harmonies violentes dans les parfums naturels qui me grisent. Délice relevé de je ne sais quelle horreur sacrée que je devine vers l'immémorial. Autrefois, odeur de joie que je respire dans le présent. Figures animales, d'une rigidité statuaire: je ne sais quoi d' ancien, d'auguste, religieux dans le rhythme de leur geste, dans leur immobilité rare. Dans des yeux qui rêvent, la surface trouble d'un énigme insondable. Et voilà la nuit—tout repose. Mes yeux se ferment pour voir sans comprendre le rêve dans l'espace infini qui fuit devant moi, et j'ai la sensation de la marche dolente de mes espérances.' ʸ

All this has been really given in the work in the way described by Gauguin himself (immediately below the quotation given just now) 'sans aucune allégorie.' Although its motifs are realistic, the real meaning of the work is 'ce qui n'est pas exprimé'—i.e., that which is not contained in the motifs as such—'il en résulte implicitement des lignes, sans couleurs ou paroles, il n'en est pas matériellement constitué.' ᶻ So this is the 'musicality' again—he speaks of his 'poème musical'—ultimately revealing the meaning of the work, in its composition, in its aesthetic arrangement.

We now have to consider the different figures and motifs as he explains them in his letter to Morice in 1901:
'Dans ce grand tableau:

    Où allons-nous?
Près de la mort d'une vieille femme,
Un oiseau étrange stupide conclut.

    Que sommes-nous?
Existence journalière.
L'homme d'instinct se demande ce que tout cela veut dire.

    D'où venons-nous?
Source.
Enfant.

235

La vie commune.

'L'oiseau conclut le poème en comparaison de l'être inférieur vis-à-vis de l'être intelligent dans ce grand tout qui est le problème annoncé par le titre.

'Derrière un arbre deux figures sinistres, enveloppées de vêtements de couleur triste, mettent près de l'arbre de la science leur note de douleur causée par cette science même en comparaison avec des êtres simples dans une nature vierge qui pourrait être un paradis de conception humaine, se laissant aller au bonheur de vivre' aa—if anywhere it is here in this last paragraph that Gauguin comes very close to Jean-Jacques Rousseau.

It is very remarkable that in this work he has represented the course his thoughts took from the right hand side to the left. ad Should this be viewed as a last effect of the influence of Japanese art which construes its compositions from right to left? ac

A last trace of Japanese influence, we said, for in contradistinction to the principal work of the first period in Brittany 'Vision après le sermon', this work is not at all Japanising in its structure. We do not look down on the scene as it were from above, and the figures are never cut at the border of the picture. Its decorative effect is due to something quite different—to a frieze-like arrangement of the figures in a few plans parallel to the front-area. It would be possible to ascribe this feature to the influence of Puvis—and there is certainly such an influence—but, as Dorival has established, we must above all bear in mind that Gauguin possessed some photos of the Burubudur friezes.[17] They exhibit a similar rhythmical arrangement of the figures side by side, also in at most a few parallel plans. The landscape in the background is a real background, one that evokes little sense of depth. Also in this case Gauguin's composition has been kept rather flat although the figures in the foreground have been given the necessary moving space. For, however satisfying the arrangement on the surface may be called, it is certainly not a 'flat' composition in the exclusively decorative sense.

In this work we are really face to face with the direct application of some of the artistic ideals he had formulated in his mythical exposition, his story of the painter 'Mani-Vehli-Zumbul-Zadi' who gives his pupils all kinds of precepts a.o. 'cherchez l'harmonie ... que tout chez vous respire le calme ... Évitez la pose en mouvement. Chacun de vos

236

personnages doit être à l'état statique . . . Appliquez-vous à la silhouette de chaque objet'. [ad] Although this writing had been made at a much earlier period [18] it certainly suits a painting like this better than his earlier art, though the latter also shows very little movement.

This painting deals with profound and fundamental problems, with the basic questions of human existence itself. As a matter of fact Gauguin has no answer to offer—a Christian answer is impossible to him, as he is of the opinion that 'se remettre entre les mains de son Créateur, c'est s'annuler et mourrir,' [al] and its vagueness is more than only a question of an artistic ideal, it is rather the expression of his resignation to its insolubility: 'L'idole (in this painting) est là . . . faisant corps dans mon rêve devant ma case avec la nature entière, régnant en notre âme primitive, consolation imaginaire de nos souffrances (mind this word 'imaginaire') en ce qu'elles comportent de vague et d'incompris devant le mystère de notre origine et notre avenir.' [af]

Later writings

After the work we have just been discussing Gauguin did not make many more paintings. He was hampered by illness, monetary difficulties and adversities. He only devoted himself more intensively to writing what might be called his memoirs embodying his creed at the same time. It is as if after the completion of his oeuvre he wishes to leave a series of reflections to posterity by way of a testament. Of course we must not expect that Gauguin now became a philosopher in the technical sense of this term—but this is not saying that his thought lacked depth or clarity. He explained his thoughts in a very sharp way, occasionally in Nietschean turns of phrase, partly as a summary of all that in the preceding ten or fifteen years he had striven after and had thought out in connection with it. But there are also new subjects, new thoughts, sharper conclusions with a new emphasis. In the writings of these years he sometimes merely repeats what he had written before, e.g. in his letters, but there is also a great deal that we have not yet come across.

Gauguin does not aim at a system—'Puis vous savez que si les autres m'ont gratifié d'un système, moi je n'en ai pas et je ne veux pas être condamné à cela. Peindre à ma guise, clair aujourd'hui, foncé demain, etc. . . . du reste l'artiste doit être libre ou il n'est pas artiste.' [ag] This explains clearly what is the issue—not some aesthetics in Sérusier's sense

with his colour circle, not a system as that which the neo-impressionists tried to formulate and to apply, not a fixed manner of working,
which would only mean a new kind of academism. All this Gauguin
scrupulously avoided. But this does not mean that he was without any
definite ideas on art, that he had no artistic ideal excluding certain
kinds of art or on the other hand that he did not want a work of art
to satisfy particular requirements. In this sense he certainly had an art-
theory, which formulated general principles and defined the relation
of a work of art to reality in a more philosophic way than any mere
formula of style, or any manner of working could do.

In fact, if anywhere it is clear in the case of Gauguin that reforms
in art never arise merely spontaneously, owing to accidental influences
and circumstances, from the character and the nature of the reformer
as such, without reflection and without any conscious mental attitude
and ideals. The artist, who as it were, automatically draws purely
from his talent and discovers what is new, is a romantic conception
which only rarely does justice to reality. Then art is considered to be
apart from any conscious reflection—and the artist is really considered
as a thoughtless improvisator, which testifies to a low rather than to
a high opinion of art.

Such a view must be rejected, for, as Gauguin himself puts it: ' . . .
si l'oeuvre d'art était de hasard, toutes ces notes seraient inutiles'. ah He
maintains that his expositions are 'tout de rayons jusqu'au centre vital
de mon art.' ai

In a negative way Gauguin always described his art as the opposite
of the academism and naturalism of the Salon artists, while notwithstanding his admiration of the great personalities among the Impressionists he rejected impressionism. 'Les machines sont venues, l'art s'est
allé, et je suis loin de penser que la photographie nous soit propice', al
thus he depreciates every scientific attitude in his concise and force-
ful way (he also denied that owing to photography an artist would,
e.g., understand a horse better) ak—'Quant à moi, je me suis reculé bien
loin, plus loin que les chevaux du Parthenon . . . jusqu'au dada de mon
enfance, le bon cheval de bois'. al By this Gauguin wanted to say that
he had dissociated himself from every system that prevailed in the
world of art before him, also mentioning the Parthenon to indicate
that even Greek art could no longer be a source of inspiration to him.
Egyptian art and that of the Burubudur—which he called the art of

238

Cambodja—they were sources of inspiration to him, for in these he found an artistic conception to which he felt akin—an art which was free of any naturalism, because it most clearly manifested the iconic element in the sense in which he understood it.[19] He considered such men as Ingres, Corot, Delacroix of the first half of the 19th century as his direct predecessors—'En somme aujourd'hui il y a un bel effort et venant bien moins directement de l'époque précédente que des romantiques.' [am]

For the art of the period immediately preceding his own time too much forgot 'le centre mystérieux de la pensée', [an] remained too superficial, was often too much of a system, a formula, too little born of the strictly human subjectivity. 'Où commence l'exécution d'un tableau, où finit-elle? Au moment où des sentiments extrêmes sont en fusion au plus profond de l'être, au moment où ils éclatent, et que toute pensée sort comme la lave d'un vulcan, n'y a-t-il pas une éclosion de l'oeuvre soudainement créée, brutale si l'on veut, mais grande et d'apparence sur-humaine? Les froids calculs de la raison n'ont pas précédé à cette éclosion, mais qui sait quand au fond de l'être l'oeuvre est commencée? Inconscient peut-être?' [ao] This is a pronouncement to which both Delacroix and Baudelaire would certainly have subscribed each in his own way.

Freedom

When at the end of his life he surveys his work he more than ever lays the emphasis on freedom: 'J'ai voulu établir le droit de tout oser: mes capacités n'ont pas donné un grand résultat, mais cependant la machine est lancée. Le public ne me doit rien puisque mon oeuvre picturale n'est que relativement bonne, mais les peintres qui aujourd'hui profitent de cette liberté, me doivent quelque chose.' [ap] The motive of freedom, which always played an important part but was formerly kept within bounds by the idea of synthesis in which reality also claimed its rights, now comes to the fore much more emphatically, at least in Gauguin's writings. He shows that this motive was ultimately the determining element in his aims. Freedom from any restrictive demand for naturalness in the sense of naturalism, from 'les entraves de la vraisemblance' [aq]—although also at this time he did not mean to take leave of recognisibility nor deliberately seeks abstraction (in the 20th century sense). Freedom also from the 'travers acadé-

miques' and from the 'travers symbolistes, autre genre de sentimentalisme'. [ar] For he also thought symbolism too cheap. To his mind it did
not dig deep enough, stuck too much to an allegorism which could
only be understood from tradition—we are referring to his rage on
receiving his portrait painted by Schuffenecker: 'Une croix, des
flammes, v'lan! ça y est, le symbolisme.' [as]

Gauguin no doubt had some very unpleasant characteristics, he
could flare up in a very disagreeable way, he was certainly not free
from a bohemien pose. But this does not mean that we are entitled to
explain his art, his work and his aims as a kind of theatrical perfor-
mance intended to evoke applause and to increase the receipts (with
however much talent it may have been accomplished).[20] He himself denied this and he never sought a cheap success.[21] A large dose of idealism
not only urged him on but sustained him in all his difficulties and
strengthened his will-power—the idealism of his hope that also owing
to his own work, there would come a better and more beautiful art,
one that would be more healthy and more meaningful. The dream
that he wanted to deliver the art of painting especially from 'the
mediocrities' [22]—insufficiently aware as he was that the latter will never
be lacking in any period, no matter the style, the attitude and the
aims of the artists: not all men are geniuses, and a mediocre talent
also has its place in the life of art, and is perhaps as important for
society, for contemporary man, as a great reformer and leader.

In the writings of his last years rather than in his art, in which he
remained a pure synthetist, he broke with synthetism and more and
more strongly emphasized freedom. The problems evoked by it, the
conflict with given reality [at] which was bound to arise he did not only
realize intellectually, but he struggled with them in the depths of his
being. No doubt in this case he was influenced by Mallarmé who also
tried to realize freedom in his own way, [23] and possibly the reading of
an article like that on Harcoland in the *Mercure de France* (which was
always sent to him)[24] drove him again on in that direction. [au] This is
clear from the following passage in *Avant et Après:* 'J'ai su, tout le
monde aussi, tout le monde le saura, que deux et deux font quatre. Il
y a loin de la convention, de l'intuition à la compréhension: je me
soumets, et comme tout le monde je dis: 'Deux et deux font quatre . . .
Mais . . . [av] cela m'embête, et cela me dérange beaucoup de mes raison-
nements.' [aw]

240

Gauguin's legacy

Indeed, the freedom preached by Gauguin in his last years especially, the heritage which he bequeathed to the next generation—as a testament— was accepted in full by the twentieth century, as well as the problems we have just indicated. In the first few years of the new century in particular Gauguin's influence was great, and no doubt contributed a great deal to the art of the Fauves, especially in their great daring, their contempt of 'vraisemblance', their relinquishing any naturalism in colour and the handling of lines. Gradually freedom is more and more stressed, reality loses more and more of its meaning until at last non-figurative art made its appearance—in particular that branch of it which may be called irrational. [ax] In art-theory it is especially the idea of 'musicality' which was carried through to absurdity. The synthesis which determined Gauguin's work was broken up, and thus Gauguin's art in which reality continued to play an important part became an out-dated standpoint. Nevertheless its humanity always makes his art so fascinating, and constitutes its great and permanent significance, precisely also on account of his adherence to reality, although he rejected naturalism.

The re-discovery of the iconic element was to prove very fruitful—not only for Art with a capital letter, but also for posters and illustrations, etc. Looked at in an historical perspective this is perhaps the greatest importance to be attached to this oeuvre—viewed not merely as a collection of paintings left by the artist but also as the demonstration of the principles in question inherent in these works. At the same time we should not underrate the importance and the influence of his writings. After all, the decorative principle of Gauguin's art, according to which a far greater emphasis was laid on aesthetic arrangement, the rhythmic and harmonious play of lines and colours than had been done in the art of the preceding period, and which was connected with his appreciation of the iconic aspect and founded in the idea of musicality, has been of primary importance for the genesis and the development of modern French art. We are referring to Matisse and the revival of tapestry art. This was made possible because in Gauguin's art the emphasis lies on the composition on the surface, whereas the spatial effect (the ordering in depth)—also because of the influence of Japanese art and later on especially of that of the Burubudur—becomes of secondary importance.

241

So Gauguin left us with the legacy of three things: the artist's freedom to find new forms apart from any tradition, an undoubtedly very fertile apprehension of the iconic character of the pictorial arts and a new appreciation of the decorative. But it was freedom he prized above all. In an inimitable way he formulated it in 1902 as the task of the new generation—and it is still the most concise formula of twentieth century artistic striving: 'Il était donc nécessaire, tout en tenant compte des efforts faits et toutes les recherches, même scientifiques, de songer à une libération complète, briser les vitres, au risque de se couper les doigts, quitter à la génération suivante, désormais indépendante, dégagée de toute entrave, à resoudre généralement le problème. Je ne dis pas définitivement, car c'est justement un art sans fin dont il est question, riche en techniques de toutes sortes, apte à traduire toutes les émotions de la nature et de l'homme, s'appropriant à chaque individualité, à chaque époque, en joies et en souffrances.

'Il fallait pour cela se livrer corps et âme à la lutte, lutte contre toutes les Écoles, toutes sans distinction, non point en les dénigrant, mais par autre chose, affronter non seulement les officiels, mais encore les Impressionnistes, les Néo-Impressionnistes, l'ancien et le nouveau public. Ne plus avoir de femme, d'enfants, qui vous renient. Qu'importe l'injure? Qu'importe la misère? Tout cela en tant que conduite d'homme.

'En tant que travail, une méthode de contradiction, si l'on veut, s'attaquer aux plus fortes abstractions, faire tout ce qui était défendu, et reconstruire, plus ou moins heureusement, sans crainte d'exagération, avec exagération même. Apprendre à nouveau, puis, une fois su, apprendre encore. Vaincre toutes les timidités, quelque soit le ridicule qui en rejaillit.

'Devant son chevalet, le peintre n'est esclave, ni du passé, ni du présent, ni de la nature, ni de son voisin. Lui, encore lui, toujours lui.' [ay]

BIBLIOGRAPHY

We have arranged the titles systematically. Completeness has not been pursued. For an almost all comprehensive list see the bibliography in Rewald's *Post-Impressionism*.

H. Dooyeweerd *A New Critique of theoretic Thought* (Amsterdam 1955).

H. Dooyeweerd *Wijsbegeerte der Wetsidee* I, II, III (Amsterdam 1935).

H. Dooyeweerd *Transcendental Problems of Philosophic Thought* (Grand Rapids, Mich. 1948).

W. Windelband *Lehrbuch der Geschichte der Philosophie,* ed. H. Heimsoeth (Tübingen 1948 [14]).

Susanna K. Langer *Philosophy in a new key, a study in the symbolism of reason, rite and art* (New York 1949 [2]).

Philosophie, beknopt handboek tot de geschiedenis van het wijsgerig denken, I, II, red. H. v. Oyen (Utrecht 1947).

E. Panofsky *Meaning in the visual arts* (Garden City, N.Y. 1955).

E. Schöne *Über das Licht in der Malerei* (Berlin 1954).

E. Bevan *Holy Images, an inquiry into idolatry and image-worship in ancient paganism and christianity* (London 1940).

E. Cassirer *Der Begriff der symbolische Form im Aufbau der Geisteswissenschaften* (Vorträge Bibl. Warburg, 1921/2, Berlin 1922).

J. Maritain, Sign and symbol, *Journal of the Warburg and Courtauld Society* (I, 1937), p. 1.

W. Embler, Symbols in literature and art. *College Art Journal* (XVI, 1, 1956), p. 47.

Ch. Saulnier, Esthétique et connaissance, caractère spécial de l'attitude esthétique du point de vue cognitif. *Revue d'Esthétique* (V, 4, 1952), p. 411.

Th. Munro, Suggestion and symbolism in the arts. *Journal of Aesthetics and Art Criticism* (XV, 2, 1956), p. 152.

A. N. Whitehead *Symbolism, its meaning and effect* (New York 1927).

C. Morris *Signs, Language and Behavior* (New York 1946).

243

Bibliography

ON ART, ART-THEORY AND AESTHETICS BEFORE THE 19th CENTURY

E. Panofsky *Idea, Ein Beitrag zur Begriffsgeschichte der älteren Kunsttheorie* (Berlin 1924).

J. Lemeere, Les concepts du Beau et de l'Art dans la doctrine platonicienne. *Revue d'Histoire de la Philosophie et d'Histoire générale de la civilisation* (VI, 1938), p. 1 e.v.

Plotinus *Enneads*. Transl. by S. MacKenna (London 1956).

Plotin *Enneade I, VI, Du Beau,* transl. M. Meunier (Paris 1926).

E. Bréhier *La Philosophie de Plotin* (Paris 1928).

J. Daniélou *Platonisme et théologie mystique. Essai sur la doctrine spirituelle de St. Grégoire de Nyssa* (Paris 1944).

H. J. Hak *Marsilio Ficino* (Amsterdam 1934. Diss.).

A. Chastel *Marsile Ficin et l'art* (Genève, Lille, 1954).

A. Blunt *Artistic Theory in Italy 1450-1600* (Oxford 1940).

E. Gombrich, Icones symbolicae. The visual image in Neo-Platonic Thought. *Journal of the Warburg and Courtauld Society* (XI, 1948), p. 163.

E. Wind, The revolution of history painting. *Journal of the Warburg and Courtauld Society* (II, 1938), p. 116.

J. J. Rousseau *Dialogues, Rêveries d'un promeneur solitaire,* annot. P. Richard, Paris 1952 [14].

I. Kant *Werke in 8 Bücher,* ed. H. Renner (Band I, II, Berlin o.J.).

F. v. Schiller *Über die aesthetische Erziehung des Menschen* (Herford 1948).

M. Lamm *Swedenborg, Ein Studie über seine Entwicklung zum Mystiker und Geistesseher* (Leipzig 1922).

E. Swedenborg *Clavis Hieroglyphica arcanorum naturalium et spiritualium per viam repraesentationum et correspondentiarum* (London 1784).

M. Matter *Emmanuel de Swedenborg, sa vie, ses écrits et sa doctrine* (Paris 1863).

E. A. Sutton *The living Thought of Swedenborg* (London 1944).

L. Venturi *Histoire de la critique d'art* (Bruxelles 1938).

PHILOSOPHY AND AESTHETICS IN THE 19th CENTURY

A. Schopenhauer *Die Welt als Wille und Vorstellung* (Leipzig 1844 [2]).

A. Schopenhauer *Pensées, Maximes et Fragments.* Ed. J. Bourdeau, (Paris 1880).

T. Carlyle *Sartor Resartus* (London 1898).

T. Carlyle *On heroes, hero-worship and the heroic in history* (London 1852).

H. Taine *L'idéalisme anglais, étude sur Carlyle* (Paris 1864).

E. Neff *Carlyle* (London 1932).

A. C. Taylor *Carlyle, sa première fortune littéraire en France (1825-1868),* (Paris 1929).

Humbert de Superville *Essai sur les signes inconditionnels dans l'art* (Leiden 1827).

E. v. Hartmann *Philosophie des Unbewussten* (Berlin 1871 [3]).

H. Taine *Philosophie de l'art* (I, II. Paris 1924).

H. Taine *Notes sur Paris. Vie et Opinions de M. Frédéric-Thomas Graindorge, recueilli par H. Taine* ... (Paris 1867).

C. Picard *H. Taine* (Paris 1909).

J. Zeitler *Die Kunstphilosophie von Hippolite Taine* (Leipzig 1901).

J. Gibelin *L'esthétique de Schelling d'après la Philosophie de l'Art* (Diss. Paris 1933).

R. Schneider *L'esthétique classique chez Quatremère de Quincy* (Paris 1910).

D. Lenz *L'esthétique de Beuron.* trad. J. Sérusier. Introduction M. Denis (Paris 1905).

L. Venturi *Histoire de la critique d'art* (Bruxelles 1938).

V. Cherbuliez *L'art et la nature* (Paris 1892).

Ph. Gauckler *Le Beau et son histoire* (Paris 1873).

J. D. Bierens de Haan *De strijd tussen idealisme en naturalisme in de 19e eeuw* (Haarlem 1929).

M. H. Abrams *The mirror and the lamp. Romantic Theory and the Critical Tradition* (New York 1953).

A. Fouillée *Le mouvement positiviste et la conception sociologique du monde* (Paris 1896).

J. Wilcox, La genèse de la théorie de l'art pour l'art en France. *Revue d'esthétique* (VI, 1, 1953), p. 1.

A. Kuyper *Calvinism and Art. Calvinism, six Stone-Lectures* (Amsterdam-Pretoria, 1899).

A. Kuyper *The antithesis between Symbolism and Revelation.* (Lecture delivered before the Historical Presbyterian Society in Philadelphia, Pa. Amsterdam-Pretoria-Edinburg, 1899).

A. Kuyper *Het Calvinisme en de Kunst.* Rede (Amsterdam 1888).

A. Kuyper, Calvinism and Art. *Christian Thought, lectures and papers on philosophy, christian evidence, biblical elucidation* (IX 1891/2, New York), pp. 259-282, 447-459, transl. Rev. J. H. de Vries.

A. Kuyper *De verflauwing der grenzen.* Rede 1892 (Amsterdam, 1892).

LITERATURE AND CULTURE IN THE 19th CENTURY (UP TO 1885)

E. A. Poe *The poems of* ... *(& Essai on the Poetic Principle, & Essai on the Philosophy of Composition).* Introd. H. N. Williams (London, New York 1900).

E. A. Poe, Lettres 1848-1849. *La Revue Blanche* (Feb. 1895).

C. P. Cambiaire *The influence of E. A. Poe in France* (Fontenay-sous-Bois, Seine, 1927).

M. Atterton *Origins of Poe's Critical Theory* (University of Iowa Humanistic Studies II, 3, n.d.).

C. Baudelaire *Histoires extraordinaires par Edgar Poe.* annot. J. Crépet (Paris 1932).

245

Bibliography

C. Baudelaire *Curiosités Esthétiques* (Paris 1921).

C. Baudelaire *L'Art romantique* (Paris s.d. circa 1910).

C. Baudelaire *Les fleurs du mal,* ed. J. Crépet et G. Blin (Paris 1942).

M. Gilman *Baudelaire the Critic* (New York 1943).

J. P. Sartre *Baudelaire* (Paris 1947 [23]).

J. Prévost *Baudelaire* (Paris 1953).

L. Horner *Baudelaire critique de Delacroix* (Genève 1956).

A. Ferran *L'Esthétique de Baudelaire* (Paris 1933).

W. Drost, L'Inspiration plastique chez Baudelaire. *Gazette des Beaux Arts* (May/June 1957), p. 321.

R. Huyghe *L'Esthétique de l'individualisme à travers Delacroix et Baudelaire* (Oxford 1955).

Maatstaf, Maandblad voor letteren, V, 3/4, p. 145—special Baudelaire number—.

R. Michaud, Baudelaire, Balzac et les correspondances, *Romanic Review* (XXIX, 3, 1938), p. 253 e.v.

G. Batault, A propos de Baudelaire et de Balzac, *Mercure de France* (April 1931), p. 216.

H. Balzac *Oeuvres Complètes XV: Etudes philosophiques I* (Paris 1869).

H. Balzac *Oeuvres Complètes XVII: Etudes philosophiques III* (Paris 1870).

H. Evans *Louis Lambert et la philosophie de Balzac* (Paris 1951).

J. v. d. Elst, Autour du 'livre mystique'; Balzac et Swedenborg, *Revue de la litterature comparée* (X, 1930), p. 88.

E. Zola *L'Oeuvre* (Paris 1893).

E. Zola *Les romanciers naturalistes* (Paris 1881 [2]).

E. Zola *Les réalistes au salon. Mes haines* (Paris 1866).

G. Flaubert *La tentation de St. Antoine* (Paris 1874).

J. Seznec, Flaubert and the graphic arts. *Journal of the Warburg and Courtauld Society* (VIII, 1945), p. 175.

M. Raymond *From Baudelaire to Surrealism* (New York 1950). (Transl.; original French.)

A. Poizat *Le symbolisme de Baudelaire à Claudel* (Paris 1919).

A. Tabarant *La vie artistique au temps de Baudelaire* (Paris 1942).

Holbrook Jackson *Dreamers of dreams. Rise and fall of 19th century idealism* (London 1948).

H. A. Hatzfeld *Literature through art. A new approach to French literature* (New York 1952).

Kenneth Clark *The gothic revival. An essay in the history of taste* (London 1928).

U. Christoffel *Malerei und Poesie. Die symbolistische Kunst des 19. Jahrhunderts* (Zürich 1948).

P. van Tieghem *Le Romantisme dans la litterature européenne* (Paris 1948).

F. Strich, Die Romantik als europäische Bewegung. *Festschrift H. Wölfflin* (1924).

M. Jean & A. Mezei *Genèse de la pensée moderne dans la litterature* (Paris 1950).

A. Viatte *Les sources occultes du romantisme* (I, II, Paris 1928).

246

GENERAL WORKS ON 19th CENTURY ART

H. Focillon *La peinture au XIXième siècle* (I, II, Paris, 1927/28).

A. Springer *Die Kunst von 1800 bis zur Gegenwart* (Leipzig 1920).

P. Colin *La Peinture aux XIX siècle. Le Romantisme* (Paris-Bruxelles 1935).

J. Rothenstein *Nineteenth-Century painting, a study in conflict* (London 1932).

H. Sedlmayr *Verlust der Mitte. Die bildende Kunst des 19. und 20. Jahrhunderts als Symptom und Symbol der Zeit* (Salzburg 1951 ⁵).

H. Beenken, Die Krise der Malerei. *Deutsche Vierteljahrschrift für Litt. Wissenschaft und geistesgeschichte* (XI, 1933), p. 421.

M. Raynal *Histoire de la peinture moderne de Baudelaire à Bonnard* (Genève 1949).

F. D. Klingender *Art and the industrial revolution* (London 1947).

Ph. Burty *Maîtres et Petits-Maîtres* (Paris 1877).

K. Berger, Poussin's style and the XIX century. *Gazette des Beaux Arts* (1955), p. 161.

J. Alazard, L'Exotisme dans la peinture française au XIXième siècle. *Gazette des Beaux Arts* (1931, II), p. 241.

E. H. Gombrich, Imagery and Art in the romantic period. *Burlington Magazine* (XCI, 1949), p. 153.

F. Jourdain, L'Art officiel de Jules Grévy à Albert Lebrun. *Le Point* (Souillac, 1949).

W. Friedlaender *David to Delacroix* (Cambridge, Mass, 1952).

J. Piper *British Romantic Artists* (London 1946).

J. Alford, Art and Reality 1850-1950. *College Art Journal* (XVII, 3, 1958), p. 228.

The two sides of the medal. French Painting from Gerôme to Gauguin (Exhib. Detroit Museum of Art, 1954).

Verkannte Kunst, Cat. Exh. Kunsthalle Recklinghausen 1957.

Catalogue illustré officiel de l'Exposition centennale de l'Art français 1800-1889 (Paris 1900).

B. Newhall, Photography and the development of kinetic visualisation. *Journal of the Warburg and Courtauld Society* (VII, 1944), p. 42.

J. Thirion, L'influence de l'Estampe japonaise sur la peinture française. *Musée de France* (Oct. 1948), p. 229.

C. Blanc *Le Trésor de la curiosité* (Paris 1958).

E. J. Délécluze *Les beaux Arts dans les deux mondes en 1855* (Paris 1856).

Th. Gautier *L'Art moderne* (Paris 1856).

H. Heine *Der Salon* I (Rotterdam 1860).

N. Lübke *Die moderne französische Kunst* (1872).

ARTISTS, PRECURSORS OF THE SYNTHETISTS

L. Lopez-Rey, Goya and the world around him. *Gazette des Beaux Arts* (1945, II), p. 129.

Bibliography

G. Levitine, Literary sources of Goya's Capricho 43. *Art Bulletin* (XXXVII 1955), p. 56.

Xavier de Salas *Miscelanea Goyesca*. *Archivo Español de Arte* (92, 1950), p. 335.

Bosch, Goya et le Phantastique (Cat. Exp. Bordeaux 1957).

T. Hetzer, F. Goya und die Krise der Kunst um 1800. *Wiener Jahrbuch für Kunstgeschichte* (XIV 1950), p. 7.

L. Lopez-Rey *Francisco de Goya* (Amsterdam-Antwerpen 1950).

E. Delacroix, sa vie et ses oeuvres (Paris 1865).

E. Delacroix *Oeuvres littéraires* I, II ed. E. Faure (Paris 1923).

Journal d'Eugène Delacroix, ed. A. Joubin (Paris 1950 ²).

Lettres de Delacroix (1815-1863), publ. P. Burty (Paris 1878).

G. Dargenty *E. Delacroix par lui-même* (Paris 1885).

Tourneux *E. Delacroix devant ses contemporains* (Paris 1886).

A. Robaut *L'oeuvre complet d'Eugène Delacroix*, commenté par E. Chesneau (Paris 1885).

P. Signac *De Delacroix au Néo-Impressionnisme* (Paris 1899).

E. Moreau-Nélaton *Delacroix* (Paris 1916).

J. Meier-Graefe *E. Delacroix. Beitrage zu einer Analyse* (München o.J.).

J. Lassaigne *Eugène Delacroix* (Amsterdam-Antwerpen 1949).

G. H. Hamilton, Delacroix, Byron and the English Illustrators, *Gazette des Beaux Arts* (XCI 1949), p. 261.

K. Badt *Eugène Delacroix, drawings* (Oxford 1946 ²).

P. Burty *Maîtres et Petits-Maîtres* (Paris 1877).

S. J. Key *John Constable, His Life and Work* (London 1948).

ART AND ART-THEORY IN THE NATURALISTIC-REALISTIC TRADITION

J. C. Sloane *French painting between the past and the present. Artists, critics and traditions from 1848 to 1870* (Princeton 1951).

C. Mauclair *Les états de la peinture française 1850-1920* (Paris 1920).

F. B. Blanshard *Retreat from likeness in the theory of painting* (New York 1949 ²).

C. E. Gauss *The aesthetic Theories of French artists 1855 to the present* (Baltimore 1949).

L. Venturi, Prémisses théoriques de l'art moderne. *Preuves* (II 1952), p. 37.

J. de Gruyter *Wezen en Ontwikkeling der schilderkunst na 1850* (Den Haag 1935).

J. Rewald *The history of impressionism* (New York 1946).

J. E. Blanche *Les arts plastiques de 1870 à nos jours* (Paris 1931).

J. Meier-Graefe *Der moderne Impressionismus* (Berlin 1903).

E. Klossowski *Die Maler von Montmartre* (Berlin 1903).

248

Sheldon Cheney *The story of Modern Art* (New York 1945).

T. Craven *Modern Art. The men, the movement, the meaning* (New York 1940).

Th. Duret *Critique d'avant-garde* (Paris 1885).

J. K. Huysmans *L'Art moderne* (Paris 1883) (nouvelle ed. 1902).

E. Zola *Les réalistes au salon. Mes Haines* (Paris 1866).

W. A. van Konijnenburg *De waarde der impressionistische schilderkunst, Ethiek en aesthetiek* (Den Haag 1908).

Duranty *La nouvelle peinture* (1876). Nouvelle ed. M. Guérin (Paris 1946).

G. Moore *Confessions of a young man* (Penguin Books, 1939).

M. Zahar *Gustave Courbet* (Amsterdam-Antwerpen, 1950).

M. Shapiro, Courbet and popular imagery, an essay on Realism and Naiveté. *Journal of the Warburg and Courtauld Society* (IV, 1940), p. 164.

Constantin Guys (Cat. exp. Vlissingen 1954).

F. Blei *Felicien Rops* (Berlin o.J.).

M. Kunel *F. Rops* (Bruxelles 1943).

G. A. Aurier, C. Monet. *Mercure de France* (IV 1892), p. 302.

W. Seitz, Monet and abstract painting. *College Art Journal* (XVI, 1, 1956), p. 34.

ART AND LITERATURE OUTSIDE THE CIRCLE OF THE SYNTHETISTS

Kerrison Preston *Blake and Rossetti* (London 1944).

J. Bronowski *William Blake* (Penguin 1950 [6]).

R. Schmutzler, Blake and Art Nouveau. *Architectural Review* (CXVIII 704, Aug. 1955), p. 91.

D. Erdman *Blake, prophet against empire* (Princeton Univ. Press, 1954).

R. Garnett, William Blake. *The Portfolio* (Oct. 1895, London).

J. C. E. Bassalik-de Vries *William Blake in his relation to Dante Gabriel Rossetti* (Diss. Zürich 1911, Basel).

A. Blunt, Blake's Pictorial Imagination. *Journal of the Warburg and Courtauld Society* (VI, 1943), p. 190.

J. Ruskin *Modern Painters I-V* (London 1909).

J. Ruskin *The arts and pleasures of England*. Lectures 1883/4 (London 1907).

Holman Hunt *Pre-Rafaelitism and the Pre-Rafaelite Brotherhood* I, II (London 1905).

W. Morris *Hopes and fears for art* (London 1896 [4]).

W. M. Rossetti *Pre-Rafaelite Diaries and letters* (London 1900).

J. L. Tupper, The subject in art. *The Germ* (1850), p. 11.

R. Ironside & J. Gere *Pre-Rafaelite Painters* (London 1948).

W. Gaunt *The Pre-Rafaelite Tragedy* (London 1943 [3]).

Jean Proix *Un mysticisme esthétique* (Paris 1928).

A. Neumeyer, Die prärafaelitische Malerei im Rahmen der Kunstgeschichte des

19. Jahrh. *Deutsche Vierteljahrschrift für Litt. Wissenschaft und Geistesge-schichte* (XI, 1933), p. 67.

Holbrook Jackson *Dreamers of Dreams. Rise and Fall of 19th century idealism* (London 1948).

H. C. Marillier *Dante Gabriel Rossetti* (London 1901).

Dante Gabriel Rossetti, Hand and Soul. *The Germ* (1850).

Dante Gabriel Rossetti *Poems* (Leipzig 1873).

W. M. Rossetti, Dante Rossetti and Elisabeth Siddall. *Burlington Magazine* (I, 1903), p. 273.

J. Cartwright & Aymer Vallence *Burne-Jones* (London 1900).

H. Pater *The Renaissance. Studies in art and poetry* (London 1928).

Holbrook Jackson *The Eighteen Nineties* (Pelican Book, 1950).

Bettina Polak *Het fin-de-siècle in de Nederlandse schilderkunst: De symbolistische beweging, 1890-1900* (Den Haag, 1955).

A. Alexander, Les Arts français à l'âge critique: Les Salons de 1889 à 1890. *Gazette des Beaux Arts* (1934, I), p. 306.

G. Geffroy *La vie artistique* I, II, III (Paris 1892/3/4).

E. Bricon *Psychologie d'Art. Les Maîtres de la fin du XIX siècle* (Paris 1900).

T. de Wyzéwa *Peintres de jadis et d'aujourd'hui* (Paris 1903).

G. Ramberg *Die moderne Kunstbewegung. Zweck und Wesen der Sezession* (Wien 1899).

G-A. Aurier, Rationations familières et d'ailleurs vaines à propos des trois Salons de 1891, *Mercure de France* (III, 1891), p. 30.

A. Fontainas *Mes souvenirs du symbolisme* (Paris, 1928).

T. Natanson, L'Art des Salons. *La Revue Blanche* (1 et 15 mai 1895).

C. Chassé *Le mouvement symboliste dans l'Art du XIXième siècle* (Paris 1947).

H. Fierens-Gevaert *Essais sur l'art contemporain* (Paris 1897).

T. Natanson, Expositions (Utamaro, Hiroshige, Toulouse-Lautrec) *La Revue Blanche* (Feb. 1893).

T. Natanson, Expositions (des Nabis), *La Revue Blanche* (V, 25, Nov. 1893), p. 236.

Fragments de Nietsche *La Revue Blanche* (Nov. 1892).

G. Coquiot *Les gloires déboulonnées* (Paris 1924).

O. Uzanne, Victor Hugo, par la plume et le crayon. *L'Art et l'Idée* (II 1892), p. 1.

La Revue Fantaisiste (1861, Paris).

J. Destrée *L'Oeuvre lithografique de Odilon Redon* (Brussel 1891).

J. Veth, Odilon Redons lithografische Serien. *Kunst und Künstler* (III 1903), p. 104.

O. Redon *A soi-même. Journal 1867-1915* (Paris 1922).

J. Rewald, Odilon Redon and Emile Bernard. Quelques notes et documents sur Odilon Redon. *Gazette des Beaux Arts* (Nov. 1956), p. 81.

Musée Gustave Moreau, Catalogue sommaire (Paris 1926).

Charles R. Sturt (pseud. for C. Ricketts), A Note on Gustave Moreau. *The Dial* (III, 1893), London.
Gleeson White, The pictures of Gustave Moreau. *The Pageant* (1897, London), p. 3.
G. le Roy *James Ensor* (Bruxelles, Paris 1922).
L. Lebeer *James Ensor, Etser* (Antwerpen 1952).

M. Vachon *Puvis de Chavannes* (Paris s.d.).
G.-A. Aurier, E. Carrière. *Mercure de France* (II 1891), p. 332.
D. Sutton, Carrière et les Symbolistes at the Orangerie *Burlington Magazine* (XCII 1950), p. 81.
O. Uzanne, A. Robida. *L'Art et l'Idée* (II 1892), p. 128.
A. Germain, Un peintre idéaliste-idéiste, Alexandre Séon, *L'Art et l'Idée* (I, 1892), p. 107.
A. Rannit, M. K. Ciurlionis, Der erste abstrakte Maler der modernen Welt. *Das goldene Tor* (Zweimonatschrift für Litteratur und Kunst. Baden Baden 1951).

S. M. Péladan *Comment on devient fée* (Paris 1893).
S. M. Péladan *Amphithéatre des sciences mortes: Traité des antinomies, métaphysique* (Paris 1901).
Salon de la Rose†Croix, Règle et Monitoire (Paris 1891).
T. Natanson, Exposition: Le 4ième salon de la Rose†Croix. *La Revue Blanche* (Avril 1895).
A. Germain, L'idéal et l'idéalisme, Salon de la Rose†Croix. *L'Art et l'Idée* (I 1892), p. 176.

E. Michalski, Die Entwicklungsgeschichtliche Bedeutung des Jugendstils. *Repertorium für Kunstwissenschaft* (46, 1926), p. 148.
E. Bayard *Le style moderne* (Paris s.d.).
S. T. Madsen *Sources of Art Nouveau* (Oslo 1956).
J. E. Blanche, Les objets d'art. *La Revue Blanche* (15 Mars 1895), p. 463.
S. Bing *Le Japon Artistique* I, II, III (Paris 1888).
C. Lancaster, Oriental Contribution to Art Nouveau. *Art Bulletin* (XXXIV, 1952), p. 297.
Um 1900—Art Nouveau und Jugendstil. Cat. Exp. (Zürisch 1952²).
O. Uzanne, Eugène Grasset. *L'Art et l'Idée* (II, 1892), p. 193.

R. Wagner *Quatre poèmes d'Opéra précédé d'une lettre sur la musique* (Paris 1861).
P. Valin, Ceux de demain. Les jeunes et leurs revues. *L'Art et l'Idée* (I 1892), p. 62.
P. Valin, La jeune littérature. *L'Art et l'Idée* (I 1892), p. 136.
M. v. Wedderkop, Paul Verlaine und die Lyrik der Décadence in Frankreich. *Pan* (1896), p. 69.

251

Bibliography

Rémy de Gourmont, Le symbolisme. Définition de ce nouveau mouvement littéraire. *L'Art et l'Idée* (II 1892), p. 47.

P. Valin, Les lettres prochaines: Essai sur les tendences des écrivains de demain. *L'Art et l'Idée* (II 1892), p. 81.

T. de Wyzéwa *Nos Maîtres* (Paris 1895).

J. Huret *Enquête sur l'évolution littéraire* (Paris 1891).

A. Kuyper *The antithesis between symbolism and revelation* (Amsterdam-Pretoria, Edingburg 1899).

C. Moore *Confessions of a young man* (Penguin Books 1939).

J. K. Huysmans *A Rebours* (Paris 1903).

C. Récolin *L'anarchie littéraire* (Paris 1898).

P. Radiot, Notre Byzantinisme. *La Revue Blanche* (Feb. 1894), p. 110.

M. Raymond *From Baudelaire to Surrealism* (New York 1950), (transl.).

A. Micha *Verlaine et les poètes symbolistes* (Paris 1957 [17]).

A. G. Lehmann *The symbolist aesthetics in France 1885-1895* (Oxford 1950).

A. Barre *Le symbolisme. Essai historique sur le mouvement symboliste en France de 1885 à 1900* (Paris 1911).

P. Valéry *Existence du symbolisme* (Paris 1939).

C. Mauclair *Servitudes et grandeurs littéraires* (Paris 1922).

A. Fontainas *Mes souvenirs du symbolisme* (Paris 1928).

A. Poizat *Le symbolisme de Baudelaire à Claudel* (Paris 1919).

E. Raynaud *Le mêlée symboliste* I, II, III (1918-1922).

G. Michaud *Message poétique du symbolisme* I, II, III (Paris 1947).

A. J. Mathews *La Wallonie 1886-1892. The symbolist movement in Belgium* (New York 1947).

CONGENIAL CONTEMPORARIES OF THE
SYNTHETISTS, WRITERS AND PAINTERS

G.-A. Aurier *Oeuvres posthumes*. Notice de Rémy de Gourmont (Paris 1893).

J. Huret *Enquête sur l'évolution littéraire* (Paris 1891).

G. Dumur, Aurier et l'évolution idéaliste. *Mercure de France* (VIII 1893).

T. de Wyzéwa *Nos maîtres* (Paris 1895).

A. Fontainas *Mes souvenirs du symbolisme* (Paris 1928).

A. Poizat *Le symbolisme de Baudelaire à Claudel* (Paris 1919).

G. Michaud *Message poétique du symbolisme* I, II, III (Paris 1947).

M. Raymond *From Baudelaire to surrealism* (New York 1950), (transl.).

A. G. Lehmann *The symbolist aesthetics in France 1885-1895* (Oxford 1950).

S. Mallarmé *Oeuvres complètes,* notes par H. Mondor & G. Jean-Aubry (Paris 1951).

S. Mallarmé *Poésies complètes,* texte et notes établies par Y. G. le Dantec (Paris 1948).

S. Mallarmé *Divagations* (Paris 1897).
G. Delfel *L'Esthétique de S. Mallarmé* (Paris 1951).
R. Michaud *Mallarmé* (Paris 1953).

A. Mellério *Le mouvement idéaliste en peinture* (Paris 1896).
Lettres à Emile Bernard de Van Gogh, Gauguin, Redon, Cézanne, Bloy, Bourget etc. (Paris 1927).
C. Mauclair *Les états de la peinture française de 1850 à 1920* (Paris 1921).
R. Rey *La renaissance du sentiment classique dans la peinture française à la fin du XIXième siècle* (Paris 1930).
J. Rewald *Post Impressionism, from van Gogh to Gauguin* (New York 1956).
F. B. Blanshard *Retreat from likeness in the theory of painting* (New York 1949).
C. E. Gauss *The aesthetic theories of French artists 1855 to the present* (Baltimore 1949).
D. Sutton, Exhibition at Wildenstein's. *Burlington Mag.* (XCV 1954), p. 193.
H. Read *Philosophy of Modern Art* (London 1952).
W. Hess *Problem der Farbe in den Selbstzeugnisse moderner Maler* (München 1953).

J. Rewald *P. Cézanne*, Correspondances (Paris 1937).
A. Vollard *En écoutant Cézanne, Degas, Renoir* (Paris 1938).
Rainer Maria Rilke *Brieven over Cézanne, transl.* (Den Haag 1945).
F. Burger *Cézanne und Hodler* (Berlin 1919 ³).
E. Bernard, Cézanne. *Kunst und Künstler* (VI, 1908), p. 426.
E. Bernard, Souvenirs sur Paul Cézanne et lettres inédits. *Mercure de France* (1-15 Oct. 1907).
E. Bernard *Erinnerungen an Paul Cézanne* (transl. H. Graber, Basel 1917).
R. Fry *Cézanne, a study of his development* (London 1952 ²).
K. v. Tolnay, Zur Cézanne's geschichtliche Stellung. *Deutsche Vierteljahrschrift für Litteraturwissenschaft und Geistesgeschichte* (XI 1933), p. 78.
J. Rewald *Cézanne et Zola* (Paris 1936).
L. Venturi *Cézanne—son art—son oeuvre* (Paris 1936).
E. Loran *Cézanne's Composition* (Berkeley-Los Angelos 1950 ²).
L. Guerry *Cézanne et l'expression de l'espace* (Paris 1950).
J. M. Carpenter, Cézanne and tradition. *Art Bulletin* (XXXIII 1951), p. 174.
G. H. Hamilton, Cézanne, Bergson and the image of time. *College Art Journal* (XVI, 1, 1956), pag. 2.

G.-A. Aurier, Les Isolés: Vincent van Gogh. *Mercure de France* (I, 1890), p. 24.
Verzamelde Brieven van Van Gogh. Uitg. J. v. Gogh-Bonger (1953).
F. Bonger-v. d. Borch v. Verwolde, Vincent van Gogh als lezer. *Maandblad voor Beeldende Kunsten* (Maart 1950).
W. Fowlie, The religious experience of Van Gogh. *College Art Journal* (IX, 3, 1950), p. 317.
K. Jaspers *Strindberg und van Gogh. Versuch einer pathologischen Analyse unter*

Bibliography

Vergleichender Heranziehung von Swedenborg und Hölderlin (Berlin, 1926).
M. E. Tralbaut *Vincent van Gogh in zijn Antwerpse periode* (Amsterdam, 1948).
W. Jos de Gruyter *Vincent van Gogh*. Introd. cat. v. Gogh. Exposition (Den Haag 1953).

G. Laprade *Seurat* (Paris 1945).
J. Rewald *Seurat* (Paris 1948).
R. J. Goldwater, Some aspects of the development of Seurats style. *Art Bulletin* (XXIII, 2, 1941), p. 117.
R. L. Herbert, Seurat in Chicago and New York. *Burlington Mag.* (C, 1958), p. 146.
J. Rewald, Extraits du journal inédit de Paul Signac. *Gazette des Beaux Arts* (1949, p. 97), (1952, p. 265), 1953, p. 27).
P. Signac *D'Eugène Delacroix au Néo-Impressionnisme*. Ed. La Revue Blanche (1899).
J. Rewald, F. Fénéon, critique d'art. *Tijdschrift voor Beeldende Kunsten* (1950), p. 67.
J. Rewald, F. Fénéon. *Gazette des Beaux* Arts (1947), p. 45.
C. Henry, L'Esthétique des formes. *La Revue Blanche* (Aug. 1894, Oct. 1894, Feb. 1895).

WRITINGS FROM OR ABOUT THE SYNTHETISTS (1885-1900)

Ch. Morice *La Littérature de tout à l'heure* (Paris 1889).
P. Gauguin et C. Morice *Noa Noa* (Paris 1924).
G.-A. Aurier *Oeuvres posthumes* (note de Rémy de Gourmont), (Paris 1893).
G.-A. Aurier, Le symbolisme dans la peinture: Paul Gauguin. *Mercure de France* (II 1891), p. 155.
G.-A. Aurier, Les peintres symbolistes. *Oeuvres posthumes,* p. 293.
Maurice Denis *Théories 1890-1910* (Paris 1912 [2]).
P. Sérusier *A.B.C. de la peinture,* suivies d'une correspondance inédite (Paris 1950).
Sérusier reproductions. *Dekorative Kunst* (IV 1899), p. 129 e.v.
Lettres à Emile Bernard (Paris 1927).
E. Bernard, Les ateliers. Notes Diverses. *Mercure de France* (XIII, 1895), p. 194.
E. Bernard, Ce que c'est que l'Art mystique. *Mercure de France* (XIII 1895), p. 28.
E. Bernard, Les musées. *Mercure de France* (XIII 1895), p. 296.
P. Gauguin, Armand Séguin, Préface inédite au catalogue de l'exposition des oeuvres de Armand Séguin. *Mercure de France* (XIII 1895), p. 222.
A. Mellerio *Le mouvement idéaliste en peinture* (Paris 1896).
O. Uzanne, La renaissance de la gravure sur bois. Un néoxylographe: Félix Vallotton. *L'Art et l'Idée* (I, 1892), p. 113.
La Revue Blanche (Paris 1891 ff.).

254

Mercure de France (Paris 1890, ff.).

L'Art et l'Idée, Revue contemporaine illustrée, publ. p. O. Uzanne, I, II (Paris 1892).

WRITINGS BY GAUGUIN

M. Malingue *Lettres de Gauguin à sa femme et à ses amis* (Paris 1946).

Lettres de Gauguin à Daniel de Monfreid, ed. Mme Joly-Ségalen (Paris 1950).

P. Gauguin *Avant et Après* (Paris 1923).

P. Gauguin, Armand Séguin: Préface inédite au catalogue de l'exposition des oeuvres de Armand Séguin. *Mercure de France* (XIII 1895), p. 222.

Notes synthétiques de Paul Gauguin, ed. H. Mahaut, *Vers et Prose* (VI, 22, Juillet-Sept. 1910), p. 51.

P. Gauguin *Ancien Culte Mahorie.* Présentation p. R. Huyghe, Le clef de Noa Noa. Facs (Paris 1951).

P. Gauguin et C. Morice *Noa Noa* (Paris 1924).

P. Gauguin *Racontars de Rapin* (Paris 1951).

P. Gauguin *Esprit Moderne et le Catholicisme* (ms. à St. Louis, Miss.) (1897-98).

B. Dorival *Carnet de Tahiti.* Facs. (Paris 1954).

R. Huyghe *Le carnet de Paul Gauguin.* Facs. (Paris 1952).

WRITINGS CONCERNING GAUGUIN

G.-A. Aurier, Le symbolisme dans la peinture: Paul Gauguin. *Mercure de France* (II 1891), p. 155.

T. Natanson, Oeuvres récentes de Gauguin (Galerie Durand-Ruel). *La Revue Blanche* (V, 26, Dec. 1893), p. 418.

J. de Rotonchamp *Paul Gauguin* (Paris 1906).

C. Morice *Paul Gauguin* (Paris 1919).

Ch. Chassé *Gauguin et le groupe de Pont-Aven* (Paris 1921).

R. Rey *Gauguin* (Paris 1924).

J. Dorsenne *La vie sentimentale de Paul Gauguin* (Paris 1927).

M. Guérin *L'oeuvre gravé de Gauguin,* I, II (Paris, 1927).

A. Alexander *Paul Gauguin, sa vie et le sens de son oeuvre* (Paris 1930).

C. Kunstler *Gauguin, peintre maudit* (Paris 1934).

J. Rewald *Gauguin* (London 1938).

M. Malingue *Gauguin* (London-Paris 1948).

R. Cogniat *La vie ardente de Paul Gauguin* (exp. Galerie Wildenstein 1936-37).

C. Estienne *Gauguin, étude biographique et critique* (Genève 1953).

Hans Graber *Paul Gauguin nach eigenem und fremden Zeugnissen* (Basel 1946 [2]).

R. Cogniat *Gauguin* (Paris s.d.).

R. Goldwater *Gauguin* (New York 1957).

D. Sutton, La perte du pucelage by Paul Gauguin. *Burlington Magazine* (XCI 1949), p. 103.

Bibliography

D. Sutton, The Gauguin Exhibition. *Burlington Magazine* (XCI 1949), p. 283.

D. Sutton, Notes on Paul Gauguin. *Burlington Magazine* (XCVIII 1956), p. 84.

H. Dorra, The first Eves in Gauguin's Eden. *Gazette des Beaux Arts* (Maart 1953), p. 189, 225.

H. Dorra, Emile Bernard et Paul Gauguin, *Gazette des Beaux Arts* (XLV 1955), p. 227.

R. Huyghe *Gauguin, Createur de la peinture moderne* (Gauguin, Exposition Centenaire, Paris 1949).

Gauguin, cat. exhibit. Tate Gallery 1955: D. Cooper *Gauguin the innovator,* p. 5.

Pola Gauguin, Paul Gauguin: Avant et Après, *Kunsten Idag* (XXVII, Oslo 1954), 1, p. 21.

B. Dorival, Sources of the art of Gauguin from Java, Egypt and Ancient Greece. *Burlington Magazine* (XCII 1951), p. 118.

D'où venons-nous, que sommes-nous, où allons-nous (M. Harriman Gallery, New York 1936).

Lee van Dowski, Gauguin als Glasmaler. *Neue Zürcher Zeitung* (4/11/'50).

R. Puig *Paul Gauguin, G. D. de Monfreid et leurs amis* (Perpignan 1958).

U. F. Marks-Vandenbroucke, Gauguin, ses origines et sa formation artistique. *Gazette des Beaux Arts* (98ième année, 1956), p. 9.

H. Rostrup, Gauguin et le Danemark, *Ditto,* p. 63.

J. Thirion, L'influence de l'estampe japonaise dans l'oeuvre de Gauguin, *Ditto,* p. 95.

Jénot, Le premier séjour de Gauguin à Tahiti, 1891-1893, *Ditto,* p. 115.

L. J. Bouge, Traduction et interpretation des titres en langue tahitienne inscrit sur les oeuvres océaniennes de Paul Gauguin, *Ditto,* p. 161.

J. Loize, Gauguin sauvé du feu. *Ditto,* p. 165.

G. Le Bronnec, Les dernières années. *Ditto,* p. 189.

G. Wildenstein, L'Idéologie et l'esthétique dans deux tableaux clés de Gauguin. *Ditto,* p. 127.

Documents. *Ditto,* p. 201.

J. Lindberg-Hansen, Discovering Paul Gauguin, the Wood-carver. *College Art Journal* (XII, 2, 1953), p. 117.

H. Read, Gauguin, return to symbolism. *Art News* 25: 122-58 (1956).

J. Rewald *Gauguin Drawings* (New York 1957).

L. Gowing, Letter on Paul Gauguin, *Burlington Magazine* (XCI 1949, p. 354).

C. Gorham *Gouden Gestalten, een roman over Gauguin* (Amsterdam 1956).

C. Chassé, Le sort de Gauguin est lié au Krach de 1882, *Connaissance des Arts* (Paris, Feb. 1959), p. 40.

F. Daulte, L'art de 'transposer' chez Gauguin, *Connaissance des Arts* (Paris, Feb. 1959), p. 44.

MEMOIRS AND WRITINGS AFTER 1900 OF EYE-WITNESSES

M. Denis *Théories 1890-1910* (Paris 1912 [2]).

M. Denis *Catalogue de l'Exposition Cross* (Paris 1910).

256

M. Denis *Nouvelles théories* (Paris 1922).

M. Denis, Introduction cat.: Französische Kunst des XIX und XX Jahrh. *Zürcher Kunsthaus* (Oct.-Nov. 1917).

M. Denis, L'Époque du symbolisme. *Gazette des Beaux Arts* (1934 I), p. 165.

M. Denis *Sérusier* (Paris 1942).

P. Sérusier *A.B.C. de la peinture,* suivi d'une correspondance inédite (Paris 1950).

W. Verkade *Le tourment de Dieu* (Paris 1926), Préface de M. Denis.

E. Bernard, Louis Anquetin. *Gazette des Beaux Arts* (1934 I), p. 108.

C. Morice *Gauguin* (Paris 1919).

T. Natanson *Peint à leur tour* (Paris 1948).

T. Natanson *Le Bonnard que je propose* (Genève 1951).

A. Barre *Le symbolisme.* Essai historique sur le mouvement symboliste en France de 1885 à 1900 (Paris 1911).

C. Mauclair *Les états de la peinture française de 1850 à 1920* (Paris 1921).

C. Mauclair *Servitude et grandeur littéraires* (Paris 1922).

A. Fontainas *Mes souvenirs du symbolisme* (Paris 1928).

J. E. Blanche *Les arts plastiques de 1870 à nos jours.* Introduction par M. Denis (Paris 1931).

LATER LITERATURE ON SYNTHETISM AND THE SYNTHETISTS

H. F., Studio-Talk—on Maurice Denis, *Studio* (1910 III), p. 235.

G. Coquiot *Cubistes, Futuristes, Passéistes* (Paris 1914).

A. Ségard *Peintres d'aujourd'hui.* Les décorateurs. H. Martin, Aman-Jean, Maurice Denis, Vuillard (Paris 1914).

Ch. Chassé *Gauguin et le groupe de Pont-Aven* (Paris 1921).

A. Vaudoyer, Maurice Denis. *Dedalo* (II 1921/2), p. 772.

J. E. Blanche *De Gauguin à la Revue Nègre* (Paris 1928).

T. Craven *Modern Art* (New York 1940).

S. Cheney *The story of modern art* (New York 1945).

S. Bavazetti-Desmoulin *Maurice Denis* (Paris 1945).

C. Chassé *Le mouvement symboliste dans l'art du XIXième siècle* (Paris 1947).

C. E. Gauss *Aesthetic Theories of French Artists 1855 to the present* (Baltimore 1949).

H. Redeker *De dagen der artistieke vertwijfeling* (Amsterdam 1950).

L. Venturi, Prémisses théoriques de l'art moderne. *Preuves* (II 1952), p. 37.

F. Dauchot, Meyer de Haan en Bretagne. *Gazette des Beaux Arts* (1952), p. 355.

D. Sutton, Paris in the 90th at Wildenstein. *Burlington Mag.* (XCVI 1954), p. 193.

H. H. Hofstätter *Die Entstehung des neuen Stils in der französischen Malerei um 1900* (1954 Diss. Freiburg i.B.).

Agnes Humbert *Les Nabis et leur époque, 1888-1900* (Genève 1954).

J. Rewald *Post Impressionism* (New York 1956).

J. Rewald, Odilon Redon and Emile Bernard. *Gazette des Beaux Arts* (1956), p. 81.

O. Hølaas, J. F. Willumsen. *Kunsten Idag* (XLIV, Oslo 1958, 2), p. 5.

R. Puig *Paul Gauguin, G. D. de Monfreid et leurs amis* (Perpignan 1958).

257

For a list of the abbreviations used, see p. 2 of the booklet at the back of the book.

CHAPTER I:

1. See Rewald *Impressionism,* p. 23.

2. Cf. W. Friedlander: *David to Delacroix* (transl. R. Goldwater), (Cambridge, Mass, 1952), pp. 7 ff.

3. Cf. Delacroix: *Oeuvres Littéraires* (1923) I, pp. 24, 25; C. Mauclair: *Les états de la peinture française 1850-1920* (1921), p. 30 passim; John Rothenstein: *Nineteenth Century Painting* (London, 1932), pp. 25 ff.

4. Quatremère de Quincy: *Essai sur l'idéal dans ses applications pratiques aux oeuvres de l'imitation propre des arts de dessin* (Paris, 1837), pp. 314 ff.

5. A. Springer: *Die Kunst von 1800 bis zur Gegenwart,* 7th edition (1920, Leipzig), fig. 197.

6. Catalogue illustré officiel de l'exposition centenale de l'art français, 1800-1809 (Paris, 1900). Cf. also: The two sides of the Medal: French Painting from Gerôme to Gauguin. Detroit Museum of Art Exhib. (1954).

7. Castagnary: *Le Salon de 1866,* in Salons 1857-'70 (Paris, 1872) I, p. 224, quoted by Rewald: *Impressionism,* p. 126.

8. George Besson: *La peinture française au XIXième siècle* (Paris, s.d.), fig. 56.

9. Van Gogh *Brieven III,* Sept. 1885, Letter 423.

10. *Cur. Esth.,* Salon 1846, V, p. 122.

CHAPTER II:

1. E. Wind: The Revolution of History Painting. *Journal of the Warburg and Courtauld Society* (II, 1938, '39), p. 116.

2. Cf. *Burlington Magazine* (XCVI, 1954), the Géricault number, pp. 233 ff.

3. Cf. W. G. Constable: A Note on the Birth of Modern Painting, as Examplified in Landscape, *Actes du XVIIième Congrès International de l'Histoire de l'Art* (La Haye, 1955), p. 480. Cf. Kenneth Clark: *Landscape into Art* (London, 1949), pp. 74 ff.

4. Cf. Ellis Waterhouse on this subject in the Introduction to the *Catalogue of the English Landscape Art* (Boymans' Museum 1955), and also J. Piper: *British Romantic Artists* (London, 1946 ²), p. 19.

5. Cf. also Rewald *Impressionism*, p. 213, with a telling pronouncement by Monet.

6. J. Ruskin: *Modern Painters* (Part VII, Chapter IV, 18) V (London, 1904), p. 162.

7. Goya: Caprichos No. 43, F. J. Sanchez Canton: *Los Caprichos de Goya y sus debujos preparatorios* (Barcelona, 1949).

8. G. Levitine: Literary Sources of Goya's Capricho 43, *Art Bulletin* (XXXVII, 1955), pp. 56 ff.

9. E. H. Gombrich: Imagery and Art in the Romantic Period, *Burl. Mag.* (XCI, 1949), pp. 158 ff.

10. Cf. E. H. Gombrich: Tobias and the Angel, 'Harvest I', 'Travel' (1948, London), p. 63.

11. A. de Vesme: *Le peintre graveur italien* (Milan, 1906), p. 382: Vari Capricci (3-12), Scherzi di Fantasia (13-35).

12. No. 76 of the series E. Lafuente Ferrari: *Goya, Desastros de la Guerra y sus debujos preparatorios* (Barcelona, 1952).

13. Van Gogh *Brieven III*, Letter 401.

14. P. Signac: *D'Eugène Delacroix au néo-impressionisme* (ed. La Revue Blanche, 1899).

15. E.g. Gauguin in 'Diverses Choses' (1902), quoted by Kunstler, p. 182.

16. Delacroix: *Journal*, 12 Oct. 1853.

17. Cf. Windelband-Heimsoeth, § 34. Die Erkenntnis der Aussenwelt, pp. 391 ff.

18. Cf., e.g., H. Heine: *Der Salon I* (Rotterdam, 1860), p. 18.

19. Delacroix: *Journal*, 27 Dec. 1853.

20. *Cur. Esth.* Quelques caricaturistes français II, pp. 411, 412.

21. P. v. Tieghem: *Le romantisme dans la littérature europienne* (Paris, 1948), p. 179 passim.

22. Margaret Gilman: *Baudelaire the Critic* (New York, 1943), pp. 65 ff.

23. W. Windelband-Heimsoeth, pp. 537, 538.

24. Delacroix: *Journal I,* May 14, 1824, e.g.

25. Baudelaire: *Art Romantique*, pp. 9, 10.

26. *Cur. Esth.*, pp. 196/198.

27. Ferran *Esth.,* p. 500.

28. Baudelaire: *Art Romantique,* p. 301.

29. Dr. A. Kuyper: *The Antithesis between Symbolism and Revelation* (1899), p. 15.

30. A. Viatti: *Les sources occultes du romantisme 1770-1820* (1928, Paris) and R. Michaud: Baudelaire, Balzac et les correspondances, *Romanic Review* (Oct. 1938 XXIX, 3), p. 254 note.

31. Literature on Swedenborg: M. Matter, *S.* (Paris, 1863); M. Lamm: *S., Ein Studie über seine Entwicklung zum Mystiker und Geisterseher* (transl. Leipzig, 1922); A. Viatti: *Les sources occultes du romantisme, I* (Paris, 1928), pp. 72 ff. H. de Geymuller: *Swedenborg et les phénomènes psychiques* (Paris, s.d.). E. A. Sutton: *The Living thoughts of S.* (London, 1944).

32. M. Lamm, *op. cit.,* p. 20.

33. Ditto, pp. 30 ff.

34. Ditto, pp. 62, 63, 111, 112.

35. Ditto, pp. 256 ff., Sutton, *op. cit.,* pp. 71 ff.

36. Ditto, pp. 51, 73, 74.

37. Ditto, p. 89; on Plotinus, cf. E. Bréhier: *La philosophie de Plotin* (Paris, 1928), pp. 47 ff.

38. Bréhier, *op. cit.,* pp. 36, 42.

39. Bréhier, *op. cit.,* p. 55; Lamm, *op. cit.,* p. 109.

40. Swedenborg's *'Clavis Hieroglyphica arcanorum naturalium et spiritualium per viam Repraesentationum et Correspondentiarum'* (1784, London), pp. 19 ff., also quoted by Lamm, *op. cit.,* p. 110, cf. Bréhier, p. 124 (Enneads V, 8, 6).

41. E. H. Gombrich: Icones Symbolae, The Visual Image in Neo-Platonic Thought, *Journal of the Warburg & Courtauld Society* (XI, 1948), pp. 167 ff., cf. also I. L. Zupnick: The Aesthetics of the Early Mannerists, *Art Bulletin* (XXXV, 1953), p. 305.

42. H. Evans: *Louis Lambert et la philosophie de Balzac* (Paris, 1951), p. 248.

43. Margaret Gilman: *Baudelaire the Critic* (New York, 1943), p. 16.

44. J. v. d. Elst: Autour du 'Livre Mystique': Balzac et Swedenborg, *Revue de la littérature comparée* (X, 1930), pp. 88 ff.

45. E.g., Gauguin, cf. Charles Morice: *Paul Gauguin* (1919, Paris), p. 37.

46. Quoted and analysed by M. Raymond: *From Baudelaire to Surréalism* (New York, 1950), pp. 17 ff.

47. R. Michaud: Baudelaire, Balzac et les correspondances. *Romanic Review* (Oct. 1938, XXIX), p. 257.

48. Cf. article quoted in note 41.

49. Cf. *Cur. Esth.,* p. 104.

50. *The Poems of Edgar Allen Poe* (London, New York, 1900), pp. 211 ff.

51. *Cur. Esth.,* p. 325.

52. H. de Balzac: *Seraphita,* Oeuvres Complètes XVII Etudes Philosophiques III. Etudes Analytiques (1870, Paris), pp. 429, 430.

53. *The Opal* (1845, Virginia ed. XIV), p. 187.

54. *Cur. Esth.,* p. 92, passim.

55. On Poe, cf. C. D. Cambiaire: *The Influence of E. A. Poe in France* (Fontenay-sous-Bois, 1927). M. Alterton: *Origins of Poe's Critical Theory* (University of Iowa Humanistic Studies, II, 3, w.d.)

56. Cambiaire *op. cit.,* p. 44, quotes from the introduction of *Histoires extraordinaires* (Paris, 1922), p. 29; ditto edition Paris 1932, p. XXVIII.

57. Thus Gautier in the Preface to Baudelaire's '*Fleurs du Mal*' (1868), quoted in Cambiaire, *op. cit.,* p. 37.

58. M. Alterton, *op. cit.,* p. 68.

59. Cf. Note 57.

60. C. Mauclair, in the *Fortnightly Review* (Sept., 1923), 'E. A. Poe as an Inspirer of Ideas', translation, quoted in Cambiaire, *op. cit.,* p. 64.

61. Schopenhauer: *Pensées, Maximes et Fragments* (par J. Bourdeau, Paris, 1880 [2]).

62. Thus Morhardt in: *Nouvelle Revue* (LXXXV, Febr. 1892), quoted in Lehmann: *Symbolist Aesth.,* p. 66.

63. Justi: *Winckelmann und seine Zeitgenossen,* especially I, p. 148.

64. Schopenhauer: *Die Welt als Wille und Vorstellung* (publ. Leipzig, 1844 [2]), par. 30, pp. 191 ff.

65. Ditto, par. 36, p. 208.

66. *Pensées,* etc. quoted in note 61, p. 140, 141.

67. Rewald *Post Impr.,* p. 298.

68. Ditto, p. 295, illustr., Coll. Q. A. Shaw Mc. Kean, Boston.

69. Th. Carlyle: *Sartor Resartus* (London, 1898), p. 193.

70. Ditto, p. 196.

71. Ditto, p. 198.

72. Ditto, p. 227.

73. Ditto, p. 252.

74. Ditto, p. 254.

75. Ditto, p. 257.

76. Ditto, p. 258.

77. Margaret Miller: Géricault's Paintings of the Insane. *Journal of the War-burg and Courtauld Society* (IV, 1940), p. 151.

78. R. Rey: *La renaissance du sentiment classique dans la peinture française à la fin du XIX siècle* (Paris, 1931).

79. Baudelaire: *Art. Romantique,* p. 54 ff.

80. See page 3.

81. Cf. Rewald *Impressionism,* p. 107 pàssim.

82. Rewald *Impressionism,* p. 126-131.

83. See f.i. R. W. Lee: Ut pictura poesis, the humanistic theory of painting, *Art Bulletin* XXII (1940), p. 228.

84. W. G. Constable: A note on the birth of modern painting, as exemplified in landscape. *Actes du Congres International d'Histoire de l'art* (La Haye, 1955), p. 476-481.

85. Revue Critique de productions de peinture, sculpture, gravure exposées au Salon de 1824, Par M.—, quoted in Gustave Geffroy, J. B. C. Corot, *Winternumber Studio* 1902/3, pag. C. VI.

86. Geffroy: *Corot op. cit.,* p. C. VII.

87. Ch. Blanc: *Les artistes de mon temps* (1876), quoted Ferran *Esth.,* p. 425.

88. For instance Castagnary and de Goncourts, see J. C. Sloane: *French Art 1850-1870* (1951), pp. 100 ff.

89. The Orpheus: Ill. C. 15 in Studio no. quoted in note 85, coll. Cottier & Co., New York and London.
The woman, ill. J. Baschet: *Pour une Renaissance de la peinture française* (Paris 1946), p. 45, Coll. M. G. Wildenstein.

90. Compare Rewald *Impr.,* p. 295/7.

91. Duranty: *La nouvelle peinture, à propos du Groupe d'artistes qui expose dans les Galeries Durand-Ruel 1876,* Nouvelle édition, ed. M. Guérin (Paris, 1946), p. 41.

92. Rewald *Impr.,* p. 176; Rewald *Post Impr.,* p. 157; Mme Thirion: L'in-fluence de l'estampe japonaise sur la peinture française. *Musée de France* (Oct. 1948), p. 229.

CHAPTER III:

1. W. Blake: A vision of the last judgment, in Kerrison Preston: *Blake and Rossetti* (London, 1944), p. 84.

2. A. Blunt: Blake's Pictorial Imagination, *Journal of the Warburg and Cour-tauld Society* (VI 1953), pp. 190 ff.

3. Cf. Note 1.

4. J. C. E. Bassalik-de Vries: *William Blake in his relation to D. G. Rossetti* (1911, Basle), p. 11. Here also more discursive on the 'correspondances'. Compare Blake *op. cit.*, p. 76.

5. Bassalik-de Vries *op. cit.*, p. 11.

6. Blake *op. cit.*, p. 82.

7. Cited from the Rossetti manuscript in Kerrison Preston *op. cit.*, p. 63.

8. Blake *op. cit.*, p. 75.

9. Bassalik-de Vries *op. cit.*, p. 8.

10. We agree with this view on Blake's profetic books. See: J. Bronowski: *William Blake* (London, 1954 [2]), pp. 24 ff.

11. Bronowski *op. cit.*, p. 127, cited from Blake's Jerusalem.

12. F. D. Klingender: *Art and the Industrial Revolution* (London, 1947), p. 105, cited from Blake's Milton.

13. Kerrison Preston *op. cit.*, p. 65.

14. For reproductions of his biblical illustrations see e.g. Catalogue of Christie's: Sale of Robertson collection, July 22, 1949.

15. John Ruskin: *Modern Painters* (London, 1909), III, p. 30.

16. Ditto, p. 158 passim.

17. Ditto, p. 264 ff.

18. Ditto, p. 327 ff.

19. Ditto, p. 326.

20. *Modern Painters* I, p. 13.

21. Ditto, p. XXXIII and XXXIV.

22. Ditto, p. 450.

23. Ditto, p. 451/2.

24. Ditto II, p. 166. Cf. p. 176.

25. Compare F. Hoffet: *L'Impérialisme protestante, Considérations sur le destin inégal des peuples protestants et catholiques dans le monde actuel* (Paris, 1948). See the author's: De constituerende factoren ener historische daad, *Philosophia Reformata* (XIX 1954), p. 129 ff. See also Ruskin: *Modern Painters* V, p. 376 ff. on unbelief and its consequences.

26. W. Holman Hunt: *Pre-Rafaelitism and the Pre-Rafaelite Brotherhood* (London, 1905), I, p. 73.

27. Ditto, p. 91.

28. Repr. R. Ironside and J. Gere: *Pre-Rafaelite Painters* (London, 1948), No. 25, Manchester Art Gallery.

29. Ditto Repr. 7, Manchester City Art Gallery.

30. Holman Hunt *op. cit.* I, p. XV.

31. Repr. Ironside & Gere *op. cit.*, p. 28 and 29, Coll. C. Anderson esq.

32. Holman Hunt II, p. 436. Repr. Ironside and Gere *op. cit.* repr. 33, Bancroft Foundation, Wilmington, Delaware.

33. 'Hand and Soul', reprinted in Kerrison Preston: *Blake and Rossetti* (1944, London), p. 88.

34. Ditto, p. 92.

35. J. C. E. Bassalik-de Vries: *William Blake in his relation to Dante Gabriel Rossetti* (Basle, 1911), p. 49.

36. Ditto, p. 17.

37. Ditto, p. 24.

38. Kerrison Preston *op. cit.*, p. 95 ff.

39. A pencil-drawing of 1855, Ironside & Gere, *op. cit.* repr. 32, Coll. Miss Munro.

40. Ironside and Gere *op. cit.* repr. 44, Tate Gallery.

41. Kerrison Preston *op. cit.*, p. 98.

42. Holbrook Jackson: *The Eighteen Nineties* (Pelican 1950 [6]), p. 286 ff.; Miss Dr. Bettina Polak: *Het fin-de-siècle in de Nederlandse schilderkunst* (The Hague, 1955), p. 255.

43. A. Muthesius-Trippenbach: Das moderne englische Bilderbuch, *Die Kunst* (München, 1902), p. 300 ff.

44. Ironside and Gere *op. cit.*, p. 18.

45. Kenneth Clark: *The gothic revival, an essay in the history of taste* (London, 1928), p. 265.

46. W. Gaunt: *The Pre-Rafaelite Tragedy* (London, 1948 [3]), p. 68.

47. Cf. a letter of Ruskin of 1862, cited by Holbrook Jackson: *Dreamer of Dreams* (1948), p. 95 ff.

48. Gaunt *op. cit.*, p. 135, G. Bell: *The art of William Morris* (1897), Holman Hunt *op. cit.* II, p. 218.

49. Holbrook Jackson *op. cit.*, p. 247 ff.

50. James Grady: Nature and the Art Nouveau, *Art Bulletin* (XXXVII, 3, 1955), p. 187; *Le Japon Artistique,* I, p. 112, 113.

51. R. Schmutzler: Blake and Art Nouveau, *Architectural Review* (CXVIII 704, Aug. 1955), p. 91.

52. Holbrook Jackson *op. cit.,* p. 23 passim and p. 31 ff.

53. Ditto p. 56.

54. Ditto p. 272 ff.

55. Ditto p. 60. Baudelaire is mentioned more than ten times in this book, although French influences as such, are not discussed.

56. These works are reproduced: Ricketts' 'Oedipus' and Sturge Moore's scenes from Coleridge, in *The Pageant* (London, 1896); 'Pan-Island' by Sturge Moore, Savage's 'Behemoth' and a woodcut by Lucien Pissarro in *The Pageant* (1897). W. Heath Robinson's Poe illustrations in *The Poems of Edgar Allen Poe* (London, New York, 1900); Beardsley's work in R. A. Walker: *The Best of Beardsley* (London, 1948); 'Pan-Island' by Sturge Moore and work by Lucien Pissarro in *The Dial,* ed. C. S. Ricketts and Ch. Shannon (London, 1897); Savage's 'Centaurs' in *The Dial,* No. 3 (1893); Savage's 'Behemoth' in *The Dial* No. 2 (1892); Ricketts' 'Daphnis and Chloe', in P. James, *English Book Illustration 1800-1900* (London, New York, 1947), p. 59; Burne Jones' works in J. Cartwright: *Life and Work of Edward Burne Jones* (London w.d.).

57. Holbrook Jackson *op. cit.,* p. 104 ff.

57a. Yeats' *Collected Works* (Stratford on Avon 1908), VI, p. 132.

58. Cited by Holman Hunt *op. cit.,* p. 365.

59. G. Geffroy: *La vie artistique* III (Paris, 1894), p. 371.

60. Cf. Kahn's writings cited Rewald *Post Impressionism,* p. 148/149, cited below, Chapter III, pag. 71, 72.

61. A. Germain: L'idéal et l'idéalisme, Salon de la Rose†Croix in *L'Art et l'Idée* (I, 1892), p. 176.

62. A. Springer: *Die Kunst von 1800 bis zur Gegenwart* (Leipzig 1920 [7]), p. 286.

63. *Mercure de France* (II April 1891), p. 236 ff. about the exposition of the XX in that year.

64. We refer to the elaborate study by Miss Dr. Bettine Polak: *Het fin-de-siècle in de Nederlandse schilderkunst* (Den Haag, 1955) (title shortened here: B. Polak).

65. B. Polak, p. 25, 89, 102, 293.

66. This even applies to a Toorop: influences of Schwabe, see B. Polak, p. 127/128 (repr. 27, 28), concerning contacts with Péladan, ditto, p. 115.

67. B. Polak, p. 28 ff.

68. For example B. Polak, repr. 47.

69. Cf. G. Michaud *Message poétique* III, p. 468.

70. Reproduced in the *'Illustration'*, special number devoted to the Salon of that year.

71. B. Polak, p. 292, repr. 41.

72. See scheme, p. 644 of Michaud *Message poétique* III.

73. Cf. Michaud *Message poétique* I, p. 34, 35.

74. Michaud *Message Poétique* II, p. 204.

75. Rewald *Post-Impressionism*, p. 148/149.

76. Cited by Morice *La Littérature*, p. 185.

77. Cf. the literature quoted in note a chapter II.

78. *Sartor Resartus*, p. 222.

79. Cf. H. Dooyeweerd: *Dictaat Inleiding tot de Encyclopedie der Rechts-wetenschap* (Amsterdam), p. 22, the same: *Wijsbegeerte der Wetsidee*, I, p. 30 ff. and II p. 252 ff.; *A New Critique of Theoretical Thought* I, p. 65 ff. II, p. 299 and the literature quoted in note a chapter II.

80. Dooyeweerd *Wijsbegeerte der Wetsidee*, I, p. 154 ff.

81. Cf. Windelband-Heimsoeth, p. 550, 551.

82. Cf. Jean Lemeere: Les concepts du Beau et de l'art dans la doctrine pla-tonicienne. *Revue d'Histoire de la Philosophie et d'histoire générale de la civilisa-tion* (VI, 1938), p. 1 ff., especially, p. 10 ff.

83. M. H. Abrams: *The mirror and the lamp, Romantic theory and the critical tradition* (New York, 1953), p. 42. ff.
E. Panofsky: *Idea, ein Beitrag zur Begriffsgeschichte der älteren Kunsttheorie* (Berlin, 1924), p. 11.

84. E. Panofsky *op. cit.*, p. 39 ff.; I. L. Zupnick: The 'aesthetics' of the early Mannerists, *Art Bulletin* (XXXV 1953), p. 302 ff.; A. Blunt: *Artistic Theory in Italy 1450-1600* (Oxford, 1940).

85. Abrams: *Mirror and the lamp*, p. 43, p. 126 ff. See also P. v. Tieghem: *Le romantisme dans la litterature européenne* (Paris, 1948), p. 271 ff.

86. Abrams ditto, p. 44.

87. R. F. Beerling: *Sjestow* (Baarn, w.d.), p. 74 ff.; see E. Panofsky on Suger *Meaning in the visual arts*, p. 132.

88. M. Denis *Théories*, p. 160.

89. H. Redeker: *De dagen der artistieke vertwijfeling* (Amsterdam, 1950), p. 31.

90. Ditto, p. 154, 155, 143.

91. Cf. page 50.

92. See Rewald *Post Impressionism,* p. 154 passim.

93. Dr. B. Polak: *Het fin-de-siècle in de Nederlandse schilderkunst* (The Hague, 1955), p. 20 ff.

94. Cf. Barre *Le Symbolisme,* p. 133.

95. See Holbrook Jackson: *The eighteen nineties,* p. 26, 60.

96. He wrote articles on the Salons, collected in *L'Art moderne* (Paris, 1902 ²) (first impression, 1883).

97. See e.g. '*Les licornes*', cat. no. 213, repr. on p. 66.

98. A. Fontainas: *Mes souvenirs du Symbolisme* (Paris, 1928), p. 326.

99. *The Dial* (1893, No. 3), p. 10 ff., article signed Charles R. Sturt, pseudonym of Ricketts, see U. Bridge: *W. B. Yeats and T. Sturge Moore, their correspondence 1901-1937* (London, 1953), letter of 7 November 1921.

100. Gleeson White: The pictures of Gustave Moreau, *The Pageant* (1897), p. 3 ff.

101. Ditto, p. 11.

102. G. Michaud *Message Poétique* II, p. 221.

103. Catalogue of etchings and lithographs by Rodolphe Bresdin, Print Room Amsterdam, 1955, cat. no. 45.

104. Rewald *Post Impressionism,* p. 166 ff.

105. Cf. e.g. Jan Veth: Odilon Redons lithografische Serien, *Kunst und Künstler* (III, 1903), p. 104.

106. E.g. Odilon Redon: '*A soi-même*', *Journal 1867-1915* (1922, Paris), p. 71.

107. In *L'art moderne* 1883, cited by Jules Destrée: *L'oeuvre lithografique de Odilon Redon* (Brussel, 1891), p. 8.

108. Michaud *Message Poétique* III, p. 644.

CHAPTER IV:

1. This term may be read in English as well as in French. Cf. Windelband, p. 377 ff.

2. Rewald *Impressionism,* p. 234, cf. p. 271 ff.

3. Cf. Windelband-Heimsoeth, p. 381, about Hume.

4. Gauss: *Aesthetic Theories,* p. 21, 22; cf. Duranty: *La nouvelle peinture,* p. 39.

5. Rewald *Impressionism,* p. 131.

6. Rewald *Impressionism,* p. 431.

7. Cf. L. Venturi: *Cézanne* (Paris, 1936), p. 29.

8. See e.g. P. A. Scholes: *The Oxford Companion to Music* (Oxford, 1947 [7]), s.v. Impressionism.

9. Fontainas *Souvenirs,* p. 91 ff.

10. Rewald *Impressionism,* p. 119.

11. Cf. Lehmann, p. 102/3.

12. P. Signac: *D'Eugène Delacroix au Néo-Impressionnisme* (Ed. La Revue Blanche, 1899), p. 21.

13. Laprade: *Seurat* (1945) cited from a letter of Seurat to Beaubourg of 1890: Le moyen d'expression est le mélange optique des tons, des teintes ... etc. (The means of expression are found in the optical mixing of tones and hues.)

14. Rewald *Post Impressionism,* p. 100 passim.

15. Cf. Rewald *Seurat,* concerning his apprenticeship, when he made copies of Rafael, Holbein, Ingres, etc.

16. Article in *L'Art Moderne* (1st May 1887), cited by Rewald *Post Impressionism,* p. 99.

17. Verhaeren: Le salon des Vingt à Bruxelles, *La Vie Moderne* (Feb. 26, 1887), cited by Rewald *Post Impressionism,* p. 104.

18. R. J. Goldwater: Some aspects of the development of Seurat's style. *Art Bulletin* (XXIII 1941), p. 124.

19. Gauguin had in his cabin at Atuana among others a photograph of Puvis' Hope—of which he had made a lithography at an earlier date. Cf. Rewald *Post Impressionism,* p. 162, 459. And in a letter to Fontainas of 1899 (Malingue CLXX) Gauguin wrote: 'Puvis de Chavannes (en) est le haut example'. (Puvis de Chavannes is the best example).

20. Cf. Aurier: Les symbolistes, *Revue encyclopédique* (April, 1892), cited by Rewald *Post Impressionism,* p. 165.

21. E. Bernard: *Erinnerungen an Paul Cézanne* (Basle, 1917), transl. H. Graber, p. 34, 35; G. Geffroy: *La vie artistique* III, 1894, p. 249.

22. Rewald *Impressionism,* p. 356, 358.

23. Cézanne *Correspondances,* p. 98/99, letter of 1866.

24. Cited in L. Venturi: *Cézanne, son art, son oeuvre* (Paris, 1936), letter to Maus of 1889 on p. 42.

269

25. Those of Gasquet and of Vollard.

26. Rewald *Impressionism,* p. 324.

27. Rewald *Impressionism,* p. 358.

28. Rewald *Cézanne et Zola,* p. 286.

29. Rewald *Post Impressionism,* p. 308.

30. Cf. F. Bonger-v. d. Borch van Verwolde: Vincent van Gogh als lezer, *Maandblad voor Beeldende kunsten* (Maart, 1950) and M. E. Tralbaut: *Vincent van Gogh in zijn Antwerpse periode* (Amsterdam, 1948).

31. Cf. *Brieven* No 423 from his early period.

32. Rewald Post *Impressionism,* p. 338, *Brieven* IV T 10.

33. *Brieven* No. 615.

34. *Brieven* No. 566—he says to do so under Delacroix' influence. Cf. IV B 19.

35. Malingue LXXVIII, letter of Dec. 1888.

36. *Brieven* 626 a, and 595.

37. *Brieven* IV B 21.

38. Karl Jaspers: *Strindberg und van Gogh. Versuch einer pathografischen Analyse under vergleichender Heranziehung von Swedenborg und Hölderlin* (1926, Berlin), p. 124 ff.

39. Rewald *Post Impressionism,* p. 371.

40. *Brieven* IV B 8, cited by Rewald *Post Impressionism,* p. 235.

41. *Brieven* No. 554, cited by Rewald *Post Impressionism,* p. 235.

42. *Brieven* No. 520.

43. *Brieven* IV R. 30.

44. Cf. R. Huyghe: *Le carnet de Paul Gauguin* (Paris, 1952), p. 78.

45. E. Klossowski: *Die Maler von Montmartre* (Berlin, 1903), p. 5 passim. A. Barre *Le symbolisme,* p. 67 ff.

46. Maurice Kunel: *Félicien Rops* (Bruxelles, 1943), p. 30 ff.

CHAPTER V:

1. Denis *Théories,* p. 160.

2. Delacroix *Journal* 9 April, 1856.

3. Aurier *Oeuvres,* p. 301.

4. Cf. Note a Chapter II.

5. Morice *Gauguin*, p. 243.

6. As is said with emphasis by Denis *Théories*, p. 33.

7. Morice *Gauguin,* p. 37.

CHAPTER VI:

1. Cf. e.g. letter from Arles to Bernard, Malingue no. LXXVIII, p. 154.

2. Rewald *Post Impressionism,* p. 74, 75, 186.

3. Rewald *Impressionism,* p. 378/9.

4. Rewald *Impressionism,* p. 323, 351.

5. Page 130.

6. Rewald *Post Impressionism,* p. 187.

7. Rewald *ditto,* p. 190.

8. Rewald *ditto,* p. 56.

9. Rewald *ditto,* p. 195 repr.

10. Cf. list of Bernard's works by H. H. Hofstätter: *Die Entstehung des 'Neuen Stils' in der französischen Malerei um 1890* (Freiburg im Breisgau, 1954) (mimeographed), p. 258.

11. Van Gogh *Brieven* B 21, cited by Rewald *Post Impressionism,* p. 363/4.

12. Cf. e.g. his statements in connection with his 'potato-eaters', collected by Dr. J. G. van Gelder: *De aardappeleters van Van Gogh* (Amsterdam, Antwerpen, 1949), p. 10 and 11.

13. See Rewald *Post Impressionism,* p. 22, 56/9; Hofstätter, p. 27/29.

14. Cf. e.g. Van Gogh *Brieven* B 9 (end of June 1888) in which Van Gogh discusses one of his poems.

15. Michaud *Message Poétique,* p. 327 ff.

16. Rewald *Post Impressionism,* p. 148.

17. Dargenty *Delacroix,* p. 125.

18. Rewald *Post Impressionism,* p. 193.

19. Denys Sutton: The Paul Gauguin Exhibition, *Burl. Mag.* (XCI 1949), p. 285, note 26.

20. Rewald *Post Impressionism,* p. 197 repr.

271

21. See Rewald *Post Impressionism,* p. 191 reproduction in connection with the letter to Schuffenecker, Malingue LXVI, p. 133.

22. Van Gogh *Brieven* 539—cited by Rewald *Post Impressionism,* p. 201.

23. See Hofstätter, p. 66.

24. Malingue **LXXV.**

25. In a letter to Schuffenecker, Malingue LXVII.

26. Rewald *Post Impressionism,* p. 192 repr.

27. Rewald *Post Impressionism,* p. 61 repr.

28. Chassé *Le mouvement symboliste,* p. 99.

29. Rewald *Post Impressionism,* p. 193 cites articles of Bernard of 1934 on Anquetin and another of 1940 concerning the history of symbolism.

30. Van Gogh *Brieven* No. 539.

31. In a letter by Gauguin to Van Gogh, Rewald *Post Impressionism,* p. 202, not published before.

32. Van Gogh *Brieven* No. 531.

33. Rewald *Post Impressionism,* p. 209, where again a not published letter of Gauguin is cited.

34. Cf. reproduction Rewald *Post Impressionism,* p. 254.

35. Van Gogh *Brieven* No. 562.

36. Rewald *Post Impressionism,* p. 255 repr.

37. Van Gogh *Brieven* B 21.

38. Ditto 533 and 555.

39. Rewald *Post Impressionism,* p. 206.

40. Denis *Théories,* p. 160.

41. Rewald *Post Impressionism,* p. 272.

42. Rewald *Post Impressionism,* p. 282 ff.

43. Cf. Malingue LXXXV, XCII, XCIV; Rewald *Post Impressionism,* p. 289.

44. Repr. Rewald *Post Impressionism,* p. 295.

45. Repr. Rewald *Post Impressionism,* p. 299; Cf. Denys Sutton: The Paul Gauguin Exhibition, *Burl. Mag.* (XCI, 1949), p. 284.

46. Repr. Rewald *Post Impressionism,* p. 299.

47. Rewald *Post Impressionism,* p. 298.

48. Morice *Gauguin,* p. 25/29; cf. Rewald *Post Impressionism,* p. 489, note 25 and p. 452.

48a. C. Chassé *Le mouvement symboliste,* p. 69.

49. Rewald *Post Impressionism,* cites a letter published by J. Loize: Un inédit de P.G., *Nouvelles Littéraires* (May 7, 1953).

50. Concerning these 'poètes maudits' and the meaning to be attached to this term, cf. P. Rodenko: Baudelaire en de 'poètes maudits', *Maatstaf* (V 3/4 Juni/ Juli, 1957), p. 198 ff.

51. Repr. Rewald *Post Impressionism,* p. 451.

52. Rewald *Post Impressionism,* p. 455.

53. Rotonchamp *Gauguin,* p. 21.

54. Malingue **CLXVI**.

55. Morice *Gauguin,* p. 37.

56. *Avant et Après,* p. 1.

57. Rewald *Post Impressionism,* p. 466/7 and Denys Sutton: La perte du Pucelage by Paul Gauguin, *Burl. Mag.* (XCI 1949), p. 103.

CHAPTER VII:

1. Cf. A. Fontainas: *Mes souvenirs du symbolisme* (Paris, 1928), p. 31 ff.

2. Morice *La littérature,* p. 175.

3. Cf. Windelband-Heimsoeth, p. 221 ff., Dr. R. J. Dam: Karakter en functie van het lelijke, *Philosophia Reformata* (VI, 1941), p. 105 ff., especially, p. 126/7;

H. Dooyeweerd: Grondthema's van het wijsgerig denken van het avondland, *Philosophia Reformata* (VI, 1941), p. 169, 170.

4. Morice *La littérature,* p. 267.

5. Rewald *Post Impressionism,* p. 454/5.

6. Cf. note a, chapter II.

7. Cf. page 77.

8. Cf. page 73.

9. Literature dealing with Mallarmé: G. Delfel: *L'esthétique de S.M.* (Paris, 1951) (review by C. Lalo *Revue d'Esthétique* (VI, 1, 1953), p. 108); A. Barre: *Le symbolisme* (Paris, 1911), p. 198 ff. M. Raymond: *From Baudelaire to Surrealism* (New York, 1950), p. 23 ff; G. Michaud: *Le message poétique du symbolisme* (I, Paris, 1948), p. 159 ff.; J. Huret: *Enquête sur l'évolution litteraire*

(Paris, 1891), p. 60 passim; A. Poizat: *Le symbolisme de Baudelaire à Claudel* (Paris, 1919), p. 70 ff.; A. G. Lehmann: *The symbolist esthetics in France 1885-1895* (Oxford, 1950), p. 50 ff. and passim; *Poésies complètes de Stéphane Mallarmé,* (textes et notes p. Yves-Gérard le Dantec, Paris 1948).

10. Cf. N. Westendorp Boerma: Engelse Verlichting van Francis Bacon to David Hume, in *Philosophia* II, (ed. H. v. Oyen, Utrecht, 1949), p. 87 on Berkeley.

11. Lehmann *Symbolist Aesthetics,* p. 162.

12. See note al.

13. Cf. G. Mauclair: *Servitude et grandeur littéraires* (Paris, 1922), p. 29 ff.

14. Here and elsewhere we have presupposed a general knowledge of Gauguin's life. Therefore we do not feel compelled to refer to existing literature when facts like these are concerned.

15. Cf. Rewald *Post Impressionism,* p. 400.

16. Cf. Malingue CII, CIII, CV, etc.

17. Malingue CXXVII.

18. Rewald *Post Impressionism,* p. 191, 192, 366.

19. Ditto, p. 366.

20. Cf. Rewald *Post Impressionism,* p. 559. This knowledge is implied in his statements on quite a number of painters.

21. Aurier 2, p. 296, 304. (Cf. note au.)

22. Aurier 2 p. 294.

23. Aurier 2 p. 301.

24. Baudelaire *Art Romantique,* p. 311 ff.

25. Cf. p. 142.

26. Aurier 1 p. 164. (Cf. note aw.)

27. Aurier 1 p. 162.

28. Cf. p. 161.

29. Aurier 1 p. 460.

30. *Lettres à Daniel de Monfreid,* Oct. 1897, p. 113.

31. Denis *Théories,* p. 162.

32. Above p. 137 ff.

33. Rewald *Post Impressionism,* p. 498, note 10, p. 536.

34. Denis *Théories,* Préface.

35. In a letter, summer 1893, to Verkade, in *A.B.C. de la peinture* (1950), p. 66.

36. Cf. p. 28 ff.

37. *Cur. Esth.*, p. 92, 272.

38. *Cur. Esth.*, p. 241.

39. Baudelaire *Art Romantique*, p. 207 ff. cited here on page 30.

40. *Cur. Esth.*, p. 274.

41. Cf. p. 15 ff.

42. Baudelaire *Art Romantique*, p. 317, cited here on page 30.

43. Cf. p. 146 ff.

44. Denis *Nouvelles Théories*, cited by Ch. Chassé: *le Mouvement symboliste* (1947), p. 155.

45. *ABC de la peinture*, p. 7 ff.

46. In a letter to Denis of 29 Febr. 1915, *ABC de la peinture*, p. 146.

47. J. E. Blanche: *Les arts plastiques*, p. 243.

48. Bernard cites: *Oeuvres de Saint Denys l'Aréopagite* (trad. p. l'Abbé Dulac, Paris 1865).

49. Cf. p. 134.

CHAPTER VIII:

1. Cited in F. D. Klingender: *Art and the industrial revolution* (London, 1947), p. 31.

2. Cf. E. Littré in *Dictionnaire de la langue française* (Paris, 1889), s.v. 'synthèse'. Also A. Lalande: *Vocabulaire technique et critique de la philosophie* (Paris, 1951).

3. See note t of this Chapter.

4. Cf. Denis *Théories*, p. 164.

5. Windelband-Heimsoeth, p. 505/512 passim.

6. Cf. a.o. Michaud: *Message poétique*, p. 200; Lehmann *Symbolist Aesthetics*, p. 37 ff.; Fontainas *Mes Souvenirs*, p. 110.

7. Cited by H. J. Hak: *Marsilio Ficino* (Amsterdam, 1934), p. 102. Cf. A. Chastel: *Marsile Ficin et l'Art* (Genève, Lille, 1954), p. 64/65.

8. Rewald *Post Impressionism,* p. 298.

9. Ditto, p. 281.

10. See pag. 182.

11. Cf. Lehmann *Symbolist Aesthetics,* p. 85 ff.

12. Cf. George Levitine: Literary Sources of Goya's Capricho 43, *Art Bulletin* (XXXVII, 1, 1955), p. 56. See also chapter II, p. 12 ff.

13. Bernard: Ce que c'est que l'Art Mystique, *Mercure de France* (XIII 1895), p. 28.

14. Aurier: Le Symbolisme en peinture, P. Gauguin, *Mercure de France* (II, 1891), p. 155.

15. *Sartor Resartus,* p. 254.

16. See Thesis IV to Hak's dissertation on Ficino: 'The theology of Ficino distinguishes itself in this from Scholasticism and Neo-Platonism, that it declares the human spirit to be independent of God and of matter and makes it the centre of the Universe.'

17. Cf. Hak *Ficino,* p. 102. Also A. Chastel *Marsile Ficin,* p. 65.

18. A. Kuyper: *The antithesis between Symbolism and Revelation,* p. 9.

19. Ditto, p. 10.

20. Ditto, p. 10.

21. R. Kroner: The year 1800 in the development of German Idealism, *Review of Metaphysics* (I, 4, June, 1948), p. 22.

22. *Ongeloof en Revolutie* (Kampen, 1904), p. 347 ff.

23. Cf., the article cited in note 21, p. 7: 'No longer do the practical issues, the ideals of moral man, the principles of volition and action dominate thought, but instead intuition and imagination, contemplation and speculation assume supremacy.'

24. Kuyper *op. cit.,* p. 13.

25. Ditto, p. 14.
26. Ditto, p. 15, 16.

27. Ditto, p. 16.

28. Lehmann: *Symbolist Aesthetics,* p. 306.

29. W. B. Yeats: *Collected Works* (Stratford-on-Avon, 1908); especially VI, Ideas on Good and Evil; concerning Magic, p. 23 ff., on symbolism in painting, p. 176, p. 224. Cf. Holbrook Jackson: *The eighteen ninetees,* p. 69, 147 ff; Lehmann: *Symbolist Aesthetics,* p. 281 ff.

276

30. Lehmann: *op. cit.*, p. 308.

31. Ditto, p. 313.

32. Ditto, p. 306.

33. M. Denis: Introduction to the *Catalogue of the exhibition 'Französische Kunst des XIX. Jahrhunderts'*, Zürcher Kunsthaus, Oct.-Nov. 1917, p. 10.

34. Morice: *Gauguin*, p. 225 e.g.

35. Ditto, p. 44.

36. See page 205/6.

37. *Poetica* I, 2 and 4. A. Gudeman: *Aristoteles über die Dichtkunst* (Leipzig, 1921), p. 1.

38. Cited by Abrams: *Mirror and the Lamp*, p. 92.

39. Edition of 1852, pp. 129/130.

40. See p. 194 and note bc.

41. Diverses Choses, cited by Rotonchamp, *Gauguin*, p. 214. Cf. note dp.

42. Ruskin: *Works* XX, Aratra Pentelici 207. Cited by C. Dougherty: Ruskin's views on non-representational art, *College Art Journal* (XV, 2, 1955), p. 114.

43. Dougherty: *op. cit.*

44. Ditto, p. 117.

45. M. Raymond: *From Baudelaire to Surrealism* (New York, 1950), p. 46/47.

46. J. Huret: *Enquête sur l'évolution littéraire* (Paris, 1891), p. 60.

47. Cf. Michaud: *Message poétique*, p. 190.

48. Ditto, p. 172.

49. Cf. W. H. Beuken: *Ruusbroec en de Middeleeuwse Mystiek* (Utrecht, Brussel, 1946); J. W. Tunderman: *Marnix van St. Aldegonde en de subjectivistische stromingen in de 16e eeuw,* Chapter II: Subjectivistische Themata in de eeuwen voor de Reformatie (Goes, z.j.), p. 26.

50. Aurier: Le symbolisme en peinture, P. Gauguin, *Mercure de France* (II, 1891), p. 159.

51. W. Haftmann: *Malerei im 20. Jahrhundert* (München, 1954), p. 77; *Dekorative Kunst,* Ill. Zeitschrift für angewandte Kunst (I, München, 1898), p. 75/76, an article by A. Endell.

CHAPTER IX:

1. Cf. B. Smith: European Vision and the South Pacific, *Journal of the Warburg and Courtauld Society* (XIII, 1950), p. 65.

2. H. La Fargue: John la Fargue and the South Sea Idyll, *Journal of the Warburg and Courtauld Society* (VII, 1944), p. 34; F. Fairchild Sherman: Some early oil paintings by John la Fargue, *Art in America* (Feb. 1920), p. 85.

3. Charles Kunstler: *Gauguin, peintre maudit* (Paris, 1934), p. 8.

4. P. Gauguin: *Ancien Culte Mahorie,* Présentation par R. Huyghe. Le Clef de Noa Noa (Paris, 1951).

5. Malingue CXXVII.

6. Morice: *Gauguin,* p. 190.

7. Noa Noa p. 29, cited by Morice: *Gauguin,* p. 199.

8. Cf. e.g. H. Kauffmann: Jan van Eyck's Arnolfini's Hochzeit, *Geistige Welt* (1950, 2), p. 45; J. G. van Gelder: *De Schilderkunst van Jan Vermeer* (Utrecht, 1958).

9. *Modern Painters* I, p. 12.

10. P. Rodenko: Baudelaire en de 'Poètes maudits', *Maatstaf* (V, 2/3, 1957), p. 220.

11. Bettina Polak: *Fin de siècle,* p. 37, 67.

12. *Sartor Resartus,* p. 193.

13. Ditto, p. 254/5.

14. Ditto, p. 306.

15. Repr. Rewald *Post Impressionism,* p. 295. Cf. D. Sutton: The Paul Gauguin Exhibition, *Burlington Magazine* (XCI, 1949), p. 284.

16. H. Taine: *L'idéalisme anglais, étude sur Carlyle* (1864), p. 108.

17. B. Dorival: Sources of the art of Paul Gauguin from Java, Egypt and Ancient Greece, *Burlington Magazine* (XCIII, 1951), p. 118.

18. See Chapter VI, note an.

19. *Lettres à de Monfreid,* p. 113, Oct. '97.

20. As e.g. Th. Craven: *Modern Art, the men, the movements, the meaning* (New York, 1940), p. 118 ff.

21. Cf. Malingue CLXVIII.

22. Ditto.

23. Michaud *Message Poétique,* p. 174; G. Delfel: *L'esthétique de Stéphane Mallarmé,* p. 34 ff.

24. Malingue CLXXVI.

The Arabic numbers refer to the pages in the book, the Roman numbers (indicating a Chapter) followed by one or two letters refer to the Notes to be found in the booklet at the back of this book.

971

TRANSLATIONS, EXPLICATIONS AND
ELABORATIONS

NOTES IN LETTERS

pertaining to

SYNTHETIST ART THEORIES

by

DR. H. R. ROOKMAAKER

The reproduction given on the title page of this booklet is from a zinkograph of Gauguin, 'Les drames de la mer, Bretagne', in the Print Room, Amsterdam.

NOTES IN LETTERS

In this booklet are given translations of all the quotations that are found in the text of the book in French, or in other non-English languages. Beside these there are some explicatory notes. The user is adverted that in some cases under one entry a translation as well as an explication or elaboration of some topic is inserted.

References and other mere indications of literature etc. are to be found at the end of the book - referred to by numbers.

Some *abbreviations* used in the notes:

Windelband-Heimsoeth: W. Windelband *Lehrbuch der Ge-schichte der Philosophie,* ed. H. Heim-soeth, (Tübingen 1948 [14])

Cur. Esth. : C. Baudelaire *Curiosités Esthétiques* (Paris 1921)

Ferran *Esth.* : A. Ferran *L'Esthétique de Baudelaire* (Paris 1933)

Malingue : M. Malingue *Lettres de Gauguin à sa femme et à ses amis* (Paris 1946)

Denis *Théories* : M. Denis *Théories 1890-1910* (Paris 1912 [2])

ABC de la peinture : P. Sérusier *ABC de la peinture suivi d'une correspondance inédite* (Paris 1950)

Other abbreviations used will be so evident that there is no need to quote them here.

CHAPTER I:

a. 'Le XIXième siècle, après avoir, quatre-vingt ans, proclamé, dans son enthousiasme enfantin, l'omnipotence de l'observation et de la déduction scientifiques, après avoir affirmé qu'aucun mystère ne subsistait devant ses lentilles et ses scalpels, semble enfin s'apercevoir de la vanité de ses efforts, de la puérilité de ses vantardises. L'homme marche toujours au milieu des mêmes énigmes, dans ce même formidable inconnu, devenu plus obscur encore et plus troublant depuis qu'on s'est déshabitué de le considérer. Bien des savants, aujourd'hui, s'arrêtent avec découragement, comprenant enfin que cette érudition expérimentale, dont ils tiraient vanité, a moins de certitude mille fois que la plus bizarre théogonie, que la plus folle rêverie métaphysique, que le moins acceptable rêve de poète, et pressentant que cette hautaine science, qu'ils appelaient en leur fierté, positive, n'est peut-être que la science des relativités, des apparences, des 'ombres' comme disait Platon, et qu'ils n'ont, eux, rien à mettre dans les vieux Olympes dont ils ont arraché les divinités et décroché les astres.' G.-A. Aurier: *Les peintres symbolistes,* pp. 293 ff.

b. 'the short-sighted copy of social anecdotes, the imbecile imitation of the warts of nature, the flat observation, the optical illusion, the glory of being as faithfully and vulgarly exact as a daguerréotype.' G.-A. Aurier: *Les peintres symbolistes,* p. 294.

c. 'At the beginning of the 19th century art is no longer a language as it used to be formerly, in every country, with the memory of beautiful traditions. It is in a way a kind of volapuk formed with the aid of recipes. A unique language taught by certified teachers, giving the assurance of perfection and of an immense mediocrity. This volapuk is still spoken . . .' P. Gauguin: *Racontars d'un rapin,* p. 61/62; here as quoted, a bit shortened, by Kunstler, p. 177.

d. They were even able to appeal to Ingres himself. Ingres, *Raconté par lui-même et ses amis,* (Paris, 1947), pp. 48/49, 64/65. See also in this connection the pictures of painters of the 'Salons' collected by F. Jourdain in 'L'art officiel de Jules Grévy à Albert Lebrun', *le Point* (XXXVII, 7, April, 1949, Souillac). They prove—and this is even more marked in these black-and-white reproductions, of course—that the nudes at the Salons, only differ from the photos obtainable at present in 'photobooks' under the style of studies from the model or 'Nudes', as far as the material—in the literal sence of the word—and the proportions are concerned. In these this 'art' has sought a 'refuge' now that the walls of the museums have been denied to it. These photos are made for the same kind of public which, however, must do without the sanction that the kind of work it desires is 'great art.'.

e. 'an obligatory brothel'. Gauguin: *Racontars d'un rapin,* p. 70.

f. There has been a recent attempt made by Sloane to promote Henri Regnault, who died in 1870, to a real master of the Salon-world. The question whether or not Regnault's work justifies such an attempt can only be settled after more work of his can be seen together. Cf. J. C. Sloane, *French Art between the Past and the Present, Artists, Critics and Traditions from 1848 to 1870* (Princeton, New Jersey),

3

1951, pp. 176 ff. Neither of the work of this artist, nor of that of Bastien-Lepage or Lhermitte, do we find a reproduction in the fiercely critical publication of Jourdain mentioned in our previous note (see note d). They are no good instances of taste-lessness and artistic emptiness.

g. 'Without your being aware of it, this academy is a mistress who prevents a warmer and more serious, more fruitful love from awakening in you—Leave this mistress alone, and fall in love over head and ears with your real beloved one, dame nature or reality... She renews, she gives fresh vigour and courage, she gives life!...' Van Gogh: *Brieven* IV, R. 4.

h. 'floods of articles of a purely commercial nature ... there would be no question at all of art, no artists, but simply of a luxury industry. *Mercure de France*, (III, 1891,) p. 30.

i. 'mediocrity ... prevails more than ever.' *Cur. Esth.* Salon 1859, I, p. 248.

CHAPTER II:

a. Humanism as a view of life and the world arose in the fifteenth century and has dominated Western Culture since that time. It is always essentially driven on by a dynamic motif of a religious character. Its basic motif is found in the human freedom to selfconstitution. However, there is no absolute freedom realizable, as in the striving after such freedom the structure of reality operates as a counter instance to which also man is bound. This is especially true with respect to the natural aspects of reality with their unavoidable laws. The attempt is then made to make this nature subservient to man by submitting to its laws in order thus to realize the humanistic ideal. This, however, entails the risk that human freedom has to suffer. In this way there arises a dialectic of a fundamentally religious nature not necessarily avowed, as the issue is the basic attitude of man in the heart of his existence towards God, His creation and His law (or His norms). Compare with this, e.g. Delacroix's pro-nouncements referred to in note aa); and also *Oeuvres Littéraires* I, p. 115: 'L'homme domine la nature et en est dominé. Il est le seul être de la création qui, non seulement lui résiste, mais la dompte ou en élude les lois et qui étende son empire par sa volonté et son activité. Mais que la création ait été fait pour lui, c'est une proposition qui est loin d'être évidente...' ('Man dominates nature and is domi-nated by it. He is the only being of the creation who does not only resist it, but subjects it or eludes its laws and who extends his empire by his will and his activity. But that the creation was made for him is a proposition which is far from evident...') Compare a more detailed account of these things in H. Dooyeweerd: *A New Critique of Theoretical Thought*, (Amsterdam 1955), pp. 169 ff.; *Trans-cendental Problems of Philosophic Thought* (Grand Rapids, Mich. 1948), p. 73 ff. and 'De transcendentale critiek van het wijsgerig denken en de grondslagen van de wijsgerige denkgemeenschap van het avondland', *Philosophia Reformata*, (VI, 1941) pp. 1 ff., and his: 'De vier religieuze grondthema's in de ontwikkelingsgang van het wijsgerig denken van het avondland', *Philosophia Reformata* (VI, 1941) pp. 161 ff.

4

b. 'a nook of nature viewed through a temperament'. On Zola, cf. L. Venturi: *Histoire de la critique d'art*, p. 300, with a.o. quotations from his Salon of 1866. Ditto, Rewald: *Impressionism*, pp. 123 ff.

c. Very telling is the text that Goya wrote on the drawing for his etching No. 43: 'Ydioma universal. El autor soñando. Su yntento solo es desterrar bulgaridades perjuciales y perpetuar con esta obra de caprichos el testimonio sólido de la verdad' ('Universal idiom. The author dreaming. His only purpose is to make an end to senseless prejudices and to perpetuate with this work of caprichos the testimony only of truth.') F. J. Sanchez Canton: *Los Caprichos de Goya y sus debujos preparatorios*, (Barcelona 1949) p. 87.

d. To prevent confusion we shall have to make a sharp distinction between the terms naturalism and realism. Naturalism refers to the way of representing things. It is the attempt to call up an image, analogous to what the eye sees, by means of lines and colours, and as accurately as possible. Realism is concerned with the subjects, the facts represented. In realism the artist only wants to depict what can be observed in the reality around him. Thus, e.g., an angel (a nonrealistic subject) may be rendered in a naturalistic way—recall van Eyck—while it is also possible to represent a realistic theme in a non-naturalistic way—e.g., by means of colour symbols, expressive lines elucidating the meaning of what is depicted, as is often done by the expressionists. As a matter of fact every caricature is realistic—non naturalistic.

e. 'these contortions, these bestial faces, these diabolical grimaces are penetrated by humanity.' *Cur. Esth.* Caricaturistes Etrangers II, p. 430.

f. 'all the vices the human mind can conceive of.' *Cur. Esth.* p. 428.

g. The first edition of articles etc. by Delacroix appeared in 1865, the editor being Piron, but this impression consisted of a very small number of copies. His 'Journal' was published in 1893, compiled by Paul Flat and René Picot, whereas some time before a number of his letters had been published by Burty, in two volumes, one of 1878 and one of 1880. Baudelaire's work was easily accessible in the publication of the Curiosités Esthétiques, Collected 'Salons', supplemented by a few other articles, in 1884, and there was also a great deal to be found of his works, e.g., in the prefaces to the translations of Poe's works.

h. 'one should make ... sketch-like pictures that had the freedom and the frankness of rough drafts.' Delacroix: *Journal*, 5 Oct. 1847.

i. 'it looks as if the tones have been assembled by luck and the lines of the composition have been arranged by chance. The poetic or expressive idea does not strike one at the first glance'. Delacroix: *Journal*, 19 Sept. 1847.

k. 'There is an impression evoked by a certain arrangement of colours, lights and shadows etc. .... This is what one would call the music of the picture ...' Delacroix: *Oeuvres littéraires*, I. pp. 63, 64, also quoted by Ferran *Esth.* p. 147.

1. 'the artist's imagination not only represents to himself such and such objects, but combines them for the purpose he wants to realize; it produces pictures, images he composes as he pleases.' Delacroix: *Oeuvres littéraires,* III, p. 45, quoted by M. Gilman: *Baudelaire the Critic,* (New York '43) p. 226.

m. 'but if, to a composition already interesting by the choice of subject, you add a disposition of lines which increases the impression, a chiariscuro which catches the imagination, a color adapted to the character, you have resolved a more difficult problem and once more, you are superior: it is harmony and its combinations adapted to a song which is unique'. Delacroix *Journal* 1853, May 20, quoted in English J. C. Sloane: *French Art 1850-1870;* (1951), p. 115.

n. 'Our moderns no longer paint the feelings, they describe the exterior, they analyse everything.' Delacroix *Journal* 9 April, 1856.

o. 'my intentions are more pronounced and useless particulars have been removed.' Delacroix *Journal,* 12 October, 1853.

p. 'the most careful execution of details will not give that unity which results from I do not know what creative power whose origin is indefinable.' Delacroix in notes for 'Le réalisme et l'idéalisme' quoted by R. Rey: *La Renaissance du sentiment classique,* p. 25.

q. Of course, we need not think of a particular philosopher, but, more generally, of the way in which the epistemological problem regarding the relation of man to reality was posited and the direction in which the answer was sought.

r. 'The fact counts for nothing because it will pass. Nothing is left but the idea; in reality the fact even exists only in the idea, since the latter lends its colour to it ... (This is) what happens when the creative faculty seizes the idea in order to animate the real world given in the transitory facts and to derive from them pictures of the imagination. It composes, i.e. it idealizes and selects.' Delacroix *Oeuvres Littéraires* I, p. 114, quoted by M. Gilman: *Baudelaire the Critic,* (New York, '43), p. 226.

s. 'These figures, these objects, which seem to be the things themselves to a certain part of your intelligent being, seem to be a solid bridge on which the imagination leans in order to penetrate to the mysterious and profound sensations of which the forms are somehow the hieroglyph.' Delacroix *Journal* 17 Oct. 1853. Cf. *Journal* 14 May 1824.

t. This old method was certainly not primitive or naïve because science had not yet advanced sufficiently and so there was no possibility of exactness. On the contrary, here we are confronted with a quite different conception of the past and its significance for the present, which was, therefore, reflected in the work of art. Cf. H. v. d. Waal: *Drie Eeuwen Vaderlandse Geschiedenis-Uitbeelding.* (Den Haag, 1952).

u. 'without this philosophy as I understand it there will be no duration for a book or a painting, or rather no existence.' Delacroix *Journal,* 17 Oct. 1853.

v. 'I wish to be taken to the dioramas whose bold and enormous magic can force their useful illusion on me ... These things are infinitely nearer to truth because they are false; whereas the majority of our landscapists are liars for the very reason that they have forgotten to lie.' *Cur. Esth.*, Salon 1859, VIII, p. 338.

w. 'a magnificent imagination'. *Cur. Esth.*, Salon 1859, VIII, p. 338.

x. 'the disorder and the shameless displays.' Ferran. *Esth.*, p. 500.

y. 'Pity me, or rather, pity us, for I have many fellows of my kind; it is the hatred of all and of ourselves that has induced us to tell lies like these. It is through the despair of ever attaining to nobility and beauty by natural means that we have painted our faces so strangely. We have so much laid ourselves out to sophisticate our hearts, we have so much abused the microscope to study the hideous excrescences and the disgraceful warts that cover our hearts and which we have a pleasure in enlarging that it is impossible for us to speak the language of other people ... We have altered the accent of nature, pulled out the decencies of virginity one by one that covered the honesty of our inner man. We have psychologized like fools who add to their folly by trying to understand it ... Woe, three times woe to our fathers who made us rachitic and undersized ...' Ferran *Esth.* p. 98.

z. We are referring here to Humanism as a view of life and the world. Cf. note a chapter II.

aa. Cf. also what Delacroix says about reality, inclusive of his own body, in his *Journal* of 4 June, 1824; 5 May, 1847; and 5 Sept. 1847; 'Est-il dans la création un être plus esclave que n'est l'homme? La faiblesse, les besoins, le font dépendre des éléments et de ses semblables ... Il ne veut non plus de la hierarchie en quoi que ce soit; c'est en quoi il trouve surtout le christianisme odieux ... soumission à la loi de la nature, résignation aux douleurs humaines, c'est le dernier mot de toute raison (et partant soumission à la loi écrite, divine ou humaine)' ('Is there in the creation a being that is more of a slave than man? His weakness, his needs make him dependent on the elements and on his equals ... He does not want any hierarchy either, in whatever it may consist; that is what he especially hates in Christianity ... submission to the law of nature, resignation to human sorrows, this is the last word of every reason (and consequently submission to the written law either divine or human)'.
The same thing also elsewhere in Baudelaire: 'La nature qui pose devant nous, de quelque côté que nous nous tournions, et qui nous enveloppe comme un mystère ...' ('Nature, which confronts us wherever we may turn, and envelops us like a mystery ...') *Art Romantique* p. 311.

ab. 'the hostility of the atmosphere'. Baudelaire: *Art Romantique*, p. 100.

ac. 'The complaint about the emptiness and nothingness of existence of a soul that had withered early in the storms of life.' M. v. Wedderkop: Paul Verlaine und die Lyrik der Décadence in Frankreich. *Pan.* (1896) pp. 69 ff.

ad. 'all this work ... is like a terrible hymn composed in honour of fatality and irremediable sorrow.' Baudelaire: *Art Romantique*, p. 30.

7

ae. 'O death!
　　Pour out your poison that it may comfort us!
　　This fire burns our brain so much that we wish
　　To plunge into the depths of the abyss, into hell
　　　　　　or into heaven, it does not matter!
　　Into the depth of the unknown to find something new.'
Also quoted by Barre: *Le Symbolisme*, p. 54.

af. 'at the bottom of the unknown.' Cf. also what he writes in connection with Hugo, *Art Romantique*, p. 318.

ag. This is why he wrote about the 'Fleurs du mal', (the flowers of evil), in which he wanted 'd'extraire la beauté du mal' (to extract beauty from evil). (*Fleurs du Mal,* ed. critique Jacques Crépet et Georges Blin (Paris, 1942), p. 211: Projet de Préface pour une édition nouvelle).

ah. 'What is pure art according to the modern conception? It is the creation of some suggestive magic comprising at once the object and the subject, the outer world and the artist himself.' Margaret Gilman: *Baudelaire the Critic*, p. 166.

ai. 'Romanticism does not exactly consist in the choice of subject, or in the exact truth, but in the manner of feeling. Above all one must know the aspects of nature and the situations of man which the artists of the past considered to be beneath them, or which they did not know.' *Cur. Esth.*, pp. 85/86

ak. 'Romanticism' here refers to Baudelaire's own ideals, not to the older movement.

al. 'la reine des facultés' (the queen of the faculties) comprises analysis and synthesis. Here the word 'synthesis' is intended to denote the opposite of analysis, and is not used in the sense indicated above—as later on the term is generally used, which we hope to prove.

am. 'It is the imagination that has taught man the moral sense of colour, outline, sound and smell. At the beginning of the world it created analogy and metaphor; it breaks up the whole of the creation, and with the materials collected and arranged according to rules the origin of which can only be found in the depths of the soul, it produces the sensation of what is new. Since it has created the world—one may put it like this, I believe, even in a religious sense—it is only right for it to rule.' *Cur. Esth.* pp. 264, 265.

an. As a matter of fact, throughout the century French contemporary philosophy had hardly any influence on the literati (and the painters), not even in those cases that clearly show spiritual affinity. Recall Ravaisson and Lachelier.

ao. 'The imagination is the queen of truth, and the possible is one of the provinces of the truth.' *Cur. Esth.* p. 263.

ap. 'The chief formula ... of true aesthetics' will be 'the whole of the visible creation is only a storehouse of images and signs to which the imagination assigns a place and a relative value; it is a kind of food that the imagination has to digest and transform.' *Cur. Esth.*, p. 274. Cf. Baudelaire: *Art Romantique*, p. 13.

aq. 'Everything must serve to illuminate the generative idea and still bear its own original colour, its livery, so to say.' *Cur. Esth.*, p. 272.

ar. 'the dream' is a vision produced by intense meditation.' *Cur. Esth.*, p. 289.

as. 'A picture must above all reproduce the intimate thought of the artist which dominates the model as the creator does the creation.' *Cur. Esth.*, p. 104.

at. This appears from his introduction to the 'Fleurs du Mal': 'In this atrocious book I have put all my heart, all my tenderness, all my religion (travestied), all my hate.' (Marcel Raymond: *From Baudelaire to Surréalism* (New York, 1950), p. 13. L'art pour l'art really meant the absolute liberty of the artist to treat anything he liked without heeding ethical or other norms. Cf. Recolin: *L'Anarchie littéraire* (Paris, 1898) p. 178, and J. Wilcox: La genèse de la théorie de l'art pour l'art en France. *Revue d'esthétique*, VI (1, 1953) p. 1 ff.

au. 'All this would have to be invented if it did not exist'. *Cur. Esth.*, p. 337.

av. 'The absence of what is just and true is equal to the absence of art', for 'the entire man has vanished.' Baudelaire: *Art Romantique*, p. 301.

aw. 'The imagination is the most scientific of the faculties, for it is the only one that understands the universal analogy or that which a mystical religion calls the 'correspondence.' *Correspondances* I, 130, publ. Gautier et le Dantec, commented on by M. Gilman: *Baudelaire the Critic*, (New York, 1943), p. 121.

ax. 'for all divine things are examples; intellectual, moral and civil things are types but the images of nature as such and things physical are merely likenesses.' M. Lamm: *Swedenborg, Ein Studie über seine Entwicklung zum Mystiker und Geisterseher*, (transl. Leipzig, 1922), p. 108, a quotation from Swedenborg's: '*Clavis Hieroplyphica arcanorum naturalium et spiritualium per viam Repraesentationum et Correspondentiarum*' (1784, London).

ay. 'The soul adds the form of the world to the four elements and provides them with it; but it is the intelligence which furnishes germinal reasons . . .' E. Bréhier: *La philosophie de Plotin* (Paris, 1928), p. 87, quoted from the *Enneads* V, 9, 3.

az. Humanistic taken in the sence of classical philology (so not in the meaning of the life and world view of modern times).

ba. The freedom motive was concretized in the life and world view (cf. note a, ch. II) as the ideal of man as an autonomous rational-moral personality, whereas the motive of nature found expression in the science-ideal, the idea that man can (only) gain an insight into reality by means of the (natural)-sciences. Cf. also the writings quoted by Prof. Dr. H. Dooyeweerd in note a.

bb. 'The eternal dialectic of idea and facts that has always tormented him is at last resolved by Balzac in favour of the idea, but the facts remain in his work as the images of the idea.' H. Evans: *Louis Lambert et la philosophie de Balzac*, (Paris, 1951), p. 250; Compare: Balzac: *Louis Lambert*, (ed. Conrad), p. 104, quoted by J. v. d. Elst: Autour du 'Livre Mystique': Balzac et Swedenborg, *Revue de la littérature comparée*, (X, 1930), p. 92.

9

bc. (It would be amazing) 'if sound could not suggest colour, or colours could not give the idea of a melody, and if sound and colour were unfit for the translation of ideas; things have always been expressed by reciprocal analogy (another word for 'correspondance') since the day God produced the world as a complex and indivisible totality.' Baudelaire *Art Romantique,* art. on Wagner, pp. 207 ff., quoted by Lehmann, *Symbolist Aesth.*, p. 264.

bd. 'We cannot but arrive at this truth that everything is hieroglyphic, and we know that symbols are only relatively obscure, i.e., according to the degree of purity, benevolence or innate clear-sightedness of the souls. Well, what is a poet—I take the word in its widest sense—if not a translator, a decipherer? With all good poets there is no question of metaphors, comparisons, or epithets which are not mathematically exact adaptations in the actual circumstances, because these comparisons, metaphors and epithets have been drawn from the inexhaustible source of universal analogy and they cannot be drawn from anywhere else.' Baudelaire: *Art Romantique,* p. 317.

be. 'It is this admirable, immortal instinct of the beautiful which makes us consider the earth and its spectacles as a summary, a correspondence of Heaven.' Baudelaire: *Art Romantique,* pp. 166-173 and: *The Poems of Edgar Allen Poe,* (London, New York, 1900) pp. 191, 192.

bf. 'The unquenchable thirst for all that is beyond and is revealed by life is the most striking proof of our immortality'. Ditto.

bg. 'It is at once by and through poetry, by and through music that the soul gets a glimpse of the splendours beyond the grave.' Ditto.

bh. 'Those tears are evidence of sensitive melancholy . . . of a nature exiled in what is imperfect, and which would immediately seize upon a revealed Paradise on this very earth.' Ditto.

bi. It might be possible to posit that Poe starts more directly from Plato, whereas Baudelaire's thought rather goes in the direction of Plotinus. For the latter has converted the Platonic Eros which strives after the highest into the knowledge of the intelligible. In the third chapter we shall revert to the relation between Plato and Plotinus.

bk. 'I wish to illuminate things with my mind and project their reflex on other minds.' *Cur. Esth.*, p. 275.

bl. This was also Delacroix's thought. 'Il est donc beaucoup plus important pour l'artiste de se rapprocher de l'idéal qu'il porte en lui, et qui lui est particulier, que de laisser, même avec force, l'idéal passagère que peut presenter la nature . . .' (*Journal* 12 Oct. 1853, II, p. 87). Cf. M. Gilman: *Baudelaire the Critic* (New York, 1943), p. 39. (It is, therefore, much more important for the artist to approach the ideal that he carries within himself and which is peculiar to him, than to give —even if it is done with vigour—the fleeting ideal presented by nature . . . ').

bm. 'The ideal is the individual restored by the individual'. *Cur. Esth.*, p. 140.

bn. This thought is also found in Delacroix, who, most probably, influenced him directly in this matter. *Cur. Esth.*, p. 105. Cf., e.g., *Journal* II, 17 Oct., 1853.

bo. 'Imagination, deserted by reason, begets impossible monsters. United with reason, she is the mother of all arts, and the source of their wonders.' Translation by Levitine. F. J. Sanchez Canton: *Los Caprichos de Goya y sus debujos preparatorios.* (Barcelona 1949) p. 87.

bp. 'intimacy, spirituality, aspiration towards the universe'. *Cur. Esth.*, p. 86.

bq. 'I have contented myself with feeling; ... I prefer to speak on behalf of feeling, of morals, and of pleasure.' *Cur. Esth.*, pp. 215, 217.

br. It is true Baudelaire here speaks of Delacroix's biblical, or his traditionally ecclesiastical pictures. But Delacroix does nothing different from what so many before him had done (since the Renaissance): he makes use of such subjects to render his own vision from his own standpoint. The term 'religion' at the beginning of our quotation can only relate to the traditional Roman-Christian subjects, but when he uses this term the second time it is clear that to Baudelaire the issue is the real all-embracing attitude and commitment of man's life and not some Roman-ecclesiastical view point. Especially when he speaks of the 'catholicité' of this basic sence of life (which might be the best translation of his word 'religion' in this case) his real meaning may be clear also in connection with 'liberté à l'individu' (the freedom of the individual person). When Baudelaire states that Delacroix is the best artist among his contemporaries as regards the painting of 'religious' subjects, he does not at all mean to describe Delacroix as a believing Roman Catholic.

bs. 'But to explain ... that only Delacroix knows how to make religion, I will point out to the observer that, if his most interesting pictures are nearly always those of which he has chosen the subjects, i.e., those of the imagination,—nevertheless the serious sadness of his talent is perfectly in harmony with our religion, a religion of universal sorrow, which on account of its very catholicity leaves the individual entirely free and requires nothing better than to be celebrated in each man's own language—if he knows sorrow and if he is a painter.' *Cur. Esth.*, p. 109.

bt. 'Poe, a new literature, the literature of the twentieth century, the scientifically miraculous, fiction by A + B ... imagination by means of analysis, Zadig judge of instruction, Cyrano de Bergerac a pupil of Arago's ... finally, the novel of the future whose call it is rather to relate things that happen in the brain of man than things that happen in his heart.' *Journal des Goncourts*, under the 16th of July, 1856, C. D. Cambiaire: *The Influence of E. A. Poe in France* (Fontenay-sous-Bois, 1927) p. 44.

bu. 'The profound sense he has of that aspect of nature and man that has not yet been observed ... the grotesque, and the horrible ... the sense of the exceptional, the spiritual sense of beauty in intensity, and lastly, the lyrical sense of science—these are the three glorious claims Poe has to eternal admiration. Ch. Morice: *La littérature de tout à l'heure* (Paris, 1889), pp. 200, 203.

11

bv. 'Matter is the artist's slave, it belongs to him.' Ch. Morice: *Paul Gauguin* (1919, Paris), p. 37—we have been unable to find out the origin of this quotation, if it is not a free summary on the part of Gauguin himself.

bw. Gauguin was fond of these books, thus C. Morice in his biography of Gauguin, (Paris, 1919), p. 37. And Sérusier writes in a letter: 'sur la table, Louis Lambert, dont je lis une page avant de travailler' (on the table Louis Lambert, a page of which I read before starting to work.) *A.B.C. de la peinture,* p. 66, in a letter to Verkade.

bx. 'The world is my conception . . .' Page 1, publ. Leipzig, 1844 [2].

by. 'As has been said, the possible transition—though it is to be considered as an exception—from the common knowledge of individual things to the knowledge of the Idea is something sudden, if knowledge detaches itself from the service of the will, so that the subject ceases to be something merely individual and is now a pure unvolitional subject of knowledge, which no longer investigates relations according to the category of sufficient ground, but rests and is merged into the fixed contemplation of the given object apart from the latter's coherence with any others . . . In such contemplation the individual thing at one blow becomes the Idea of its class, and the contemplating subject becomes the pure subject of cognition.' *Ditto,* par. 34, pp. 201-202.

bz. 'Its (i.e. of art) sole origin is the knowledge of the Ideas, its sole purpose is the communication of the Ideas . . . the essence of genius is the predominant capacity for such contemplation.' *Ditto,* par. 36, pp. 208, 209.

ca. 'The world is hell, and men are divided into tortured souls and torturing devils.' Schopenhauer: *Pensées, Maximes et Fragments* (par J. Bourdeau, Paris, 1880 [2]), p. 41.

cb. 'A novel is of an order which is all the more noble and elevated as it penetrates deeper into the inner life, and has fewer adventures . . . The novelist's task is not that of telling about great events, but that of making small things more interesting. Style is the physiognomy of the spirit' Ditto, p. 139.

cc. 'speculative results obtained by the inductive method of natural science.' E. v. Hartmann: *Philosophie des Unbewussten* (Berlin, 1871 [3]) p. 11—in 1877 a French translation appeared in two volumes: *La Philosophie de l'Inconscient,* trad. p. M. D. Nolen—.

cd. 'The facts seized upon by this vehement imagination melt away as in a flame . . . The ideas, changed into hallucinations, lose their solidity; beings resemble dreams . . . Mysticism makes its appearance like smoke within the over-heated room of the intellect which bursts.' G. Michaud: *Messages Poétiques du Symbolisme* (Paris, 1947) p. 203 quot.

ce. According to Baudelaire we see here 'marching past before your eyes in its fantastic and harrowing reality all the living monstrosities a great city may contain.' *Cur. Esth.,* p. 405.

12

cf. We here concentrate on the important years in which he struck out new paths and so caused a great deal of discussion. In his work after 1860 his strict realism was broken through or mitigated—recall his nudes and his landscapes.

cg. 'I have been astonished at the vigour and dash of his principal painting; but what a painting! what a subject! The vulgarity of the forms would not matter, it is the vulgarity and uselessness of the idea that are abominable; even if this idea as such was clear.' Delacroix: *Journal*, 15th April, 1852.

ch. 'Painting is an essentially concrete art and can only consist in the representation of things that exist really. An abstract object, invisible, does not belong to the domain of painting. The imagination in art consists in finding the most complete expression of an existing thing . . .' *Courrier du Dimanche*, 25th December, 1861, quoted by L. Venturi: *Histoire de la critique d'art*, p. 291.

ci. 'Beauty, like truth, is something relative to the time in which we live and to the individual's aptitude to conceive it.' Ditto.

ck. This term is used in a very broad sense here, comprising eighteenth century French scientialism and 19th century positivism proper, not restricting ourselves to Comte.

cl. 'And then he falls into the notorious modern error originating in a blind love of nature, of nothing but nature; he takes a simple study for a composition.' *Cur. Esth.*, p. 329.

cm. 'I understand that a mind applying itself to taking notes cannot indulge in the stupendous day-dreams contained in the scenes of present nature.' *Cur. Esth.*, p. 333.

cn. 'And the purpose of the drawing according to the ideals of these moderns is exactly to reconnoitre nature so accurately, to embrace it so strongly, that the drawing is irreproachable with respect to the coherence of the forms, that it captures the inexhaustible diversity of the characters. Farewell to the human body treated as a jar from the viewpoint of the decorative vase; farewell to the uniform monotony of the frame, to the anatomy of the limbs showing under the nude; what we want is the special note of a modern individual in his clothes, in the midst of his social habits, at home or in the street. The job becomes particularly tricky now, it is like the fitting of a torch into its shaft with a pencil, it is the study of habits reflected in the faces and by the dress, the observation of the intimacy of man with his apartment, of the special trait imprinted on him by his profession, the gestures it entails, the aspects by which he manifests and assert himself best.' Duranty: *La nouvelle peinture, à propos du Groupe d'Artistes qui expose dans les Galeries Durand-Ruel 1876*, Nouvelle édition, ed. M. Guérin, (Paris, 1946) p. 42.

co. 'a new aesthetics, an aesthetics allowing greater freedom, a drawing at first sight, an exuberant fantasy and at the same time a servility of the right kind to follow nature in its most rapid transformations.' A. Renan: La Mangua de Hokusai, *Le Japon Artistique*, Documents d'Art et d'Industrie réunies par S. Bing, (Paris, 1888) I, p. 93.

13

cp. We do not enter into a discussion of the question whether or not Renan and his contemporaries interpreted Japanese art correctly, and whether they did not too much overlook its strong stylization according to a fixed traditional pattern. Perhaps painters like Gauguin and his fellows had a better understanding of these things.

cq. 'It is evident that there are two men in the author of the Mangua: the naturalist and the idealist. The latter term need not astonish anybody. Hokusai is not only in love with visible nature; he is also a dreamer, an imaginative painter. A. Renan: La Mangua de Hokusai, *Le Japon Artistique*, Documents d'Art et d'Industrie réunies par S. Bing, (Paris, 1888), p. 109.

cr. 'Is not it something remarkable to find the plastic realization of these dreams of 'the beyond' with an artist of the Far East, nostalgic dreams that the most advanced literary art in Britain and France believed to have had an exclusive glimpse of?' A. Renan, *op. cit.*, p. 110/111.

CHAPTER III:

a. Contradictory thought proceeds from a view of the cosmos as a co-incidentia oppositorum. This view was introduced into Western thought by Heracleitos (cf. Dr. D. H. Th. Vollenhoven: *Geschiedenis der Wijsbegeerte I*, (Franeker, 1950) pp. 74 ff.) and it is more than once found again with the mystics—e.g. in Eckhardt (cf. Windelband-Heimsoeth, p. 282) and in Sebastian Franck (ditto, p. 306, 308 and J. W. Tunderman: *Marnix van St. Aldegonde en de subjectivistische stromingen in de 16e eeuw*, (Goes, n.d.) p. 123 ff.). Blake's Heracleitism is very clear in Kerrison Preston's Summary (*Blake and Rossetti*, p. 62): 'Blake's way of Twofold vision, of seeing the soul through the body, the universal through the particular, the eternal through the temporal, can be acquired by anybody with Imagination, which is the Divine Vision, but Blake wanted everyone to go farther and 'be an Artist', or Prophet, completing the process of vision by reversing it, taking in and also giving out, like continuing the circumference of a semi-circle to the starting-point and making the perfect round. This means translating the universal back into the particular, giving the soul a visible body, manifesting eternity in time and space, as an artist does with paint and paper.' This also shows the background of his method of working, which will be discussed in more detail in what follows. Bronowski: *William Blake*, (London 1954 [2]), p. 63. Kerrison Preston: *Blake and Rossetti*, (London 1944), p. 62.

b. Naturalism refers to the way of representing things, in a plastic manner, in three dimensions, e.g., by means of perspective, etc., so it refers to the way of depiction and not to the subjects.

c. In our opinion there is here some misconception on the part of Ruskin. Also the great Dutch landscapists such as Van Goyen and Ruysdael are rather concerned with a total view, a summary of the structure of, e.g., a Dutch riverscape or of a Guelder wood than with a meticulous representation of a particular subject. The latter is found with the (later) topographically-minded painters. The distance in this respect between Van Goyen and Turner is certainly not so very great. The difference is the consequence of a different kind of vision. As a matter of fact we often get the impression that this Dutch art suits Ruskin's theories better than the often rather too romantically vague achievement of Turner—who gives his 'imagination' (in Ruskin's sense) rather too much rein (cf. what follows in this paragraph). In addition, it is remarkable that Ruskin has so little to say about Constable, who had certainly also studied nature in its forms of appearance and its structures in a way similar to Ruskin's—e.g. by his study of clouds. Ruskin's criticism of Constable in a note to the preface of the second edition of *Modern Painters* (ed. 1909, p. XLIV) is, however, far from clear.

d. Man has in his soul inborn feelings that will never be satisfied with real things, and to these feelings the imagination of the painter or the poet is able to give a form and life . . . The most accurate execution in details will never give this unity that results from I know not what creative power of which the source is informulatable.' Delacroix, cited R. Rey: *Le Renaissance du sentiment classique*, p. 25.

e. 'Breakfast on the grass'. Louvre, Paris. Cf. P. Fehl: The hidden genre: a study of the Concert Champêtre in the Louvre, *Journal of Aesthetics and Art Criticism* (XVI, 2, 1957), p. 153.

f. Gauguin visited England. This follows from some comments in a letter to Mette, in which he compares Sidney and Melbourne to London (Malingue *Letters* CXXIV 1891). Cf. D. Sutton: Notes on Paul Gauguin, *Burl. Mag.* (XCVIII 1956), p. 84 ff. Gauguin was still with his children in the early eighties, and he may have looked into these books with them. He certainly has known them, see D. Sutton: The P. Gauguin Exhibition, *Burl. Mag.* (XCI 1949), p. 285, note 26.

g. Whistler's art was intermediate between Impressionism and the Pre-Raphaelites discussed here, and also underwent Japanese influences. He is a typical exponent of this period, although characteristically his own in his poetry. He stood apart from the tendencies and schools of his time. Yet this generation of 1890 could welcome him as a congenial spirit.

h. It is not so easy to classify Watts. He no doubt shows affinity with the Pre-Raphaelites, both with those who worked in the same direction as Holman Hunt, and with those who were rather of Rossetti's mind. Yet his work is more akin to the style of the Salon art. He did not play an important part in either of the groups, however, and he had no influence of any importance. This is why it was unnecessary to discuss him more elaborately. Cf. M. S. Watts: *George Frederick Watts*, (London, 1912).

i. ' . . . who up to a certain point have accomplished in France a work analogous to that of the English Pre-Raphaelites, or at least to that of some of them, notably Rossetti, Watts, and Burne-Jones. This has been a protest against the academy and against realism, and in this respect it is an interesting subject for study.' C. Mauclair: *Les états de la peinture française* (1921), p. 83.

15

j. 'still-born images'.

k. 'We should simply have been permitted to witness the concentration of the idealistic forces, the renewal of mysticism finally victorious over science, materialism, the Revolution, modern times.' G. Geffroy: *La vie artistique* II, Le symbolisme—article of March, 11, 1892 discussing the Salon de la Rose†Croix.

l. 'Art is neither a torso, nor a head, or a body, it is the soul, faith, passion, sorrow ... All art is ideographic'. A. Germain: Un peintre idéaliste-idéiste, Alexandre Séon (symbolisme des teintes), *L'Art et l'Idée* (I, 1892), p. 107.

m. 'the outward appearance of things, but the beautiful remembrance that has remained' ... 'for example as a sharply outlined piece of white colour ... with little stars round it, lines which move quietly and say how beautiful she was, how delicate her whole existence, that she was só perfect.' Dr. Bettine Polak: *Het fin-de-siècle in de Nederlandse schilderkunst* (Den Haag, 1955), p. 173.

n. ' symbolist whim, another kind of sentimentalism.' *Lettres de Gauguin à Daniel de Monfreid*, ed. Mme Joly-Segalen (Paris 1950, letter of June 1901), p. 177 ff.

o. 'So, measure figure and form, fit one's composition into a framework of decorative arabesques, choose luminosity and tints in accordance with the subject to be dealt with ... enclose one's fiction in the verisimilitude.' A. Germain: Un peintre idéaliste-idéiste, Alexandre Séon, *L'Art et l'Idée* (I, 1892), p. 107 ff.

p. 'the miserable deformations of the symbolists'. B. Polak, *op. cit.*, p. 19.

q. 'painters of the soul'. M. Denis: *Théories 1890-1910, Du symbolisme de Gauguin vers un nouvel ordre classique* (1912 [2], Paris), p. 33.

r. 'to confound mystic and allegoric tendencies, i.e., the search for the expression by means of the subject, with the symbolist tendencies to seek for the expression by means of the work of art. Denis *Théories*, p. 17.

s. 'Motifs' is here intended in the sense of subject-matter, thought, themes, and not in that of visual objects—in which sense e.g. Cézanne uses the term.

t. 'Well, I can see nothing in the symbolic art of painting but the most extreme individualism, which is possessed by the delusion of expressing universal metaphysical things, so the opposite of individual things, and has arrived at this delusion by the element of reflection, and the handling of anti-naturalistic motifs. But what is anti-naturalistic is not therefore supra-naturalistic, still less metaphysical and approaching the absolute'. B. Polak, p. 205, citation.

u. 'the sad verses', 'the egotist rêveries', 'decadent poetry'. Michaud *Message Poétique* II, pp. 314 ff., p. 328.

v. The terminology is not simple. For in this period there was often a sharp opposition between the various tendencies that we have distinguished here, but it was rarely attempted to give one's own group a name which was clearly different from the other groups. As a matter of fact such distinctive names are not found before the first decades of the 20th century. Yet we have tried to keep as closely as possible to the linguistic usage of that time and to abstain from introducing new names and new characterizations. It is, therefore, always indispensable to realize what a particular name means. We shall stick to the following terms: by symbolists we refer to the poets mentioned above who were of the same mind as the synthetist painters—Gauguin, etc.—whereas 'decadents' is the name for the men of letters who are akin to symbolist painters such as Toorop, etc. Thus we get the same name for two different groups, but this is unavoidable if we do not want to introduce artificial terms.

w. 'This is the content of decadent poetry: the inner world but reduced to its lowest levels, to its undefinable emotions, its most exasperated sensations, to dreams ruled by repressed desires and by the demands of the flesh . . . a new expression: . . . a subjective correspondence between the music of the words and the music of the soul caught in its mobile and fugitive course'. Michaud *Message Poétique* II, p. 404.

x. In one term we see here the great difference from the attitude of life founded in Holy Scripture: a believer is at home in this world (in the sense of: this cosmos, the creation of his Heavenly Father), and a stranger in the midst of the world (by which the unbelievers are meant, human society following the lead of conceptions which are often contrary to the Scriptures). The unbeliever, however, the worldling, is at home among his fellows who constitute the majority, but feels himself as a stranger in the cosmos (called 'nature' here) from which he has got estranged by refusing to recognise the Creator as such. The latter attitude justifies our term: a negative sense of reality.

y. 'Thus seeing relations in things that are hardly there and seeking for what I shall never obtain, a stranger in the real world, ridiculous among men, I shall have only vain affectations and whether I live in accordance with my own taste, or in accordance with the way of other men, I shall not have anything but the eternal torment of a permanently suppressed and miserable life—in the oppression from outside or in my own limitation. Cited by Morice *La Littérature*, p. 184, note.

z. 'I seek elsewhere, for some unknown good the urge for which pursues me. Is it my fault if I find boundaries everywhere, if all that is finite has not any value to me?' Thus the main person in Chateaubriand's 'René', cited Barre *Le symbolisme*, p. 35.

aa. By 'religious' we do not mean the cult in the service of God, nor a Christian attitude of life. By 'religious' we mean to say that it is a matter of the heart. The issue is the fundamental and most central commitment of man with respect to God—and hence also with respect to His creation and to his fellowmen, his fellow-creatures. The religious commitment of the heart is decisive for man's attitude with regard to things, it directs all his efforts and determines his aim, and is manifested in his view of life and the world. Chapter II, note a and the literature mentioned

17

there, and also the writer's 'De constituerende factoren ener historische daad', Chapter IV, *Philosophia Reformata* (**XIX**, 1954), pp. 169 ff.—English summary on page 191.

ab. 'In order to find and to combine the evolutions and sudden changes of his poem and his drama he had only to carry to their extreme consequences his feelings, imaginary but sincere, the feelings that upset his soul when exalted by the very fumes of his genius and by the electricity of the stormy air: If I were omnipotent, what should I do to my enemies, what to the world?' Morice *La Littérature,* p. 124.

ac. 'his king, his priest, and his god.'

ad. As such it is the concrete form of the Humanistic freedom motive.

ae. 'if, in a delicate way, proportionate to the new enjoyments brought by it (i.e. by the ideal of science) the indefinite progress would not be man's most ingenious and most cruel torture; if, proceding with the obstinate negation of himself, it would not be a method of incessantly renewed suicide, and if, enclosed within the fiery circle of divine logic, he did not resemble a scorpion that pierces its own body with its terrible tail, this eternal yearning which causes his eternal despair?' *Cur. Esth.*, p. 220.

af. 'In the uniform mask that science casts on nature wherever it is in direct relation to man, he has seen mankind lose its hold on things, and in a menacing silence things resuming their own individual lives, alien to humanity, thus vanquished by its victory and unable to reconquer its ruins which return to nature.' Morice: *La Littérature,* p. 221.

ag. 'the robe of Nessos from which nothing can deliver us.' Lehmann *Symbolist Aesthetics,* p. 238, cited from *Nouvelle Gauche* XI, 1882.

ah. 'only he who dreams us would do well to hasten the hatching of his opium.' Lehmann *Symbolist Aesthetics,* p. 49, cited from Laforgue: *Mélanges posthumes* (1882), p. 280.

ai. 'As our life is such a terrible thing that art has not had the means for a perfect realization of our dreams of happiness, it was really necessary to maintain ourselves mourning for the joys that life denies to us and which could only be realized in dreams.' Morice: *La Littérature,* p. 203.

aj. that was 'the impotence from which especially the artists suffered, incapable of fully realizing their dream, i.e., clothing an eternal idea in a truly real form . . .' Pierre Valin: Les lettres prochaines, *L'Art et l'Idée* (II, 1892), p. 83.

ak. 'the advice of perversity which wants all things to be dislodged from their proper cadre and deprived of their natural balance.' Pierre Valin: Les lettres prochaines, *L'Art et l'Idée* (II, 1892), p. 84.

al. 'the spirit has become incapable of hierarchy.' P. Radiot: Notre Byzantinisme, *La Revue Blanche* (Feb. 1894), p. 111.

18

am. 'It is no longer the soul as commander-in-chief which speaks but each of the mutinous soldiers, the so-called senses'. P. Radiot: Notre Byzantinisme, *La Revue Blanche* (Feb. 1894), p. 111.

an. 'The present only hurts and is ugly only on account of its being material.' . . . 'While believing that we are inventing the most fabulous chimeras we do nothing but call up the visions we remember unconsciously of the times when our souls relaxed in the marvellous garden of the Eden of the pure Ideas.' G.-A. Aurier: *Oeuvres*, p. 31.

ao. 'Because it indulges in the sweet ephemera of contingency; immortal because it can lift itself to the Paradise of the absolute . . .' G.-A. Aurier: *Oeuvres*, p. 31.

ap. 'The starting-point of the speculative thought of Plotinus . . . is a feeling of uneasy discomfort, the feeling that in its actual form human life is a checked sort of life diminished by obstacles caused by bodies and passions.' E. Bréhier: *La Philosophie de Plotin* (Paris 1928), pp. 24 ff.

In this connection it is interesting to find the following distinction made by Gregorius of Nyssa: there are three stages of knowledge: Chaldaean philosophy related to appearances, symbolic philosophy related to abstract truths, and apophatic philosophy,—apophainoo is no doubt used here in the sense of 'to reveal'— directed to spiritual reality. Each of these ways of knowledge corresponds to special organs: aisthesis for the forms of appearances, phantasia katalèptikè for abstractions, pistis for reality (Jean Daniélou: *Platonisme et théologie mystique. Essai sur la doctrine spirituelle de St. Grégoire de Nyssa*, (Paris, 1944), p. 155). It is typical of the strong bond with old traditions that these distinctions could be so readily used by the symbolists—in the wide sense of the word—. The first way was the science of nature characterized by them in a similar manner; the second was concerned with themselves (in this even the 'imagination' was applied in an identical way), while the third method was rejected by them as an impossibility, as all of them, with a few exceptions only, refused to recognise the divine revelation—so that they often assigned to art the rôle of revealing reality, thus remaining within the limits of Gregorius' second way of knowledge.

aq. 'his need to escape from the horrible reality of existence, to cross the borders of thought, to grope for some certainty without ever arriving at it, in the mist of the beyond of art' J. K. Huysmans: *A Rebours*, (Paris 1903), p. 143.

ar. 'the natural order, so that if all that lives lives as a slave, there is nothing in accordance with the laws of nature, as each life is chained by an other life, or by a vice, or by artificial obligations outlined by society as it is. Morice *La Littérature*, p. 367.

as. 'Anywhere out of the world' is a quotation form Thomas Hood's 'Bridge of Sighs', a poem that Morice perhaps knew from Poe's 'The Poetic Principle' in which it occurs in full. (Poe: *The Poetic Principle*, pp. 202 ff.)

at. 'This complaint is something of our time, and it is a great deal more than a complaint: it is the supreme law of supreme art.' Morice *La Littérature*, p. 282.

19

au. 'he withdrew more and more from reality, and above all from the contemporary world which he considered with increasing horror; this hatred had strongly influenced his literary and artistic tastes, and he turned away most from pictures and books whose limited subjects were relegated to modern life.' Huysmans: *A Rebours*, p. 238, compare p. 136.

av. 'Nature is ugly, and I prefer the monsters of my fantasy to the trivial positive.' *Cur. Esth.*, p. 263.

aw. 'I have found the definition of what is beautiful, of what I call beautiful. It is something passionate and sad, something a little vague . . . I can hardly conceive a type of beauty (would my brain be an enchanted mirror) in which there is no despair. Supported—others say obsessed—by these ideas I think that it would be difficult for me not to arrive at the conclusion that the most perfect type of manly beauty is Satan—after the manner of Milton.' From the *Journaux Intimes, Oeuvres complètes*, ed. 1e Dantec 1938 II, p. 633, cited by Denys Sutton: The Paul Gauguin Exhibition, *Burlington Magazine* (XCI 1949), p. 284; Cf. Projets de Préface pour une édition nouvelle, *Les Fleurs du Mal*, in the edition of Jacques Crépet et Georges Blin, (Paris 1942), p. 211; see also Marcel Raymond: *From Baudelaire to Surrealism*, (New York 1950), p. 13 both notes.

ax. 'And as a painter proud of my genius
    I should enjoy in my picture
    the intoxicating monotony
    of metal, marble and water
    and heavy cataracts
    hanging down like crystal curtains
    dazzling from crystal walls'
Cited by Ch. Chassé: *Le mouvement symboliste,* (1947), p. 24.

ay. 'In his erudite works full of despair there was a singular enchantment, a kind of incantation that stirs you to the bottom of your soul like certain poems by Baudelaire . . .' Huysmans: *A Rebours,* (1903), pp. 71 ff.

az. 'A satanic Decameron. This island of fantastic dreams encloses all forms of passion, fantasy, and caprice in the woman, woman in her primary essence, the unconscious being fond of the unknown, the mysterious, in love with evil in the form of a perverse and diabolic seduction. The dreams of children, of the senses, monstrous dreams, melancholy dreams, dreams that carry the spirit and the soul into the unknown of the spaces, into the mystery of gloom, everything must experience the influence of the seven deadly sins, everything is found in these satanic precincts, in this circle of the vices and the guilty ardours, from the as yet innocent germ to the monstrous and fatal flowers of the abyss . . . In the distance, the dead town with the dormant passions. And this town is real life, true life, that which is hidden, enclosed within the sombre walls, under flat roofs. But the mountainous roads . . . rise and some figures . . . are climbing while always clinging to the sharp points of that barren and hard rock . . . Perhaps they will arrive at that redemptory cross that rises humbly in the ether, the last stage of life, the last evidence of what is creative and beneficent, the last refuge of a being that has been able to avoid or to vanquish the visionary dream after the cruel afflictions, the terrible dream of ruin, of sorrow and death.' *Catalogue Musée Moreau*, 1926, No. 39, p. 11/12, ill. p. 42.

ba. 'bends its head sadly full of regret that it is enslaved and in exile, while at his feet are assembling the gloomy phalanx of the monsters of Erebus and the Night ... (while there is) an ascension to the higher spheres, to the Divine, (by which) 'the great mystery is accomplished.' *Catalogue Musée Moreau,* p. 2, no cat. no., with reprod. Cf. text concerning cat. no. 13, p. 4, 'Oedipus and the Sphinx'.

bb. 'The Salome by Gustave Moreau haunted us.' A. Fontainas: *Mes souvenirs du Symbolisme*, (Paris 1928), p. 96.

bc. 'The lawless concrete—all that remains to man after the departure of the gods—the civilized supra-nature, irrational, and psychic, creates phantoms which people the Black Novel. The phantom does not express the myths of nature or the infinity of what is real like a Greek god or like a fairy. It is a particular event that is transformed into a psychism, a part of reality transposed to the interior of man and which is reincarnated—in irreality. These immaterial creations express the terror of men threatened by the exterior evil which has become a psychism.' Marcel Jean & Arpad Mezei: *Genèse de la pensée moderne*, (Paris '50), p. 44.

bd. 'What is found everywhere in his work, from one end to the other, is man in love with solitude, flying from the world, flying desperate and homeless under the sky, into the terrors of an exile without hope and without end.' Odilon Redon: '*A soi-même*', *Journal 1867-1915*, (1922 Paris), p. 161.

be. Ensor might have been mentioned here, but he was of no importance to France—at least we have not found any reference to his work. The question might be asked whether Ensor's prints of the eighteen-eighties had been created under the influence of Redon's lithographs.

bf. 'by this semblance of truth.' Odilon Redon: '*A soi-même*', *Journal 1867-1915*, (1922 Paris), p. 93.

bg. (he puts) 'the logic of the visible at the service of the invisible as much as possible.' Odilon Redon: '*A soi-même*', *Journal 1867-1915*, (1922 Paris), p. 29.

bh. 'pain of life'. Cf. Redon *op. cit.*, p. 84.

bi. 'shiver with fear in the endless night.' G.-A. Aurier *Oeuvres*, p. 306.

bj. 'Nature is ugly, and I prefer the monsters of my fantasy to the triviality of what is positive.' *Cur. Esth.*, p. 263.

bk. 'But I think these melancholies of Meryon's utterly horrible.' Van Gogh *Brieven*, letter 546.

CHAPTER IV:

a. Here we again give a brief summary of the terminology used by us. Decadents are the men of letters that came to the fore about 1885 in the footsteps of Verlaine and Huysmans. To these the symbolistic painters of the Rose†Croix were akin. A different milieu was formed by the symbolistic writers round Mallarmé, with whom we class Aurier and Morice. They are nearest akin to the synthetist painters.

This terminology has been chosen because it is nearest to the little systematic and often confusing terminology used by their contemporaries. We have been unable to avoid using the same term for two different movements. But we prefer this to the introduction of names of our own devising.

b. 'Beware of the Pre-Raphaelites . . .' J. Rewald: Lucien Pissarro: Letters from London 1883-1891, *Burl. Mag.* (XCI, 1949), p. 192. Cf. Van Gogh *Brieven III*, letter 615.

c. Here the 'Synthetists' are meant.

d. 'the mystic and the allegorical tendencies, i.e. the search for the expression by means of the subject, and the symbolistic tendencies, i.e., the search for the expression by means of the work of art.' Denis *Théories*, p. 17.

e. 'Treatise on sensations'. Windelband-Heimsoeth, p. 383.

f. 'The eye and the hand! ah! superb, and it was enough: but nothing else.' Mauclair: *Servitude et grandeur littéraires*, (Paris, 1922), p. 192.

g. 'At bottom they had nothing in common, it was their common reaction against the ill-will of the press which united them.' Mauclair: *Servitude et grandeur littéraires*, (Paris, 1922), p. 194.

h. They also tried to stimulate this 'dream' (rêverie) in the parks laid out in the second half of the 18th century. Cf. H. Sedlmayer: *Verlust der Mitte* (Salzburg 1951 [5]), p. 19 ff. This is very clear in the theories of C. C. L. Hirschfeld: *Théories de l'art des Jardins* (traduit de l'allemand) (Leipzig 1780, 5 volumes), from which we quote, II, p. 76: Lorsque nous entrons sous des voûtes ténébreuses de feuillage, le repos se répand sur tous nos sens: notre âme se trouve soudain dans une situation qui lui fait retirer son activité en elle-même; bientôt elle ne s'occupe plus que de soi, elle commence à se livrer entièrement à l'imagination . . .' (When we enter underneath the dark arches of the foliage, the feeling of repose spreads over all our senses: our soul is suddenly in a situation which makes it withdraw its activity into itself; soon it is only occupied with its own self, it commences to deliver itself entirely to the imagination . . .') Monet's 'Nymphéas' represents a similar attitude towards nature, although very probably Monet never occupied himself with Rousseau, and even less with such a kind of literature as we have just quoted. After all Rousseau's ideas had penetrated all French thought. Cf. Lehmann, p. 81 ff.; J. J. Rousseau: *Dialogues, Rêveries, Correspondance* (ed. P. Richard, Larousse 1938), p. 17 ff.

i. '. . . it is permissible . . . to take exception to this constant sacrifice of significant forms and this deliberate plunging of beings into those atmospheres which have been so splendidly conceived that those beings seem to be vaporized in them; it is, no doubt, just as well legitimate to wish for an art that is less immediately, less directly sensational, an art of a more distant dream and of the idea . . .' Aurier: C. Monet. *Mercure de France* (IV, 1892), p. 302.

k. 'of instinct and momentaneousness' P. Signac: *D'Eugène Delacroix au Néo-Impressionnisme* (Ed. La Revue Blanche 1899), p. 58.

l. Also Baudelaire had advanced thoughts on colour that were found again in Seurat and his fellows. Thus, e.g., in the section 'De la couleur' in the Salon of 1846, *Cur. Esth.*, p. 87. The 'Curiosités Esthétiques' had appeared in 1884, and it is hardly conceivable that such a man as Seurat should have remained ignorant of it. This is a clear instance of the confluence of Baudelaire's and Delacroix's influence on this generation of painters. P. Signac: *D'Eugène Delacroix aux Néo-Impressionnisme* (Ed. La Revue Blanche 1899), p. 62.

m. 'to confer authenticity on nature tired at last of its precarious reality.' P. Signac: *D'Eugène Delacroix au Néo-Impressionnisme.* (Ed. La Revue Blanche 1899), p. 76. Cf. Rewald: *Post Impressionism*, p. 84.

n. 'To synthetize a landscape in a definitive aspect that perpetuates the sensation it gives.' J. Rewald: *Seurat*, (Paris 1948), p. 81. (from an article of F. Fénéon in *L'Art Moderne*, 1887).

o. 'Art is harmony. Harmony is the analogy between contrasts, the analogy of simularities of tone, colour, line, viewed against the dominant element and under the influence of a particular light, in gay, calm or sad combinations.' Quotation from beginning of a letter of Seurat to Beaubourg of 1890. Laprade: *Seurat*, (1945).

p. Typical of this is the announcement of the 'Bibliothèque scientifique internationale', including also Brucke and Helmholz: *Principes scientifiques des beaux-arts, suivis de l'optique et la peinture,* (trad. 1878); a.o. it says: 'La Bibliothèque scientifique internationale ne comprend pas seulement ouvrages consacrés aux sciences physiques et naturelles, elle aborde aussi les sciences morales, comme la philosophie, l'histoire, la politique et l'économie sociale, la haute législation, etc. mais les livres traitant des sujets de ce genre se rattacheront encore aux sciences naturelles, en leur empruntant les méthodes d'observation et d'expérience qui les ont rendues si fécondes depuis deux siècles.' (The 'Bibl. scientifique internationale' not only comprises works devoted to physical and natural sciences, it also deals with moral sciences, such as philosophy, history, politics, social economics, legislation, etc.; but the books dealing with such subjects will be connected with the natural sciences by borrowing from them the methods of observation and experience which have rendered these so fruitful for two centuries already.') This announcement is found at the back of Schopenhauer: *Pensées, maximes, et fragments,* (éd. J. Bourdeau, Paris, 1880 ²).

q. Later on (in Chapter VIII) we shall enter in more detail into the iconic aspect. For the present only briefly this: by 'iconic' we mean that in the picture something is told about reality in a manner analogous to language. Also outside art

23

proper we find iconic representations (just like language, which also exists apart from literature or poetry)—a pure, non-artistic, use of iconic means is found, e.g., in maps, image-statistics, etc.

r. 'subordinating colours and lines to the emotion that he has felt and wants to render, the painter will do the work of a poet, of a creator.' P. Signac: *D'Eugène Delacroix au Néo-Impressionnisme*. (Ed. La Revue Blanche 1899), p. 59.

s. 'Rules do not hinder the spontaneity of the inventive power or that of the execution in spite of their absolute character . . . Science delivers us of all uncertainties and permits us to move in perfect freedom and within a very vast circle. As all rules have been derived from the laws of nature themselves, there is nothing so easy to know in principle, nor so indispensable. In the arts everything must be planned.' Rewald: *Seurat*, p. 119, cited out of D. Sutter: Les phénomènes de la vision, *L'Art* (1880). Cf. Rewald *Post Impressionism*, p. 86.

t. 'We must see nature with the eyes of the mind and not exclusively with the bodily eyes like a creature destitute of reason.' Ditto quotation from Sutter.

u. 'A scientific Aesthetics' *Revue contemporaine* (II, August 4, 1885). Also cited by Morice: *La littérature*, p. 275, note.

v. 'The Aesthetics of Forms'. *La Revue Blanche* (August and October 1894) illustrated by Signac.

w. 'The Chromatic Circle and the Sensation of Colour'. *Revue Indépendante* (VII, 19 May 1888).

x. 'He had the merit of attempting to regulate impressionism . . . this first effort against freedom.' M. Denis *Théories*, p. 257.

y. 'They have not been disincorporated by some vain caprice, but figured strictly in accordance with the essential necessities of matter.' Fontainas *Souvenirs*, p. 99.

z. 'for all clear ideas there exists a plastic thought that translates it.' Quoted Denis *Théories*, p. 50, by Chassé: *Le Mouvement Symboliste*, p. 52 also by Rewald *Post Impressionism*, p. 162.

aa. 'I seek a scene that translates the idea exactly.' Cited by Denis *Théories*, p. 50.

ab. 'a means to express sensation'. Cézanne *Correspondance*, p. 153, letter of 1878.

ac. 'on nature'. Cézanne *Correspondance*, p. 264, letter of July 1904.

ad. 'All the theories on Cézanne's pictorial genius, all the praise of his synthetic art have been made afterwards, I saw their birth.' Mauclair: *Servitude et grandeur littéraires* (1922), p. 189.

ae. This is a clear refutation of the view that art will be all the better, greater, and more profound as the artist is poorer and more lonely. On the contrary, it is only very human that exactly by being recognised, and stimulated also by purchases, etc. the artist will be encouraged to go on in a particular direction and to give the best he can—unless he has such a weak character that he will soon fall a victim to the urge of winning an easy and immediate fame, and is thus forced to pander to the taste of his patrons. It is very doubtful whether in such a case the artist would have achieved anything of importance if he had been obliged to strive against the stream of indifferent neglect.

af. 'make of impressionism something solid and durable like art in museums.' Denis *Théories,* p. 242. This as well was written down later, and it is not possible to know whether Cézanne would have said this in the eighties.

ag. 'Look at Cézanne, who was not understood, who had the essentially mystical nature of the East . . . in the form he loves a mystery and the heavy tranquility of a man lying down to dream, his colours are grave like the character of orientals . . .' 'the farther I go the more I come to work in the way of translating thoughts by entirely different means from those of literature . . .' Malingue *Lettres* XI, Letter of January 14, 1885. See also chapter VI, note p.

ah. 'What is needed is to renew Poussin looking at nature.' Vollard, *En écoutant Cézanne,* p. 50. Cf. the statement as given by Bernard: 'Wir müssen durch die Natur, d.h. durch die Sinneseindruck wieder klassisch werden' (We have to become classic again through nature, that is through sensation), in *Erinnerung an P.C.,* p. 27.

ai. 'In a painter there are two things: his eyes and his brains, which should help each other; we must try to further their mutual development, but as a painter: the eye by looking directly at nature, the brains by means of the logic of the organized sensations which supply the means of expression.' Rewald: *Cézanne et Zola,* p. 274.

ak. 'One is neither too scrupulous, nor too sincere, nor too much submissive to nature; but one is more or less master of one's model, and above all of one's means of expression. Penetrate what one has in front of one and persevere expressing oneself as logically as possible.' Cézanne *Correspondances,* p. 262, letter of 1904.

al. 'nature is always the same but nothing of it remains of what appears to us. Our art should give us a shiver of its duration with the elements, the appearances of all the changes.' L. Guerry: *Cézanne et l'expression de l'espace* (1950), p. 187, note 28, cited from Gasquet.

am. 'The painter concretizes his sensations and his perceptions by means of the design and the colours.' Cézanne *Correspondances,* p. 262, letter of 1904. Cf. p. 257, letter of 1904, in which he speaks of his 'sensation forte de la nature' (strong sensation of nature).

an. 'the knowledge of the means of expressing emotion.' Cézanne *Correspondances,* p. 257, letter of 1904.

ao. 'I have wanted to copy nature—I have not been successful. I was satisfied about myself when I discovered that, e.g., the sun (the objects in the sunshine)

25

could not be reproduced, but that it was necessary to represent it by something else than by what I saw—by colours . . .' Denis *Théories*, p. 259, note 2.

ap. 'The reconstruction of Art started by Cézanne with the means of impressionism has been continued by Gauguin with less sensibility and scope, but with greater theoretical rigour. He has rendered Cézanne's thought more explicit.' Denis *Théories*, p. 262.

aq. 'It is undoubtedly wise and just to be moved by the bible, but the realities of today have so taken hold of us that, even when attempting abstractly to reconstruct ancient times in our thoughts, our meditations are broken into by minor events of our daily life and we are brought back forcibly by our own experiences into the world of personal sensations—joy, boredom, suffering, anger and laughter.' *Brieven* IV B 21, cited by Rewald *Post Impressionism*, p. 307/8.

ar. The word 'instinctive' is properly speaking incorrect. For this 'instinct' is the result of the formation of ideas under the influence of a particular view of life and the world for centuries at a stretch, a formation which will continue its influence even a long time after this view of life has lost its hold on people. Cf. again F. Hoffet: *L'Impérialisme protestante. Considérations sur le destin inégal des peuples protestants et catholiques dans le monde actuel.* (Paris, 1948) This 'instinct', therefore, is not something natural implied in the structure of man as such, but a complex of standards of judgment that has been formed in the cultural process.

as. 'the melancholy after the manner of Meryon.' Van Gogh *Brieven*, letter No 546.

at. 'That academy is a mistress preventing a more serious, more ardent, more fruitful love from awakening in you—Leave that mistress alone and fall in love over head and ears with your proper beloved lady nature or reality.' *Brieven* IV, R 4.

au. 'Well, one loses that general harmony of tones in nature by painfully exact imitation; one keeps it by recreating in a parallel color scale which may be not exactly, or even far from exactly, like the model.' Van Gogh, *Brieven* No. 429.

av. 'He is no doubt very conscious of pigment, of its importance and beauty, but also, and most frequently, he considers his enchanting pigment only as a kind of marvelous language destined to express the Idea. Almost always he is a symbolist . . . feeling the constant urge to clothe his ideas in precise, ponderable, tangible forms, in intensely corporeal and material envelopes.' Aurier: Les Isolés: Vincent van Gogh, *Mercure de France* (Jan. 1890) cited by Rewald *Post Impressionism*, p. 368.

aw. 'I am always in the hope of making a discovery there, to express the love of two lovers by a marriage of two complementaries, their mingling and their opposition, the mysterious vibrations of kindred tones. To express the thought of a brow by the radiance of light tones against a somber background . . .' Van Gogh *Brieven* IV B 8, cited by Rewald *Post Impressionism*, p. 235.

ax. 'and this is not the way to synthesize'. Van Gogh *Brieven* No. 614.

ay. 'I cannot work without a model. I don't say that I do not frankly turn my back upon nature in order to transform a study into a picture by arranging the colours, by enlargement and simplification.' Van Gogh *Brieven* IV B 19.

az. The latter also applies to the classicists who depict an ideal world, as they conceive of it, in a naturalistic way, while correcting the real object by purifying it from its (supposed) faults. In this case we need not at all speak of the Salon artists, for they were in actual fact the adherents of the most rigorous kind of naturalism (cf. Chapter I).

ba. 'it is not a return to romanticism or to religious ideas, no. However, by passing by Delacroix even more than it appears, by colours and by the drawing which are much more arbitrary than deceptive exactness, one would express a country scene . . .' Van Gogh *Brieven* No. 595, cited by Rewald *Post Impressionism* p. 337.

bb. ' . . . to remind you that to create an impression of agony one may try to perform this without straightway aiming at a Garden of Olives in historical Gethsemane, in order to give a sweet and consoling motif it is not necessary to represent the characters of the Sermon on the Mount.' Van Gogh *Brieven* IV B 21.

bc. ' rather come back to what I sought before coming to Paris, and I do not know if any one before me spoke about suggestive colour, but Delacroix and Monticelli produced it without having talked about it.' Van Gogh *Brieven* No. 539.

bd. 'Rops has nothing mystical or neurotic. He is a sane mind in a sound body disdainful of all weak bashfulness, happy in exalting his virility . . .' Maurice Kunel: *Félicien Rops* (Bruxelles 1943), p. 30.

be. 'I simply and stupidly try to render what I feel with my nerves and what I see with my eyes: this is the whole of my theory of art.' Maurice Kunel: *Félicien Rops* (Bruxelles 1943), p. 30.

bf. 'Up till now nobody has so profoundly handled the catholic notion of lewdness, the demoniac pleasure of perversity, that which lies beyond evil.' Kunel, *op. cit.*, p. 32.

bg. 'Telling about the life of every day, showing the ridiculousness of certain sorrows, the sadness of a great many joys, and stating roughly sometimes in what a hyprocritical manner vice is inclined to manifest itself in us: this is my project. I am an imaginative seeker, I will go everywhere endeavouring to render distinctly and immediately, and as sincerely as possible, the impressions and emotions that I feel.' G. Geffroy: *La Vie Artistique* (III, Paris 1894), p. 227 ff.

bh. 'The symbolists looked down upon the Chat-Noir and on the artists of Montmartre: they were of the 'Rive Gauche' (the left bank of the Seine), stand-offish, rather lofty, and though they allowed humour, they would have thought laughter at a joke unworthy of themselves.' C. Mauclair: *Servitude et grandeur littéraires*, (Paris 1922), p. 47.

27

bi. Realism in this case is what we have called naturalism.

bk. 'It is not the deceptive appearance of realism but is it not something really existing?' Van Gogh *Brieven* No. 531.

CHAPTER V:

a. 'we went to those who had done not only with academic teaching but also and above all with naturalism, either of the romantic or the photographic kind, then universally acknowledged as the sole theory that was worthy of a scientific and democratic epoch.' Denis *Théories*, p. 254.

b. 'The natural sciences, or the inexact sciences, in opposition to rational or exact sciences which are by definition insusceptible of absolute solutions, have the fatal tendency to lead to scepticism and to the fear of thought. We must, therefore, accuse them of having made for us this society without faith, so common-place, incapable of those thousand intellectual or sentimental manifestations that might be comprised under the name of devotion. They are, consequently, responsable . . . for the poverty of our art to which they have assigned imitation as its unique domain, the only aim that can be verified by experimental methods.' Thus we have arrived at 'pure animality'. 'We must again cultivate the higher qualities of the soul.' Aurier *Oeuvres*, p. 175, 176, 202.

c. It is remarkable and striking that here Baudelaire simply speaks of 'vrai' (true), thus implicitly accepting positivism. Only as a guide for artistic creation it is depreciated. It appears that positivism was by no means overcome and subjected to an intrinsic criticism—its 'truth' was recognised as such.

d. 'With us the painter of nature is almost a monster. The exclusive preference for truth suppresses and suffocates the sense of what is beautiful . . . He (the artist) feels or rather judges in succession, analytically.' *Cur. Esth.*, p. 257.

e. 'We have lapsed into the abominable error of naturalism.' Morice *Gauguin*, p. 27—it is cited by Morice from memory.

f. 'They sought what was visible round about them and not what was in the mysterious centre of thought, and thus they fell into scientific reasonings.' *Lettres de Gauguin à Daniel de Monfreid*, (Paris 1950), p. 121, letter of March 1898.

g. 'the force to create'. Malingue CLXXXI, April 1903 to Morice, p. 319.

h. 'The short-sighted copy of social anecdotes, the flat observation, the imbecil imitation of the warts of nature, the trompe l'oeil, the glory of being as truly and as trivially exact as a daguerréotype, no longer satisfies any painter worthy of the name.' Aurier *Oeuvres*, p. 294.

i. 'They have propagated the hatred of naturalism.' Denis *Théories*, p. 26.

k. 'Where does the execution of a picture begin and where does it end? At the moment when the extreme sentiments are being fused in the deepest of being, when they explode and all thought is thrown out like lava from a volcano, is not there a breaking forth of the work which is suddenly created? The cold calculations of reason have not preceded this explosion.' *Lettres à Daniel de Monfreid*, March 1898, p. 206. Cf. Delacroix's pronouncement: '. . . l'unité qui résulte de ce je ne sais quelle puissance créatrice dont la source est indéfinissable.' (the unity that is the result of I do not know what creative power whose source is indefinable) (From his notes for 'Le réalisme et l'idéalisme', quoted in R. Rey: *La renaissance du sentiment classique*, p. 25). There is also a striking agreement with the thought expressed in a stanza of Poe's
These were the days when my heart was volcanic
As the scoriac rivers that roll—
As the leaves that restlessly roll
Their sulphurous currents . . .
(from the second stanza of Ulalume, in *The Poems of Edgar Allan Poe*, (London, 1900), p. 23).

It is possible that Gauguin knew this, maybe as a result of his contact with Mallarmé. The image however can be traced much farther back in history. 'The familiar Neoplatonic figure of the soul as a fountain, or an outflowing stream, is also frequent in romantic poetry, although this, too, is usually reformed to imply a bilateral transaction, a give-and-take, between mind and external object.' (M. H. Abrams: *The mirror and the lamp, Romantic theory and Critical Tradition* (New York 1953), p. 61—a book dealing chiefly with English writers like Shelley and Coleridge—). In a later context we shall revert to this very old Neoplatonic tradition which has penetrated very deep into Western thought (especially in artistic circles). This general state of affairs is not in the least affected by the possibility that Gauguin must have been indebted to Poe for his image—Poe, who of course, was himself much more directly influenced by the English authors such as Coleridge and/or by German Romantic thought.

l. 'Instead of working round about the eye we looked for the mysterious centre of thought', as Gauguin put it. The imagination again became the queen of the faculties, as Baudelaire had already demanded. Thus we liberated our sensibility, and instead being the copy of nature art became the subjective deformation of nature.' Denis *Théories*, p. 260.

m. (reality) 'seen through the medium of a temperament.' . . . The work of art as such should be 'a visible sign of this temperament' . . . 'The symbol of the ideational and sensitive totality of the worker.' Aurier *Oeuvres*, p. 298.

n. 'We strove after the joy of self-expression as the young authors demanded at that period.' Denis *Théories*, p. 164.

o. 'What is a poem? A synthesis of all the general ideas perceived by a given self.' Aurier *Oeuvres*, p. XIV.

29

p. 'Pure art according to the modern conception; the creation of a suggestive kind of magic containing the object simultaneously with the subject, the outer world and the artist himself'. M. Gilman: *Baudelaire the Critic* (New York 1943), p. 166, cited from a not finished article 'L'art philosophique' in *Oeuvres* (II Le Dantec), p. 367.

q. 'The artist does not reveal but himself . . . He has been his own king, his own priest and his own god.' *Cur. Esth.*, p. 221.

r. Motive has really been derived from movere.

s. 'Primitive art proceeds from the spirit and uses nature. So-called refined art proceeds from sensuousness and serves nature. Nature is the servant of the former, the mistress of the latter. But the servant cannot forget her origin, she vilifies the spirit in allowing herself to be adored. This is how we have fallen into the abominable error of naturalism.' Morice *Gauguin*, p. 26, 27 (cf. note e). It is not impossible for Gauguin to have borrowed this thought from Van Gogh. He already expresses it in a similar way in a letter to Van Rappart, *Brieven* IV R 4.

t. This refers to Cross.

u. 'In Paris, every year, with the Independents . . . he sees what work is going on, apparently towards more freedom, in reality towards more reason and order, a new order, paradoxical, an order derived from the symbolist arduous toil and whose success indicated the triumph of the spirit of synthesis over that of analysis, of the imagination over sensation, of man over nature.' Denis: Introduction to *Catalogue Exposition Cross*, (Paris 1910).

v. Abstraction here has nothing to do with the use of this term in the first decades of the twentieth century by modern painters. Here it refers to the forming of images, of iconic representation. The term is used in opposition to the direct 'imitation' of the naturalists. Compare also Van Gogh's use of the term in his letter to Bernard, B 21, in which he characterizes his work after the manner of Gauguin, e.g. the Berceuse, in this way.

w. 'While taking into account the efforts and the investigations, even those of science, it was, necessary to think of a complete liberation, to break the window-panes at the risk of cutting one's finger, leave to the next generation, henceforth independent, free from any shackles, to solve the problem completely. I do not say definitively, for it exactly means an art without strict boundaries, rich in all kinds of technique, fit to translate all the emotions of nature and man. For this purpose it was necessary to risk body and soul in the struggle, a struggle against all the Schools, all of them without any distinction, not by disparaging them, but by something else, by offending not only the officials but also the Impressionists, the Neo-Impressionists, the older and the newer kind of public . . . And as to the work, a method of contradiction, if you like, attacking the strongest abstractions, doing all that was forbidden, and reconstructing more or less happily, without any fear of exaggeration, even with exaggeration. Learning anew, and then, once having learnt, learn again. Conquer any timidity however much ridicule it may occasion. In front of his easel the painter is no slave, either of the past or of the present, either of nature or of his neighbour. He is himself, again himself, always himself. This effort of which I am speaking was made twenty years ago in silence in a state of ignorance, and then it began to assert itself.' Gauguin: *Racontars de rapin* (Paris 1951), p. 75 ff.

x. 'Their ideal is no doubt different from that of Romanticism; they took no pleasure in the vehement expression of the passions nor of the feelings of the heart... they clothe an abstract truth in the garb of dazzling realities.' P. Valin: Ceux de demain, Les jeunes et leurs revues, in *L'Art et l'Idée* (I, 1892), p. 62 ff.

y. 'It is not the deepest essence of the passions, it is their exterior gesticulation, their active manifestation.' Morice *La litterature,* p. 110.

z. 'painters of the soul'. Denis *Théories,* p. 33.

aa. Cf. Michaud: *Message poétique,* p. 416: 'La poésie ne saurait plus s'opposer à la science... pas de cette science qui faisait abstraction du monde psychique et intellectuel... mais de la science véritable, celle qui se propose pour objet de connaître la réalité tout entière.' (Poetry could no longer be opposed to science... not that science which abstracts from the psychic and intellectual world... but to true science, that which aims at knowing the whole of reality.) And also: A. Fouillé: *Le mouvement positiviste et la conception sociologique du monde,* (Paris 1896), p. 1: 'Montrer comment, dans leurs conclusions ultimes, peuvent ce concilier la philosophie positive et la philosophie idéaliste, tel est le but de cet ouvrage', which will bring about 'une représentation plus large de l'humanité et du monde.' (To show in their ultimate conclusions how positive philosophy and idealistic philosophy can be reconciled, this is the purpose of the present work', which will bring about 'a much more ample representation of humanity and the world'.)

ab. 'They were minds with a passion for truth, living in communion with nature... If they were induced to deform, to compose... it was also in order to achieve greater sincerity in the rendering of their sensations...' Denis *Théories,* p. 33.

ac. 'that intense contemporaneous desire ot the human mind to combine the mystic and the scientific stream into one large and living river of Beauty united with Truth in joy.' Morice *La Litterature,* p. 175.

ad. 'Integral Art.' Morice *La Litterature,* p. 60.

ae. 'I pretend that any one who plunges into allegory will be compelled to find such strong, novel and sublime ideas that without this resource with Pallas, Minerve, the Graces, Amor, Discord, etc., turned a hundred different ways, he will be cold, obscure, flat, common.' Delacroix *Journal* II, p. 343.

af. On the co-operation of Morice and Gauguin, cf. R. Huyghe: *Présentation de l'Ancien culte Mahorie,* (Paris, 1951) Introduction.

ag. '(The artist) is master of truth, of life. He brings you living nature. The invention that you reproach him for, which you mistrust, is precisely the soul of his

31

work, the breath that makes it alive, the warmth and the water that flowers cut of from their stem lack, causing them to wither too soon—Invention is the life of the works, the invention that circulates like blood through the elements borrowed from Nature by imitation . . .' 'a great artist has crowned some one of the innumerable beautiful figures of Nature with his genius, when the artist, himself a child of nature, nourished by her, living on her, rises to express the beauty of his mother: when nature has one of the changing aspects of her mysterious countenance eternalize the word of her enigma in the work of art.' Gauguin & Morice: *Noa Noa* (Paris 1924), p. 10.

ah. Actually Gauguin never let go reality, 'nature', and the following pronoun-cement of Morice is quite correct: 'Gauguin a une constante préoccupation de la réalité. Dans les contrées lointaines et primitives où il est retiré . . . il observe sans cesse, directement, il se renseigne, accumulant les documents, croquis . . . notes écrites . . .' (Morice *Gauguin*, p. 190). (Gauguin is constantly concerned with reality. In the remote and primitive parts where he has withdrawn from the world . . . he unceasingly observes, directly, he makes inquiries, accumulates documents, sketches . . . written notes . . .')

ai. Here creation is synonymous with nature, the created world.

ak. 'Perhaps one day they will attain to nature: i.e., that their conception of things will possibly become complete and profound enough for the work of art realized by them to preserve all the logical relations that form the essential character of living Nature, and thus there will be a greater analogy between the object and the subject, between the creation and the image that they will have reconstructed . . .' Denis *Théories*, p. 28.

al. 'From the canvas itself, a flat surface covered with colours, springs the bitter or the soothing emotion, 'literary' as the painters put it, without any need to inter-pose the memory of another old sensation (like that of the motif of nature utilized). In the one the form is expressive, in another nature wants to be so.' Denis *Théories*, p. 10.

Of course the controversy is carried on here against naturalism, but perhaps much more directly against (pictorial) symbolism, for the latter sought the new art in the first place in the choice of subjects, which were strongly allegorical.

am. 'Look about you in the immense creation of nature and you will see if there are no laws to create all human sentiments with altogether different means and yet similar in their effect.' Malingue XI, 14/1/1885, p. 44.

an. 'Instead of evoking our mental states by means of the subject represented, it was the work itself which was to transmit the initial sensation and perpetuate the emotion.' Denis *Théories*, p. 245.

ao. 'To remember that a picture—before being a war-steed, a naked woman, or no matter what anecdote,—is essentially a flat surface covered with colours put together in a particular order. Denis *Théories*, p. 1. Cf. the elaborate discussion on page 164 ff.

32

CHAPTER VI:

a. Cf. Page 103 ff.

b. A name for synthetism.

c. 'It was necessary to justify (ideist art) by abstract and complicated reasonings, so much did it seem to be paradoxical to our decadent civilizations that had forgotten all about initial revelation . . .' Aurier *Oeuvres*, p. 163.

d. 'Besides, Sérusier proved to us by means of Hegel, and the difficult articles by Albert Aurier insisted on the fact, that logically and philosophically speaking, Gauguin was right.' Denis *Théories*, p. 164.

e. Gauguin was certainly a reader of books. This is clear from the letter Malingue CLXVI to Morice, Tahiti November 1897.

f. It is impossible to prove this from the direct source material.

g. In 1885 the following books were published: A. Robaut, *L'Oeuvre Complet de Eugène Delacroix*, commenté par E. Chesneau, with an introduction by the latter; and also P. Dargenty: *Eugène Delacroix par lui-même*. But Gauguin will not yet have been able to read either of them in January when he wrote his letters from Kopenhagen. But some older publications, like e.g., the *Lettres de Delacroix*, publ. p. Phil. Burty, Paris 1878—although this contains little that is important in an art-theoretical respect—and the important *Oeuvres littéraires de Delacroix*, published in 1865—although much rarer—he may have known. Some of Delacroix's thoughts were also spread by means of articles. Van Gogh, e.g., at Nuenen already knew about Delacroix's theories (cf. *Brieven* 401).

h. 'It is a happy thing to dream, and it would be glorious to express what one dreamt.' *Cur. Esth.*, p. 262.

i. 'There are gay and playful tones, playful and sad ones, rich and gay ones, rich and sad ones, common and original ones.' *Cur. Estĥ.*, p. 92.

j. 'The work of Eugène Delacroix contains feeling, constant emotion, sharp emotion leading the spectator instantly through all the phases of the excited intellectual activity. The fixed idea of the master, if I am not mistaken, has been to render the struggles going on in the secret chambers of the soul and to make them, so to say, palpable, visible by means of colours and forms.' Robaut: *L'oeuvre complet de Eugène Delacroix* (commenté par E. Chesneau, 1885), Paris, p. XXXIX (cited from an article of Chesneau of about 1863).

k. In *Lettres à Daniel de Monfreid* is reproduced on page 178 a water colour that bears strong resemblance to the painting of Delacroix referred to. Is it a copy after this by Gauguin, or has he made it from memory?

l. 'In the same way with Delacroix arms and shoulders are always turned round in a manner that is foolish and impossible to reason, but nevertheless express the real in the passion' . . . 'Nothing but the painting, no trompe l'oeil' . . . 'The essential line with him (is) a means to accentuate an idea'. Malingue *Lettres* XXII, p. 62, 63.

33

m. This formulation looks paradoxical. It is not meant as such, however, but Gauguin had not yet the correct words for the new thoughts he tried to formulate. He means to say: we must seek for pictorial means to express the human view of things iconically—which may result in an image that deviates strongly from that of the naturalists—in which, however, the structure of the given object should be retained.

n. 'To me the great artist is the formula of the greatest intelligence, to him occur the most delicate and, therefore, the most invisible feelings and translations of the brain. Look about you in the immensity of the creation of nature and see if there are no laws to create all the human feelings with means that are totally different and yet similar in their effect.' ... 'From this I draw the conclusion that there are noble lines, mendacious ones, etc.' Malingue XI.

o. Humbert de Superville mentioned it in his *Essai sur les signes inconditionnels dans l'art* (1827). It is very doubtful if Gauguin had known this work. Perhaps Seurat had read it and told him about it. (Seurat himself wrote about the meaning of the direction of the lines only later on). Aurier turned out to have read it later on (in his article 'Les peintres symbolistes', *Oeuvres posthumes*, p. 302).

p. Malingue here has: 'abonde', which does not make sense, in our opinion. The emendation is ours,—abonde may very well be a clerical error. The same thing applies to the word 'pour', which we changed into 'par'.

q. 'Colours are even more explanatory although less manifold than lines owing to their power over the eye. There are noble tones, others are common, tranquil harmonies, soothing ones, others that exite you by their audacity.' ... 'would not lines and colours also give an impression of the more or less grandiose character of the artist?' ... 'The further I get the more I feel the necessity to render thought by something quite different from literature.' ... 'work in freedom and like mad ... a great feeling can be rendered immediately, dream about it, and find its simplest form.' Malingue *Lettres* XI, p. 45-47.

r. Rewald *Gauguin*, p. 16 note 73; cf. also H. H. Hofstätter: *Die Entstehung des 'Neuen Stils' in der französischen Malerei um 1890,* (Freiburg im Breisgau 1954) (nimeographed), p. 22. Even though Devallée, who tells us about it, is perhaps not entirely reliable, (Rewald *Post Impressionism*, p. 185 and note 2, page 239), we need not suppose with Hofstätter that at this time Gauguin meant something different by synthesis than later on, or that he had not yet thought of synthesis at all. The term is characteristic enough of Gauguin's thought and aims, also in the time immediately after 1885.

s. It is true, Gauguin's keramic work is quite different from what was made by others in this period. It shows strong Peruvian elements. We may no doubt refer in this case to Gauguin's reminiscences of his youth, when he must have seen Inca-pots in his childhood in Peru. Cf., e.g., the pot in the portrait of Laval (reproduced in Rewald *Post Impressionism*, p. 187) and very especially the pot with the portrait head of Gauguin himself (Rewald, *op. cit.*, p. 442 which also occurs in the still-life represented on page 443 there).

t. Rewald *Post Impressionism*, p. 289.

So we do not agree with Hofstätter who discovers all kinds of new elements in this work—p. 25 of his *Entstehung des neuen Stils*.

u. 'I have never had such a clear and lucid painting (a great deal of fantasy, for instance)'. Malingue LVII, p. 117.

v. A few times, as, e.g., in the landscape of St.-Briac reproduced in Rewald *Post Impressionism*, p. 192.

w. Here we use the term in the same way in which he operates with it. This indicates that in the work the emphasis is laid on the play of lines over the surface, and on the mutual relations between the colours.

x. E.g., the oval shape on Bernard's work in 1887, reproduced in Rewald, *op. cit.*, p. 195.

y. We express ourselves so cautiously on purpose, for it does not seem quite certain that Bernard pronounced or wrote down these opinions in 1888 literally like this. The quotation is from E. Bernard: *Souvenirs inédits sur l'artiste peintre Paul Gauguin et ses compagnons,* (1939), p. 11—quoted by H. Dorra, Emile Bernard and Paul Gauguin, *Gazette des Beaux Arts,* (April, 1955), p. 227 ff. The remarkable elliptic form of this sentence we leave as it is without any attempt at correction. The meaning will no doubt be clear. This quotation is a very good illustration of Puig's pronouncement on Bernard's style of writing: 'Et ce style était souvent un peu compliqué, et même prétentieux'. (And this style was often a little involved and even pretentious). R. Puig: *P. Gauguin, G. D. de Monfreid, et leurs amis,* (Perpignan, 1958), p. 73.

z. 'Since the idea is the form of things acquired by the imagination, one should not paint in front of things but by calling them back into the imagination that had acquired them, which preserved them in the idea; thus the idea of a thing gave the suitable form to the subject of the picture, or rather to its ideal (the sum total of the ideas) it gave the simplification purporting to be the essential in things perceived, and consequently details are rejected. E. Bernard: *Souvenirs inédits sur l'artiste peintre Paul Gauguin et ses compagnons* (1939), p. 11, cited in translation by H. Dorra: E. Bernard and Paul Gauguin, *Gaz. Beaux Arts* (1955), p. 238.

aa. 'fantastical poetry' (of Rimbaud c.s.). Cf., p. 71.

ab. Quoted by us on page 17.

ac. 'the symbolic meaning that the abstract and mystic drawing may contain . . .' 'your investigations with regard to the properties of lines with opposite movements.' Van Gogh *Brieven* B 14—in B 15 van Gogh says he is happy that B. is with Gauguin at that moment, which implies that the letter to which Van Gogh refers in B. 14 was at any rate written before this contact.

ad. ' body of psychological and quasi literary ideas' . . . 'the absolute predominance of the decorative principle in all the branches of art.' . . 'a natural talent for synthesis', 'a marvellous instinct for the resources of colour', 'a profound knowledge of their harmony,' 'infinite delicacy in varying their use.' *Le Japon Artistique,* (documents d'art et d'industrie réunis par S. Bing, publication mensuelle, le fasc. March 1888), p. 13, 14.

The head at the right hand side of the bottom of Bernard's 'Bretonnes dans la prairie', reproduced in Rewald, *Post Impressionism*, p. 251, shows a striking resemblance to a head in Hokusai's composition representing a row of men, depicted with the article quoted here. It might very well be a borrowing, but this is not so evident on the other hand, that we should be warranted in drawing the conclusion that Bernard had read this article.

ae. Hofstätter also mentions this influence in his *Entstehung des neuen Stils,* and then refers to Mackmurdo, an English artist we do not know anything about, and who was certainly not a prominent personality.

af. In this part of our study we do not intend to repeat the excellent articles on this period and these artists written by Huyghe, Dorra, Rewald and a few others. We are exclusively concerned with the art-theories of these painters, but in the discussion about them it is unavoidable for us to enter into their art as such.

ag. On the origin of this term, cf. Rewald, *Post Impressionism*, p. 194. It will have been used by Dujardin to denote some analogy with Limoges enamel.

ah. 'it is not at all like Degas'.

ai. '(Gauguin) truly saw in my work and learnt from the exposition of my ideas all that could be derived from Cézanne.' Chassé: *Le mouvement symboliste,* p. 100 cites a letter of Bernard to the writer.

ak. This is confirmed by a later letter of Gauguin's, published in Rewald, *Post Impressionism*, p. 283—Nov. 1889 of Gauguin to Theo Van Gogh (cf. Rewald *op. cit.*, p. 311, note 21).

al. In this connection Denis' remark is remarkable as well as elucidating: 'La reconstruction d'art que Cézanne avait commencée avec les materiaux de l'impressionnisme, Gauguin l'a continué avec moins de sensibilité et d'ampleur, mais avec plus de rigeur théorique: Il a rendu plus explicite la pensée de Cézanne.' (Denis *Théories*, p. 262). (The reconstruction of art begun by Cézanne with the materials of impressionism has been continued by Gauguin with less sensibility and fulness, but with more theoretical rigour: he has made Cézanne's thought more explicit).

am. Delacroix had already developed similar ideas. Cf. his *Journal,* 12 October 1853.

an. We express some reserve because we are not at all certain that Morice's note to the story we are quoting is correct: 'Ces lignes datent de son second séjour à Pont-Aven (1888)' (These lines date from his second stay at Pont-Aven). (Morice, *Gauguin,* p. 230 ff.) Rotonchamp in his book on Gauguin gives the same 'legend' of Mani-Vehli-Zumbul-Zadi (p. 215) adding: 'Gauguin a lui-même exposé, en une fantaisiste parable, les éléments de sa technique propre.' (Gauguin himself has shown the elements of his own technique in a fantastic parable). Its source is not given here either. Finally we find this story in *Avant et Après* (p. 55)—if we should have to look upon this passage as the original source, Morice would have been mistaken, and ought to have said: 1898, during the second stay in Tahiti. The ideal to give quiet, stately figures in the art of painting, which is also expressed in this story, admirably suits the work of this period, better than it would do the earlier one.

R. L. Herbert (Seurat in Chicago and New York, *Burlington Magazine* (C 1958), p. 151, note 21) tells us that before 1886 Gauguin had lent a manuscript to Seurat containing the copy of a Turkish painter's guide, that of the Turkish poet Vehli Mohamed Zumbul Zadé († 1809). If the source from which Herbert draws in this case should have to be considered as reliable, it would be very interesting, because then this manuscript might have influenced Seurat in the direction of a classical ideal of style. But then the question remains where Gauguin had copied the fragment from. The *Encyclopaedie des Islam* IV (Leiden-Leipzig 1934) and J. v. Hammer-Purgstall: *Geschichte des osmanischen Dichtkunst* (Pesth, 1838) IV, pp. 554-573 and E. J. W. Gibb: *A History of Ottoman Poetry*, (ed. E. G. Browne, London, 1905) IV, pp. 242-265, give all of them elaborate views of Sumbulzade Wehli, and the only work relevant to this question seems to be the Lutfiyya. However, there is nowhere any mention made—in spite of the extremely detailed bibliographies—of a translation of this work into French or into any other West-European language. The only possibility would be for a Turcologist of the middle of the 19th century, such as, e.g. C. A. C. Barbier de Meynard, to have given a translation of some passage in a non-scientific publication. In the bibliographies bearing on this there is however not even the merest indication of such an article to be found. But the character of the Turkish poet's work, and in particular that of the Lutfiyya, in no way suggests that such a passage resembling Gauguin's story really occurs in it. And in addition it is questionable whether a Turk would speak of the art of painting in such a way, while on the other hand it is certainly possible for Gauguin to have formulated similar views of the nature of the art of painting, also about 1885.

We think we are warranted to suppose that this story was written by Gauguin himself—in which case it is difficult to fix the date with any degree of certainty. Gauguin would then have introduced the figure of Mani-Vehli-Zumbul-Zadi, because he somewhere found this name and thought it poetical, strange and remote enough to function as the principal character of this legend. There is a certain analogy in it with Nietsche's *Also sprach Zarathustra,* which was published in 1884. So Gauguin may have heard or read about it. The addition of 'Mani' to the Turkish poet's name, which was not very accurate either, points in this direction. It is not a falsification, but may be a legend invented by Gauguin in order to express some of his ideas in a literary form.

ao. 'It is better to paint from memory, in that way your work will be yours; your sensation, your intelligence and your soul will then survive for the eye of the amateur . . . Seek harmony.' Morice *Gauguin,* p. 213.

ap. Abstraction in this case has little or nothing in common with the abstraction intended or practised after 1900 (synonymous with nonfigurative). Cf. chapter V, note v. We again refer to this in connection with the note given by Malingue with Letter LXVII of August 1888 to Schuffenecker. 'Abstraction' is here perhaps best translated by 'stylization' although the former term implies a little more than the rather technical ring of the word 'stylization'.

aq. 'A piece of advice, do not paint too much from nature. Art is an abstraction, borrow it from nature by dreaming in front of it and think more of the creation that will result.' Malingue LXVII.

ar. 'only using colour as a combination of tones, as different harmonies, they still give the impression of warmth, etc.' Malingue LXXV.

as. 'In a way the shadow is at your service.' Malingue LXXV.

at. ' a synthesis of form and colour while only considering the dominant'. Malingue LXVII (cited by Rewald *Post Impressionism*, p. 196).

au. 'Why do you talk to me about my terrible mysticism. Be an impressionist to the end and fear nothing.' Malingue LXXIII.

av. It is very well possible that Schuffenecker here reacted to a letter in which Gauguin explained his thoughts. We must certainly not exclude the possibility of some letters having got lost. Another possibility might be found in letter LXXI, in Malingue. There is also the chance of oral communication via men like Sérusier of the ideas of Gauguin, while finally, apart from all this, (or in collaboration with it) it is quite possible that Schuffenecker wrote in response to some pictures he had seen (e.g. 'Vision après le sermon') but had not quite understood.

aw. In the manner of working of the 'Vision après le sermon' it is very plausible that Gauguin was influenced by Bernard—in the cloisonné. But, quite different from what Bernard pretented, this was not the essential thing (to Gauguin). For a short time after he again made various other works in which he experimented with different techniques. We are referring to the works reproduced in Rewald *Post Impressionism*, p. 248, 259, 258. With Gauguin the strict cloisonnéism is only a very transitory phase.

ax. 'I think I have to make Puvis mixed with the Japanese manner.' Malingue LXXV.

ay. 'a source of fine modern style'. Malingue LXXV.

az. ' a remembrance of our garden at Etten.' Van Gogh *Brieven*, No. 562.

ba. 'I leave it to the critics to say whether or not I have already sung a lullaby with the colours . . .' Van Gogh *Brieven*, No. 571a.

bb. 'Perhaps in the 'Berceuse' (the cradle) there is an effort to compose some colour-music about here . . .' Van Gogh *Brieven*, No. 567.

bc. 'decadent literature'. Denis *Théories*, p. 160 ff.

bd. For this purpose he could consult the elaborately annotated French translation made by M. N. Bouillet, and published in 1875.

be. 'a formless landscape, by dint of being formulated synthetically, in violet, vermilion, veronese green and other pure colours as they come out of the tube almost without any mixture with white.' 'How do you see that tree? Gauguin had asked in front of a nook in the Bois d'Amour; is it green? Put on green then, the most beautiful green of your palette; and that shade, rather blue? Be not afraid to paint it as blue as possible.' Denis *Théories,* p. 160.

bf. 'Thus, in a paradoxical, unforgettable form, we were for the first time presented with the fertile concept of 'the surface covered with colours assembled in a particular order.' Ditto.

bg. 'every work of art was a transportation, a caricature, the passionate equivalent of a sensation received.' Ditto.

bh. 'Gauguin was no teacher ... On the contrary, he was an intuitive person. In his conversation as in his stories there were happy aphorisms, profound insights, finally assertions of a logic that was stupefying to us.' Denis *Théories,* p. 162.

bi. Also later on Sérusier repeatedly came back to Le Pouldu.

bj. In this case we follow Rewald's on the whole convincing chronology. Rewald *Post Impressionism,* p. 310, note 4 and p. 283.

bk. It is not clear why Rewald dates this work in 1890 (p. 441). From Letter XCIII in Malingue, dated (not by way of conjecture) November 1889, it appears clearly that the work was finished then.

bl. 'The fox an Indian symbol of perversity'. Malingue LXXXVII.

bm. 'we have to work in both directions'. Malingue LXXXVII.

bn. 'lack of the beyond'. Ditto.

bo. It will not be easy to discover the exact meaning of this indication of the day. Probably this is an instance of the esoteric jargon the 'Nabis' used among themselves.

bp. 'What has especially embarrassed me is this: what should be the part of nature in the work? Where should one stop? and finally, from the material point of view, the execution, should we work from nature or only look and remember?' Sérusier, *A.B.C. de la peinture,* p. 39.

bq. 'I am sorry for what I have said about Gauguin, he has nothing of the humbug, at least with regard to those who he knows can understand him.' Ditto, p. 42.

br. We may suppose that by this he means those theories that he had mentioned to Denis in his letter from Le Pouldu 1889 under a): 'Principes immuables' (*ABC de la peinture,* p. 42).

bs. 'Of all my theories that have been tried this winter only this simple law is left: avoid bringing together two tones that are too wide apart as values if at least there is no connection between them.' Ditto, p. 45.

bt. 'Primitive art proceeds from the mind and uses nature. So-called refined art proceeds from sensuality and serves nature. Nature is the servant of the former and the mistress of the latter, but the servant cannot forget her origin and degrades the mind by allowing him to adore her. This now is how we have fallen into the abominable error of naturalism...' Morice *Gauguin,* p. 25/29; cf. Rewald *Post Impressionism,* p. 489, note 25 and p. 452.

It is at most the formulation which is new. For similar thoughts had already clearly occurred in his earlier letters, as we have already seen more than once.

bu. 'Gauguin is coming back, I have received his tidings. He tells me he has studied without looking for symbolism. Oh! all the better. He has risen above people that make me even detest this word.' Sérusier, p. 63.

bv. 'the shackles of symbolism'. *Gauguin à Daniel de Monfreid,* Nov. 1901, p. 333.

Symbolism is here clearly intended in the sense of the art of Moreau, the people of the Rose†Croix, etc. As has been explained before, it is very difficult to find a terminology which is clear and does not deviate too much from the terminology used in the nineteen-nineties. As a matter of fact we have been content to adopt the inconsistent terminology of the period, and preferred it to a series of neologisms, although we are thus compelled every time to describe in more detail what was meant in our opinion.

CHAPTER VII:

a. 'He 'philosophizes' when he demonstrates his way of understanding general ideas... (saying) 'Philosophy is difficult if it is not in me by instinct. It is sweet in our sleep with the dream that adorns it—it is not science... it is not a logical conclusion as grave persons would like to teach us, but it is a weapon that we make for ourselves as savages. It does not present itself as a reality, but as an image: like a picture, admirable if the picture is a master piece.' Morice *Gauguin,* p. 82/83.

b. 'elevate to dogmas that will have no heretics among true poets'. Morice *La littérature,* p. 267.

c. 'the popularization of the sciences'. Ditto, p. 2.

d. 'Mediocrity. The fatal product of the diffusion of light—the enormous joke, that monstrous modern ecstasy.' Ditto, p. 2.

e. 'they want nothing but formulae, 2 and 2 are 4, there is only this at the back of everything.' Ditto, p. 7.

f. Morice's mysticism is characteristically intellectualistic, like that of Plotinus. Cf., e.g., his pronouncement: 'Poète... n'oublie pas... que ta joie doit être cérébrale.' (Poet, do not forget that your joy is cerebral.) (*Littérature de tout à l'heure,* p. 360).

g. 'Emanations of God, sparks escaped from the fire of the All-Light, they —the poets—return into it.' Ditto, p. 14, cf. Dr. D. Loenen: De wijsbegeerte van den hellenistisch-romeinschen tijd, in *Philosophia* I (editor H. van Oyen, 1947), p. 134/5 (where Plotinus is discussed).

h. 'the universal law of life, of the souls.' . . . 'These souls are the exterior manifestations of God who emits them with the mission to co-operate, each in their own way, to the luminous harmony of the world.' Morice *La littérature,* p. 14.

i. 'A book, a work of art, a musical phrase, pure thought itself . . . are eternalizations of the I. From this we make as many means to disengage our I-ness from contingencies, and it is in this way also that the human I comes back as soon as it escapes from contingencies to the seat of the absolute, to the metaphysical place of the Ideas, to God.' Ditto, p. 30.

k. 'the form in the work that is thus perfect and ideal is only the bait offered to seduce the senses to let themselves be appeased; they have fallen asleep in a delicious drunkenness and leave the spirit free, the senses are enchanted to recognise the lines and the primitive sounds, the forms that have not yet been betrayed by an artifice and which a genius finds in his communion with Nature.' Ditto, p. 33.

l. (to the liberated spirit is left) 'the vague and charming apparition of a divine entity of the Infinite'. Ditto, p. 33.

m. 'understood thus, art is only the revelator of the Infinite, it is the very means to penetrate into it. It goes much deeper than any philosophy, it prolongs and reverberates the revelation of a Gospel . . .' Morice *La littérature,* p. 33.

Here Dr. Abraham Kuyper's criticism started, which we will examine more closely in the following chapter.

n. 'Here is the great, the most important, the first sign of a new Literature, here, in this ardour to unite Truth and Beauty, in this desirable unity of Faith and Joy, Science and Art—'Integral Art'. Ditto, p. 59.

o. 'We seek the truth in the harmonic laws of Beauty, deducting from the latter all metaphysics—because the harmony of the nuances and the sounds symbolises the harmony of the souls and worlds—and all morals . . .' Ditto, p. 65.

p. 'to let join them each other in a single grand and living river of Beauty united with the Truth in Joy the mystic and the scientific movement.' Ditto, p. 177.

q. 'While waiting for the moment when science has decidedly turned to mysticism, the intuitions of the dream forstall science, celebrate such an as yet future and already definitive alliance of the religious with the scientific sense in an aesthetic fête where the very human desire for a reunion of all the human powers is glorified by a return to original simplicity.' Morice *La littérature,* p. 355.

r. Morice also uses the word 'simplicity' with respect to painting. Cf. *La littérature de tout à l'heure,* p. 283.

s. 'to suggest the whole of man by the whole of art.' Ditto, p. 358.

41

t. 'the synthesis cannot be localized in a pure psychology of the passions, nor in a dramatization of the sentiments, nor in the pure observation of the world as we see it immediately round us, for then it would run the risk of ceasing to be a synthesis and become analysis again.' Morice *La littérature,* p. 358, 359.

u. 'The work of art is a transaction between the temperament of the artist and nature.' Morice *La littérature,* p. 362.

v. We have the word 'christian' printed in small type on purpose, not in capital letters: the search for a synthesis between Christian—i.e. Biblical—Truth and ancient pagan philosophy was certainly understandable in the earliest Christian thinkers who themselves had been educated and formed in the ancient pagan spirit —the conversion of an entire manner of thought and of a mental attitude is not such a simple and immediately realisable process. And sometimes this synthesis will have been unconsciously due to the fact that long-established terms were used which, somehow, carried along something of their own original 'burden'. But this synthesis as such is not typically Christian, and more than once it actually caused the Christian thinkers, against their will, to get into conflict with Holy Scripture itself. Especially in mystical circles this 'christianized' Neo-platonic thought had a prolonged influence, and a little more than half a century ago its influence was still strong.

w. 'In art the soul regains its own depth in order that (!) the soul may free itself from all fetters for the joy and the understanding of the world and itself.' Morice *La littérature,* p. 367.

x. 'Every life is chained to another life' . . . 'the disorder of the world'. Morice *La littérature,* p. 367.

y. 'This recovery of the self through freedom'. Ditto, p. 170.

z. 'a feeling of unlimited power.' Ditto, p. 170.

aa. 'Man's glory in the world is that instead of the dubious honour of being elected for kingship (what a chimera!)—this is an obvious allusion to the Biblical Christian view—he is really reduced to being merely the servant of Nature (with a capital letter) and its confident. Here, natural science intervenes to make a pact for a fertile alliance with metaphysics . . .' Ditto, p. 170.

ab. 'the contemporary moment' . . . 'The Dream that escapes himself may reach the appearence of everyday reality.' Ditto, p. 373.

ac. 'Suggestion can do what expression can not. Suggestion is the language of the 'correspondences' and of the affinities of the soul and nature' . . . 'Suggestion alone can render in a few lines the perpetual crossing and recrossing and the mingling of details to which expression would devote whole pages' . . . 'it has ascended to the very source of all language, to the laws of the adaption of the sounds, and the colours, of the words to the ideas.' Ditto, p. 378.

42

ad. 'A poet is the necessary intermediary not only between humanity and nature, but also between man and thought. The arts form a hierarchy according to the more or less numerous means with which they furnish the poet for the accomplishment of his function as an intermediary.' H. Mahaut: Notes synthétiques de Paul Gauguin, *Vers et Prose* (VI, 1910), p. 51 ff.

ae. 'Painting is the most beautiful of all the arts, all the sensations are summarized in it, looking at it everybody can create a novel, according as his imagination prompts him, at one glance he can have his soul overwhelmed by profound remembrances; with no efforts of the memory everything is summarized in one single instant.—A complete art, comprising all the others and completing them—.' Ditto.

af. 'the art of the colorist' ... 'to enter into an intimate relation with nature.' Ditto.

ag. 'you can freely dream while you listen to music just as when you look at a picture.' Ditto.

ah. 'The divine transposition for whose accomplishment man exists goes from the fact to the ideal.' Mallarmé *Divagations* (Paris 1897, p. 121, cf. A. Micha: *Verlaine et les poètes symbolistes* (Paris 1943 [17]), p. 53.

ai. This quotation is very difficult to translate; it is certainly incapable of anything like a literal rendering, as Mallarmé's style is strongly suggestive and even relies for its meaning and effect on the sound of his language. The following attempt is, therefore, only an approximation:
'Abolished is the pretention—aesthetically speaking an error, although it dominates master-pieces—that it would be possible to put on the thin paper of a volume anything else but, e.g., the horror of the wood or the threat of thunder silently waiting scattered in the foliage: not the wood as a whole in the density of its trees ... Monuments, the sea, the human face, in their inherent fulness, retain a force so much more lovable that a description would only veil them, which ought to be said by evocation, an allusion I know, suggestion. This terminology is a little at random and testifies to the tendency, perhaps a very decisive one, to which literary art has been subjected, and by which it has been determined as well as freed. Magic it has if it only liberates, loose from a handful of dust or reality, without binding it in the book, even (if understood) as a text, the volatile dispersion that is the spirit, which is only concerned with the musicality of the whole.' Mallarmé *Divagations,* p. 245/6.

ak. 'nothing would reveal the meaning of the allegory to us.' Malingue CLXX.

al. It is not quite clear what this remark refers to, to what precedes or to what follows? In either case the influence is clear. But we have not been able to locate the literal wording of the quotation—Gauguin may be quoting something from memory that he had heard from Mallarmé on one of the occasions of his meeting him. For it is clear that Mallarmé's thought turned in this direction. We refer, e.g., to his pronouncement: 'Nommer un objet, c'est supprimer les trois-quarts de la jouissance d'un poème qui est faite du bonheur de deviner, peu à peu . . .' (Giving a thing a name is suppressing three quarters of the enjoyment of a poem which is constituted of the happiness of divining little by little . . .) (J. Huret, *Enquête sur l'évolution littéraire*, p. 57).

am. 'my dream is not tangible, it does not contain any allegory; like a musical poem, it can do without a libretto. (Quoted from Mallarmé). Consequently the essential thing in a work (of art) is immaterial and superior and consists exactly in 'that which has not been expressed: it results from the lines, without the colours or the words, it has not been constituted in a material sense.' Malingue CLXX, Tahiti, March 1899, p. 288.

an. 'Fly! Yonder! Fly! I feel that the birds are intoxicated
Because they are in the foam of the unknown waves and in
the heavens

. . .

I will go! Steamer with thy dancing masts
Weigh anchor to depart for an exotic nature!'

Ch. Chassé: *Le mouvement symboliste* (Paris 1947), p. 86, from 'Brise Marine' of 1865, published 1886, 1887, 1893 (and 1899). *Oeuvres Complètes* (1951), p. 38 and p. 1432/3.

ao. 'Free at last, without any financial worries, and I shall be able to love, sing and die.' Malingue C.

ap. 'The Western world is corrupt and whoever is a Hercules can obtain new strength by touching the soil over there, like Antaeus.' Malingue CVI.

aq. 'My artistic centre is in my brain and nowhere else, and I am strong because I am never led astray by the others and because I make what is in me.' Malingue CXXVII.

ar. 'If . . . I take . . . an intelligent (person) and transport him into a remote country I am sure . . . this will create a new world of ideas in him . . . all this unknown vitality will be added to his own vitality; some thousands of ideas and sensations will enrich the dictionary of his mortal being . . .' *Cur. Esth.*, p. 213/214.

as. 'Besides Madagascar offers more resources with respect to types, religion, mysticism, symbolism.' Malingue CIX.

It is also possible to think of a distant influence of Plotinus about whom one of those who were acquainted with the subject in this respect may have talked to him, such as Morice, Meyer de Haan, Bernard, or Sérusier. Bréhier summarizes Plotinus' view as follows: 'Plotin allait demander aux Barbares . . . la réalité, l'intuition vivante que risquaient de faire perdre les constructions savantes et compliquées de la philosophie grecque.' (Plotinus would demand from the barbarians . . . reality, the living intuition, the loss of which was risked by the learned and complicated constructions of Greek philosophy), p. 124.

at. He calls them symbolists himself.

44

au. 'this formidable unknown'. G.-A. Aurier: Les peintres symbolistes, in *Oeuvres Posthumes* (1893), p. 293. We will refer to this article as Aurier 2.

av. 'guardians of eternal knowledge'. Aurier 2, p. 294.

aw. 'the antinomy of all art: concrete truth, illusionism, 'trompe-l'oeil'. Aurier: Le symbolisme en peinture, Paul Gauguin. *Mercure de France* (II 1891), p. 162— we will cite this article as Aurier 1.

ax. 'the short-sighted copy of social anecdotes, the imbecil imitation of the warts of nature, vulgar observation.' Aurier 2, p. 294.

ay. 'poor, stupid prisoner of Plato's allegorical cave.' Aurier 1, p. 159.

az. This 'Azure' is found in a poem entitled: L'Azur by Mallarmé. 'L'azur symbolizes the poet's artistic ideal', says A. Micha—note 4, to page 54 in: '*Verlaine et les poètes symbolistes*'. It has been printed here. Originally it was published in *L'Artiste*, later on in *Le Parnasse contemporain*.

ba. 'Everywhere they are vindicating the right to the dream, the right to pasture in the azure heavens, the right to wing their way towards the stars to which the absolute truth has been denied.' Aurier 2, p. 294.

bb. 'They have made efforts to understand the mysterious meaning of lines, the effects of light, and shadows, in order to use these elements, like the letters of an alphabet, to write the beautiful poem of their dreams and of their ideas.' Aurier 2, p. 296.

bc. 'these directly signifying characters (forms, lines, colours, etc.)' Aurier 1, p. 164.

bd. 'art, the supreme way of expression, could not express the universality of the souls.' Aurier 2, p. 299.

be. Bréhier translates 'Nous' by Intelligence (cf. Bréhier *La Philosophie de Plotin,* p. 81), compare also note bh.

bf. 'the form, ... the body of every object is ... the tangible modality of its being, i.e., the visible signification of a 'pensée'. Aurier 2, p. 299/301.

bg. 'through all this repulsive jargon and through all this hoary scholasticism'. Aurier 2, p. 299/301.

bh. This is also found in Plotinus. About this Bréhier says: 'The Intelligence corrresponds with the platonic ideas'. (*op. cit.,* p. 81).
'In nature everything is ultimately only a signified Idea'. Aurier 2, p. 299/301.

bi. 'the superior minds of our poor blind humanity'. Aurier 2, p. 301.

bk. '(He is) the expressor of the absolute Beings' ... 'as a superior man he is the tamer of the monster illusion; he knows how to walk as a master in this temple of fantasy 'where living columns sometimes utter confused words', whereas the imbecil human herd, duped by appearances that make them deny the essential ideas, will pass by in eternal blindness, watched by the forests of familiar looking symbols.' Aurier 1, p. 161/2, quoted from Baudelaire's poem 'Correspondances'.

bl. 'The various combinations of lines, plans, shades, colours, constitute the vocabulary of a mysterious language which is miraculously expressive'. Aurier 1, p. 161/2.

bm. 'this language, like all languages, has its alphabeth, its orthography, its grammar, syntax, even its rhetoric which is: the style'. Aurier 2, p. 302.

bn. 'Many persons say I cannot draw, because I make special forms. When will they understand that the execution, the drawing, and the colour (the Style) must be in accordance with the poem?' Morice *Gauguin*, p. 122—a letter to Morice from Tahiti concerning Gauguin's 'D'où venons-nous . . .'

bo. 'In a way I work like the Bible of which the doctrine . . . announces itself in a symbolic form presenting a double aspect, a form which first materializes the pure Idea in order to make it better understandable . . . this is the literal, super-ficial, figurative, mysterious meaning of a parable; and then the second aspect which gives the Spirit of the former sense. This is the sense that is not figurative anymore, but the formed, explicit one of this parable.' Malingue Lettres CLXXII.

This view of the Bible shows close agreement with Swedenborg's, which Gauguin may have known via Balzac, whose *Séraphita* was one of the painter's favourite books and in which similar ideas were expounded (p. 154).

bp. 'as a minimum it is a fragment of the spirituality of the artist, as a maximum it is this whole spirituality of the artist with added to it the essential spirituality of the various objective beings.' Aurier 2, p. 303.

bq. 'which is the synthesis of two souls, the soul of the artist and that of nature.' Ditto.

br. 'It is this influx, this sympathetic radiation felt at the sight of a master piece which is called the feeling of beauty, the aesthetic emotion.' Ditto.

bs. 'The aesthetics of Plotinus is really impregnated with this idea, that beauty is not added to things as an exterior accidental quality but constitutes their true essence (*Ennéades* I, 2) . . . beauty must, therefore, be the reflex of an Idea which makes this being what it is. Aesthetic value and intellectual value coalesce.' E. Bréhier: *La Philosophie de Plotin*, (Paris 1928), p. 85.

bt. 'some muddy sexuality' . . . 'pure and simple animality' . . . 'we must again learn what is love, the source of any comprehension.' Aurier *Oeuvres*, p. 202 (from a not previously published 'Essay sur une nouvelle methode de critique').

bu. It is characteristic of Aurier to accept the results of positivism, nothwith-standing, however much he may have depreciated it. He does not suggest a new view which is really directed against the fundamental tenets of positivism and is therefore able to regret its results.

bv. 'Only one love has still been permitted to us, that of works of art. Let us throw ourselves on that last plank of salvation.' Aurier *Oeuvres*, p. 202.

46

bw. In the next chapter we will revert to this thought and examine Dr. A. Kuyper's criticism of it (especially in connection with the conceptions of the meaning of a symbol).

'Understood thus, art is merely the revealer of the Infinite . . . So by nature, and in essence, art is religious.' Morice *Littérature,* p. 34, 35, cited by Lehmann *Symbolist aesthetics,* p. 116.

bx. 'besides, it is found to be at bottom identical with primitive art, art as it was discovered by the instinctive geniuses of the earliest times of humanity.' Aurier 1, p. 163, cf. 2, p. 304.

by. 'It is the plastic interpretation of platonism done by a savage genius.' Aurier 2, p. 305.

bz. 'Ideational, for its unique ideal will be the expression of the Idea.' Aurier 1, p. 162.

ca. 'Symbolistic, for it expresses this Idea by means of forms.' Ditto.

cb. 'Synthetistic, for it will write these forms, these signs, according to a method which is generally understandable.' Ditto.

cc. 'Subjective, for the object will never be considered as an object but as the sign of an idea perceived by the subject.' Ditto.

cd. '(It is consequently) decorative—for decorative art in its proper sense, as the Egyptians, very probably the Greeks and the Primitives understood it, is nothing but a manifestation of art at once subjective, synthetic, symbolic and ideational.' Ditto.

ce. for 'Sérusier proved to us by means of Hegel,—and the abstruse articles by Albert Aurier insisted on the fact—that logically, philosophically, Gauguin was right'. Denis *Théories,* p. 162.

cf. 'Remember that a picture—before being a war horse, a naked woman, or whatever anecdote—is essentially a surface area covered with colours assembled in a certain order.' Denis *Théories,* p. 1.

cg. 'Thus for the first time the future concept of 'the surface area covered with colours assembled in a certain order' was given us in a paradoxical, unforgettable form'. Denis *Théories,* p. 161.

ch. 'Thus we came to know that every work of art is a transposition, a caricature, the passionate equivalent of a sensation perceived.' Ditto.

ci. 'There is art when the figures are given with plastic rounding.' Ditto, p. 10.

ck. 'From the canvas itself, a surface area coated with colours springs the bitter or the consoling emotion, 'literary' as the painters say, without there being any need to interpose the memory of another earlier sensation (like that of the given natural object used)'. Ditto.

47

cl. 'A Byzantine Christ is a symbol, the Jesus of modern painters, even if provided with a most accurate kiffyed, is merely literary. In the first it is the form which is expressive, in the second nature (being imitated) wants to be so as such.' Denis *Théories*, p. 10.

cm. By 'in its proper sense' we mean: in the sense in which this term was generally used by the painters. Properly speaking, the term is wrong, as 'literary' is not at all identical with naturalistically descriptive.

cn. Here 'symbolist' means 'synthetistical'. By that mystical tendency he refers to those we have called symbolists, the painters who were related to the decadent poets.

co. 'We are astonished that informed critics ... take pleasure in confusing mystical and allegorical tendencies, i.e., the attempt to express oneself by means of the subject and the symbolistic tendencies, i.e., the search for an expression by means of the work of art.' Denis *Théories*, p. 17.

cp. 'The inaugurators of synthetist art were landscapists, still-life painters, not at all 'painters of the soul'. Denis *Théories*, p. 33.

cq. Deformation is not used here in the sense of twentieth-century art, which interferes with the structure of the natural object. Here we use it in such a way that we can also say: Raphael deforms.

cr. By 'content' we mean that which Panofsky renders by the word 'meaning' (in his introduction to his *'Meaning in the visual arts'* (Garden City, N. York, 1955), page 40 passim.

cs. 'hermetique' here means 'lofty', 'elevated above reality'.

ct. 'Art is the sanctification of nature, of the nature of everybody who is content to live. What is the great art that is called decorative, the art of the Hindus, the Assyrians, the Egyptians, the Greeks, the art of the Middle Ages and the Renaissance (i.c. all art that has ever been important) and the decidedly superior modern art works (he may be referring to Cézanne and Gauguin)? What else is it but disguising common sensations—of natural objects—as sacred icons, hermetic, impressive.' Denis *Théories*, p. 12.

cu. We use the term 'realistic' here in a sense which is not identical with 'naturalistic'. By 'realistic' we mean that the subject has been derived from everyday reality, whereas 'naturalistic' refers rather to the manner in which the subject-matter (which is perhaps, not at all realistic, e.g., in Bouguereau) has been rendered. And, in addition, we use the term 'motifs' in the same sense as Panofsky does in his introduction just mentioned (note cr)).

cv. 'The universal triumph of the imagination of the aesthetes over the stupid efforts at imitation; the triumph of the feeling of beauty over the naturalist lie.' Denis *Théories*, p. 12.

48

cw. 'They (i.e. the first generation of the new art) were willing to submit to the laws of harmony governing the relations between the colours, the arrangement of lines (the researches of Seurat, Bernard, C. Pissarro); but it also served to bring more sincerity in the rendering of their impressions' ... 'There was, therefore, a close correspondence between forms and sensations.' Denis *Théories*, p. 33.

cx. 'From an objective standpoint the decorative, aesthetic, and rational composition ... became the counter-part, the necessary corrective of the theory of the equivalents. The latter justified all possible transpositions with regard to the expression, even those that had the character of caricatures, any excessive rendering of character: the objective deformation in its turn compelled the artist to transpose everything into Beauty. In summary: the expressive synthesis, the symbol of a sensation or a feeling, was to be an eloquent transcription, and at the same time an object that had been composed to be a pleasure to the eye. Denis *Théories*, p. 260.

cy. 'We made a singular mixture of Plotinus, Edgar Poe, Baudelaire and Schopenhauer'. Quoted from *Nouvelles théories,* cited by Ch. Chassé: *Le mouvement symboliste* (1947), p. 152.

cz. Cf. Agnes Humbert: *Les Nabis,* p. 54 passim, W. Haftmann: *Malerei im 20. Jahrhundert,* (München 1954), p. 51.

da. 'a collection of rules required by the organisation of the spiritual being.' *Cur Esth.,* p. 274.

db. 'by the whole, by the profound, complete harmony between his colour, his subject, his drawing, and by the dramatic gestures of his figures.' *Cur. Esth.,* p. 243.

dc. 'There was, consequently, a close correspondence between forms and sensations.' Cf. note cx.

dd. 'I want a firm, simple and finished drawing. By this I do not mean that it should contain all the details, but that each line should be planned and have its own function, its expressive and decorative rôle in the whole; I wish every line to be necessary. But if this end is to be attained one should know one's subject thoroughly.' *ABC de la peinture,* p. 61.

de. 'The direct spectacle of nature exciting the feelings—the memory which calls them back to the mind—the imagination that creates them by means of combinations—bring us into an involuntary mental state. Then the Idea is formed in our mind. It is superior to our lower nature on account of its logic, and its harmony appearing to the artist. He exerts himself to express it in its integral intensity, a result that he can all the better achieve if he ignores details and only retains the characteristics. Then the artist puts the spectator in the same frame of mind that he was in—which is the purpose of art.' Mellerio: *Le mouvement idéaliste,* p. 45.

df. 'We have followed the right ways seeking the Idea expressed by decorative forms, explained by simple colours.' *ABC de la peinture,* p. 77.

49

dg. In our discussion of the preceding writers we have not repeatedly dealt with this question, above all in order not to lay too heavy a burden on our argument. But we purposely bring in this problem here because in Sérusier the synthesis has been realized in the purest way, and his expositions have been least mixed with all kinds of secondary motifs and ideas derived from Plotinus and others. When studying Bernard and also in the next chapter we shall enter into more detail about the problems indicated.

dh. 'I believe that our age is rather less advanced as far as Christian art is concerned, than the earliest times of Christianity. So I believe that we can apply to our age what he (P. Didier) says about these times: that the search for beauty would prevent the direct and natural expression of the ideas; let us express ourselves anyhow and above all let us be sincere with ourselves: this constituted the spirit of the primitives; the correction will come little by little, it cannot precede the ideas without barring them the way. For the rest, there is no agreement among us about the meaning of the word. Beauty ... I think you take this word in an objective sense, whereas I take it in a subjective meaning. This difference separates the schools of this century, which have ended in Cabanel and Bouguereau from those to which I have belonged ...' *ABC de la peinture,* p. 117.

di. 'I now believe that the only thing that can make an artist is the establishing of a harmony in forms and colours. Harmony is the only means, like prayer, to bring us into communion with God. All the rest in art is only illustration, personal sentiment, individualism, human poetry. As to copying natural objects, especially models that are not even natural, I think it horrible.' *ABC de la peinture,* p. 122.

dk. No doubt in this connection Desiderius Lenz of the Beuroner School had some influence on him. Here, however, this influence is chiefly concerned with the elaboration of details, for at bottom the Beuroners and Sérusier were of the same mind before they entered into a more intensive discussion with each other. This is why we shall not go into these matters which were certainly not unimportant to Sérusier personally. Sérusier translated Lenz's German work of 1865: D. Lenz *L'esthétique de Beuron,* (trad. Sérusier, Paris, 1905), cf. Agnes Humbert: *Les Nabis,* p. 56/7.

dl. In passing we would refer to the agreement with Aurier's idea of style (cf. page 160). Of course, Sérusier may have learnt and borrowed something from it.

dm. 'A superior quality, a language which is common to every human intelligence. Without some trace of this universal language there does not exist any work of art ... These elements are inherent in our constitution, therefore inborn.' *ABC de la peinture,* p. 12.

dn. There occurs a remarkable passage on page 21 of his *ABC de la peinture:* 'Il est une notion sans laquelle aucun être animé, même le végétal, ne pourrait exister: C'est celle de l'équilibre. La ligne droite horizontale et la verticale sont les signes de l'équilibre; la première pour la matière dite inerte, la seconde pour la matière vivante. Il est à remarquer que ces deux lignes n'existent pas dans la nature; elles sont des conceptions de notre esprit ... alors que la nature ne procède que par des courbes . . . Tout manque d'équilibre est une souffrance.' ('There is a notion without which no animate being, even of the vegetable kind, could exist: it is that of equilibrium (balance). The horizontal straight line and the vertical line are signs of balance; the former for so-called inert matter, the latter for living matter. It must be observed that these two lines do not exist in nature; they are conceptions of our mind . . . whereas nature does not proceed except along curved lines . . . Every lack of equilibrium is distress.') The passage is remarkable on account of the close resemblance to the ideas of Mondriaan and his circle. In the first place both speak of balance. Thus Mondriaan considered as his ideal purpose:

'Universal harmony; to be realized in art, but in life as well. In art and life, it means the reign of serene, unchangeable equilibrium.' (H. L. C. Jaffé *De Stijl, 1917–1931* (Amsterdam 1956), p. 129).

Further in his distinction of natural forms from artistic ones (compare Sérusier's pronouncement just quoted with those of Van Doesburg (Mondriaan's nearest congenially minded fellow-artist) quoted on p. 55 of Jaffé, *op. cit.,* taken from the periodical *De Stijl*). It is not impossible for Sérusier to have heard this—it is even possible that Sérusier had heard Van Doesburg speak at Paris in 1921 (Jaffé *op. cit.,* p. 177), as precisely in this latter year the former published his *ABC de la peinture*.

Another agreement is seen in their positing the meaning of what is vertical and horizontal, although Sérusier's formulation is slightly different. Van Doesburg summarizes Mondriaan's 'equations' as follows: Vertical = male = space = statics = harmony; horizontal = female = time = dynamics = melody, etc. (Jaffé *op. cit.,* p. 58). Finally the thought that the breaking of harmony entails pain, has its parallel in Mondriaan's ideas of the tragical in this connection. (Cf. Jaffé *op. cit.,* p. 130 passim). Although we should certainly consider the possibility of Sérusier being influenced by 'De Stijl', we should not think of some direct dependence—for such dependence the formulations are not sufficiently identical. As a fact, Sérusier borrows nothing from the philosophical-theosophic implications, nor from Mondriaan's utopistic doctrines, while he does not in the least attempt to defend abstraction qua talis. On the other hand we should also take into account the possibility that Sérusier himself may have influenced the formation of the ideas of 'De Stijl', perhaps in a direct way, perhaps via (the work of) Delaunay, at the time when Mondriaan and Van der Leck were at Paris. (Cf. Jaffé, *op. cit.,* p. 48 passim, and W. Haftmann: *Malerei im 20. Jahrhundert* (München 1954), p. 165/6).

do. Cf. Aurier's pronouncement quoted on p. 159/60.

dp. 'Thoughts and moral qualities can only be represented by formal equivalents. It is the faculty of perceiving these correspondences which makes the artist.' *ABC de la peinture,* p. 23.

dq. 'The exterior world in its laws and not in its accidents'. *ABC de la peinture,* p. 33.

dr. Compare, e.g., Sérusier's 'Die Sage' (The saga) (reproduced in *Dekorative Kunst,* Band IV, 2nd year, p. 129), with Gauguin's 'Vision après le sermon', from which it derived its inspiration. Sérusier's work is really what it has been called in this magazine, a 'dekoratives Gemälde' (a decorative painting), and reduces the whole fascination of Gauguin's conception to something that is at bottom far less new. This is immediately discovered when we realize how Gauguin represents his subject 'after the Japanese manner', as if he had looked down upon it from the top, whereas Sérusier's 'direction of observation' lies much nearer to the horizontal, in conformity to Western tradition. The figures, too, are much more 'academic' as to the drawing. And lastly, the remarkable kind of realism inhaerent in Gauguin's painting has been turned into a poetic-symbolistic vision ('real' people in the foreground see, behind trees, a procession of figures belonging to a saga), which, indeed, is much more in accordance with the poetry of the nineteen-nineties. But on the other hand, there is after all a clear distance from the Art Nouveau and the symbolistic painters (in the sense defined above).

ds. Cf. on this H. Dooyeweerd: *Transcendental Problems of Philosophic thought,* (Grand Rapids, Mich. 1948), p. 62 ff. and H. Dooyeweerd: Grondthema's van het wijsgerig denken van het avondland, *Philosophia Reformata* (VI 1941), p. 164 ff. As a short summary we would submit the following quotation from this article: 'The form-matter-scheme of Greek philosophy . . . was . . . deeply rooted in the Greek religious consciousness of an irreconcilable tension between the older, tellurian, chtonic and ouranic religions of nature on the one hand, . . . and the younger cultural religion of form, measure, and harmony on the other . . .' These thoughts have been elaborately treated in: H. Dooyeweerd, *Reformatie en Scholastiek* (I, Franeker, 1949) and in his *A New Critique of Theoretical Thought* (Amsterdam 1955), I, p. 62 ff.

dt. In the philosophical elaboration of this theme there are a great variety of conceptions possible—which give an answer to such questions as, e.g., in what is the principium individuationis to be found, or where does the caesura lie between the sphere of the principle of matter and that of form. Of course, we shall leave these questions for what they are. Cf. D. H. Th. Vollenhoven: *Geschiedenis der Wijsbegeerte* (I, Grieksche Philosophie, Franeker 1950) a.o., p. 40 ff. Compare also the work of H. Dooyeweerd, mentioned in the previous note, in which these problems are further examined especially in connection with Plato's philosophy.

du. The basic motives mentioned here are of a religious nature. Cf. note a chapter II and the literature quoted there.

dv. Cf. on this synthesis: D. H. Th. Vollenhoven: Christendom en humanisme van Middeleeuwen tot Reformatie, *Philosophia Reformata* XI, 1946, p. 102 ff.; H. Dooyeweerd, Grondthema's van het wijsgerig denken van het avondland, *Philosophia Reformata,* VI, 1941, pp. 169 ff; Windelband-Heimsoeth, pp. 210 ff. H. Dooyeweerd: *Transcendental Problems of Philosophic thought* (Grand Rapids Mich. 1948), p. 70 ff.

dw. 'For if visible things are the figure of things invisible, man's essence partaking of the divine and endowed with harmony, coordinates and transforms nature according to its own supremacy in order to make it express his real supranatural origin.' Bernard: Ce que c'est que l'Art mystique? *Mercure de France* (XIII, 1895), p. 29.

dx. 'So through God there is a latent creation in man which is superior to the visible world.' Ditto.

dy. The passages quoted by Bernard are the very same in which a doctrine has been explained that shows a close resemblance to that of Swedenborg, so exactly those thoughts that also Gauguin advanced as more or less self-evident. Cf. p. 160 (Pseudo) Dionysius represents a phase in early christian thought which seeks for a marked synthesis with Neo-platonic philosophy, but in which there is not yet any question of the nature-and-grace-scheme which was to dominate mediaeval philosophy later on (we might say that the division between the Christian and the Greek inheritance has not yet been realized).

dz. 'The beautiful which is the result of a special illumination and which is the gift of the Holy Ghost'. Bernard quotes *Oeuvres de Saint Denys l'Aréopagite* (trad. p. l'Abbé Dulac, Paris 1865), p. 39.
This is greatly emphasized in Bernard's thesis, that only a Christian can be a synthetist, i.e., only he who possesses the 'donum super additum'. For he said: 'Le symbolisme est d'essence chrétienne. C'est l'invisible manifesté par le visible et c'est cela qu'à la faveur de la foi chrétienne je tentai de ressusciter en 1890. Pour y parvenir, il fallait être croyant et professeur des théories catholiques.' (Symbolism is essentially Christian. It is the invisible manifested by the visible, and this is what I tried to restore to life again for the benefit of the christian faith in 1890. To attain it one must be a believer and profess catholic theories.) (Quoted after P. Normand, by R. Puig: *Paul Gauguin, G. D. de Monfreid et leurs amis,* (Perpignan 1958), p. 74).

ea. 'The lines are arranged in a coherence which is more or less significant, colours are characters (= alphabetical symbols), their combinations are phrases ... Young and old formulas are, therefore, a kind of script that we should always understand, always know and not deny.' Bernard *op. cit.,* p. 39.

eb. 'In nature there is no form that is not a sign for the spirit (this is the Greek 'nous' concept, or Aurier's notion of 'pensée'); all nature is, therefore, a symbol as such.' *Lettres à Emile Bernard* (1927), p. 62.

ec. 'There is an internal work done unconsciously; all that cannot be united with my temperament is effaced from me; what is left is in accordance with myself.' Ditto.

ed. 'the great directions of the lines, the simplification of colours which become more significant for the subject than representative of light and tone ...' Ditto, p. 63.

ee. For the sense of these terms, cf. W. Schöne: *Über das Licht in der Malerei,* (Berlin, 1954), p. 112, p. 188 ff., and 218/9; 'Indifferenzlicht' is light in a picture which is neither 'natürliches' (natural), nor 'künstliches' (artificial), nor 'sakral

53

Leuchlicht' (the sacral light of Christ or an angel), so light that can not somehow be explained from the scene represented, but on the other hand is not the same light found, e.g., in Ottonian miniatures, which Schöne calls 'Eigenlicht' *op. cit.,* p. 14, 12). It is exactly on these points that the great difference is seen between the new art of synthetism and the older 19th century art which would only use light that could be explained naturally when rendering the given object (cf. note 362 on p. 193 in Schöne, *op. cit.*).

ef. 'unite the visible truth of the outer world and the divine of the inner life.' E. Bernard: Note relative au symbolisme pictural 1888—1891 in *Lettres à Emile Bernard* (1927), p. 190.

CHAPTER VIII:

a. 'So-called refined art proceeds from the senses and serves nature;' whereas the art that should be practised now 'proceeds from the spirit and employs nature.' Morice, *Gauguin*, p. 26.

b. 'Thus by choice and synthesis there is a certain habit formed by the modern artist, an eclectic and exclusive habit of interpreting optical sensation,' Denis, *Théories*, p. 2.

c. 'It is... above all the complete neglect of style, of a true style which at bottom is nothing but the comprehension of the intellectuality of the forms, and which has become impossible, in the first place on account of the neglect of any synthesis in art...'
G-A. Aurier: Rationations familières et d'ailleurs vaines à propos des trois salons de 1891, *Mercure de France* (III, 1891), p. 37/38.

d. 'his last canvases, of a poetic kind of symbolism, a beautiful and skilful synthesis of lines and colours, hold out a promise of an artist of the first class.' G-A. Aurier: Les symbolistes, Littérature et Beaux Arts, *Revue Encyclopédique* (Avril 1892), quoted by Sérusier, *ABC de la peinture*, p. 56 note.

e. 'The synthesis consists in embodying all forms in the small number of forms in which we can think, straight lines, some angles, circular arcs and ellipses; if we depart from there we get lost in an ocean of varieties.' Quoted by C. Chassé: *Le mouvement symboliste* (1947), p. 129—cf. *ABC de la peinture*, p. 161.

f. 'What dominates is the idea of synthesis. There is not a classic who is not sparing of his means, who does not subordinate all the graces of detail to the beauty of the whole, who does not attain to greatness by conciseness.' Denis *Théories*, p. 228.

g. It is remarkable that somebody who was far away from France and from the circle of people that we are studying here wrote: 'He (the savage) had begun first by making a complete synthesis of certain points that interested him and...

54

had assumed to himself and others that this synthesis—which was not a copy of nature, this arrangement and coordination of certain facts of sight—would be understood by others and represent the thing seen' John La Fargue, quoted by R. Berenson Katz: John la Fargue, Art Critic, *Art Bulletin* (XXXIII 1951), p. 105. In the next chapter we intend to revert to La Fargue again.

h. 'The triumph of the spirit of synthesis over that of analysis, of the imagination over sensation, of man over nature.' Denis, Introduction to Catalogue Cross Exhibition 1910.

i. 'He feels, or rather, he judges successively, in an analytic way',... 'they feel immediately, everything simultaneously in a synthetic way.' *Cur. Esth.*, p. 257.

k. 'the synthetic language': 'which expresses complex relation in one single word, and which groups accessory ideas round the principal idea in rounded sentences.' A. Hatzfeld, A. Darmesteter: *Dictionnaire général de la langue française*, (Paris w.d.) (after 1871).

l. One of the writers of the dictionary which we have just quoted, viz. Darmesteter, is mentioned by Fontainas (in his *Mes souvenirs du symbolisme*, p. 110): 'En linguistique on prônait Littré... Darmesteter.' ('In linguistics they extolled Littré... Darmesteter'.)

m. See p. 190.

n. This term is used thus at a very early date by Mallarmé—in a letter of the 5th August 1867: 'En créant une parfaite synthèse des choses...' (by creating a perfect synthesis of things...) (Michaud, *Message poétique*, p. 178). Possibly Mallarmé was the man who circumscribed this term in the sense intended here and under whose influence it became popular in this environment.

o. 'At the bottom of their thought there is the longing for ALL. Aesthetic synthesis that is what they are after.' Morice *La littérature*, p. 297.

p. 'It is there, in this ardent wish to unite Beauty with Truth, in this desirable unity of Faith and Joy, Science and Art.' Ditto, p. 59.

q. Very clearly and explicitly the two poles of the Humanistic view of reality are opposed to each other in what follows: 'Tout objet a deux aspects: l'aspect matériel et l'aspect idéal. Il y a donc bien authentiquement deux mondes: l'un phénoménal, frappant l'âme par les sens et s'y introduisant en notations directes, l'autre intuitif, produit de l'âme, et empruntant pour se traduire les formes du premier... Il s'ensuit que le réalisme et l'idéalisme sont deux tournures de l'esprit, deux manières d'envisager la vie.' (Dumur: Aurier et l'évolution idéaliste, *Mercure de France* (VIII, 1893), p. 295). (Every object has two aspects: the material aspect and the ideal aspect. There are, therefore, really two authentic worlds: the one is phenomenal and strikes the soul by means of the senses and enters into it in direct notations, the other is intuitive, a product of the soul, and borrows the forms of the first one to express itself... from this it follows that realism and idealism are two attitudes of the mind, two ways of considering life).

r. 'What is a poem? The synthesis of all the general ideas perceived by a given self. The synthesis of the sensations constitutes the sciences. The synthesis of the sciences constitutes the philosophies. The synthesis of the philosophies constitutes the dogmas. The synthesis of dogmas constitutes a poem. A poem is, therefore, pre-eminently an intellectual conclusion; a poem is the essential synthesis of the self.' Aurier *Oeuvres*, p. XV.

s. 'a new being . . . since it has to animate it a soul which is the synthesis of two souls, the soul of the artist and the soul of nature . . .' Aurier *Oeuvres*, p. 303.

t. 'The purpose . . . of introducing contemporary life into literature constituted one of the newest tendencies, one of the boldest . . . of the romantic movement; also the most difficult one to realize if one insisted on maintaining and developing the rights of the imagination, sensibility, the ideal, on keeping the divine mantle of poetry free of any dirt in the contact with prosaic reality, on avoiding the prosaic form and the vulgar content.' Van Tieghem *Le Romantisme*, p. 345.

u. Here synthesis does not mean more than artistic form-giving, style. This passage, however, was written before Morice and the synthetists had said and written such a great deal about synthesis. Here we clearly see the transition from a neutral technical use of the word to an accurately defined use for the purpose of denoting only one movement.

v. 'Modern life does not remain forbidden to us . . . But it will be permitted to transfigure it in a synthesis different from that hitherto given by the impressionism of the novel. We shall not paint it as it subjectivizes itself in the brain of a stable-boy or of a signboard painter, but as our individual retina makes it to us, our much more comprehensive vision. We shall put in the phantoms of our dream, our hallucination, our remembrance, the imaginary evocations, for all this is found in life and constitutes it.' P. Adam: La Presse et le Symbolisme, *Le Symboliste*, 7/14 Oct. 1886, cited by Barre, *Le Symbolisme*, p. 118/119.

w. 'Here are the rejected subjects . . .: Any representation of contemporary private or public life.' Good is: 'The interpretation of oriental theogonies except those of the yellow races' . . . 'an allegory should be expressive like 'modesty and vanity', or decorative like the work of Puvis de Chavannes.' *Salon de la Rose†Croix, Règle et Monitoire* (Paris 1891), p. 8/9.

x. With the impressionists the artist's personality is expressed in the manner of painting. The composition thereby gets much less emphasis. With them there is really no question of 'objective deformation', and this on purpose.

y. 'Instead of being the copy of nature art became the subjective deformation of nature. From the objective viewpoint the decorative aesthetic and rational composition, of which the impressionists had not thought because it ran counter to their preference for improvisation, became the counter party, the necessary corrective of the theory of the equivalences. With respect to the expression this theory authorized all the transpositions, even caricatural, all the excesses of cha- racter: the objective transformation in its turn compelled the artist to turn everything into Beauty. To recapitulate: the expressive synthesis, the symbol of a feeling, had to be an eloquent transcript of it and at the same time an object composed to please the eyes. Denis *Théories*, p. 260.

z. 'Among all the others painting is the art that will pave the way to resolve the antinomy of the sensible and the intellectual world.' Quoted in Gauguin: *Avant et Après*, p. 40.

aa. 'Real and ideal are posited in our mind as equally original and related to each other.' Windelband-Heimsoeth, p. 489/90.

ab. 'In the field of human rational activity the desired synthesis of freedom and nature, of teleology and necessity, of the practical and the theoretical function is represented by Genius which produces the works of the fine arts in a teleology without utility.' Windelband-Heimsoeth, p. 474/5, cf. Kant *Kritik der Urteilskraft*, Einleitung IX and § 30 and § 44 ff.

ac. Aurier quotes Schiller (Oeuvres, p. 176) from: *Lettres sur l'éducation esthétique*. We have not been able to find a possible French edition. The quotation is taken form '*Ueber die aesthetische Erziehung des Menschen*'. (Herford, 1948, pp. 22/23).

ad. A. Delaroche mentions Schelling in his article on Gauguin taken over in *Avant et Après*, p. 41. In his *Histoire de la critique d'art* L. Venturi summarizes Schelling's ideas as follows: 'Le génie artistique fait coincide le fini et l'infini, le conscient et l'inconscient, alors que la science opère sans génie uniquement sur le fini et le conscient.' (The artistic genius causes the finite to coincide with the infinite, the conscious with the unconscious, whereas science operates without genius exclusively on the finite and the conscious). These ideas have been explained in Schelling's '*Ueber das Verhältniss der bildenden Künste zu der Natur*', 1807. The French were probably informed of Schelling's work by such treatises on him as, e.g., M. Matter: *Schelling ou la Philosophie de la Nature et la Philosophie de la Révélation,* (Paris, 1845). We have not been able to find a 19th century French translation of Schelling's work.

ae. Nowhere does one find the dialectics of the Humanistic basic motive elaborated more clearly than precisely in Kant. Cf., e.g., his *Kritik der Urteilskraft*, Einleitung II. The personality-ideal and the science-ideal have each its own domain assigned to them in Kant's attempt to do justice to both of them, the former being treated in the *Kritik der praktischen Vernunft*, the latter in the *Kritik der reinen Vernunft*. In his *Kritik der Urteilskraft* Kant makes an attempt to effect a synthesis. This term is found rarely as such, only in a note at the end of the Einleitung. It is true we come upon the term in the *Kritik der reinen Vernunft,* viz. as the combination of a plurality of representations brought about by the subject (§ 15). So we do not find this term synthesis with respect to art used in the *Kritik der Urteilskraft*. Windelband's use of the term in the quotation given in the text (on page 208) is not Kant's, although the idea is virtually there in the *Kritik der Urteilskraft*.

af. 'The movement to which we belong was anterior to the German influences. In philosophy we spoke about Plato, Aristotle, the Neo-platonics and never about Kant.' Sérusier in a letter to Denis, 29-2-1915, *ABC de la peinture*, p. 146.

ag. '. . . in it the Mind appears as the synthetic function which creates plurality out of its own higher unity. From this general point of view the Neo-platonics worked out the psychology of knowledge under the principle of the activity of consciousness. For according to this view the 'higher soul' can no longer be considered as passive, but in accordance with its essence only as active also in all its functions. All of its insight rests on the synthesis of various moments; even where knowledge is related to the sensible datum the body only is passive, whereas the soul is active in becoming conscious of it; and exactly the same thing holds for sensory feelings and affects.' Windelband-Heimsoeth, p. 195.

We shall not examine whether Windelband does not slightly distort Plotinus' thought owing to the fact that W. (as a neo-Kantian) considers him too much from the standpoint of W.'s own basic idea, and, therefore, too little from the ancient Greek idea. Cf. however the next paragraph.

ah. Whosoever looks for a genuine art-theory in Plotinus will be disappointed. Windelband's conclusion (p. 208 *op. cit.*) is, therefore, not quite supported by the texts: '. . . die Schönheit, welche die Griechen geschaffen und genossen hatten,— sie wird nun erkannt als das sieghafte Walten des Geistes, in der Veräuszerlichung seiner sinnlichen Erscheinungen. Auch dieser Begriff ist ein Triumph des Geistes, der in der Entfaltung seiner Tätigkeiten zuletzt sein eigenes Wesen erfasst und als Weltprinzip begriffen hat.' (. . . the beauty that the Greeks have created and enjoyed—it is only now recognised as the victorious rule of the Spirit, in the exteriorization of its sensory appearances. This concept, too, is a triumph of the Spirit which in the development of its activities has at last grasped its own essence and has recognised it as the principle of the world). When Plotinus speaks of beauty he does not emphasize what we call art, but an internal kind of beauty. What arouses love of beauty? 'No shape, no colour, no grandeur of mass: all is for a soul, something whose beauty rests upon no colour, for the moral wisdom the soul enshrines and all the other hueless splendour of the virtues. It is that you find in your-self or admire in another, loftiness of spirit; righteousness of life; disciplined purity; courage of the majestic face; gravity, modesty that goes fearless and tranquil and passionless; and shining down upon all, the light of godlike Intellection. All these noble qualities are to be reverenced and loved, no doubt, but what entitles them to be called beautiful?' (*Enneads* I, 6, 5). In his aesthetics Plotinus wants to give an answer to the latter question, and while doing so he also sometimes speaks of sensory beauty in things as if in passing (e.g., *Enneads* I, 6, up to and including 3, and especially V, 8, 1 up to and including 6). Perhaps we should rather credit Ficino (cf. A. Chastel: *Marsile Ficin et l'Art* (Genève, Lille, 1954), pp. 64/65) with the achievement that Windelband attributes to Plotinus.

ai. 'The synthetic relation of the idea with its appearances can only be fixed by an archetypal and complex style.' Barre *Le Symbolisme*, p. 221.

ak. 'synthesis of a form and a colour without considering the dominant.' Malingue *Lettres* LXVII.

al. Rewald *Post Impressionism,* p. 206 and p. 239, note 28.
This quotation would seem to be a very good summary. It cannot be a real source, because this document is too late and too much derived for that. But thus we avoid giving quotations that have already been used before and at the same time we can be concise.

am. 'the true manifestation of the unity of being by finite phenomena.' Gauckler, p. 44.

an. 'Modern' here very probably means the naturalism of the Salons.

ao. 'Dragged through the mire by the moderns, who did not understand it and thought it beneath them to understand it, it was highly appreciated by the Ancients who under the name of inspiration assigned to it a divine origin.' Gauckler, p. 55.

ap. 'nature is nothing but a dictionary' . . . 'Those who have no imagination copy the dictionary. The result is a great vice, the vice of banality.' Baudelaire *Art Romantique,* p. 10.

aq. 'the true art of painting is that in which the imagination speaks above all.' Delacroix *Journal,* 12 Oct. 1853 II, p. 85.

ar. 'With the artist the imagination does not only represent such and such objects, but it combines them for the purpose he wants to reach, it makes pictures, images that he composes at will.' Delacroix *Ditto,* Notes pour un Dictionnaire des Beaux Arts, s.v. Imagination, III, p. 242.

as. 'In stead of working round the eyes we sought in 'the mysterious centre of thought' as Gauguin said. Thus the imagination again becomes the queen of the faculties according to the wish of Baudelaire.' Denis *Théories,* p. 259.

at. 'The dream, the dream! friends, let us embark for the dream . . .' Cited by Michaud, *Message poétique* II, p. 260. The book was by G. Vicaire & H. Beauclair.

au. 'His dream of art began to take shape . . .' Vollard, *En écoutant Cézanne* **(1938), p. 11.**

av. 'What deceives the eye is identity. What delights and elevates the mind—for a picture is first of all a dream written down and from a certain viewpoint a kind of illusory spring-board for the mind itself—is harmony, what has been felt.' Bernard: Les ateliers, *Mercure de France* (XIII 1895), p. 203.

aw. 'A waking dream, almost the same thing as a dream in sleep. The dream in sleep is often bolder, sometimes a little more logical.' Gauguin *Avant et Après,* p. 112.

ax. This term has been aptly translated in the *Catalogue of the Gauguin-Exhibition* in London in 1955: under No. 56—Te Rerioa (Le Rêve, Day-Dreaming).

ay. 'Everything is a dream in this picture; whether it is the child, the mother, the horseman on the path, or the painter's dream! All this is beside the painting, they will say. Who knows? Perhaps not.' *Lettres de Gauguin à Daniel de Monfreid* March 12, 1897, p. 102.

az. 'But the dream is also a means to acquire knowledge, a mode of perceiving what is real or rather some super reality of which our stable universe is only a simplification and, so to say, a caricature.' Cited by Michaud *Message poétique*, p. 57 from *Paradis Artificiels* III.

ba. 'He admits the reality of the world, but he admits it as the reality of fiction. Nature with its shimmering fairy-scenes, the rapid and coloured spectacle of clouds, and the startling human societies are dreams of the soul; real: but are not all dreams real?' Wyzéwa in *Vogue* 11, 5/VII/1886, quoted by Lehmann *Symbolist Aethetics*, p. 89.

bb. a paper 'that notes the events in the light that is proper to a dream.' . . . 'Reality is an artifice suitable to orientate an average intellect among the mirages of a fact; but owing to this it rests on some universal agreement: let us therefore see if in the ideal there is not a necessary, evident, simple aspect serving as a type.' *Divagations*, p. 20 and *Poésies complètes de Stéphane Mallarmé*, textes et notes par Y.G. le Dantec (Paris s.d.) (1948), p. 180.

bc. See D. H. Th. Vollenhoven: Hoofdlijnen der logica, *Philosophia Reformata* XIII 1948, p. 93, 96.

For this reason it seems to us that Michaud's observation (*Le message poétique*, p. 200) is quite right: 'Si, pour certains, le criticisme kantien semblait préparer les voies de la science moderne en fixant les limites de la raison, du même coup son idéalisme transcendental, affirmant la subjectivité de tout connaissance, rendait au moi et à l'esprit une prépondérance qui allait permettre toutes les audaces . . .' ('If, to some people, the Kantian criticism seemed to pave the way for modern science by fixing the limits of reason, his transcendental idealism, asserting the subjectivity of all knowledge, gave to the self and to the mind a preponderance that would permit all kinds of audacities . . .')

bd. 'Beauty . . . the dream of the true. But what is this delight of the 'spiritualized sense' if not the radiation of truth in symbols that deprive it of the dryness of abstraction and complete it in the joys of the dream?' Morice *La Litterature*, p. 33.

be. We have not entered into the discussion of the use of the terminology of men like Redon, or of men of letters like Rémy de Gourmont, etc. We abstained from it on purpose as we wanted to restrict ourselves to the circle of the synthetists. As a matter of fact we followed this policy everywhere in this chapter and elsewhere.

bf. 'The idol . . . embodying my dream . . .'; 'And all this is sadly singing in my soul and in my scenery, while I am painting and dreaming at the same time . . .'; 'I close my eyes in order to see without understanding the dream in the infinite space receding before me...' Malingue *Lettres* CLXX, p. 288/9.

This reminds us of Clovio's letter rediscovered shortly after 1920 containing the story of El Greco refusing to go out one fine day, because the daylight would disturb his inner light—he planned his projects with his eyes shut. Quoted in Panofsky, *Idea*, p. 56.

bg. 'There is only symbolism at this price: a symbol is nothing but the mind presented in a form, the ideal in the sensible.' *Lettres à Emile Bernard:* Note relative au Symbolisme Pictural de 1888—1890, p. 190.

bh. For the difference between the two movements is found in the first place in the subjects and the style. Only with respect to what we call the iconic element (which we shall examine further later on) they go clearly different ways, also as far as theory is concerned, whereas (as far as we can see) the term (and the idea of) 'synthesis' is less frequent among the symbolistic painters (and decadent men of letters).

bi. 'The decadents had rallied to subjectivism... they no longer looked at things except through the distorting mirror of their dreamy souls. And as on the other hand they were great reasoners, they very soon came to look upon things, thus thought of and immaterialized, as merely emblems and symbols.' Poizat *Symbolisme*, p. 145.

bk. The use of the image of a bouquet here is characteristic. It is also found in Balzac's *Seraphita* and in Baudelaire's *Fanfarlo*—in which case the flowers have a symbolic sense as to their choice and arrangement. The connection is undeniable in this case.

bl. 'Tones, words, colours, and forms, phenomena in general, are merely symbols of the idea, symbols arising in the soul of the artist when he is moved by the holy spirit of the world, his works of art are only symbols by means of which he communicates his own ideas to other souls... Is the artist so entirely free in the choice and the arrangement of his mysterious flowers? Or does he only choose and combine because he has to do so? I answer this question about a mystical constraint in the affirmative... In art I am a supernaturalist. I believe that the artist cannot discover all his types in nature, but that the most significant types are, as it were, revealed to his soul as the innate symbolism of inborn ideas.' H. Heine *Der Salon* (I, Rotterdam 1860), p. 27/28.

bm. Baudelaire himself also quotes the passage from Heine just mentioned: *Cur. Esth.*, p. 103.

bn. 'With the most excellent poets there is no metaphor, comparison or epithet which is not a mathematically exact adaptation in the actual situation, because these comparisons, metaphors and epithets have been drawn from the inexhaustible fund of the universal analogy and cannot be drawn from anywhere else.' Baudelaire *Art Romantique*, p. 317.

bo. '(For the poet to compose) the sole worthy vision: the real and suggestive symbol in which the primary and final Idea, or truth, will rise in its naked integrity palpitating for the dream. R. Ghil: *Traité du Verbe*, (1885), p. 33, cited by Michaud *Message poétique*, p. 329.

bp. 'We, therefore, have some difficulty to believe words relating to divine mysteries which we only contemplate through the veil of sensory symbols . . . the various forms in which a sacred symbolism clothes the divine, for, looked at from outside, are they not full of some inadmissible and imaginary monstrosity?' Bernard: Ce que c'est que l'Art mystique, *Mercure de France* (XIII 1895), p. 30, cited from *Oeuvres de Saint Denys l'Aréopagite*, trad. Abbé Dulac, Paris 1865).

bq. 'one should seek the eternal in the diversity of the momentaneous forms, the truth that remains in the False that will pass away, perennial logic in the instantaneous illogical.' Remy de Gourmont: Le Symbolisme, Définition de ce nouveau mouvement littéraire. *L'art et l'Idée* II, p. 51.

br. 'Well if this has been admitted, then the possibility and the legitimacy have been granted for the artist to be pre-occupied in his work by that ideistic substratum that is found everywhere in the universe and which, according to Plato, is the sole true reality.' Aurier, *Oeuvres*, p. 301.

bs. 'The work of art which reveals, and whose perfection of form above all consists in effacing that form in order not to let anything persist to disturb thought but the vague and charming appearance, the charming and dominating, the dominating and fecund appearance of a divine entity of the Infinite.' Morice *La littérature*, p. 33.

bt. 'a simple imitation of material things which does not signify anything spiritual is never art, in other words there is not, there is never art without symbolism'. Aurier *Oeuvres*, p. 298.

bu. 'What is a poet? He is one of the incarnations in which is manifested the Revealer, the Hero, the man whom Carlyle calls: 'a messenger sent by the impenetrable Infinite with tidings for us.' This conception of the Hero, expressed by a visionary genius is the direct consequence of another conception which is universally admitted by occultists and mystics and was formulated as follows by Novalis: 'Every created being is a revelation . . .' V. E. Michelet: *De l'Esotérisme dans l'art* (1891), p. 9, cited by Michaud *Message poétique* III, p. 468.

bv. 'Somewhere outside of the world, in the heaven of joy and beauty it is the day of the supreme epiphany when a great artist has crowned with his genius one of the innumerable beautiful figures of Nature, when the artist, himself the child of Nature, fed by it, living on it, rises to proclaim the beauty of his mother: when Nature allows one of the changing aspects of its mysterious visage to eternalize the word of its enigma in a work of art.' *Noa Noa* (ed. 1924), p. 11.

bw. 'Art is nothing but the revealer of the Infinite: for the poet it is even a means to penetrate into it. He penetrates much deeper than any philosophy, he prolongs and re-echoes in it the revelation of a Gospel, he is a light that calls up light . . .' Morice *La littérature*, p. 33.

bx. 'We sought the truth in the harmonic laws of Beauty and deduced all metaphysics from the latter—for the harmony of nuances and of sounds symbolizes the harmony of the souls and the worlds—and all morality...' Morice *La litté-rature,* p. 65.

by. The examination of Kuyper's correspondence preserved in the Kuyper-huis at the Hague did not yield a single indication of the reason why he delivered his speech on 'The Antithesis between Symbolism and Revelation' for the 'Historical Presbyterian Society' at Philadelphia in 1898/9. He was in the U.S.A. for the Stone Lectures, but by the side of it he gave very many other addresses. Nowhere does Kuyper appear to possess special knowledge of art, but he has no doubt occupied himself with it. A number of publications are evidence of his interest. In addition to the lecture discussed here we may mention: 'Calvinism on Art' in *'Christian Thought', Lectures and Papers in Philosophy, Christian Evidence, Biblical Elucida-tion* (IX 1891/2, New York), pp. 259-282, 447-459, translated by Rev. J. H. de Vries, *Het Calvinisme en de Kunst,* (rectorial address, 1888, Amsterdam); 'Calvinism on art', one of the *Stone Lectures,* (1899, Amsterdam-Pretoria).

bz. There is no doubt some connection between the Liturgical Movement in Protestant Churches then and now—it may be a movement which asserts itself at different times with varying emphasis. Cf. also the book cited in the next note, pp. 63, 158.

ca. We may think of the oecumenic movement which arose with increasing force in those years and of which the World Council of Churches constituted after the last world-war is an important result. Cf. C. van der Waal: *Antithese of Syn-these? De oecumenische beweging beschreven en getoetst.* (Enschede, 1951), pp. 29 ff.

cb. He means the orthodox Calvinistic Churches.

cc. 'Poor child! Don't be sad... There is redemption. Where I would find it? In yourself... Descend into your soul... Do I have in myself, without knowing it, such a power? Do I carry a whole universe in my flesh?—A universe, my child, greater and finer than the universe! A universe of which you are the god... When we believe we invent the most fabulous chimera do we not do anything else but call up visions that we remember unconsciously from the times when our souls relaxed in the marvellous Eden of the pure ideas?' Aurier *Oeuvres,* p. 11.

cd. The text says: 'beautiful'. We thought we were entitled to correct this—the English of this lecture is sometimes far from beautiful, and obviously the work of a translator who had great difficulty with the text.

ce. The thought briefly formulated here had already been Kuyper's in 1892, and was elaborately developed in his rectorial address: *'De Verflauwing der Grenzen'* (Amsterdam, 1892), pp. 12 ff.

cf. Baudelaire, too, had discovered that this revelation via art was in reality nothing but the positing of the artist's view from the standpoint of the latter's view of life and the world—cf., p. 24.

cg. Morice, who had originated from a Roman-Catholic environment, probably refers to saints' legends, to the belief in relics, etc.

ch. 'Modern criticism does not allow us to believe unbelievable things, and yet the modern mind, like the ancients, remains eager for beautiful mysteries: has Wagner not understood that, since religion cannot live for art unless it veils its element of truth in an ever increasing accumulation of unbelievable things, and since men do not want these beautiful chimeras proposed to their reason, they must exclusively be offered to their imagination?' Morice *La litterature*, p. 199.

ci. Even the most naturalistic way of representation only seemingly copies reality—and does so merely because of the age-long custom of using a particular kind of pictorial means (such as perspective, etc.). Thus the idea got fixed in the minds of both adherents and opponents that art was really an 'imitation'.

ck. In literature it will no doubt always be realized that we are dealing with language, even though the peculiar nature of language may have been lost to sight because of the view that a word is identical with an idea or a concept. However this may be, also naturalism in literature had caused a great deal of the peculiar character of art to be lost, for art is more than 'copying' the life of every day. Thus Lehmann's thesis quoted above, which bears on literature, can be understood.

cl. The term 'iconique' even occurs a few times. For instance: '(les) milles nuances (de la couleur) sont aptes à complémentariser la symbolisation iconique d'un état d'âme...' (the thousands of shades (of colour) are suitable to complement the iconic symbolization of a state of mind...' A. Germain: Un peintre idéaliste-idéiste, Alexandre Séon (Symbolisme des Teintes), *L'Art et l'Idée* (I, Paris 1892), p. 109.

cm. By modalities we mean the different aspects of reality, which are facets that (in principle) can be discovered in everything, or spheres of experience in which every human being functions as a subject. They are not modes of thought—whoever should assert this would thereby reduce all the aspects of reality to subordinate parts of the logical modality. On the theory of the modalities, cf. H. Dooyeweerd, *Wijsbegeerte der Wetsidee* II, pp. 1 ff., or the same: *A New Critique of Theoretical Thought*, II, pp. 3 ff., or the same: *Transcendental Problems of Philosophic Thought* (Grand Rapids, Mich. 1948), p. 42 ff.

cn. We might mention as an example the Japanese way of representing depth in works of art with the aid of entirely different means from that of perspective. In this example we point out differences in pictorial representation in different cultural spheres.

co. 'There are no outlines nor touches in nature. We must always come back to the conventional means in each art which are the language of art.' *Journal*, 13 January 1857.

cp. See chapter VI, note p, q.

cq. 'You discuss with Laval about shadows and ask me if I don't care about it. As far as the explanation of light is concerned, yes. Look at the Japanese who nevertheless make such excellent drawings and you will see life in the open and in the sun without any shadows. They only use colour as a combination of tones, various harmonies giving the impression of heat, etc.' Malingue LXXV.

cr. '. . . all these fabulous colours, this glowing but sifted, silent air. But all this does not exist! (this is the critic's objection; Gauguin replies): Yes, this exists as the equivalent of that grandeur, that depth, of this mystery of Tahiti when one has to express it on a canvas of a square yard.' Cited Rotonchamp *Gauguin*, p. 122 spoken in connection with the exposition of 1893. Cf. Malingue CLXX.

cs. 'The ideistic painter's duty is, therefore, to bring about a reasoned selection from the many elements combined in objectivity, to use in his work only the lines, forms, general distinctive colours serving to describe the ideistic signification of the object clearly . . .' Aurier: Le symbolisme en peinture, *Mercure de France* II 1891, p. 162.

ct. 'This boils down to saying that the objects, i.e., abstractly, the various combinations of lines, planes, shadows, colours, constitute the vocabulary of a mysterious language, but wonderfully expressive, which one must know in order to be an artist. This language, like very language, has its own handwriting, its orthography, grammar, syntax, even rhetoric, which is 'the style'. Aurier *Oeuvres*, p. 302.

cu. We are referring to those who may call themselves Iconologists, and to S. K. Langer in the field of art-theory, in her *Philosophy in a New Key* (New York, 1949 [2]).

cv. The new insight was expressed most clearly by an artist who was strongly influenced by Gauguin in the years 1890-1892, viz. J. F. Willumsen, a Danish painter. On an etching entitled 'Fertility', of 1891, he wrote: 'L'art ancien a son ancienne langue que le monde peu à peu a appris à comprendre. Un art nouveau a une langue nouvellement formée que le monde doit apprendre avant de la comprendre.' (Ancient art has its ancient language which the world has gradually learnt to understand. A new art has a newly formed language which the world must learn before understanding it). (Reproduced in *Kunsten Idag* (XLIV, Oslo, 1958, 2), p. 13).

cw. 'Let us consider this word of Cézanne's: I have wanted to copy nature. I did not succeed. I have been satisfied about myself since I discovered that the sun, for instance (things lit up by the sun) could not be reproduced, but that one must represent it by something else than what I saw—by colour . . .' Denis *Théories*, p. 259, note 2.

cx. 'We have replaced the idea of 'nature seen through the medium of a temperament' by the theory of the equivalence or the symbol. We assert that the emotions or states of the soul evoked by some spectacle involved in the artist's imagination are signs or plastic equivalents capable of reproducing these emotions

65

or states of the soul without the necessity to furnish the copy of the initial spectacle; that with every condition of our sensibility there must be a corresponding objective harmony which is capable of translating it.' Denis *Théories*, p. 267.

cy. 'Well, thoughts and moral qualities can only be represented by formal equivalents.' . . . 'This faculty of perceiving those correspondences constitutes the artist. Every man possesses this faculty as a possibility already at birth; his personal work can develop it, a bad education may annihilate it.' Sérusier *ABC de la peinture*, p. 23.

cz. ' . . . at last I understood again that in an icon . . . everything must be imprinted with a simple, explicative, exact and symbolic character, that every actor should have a dimension proportionate to the importance of his rôle.' Bernard: Ce que c'est que l'Art mystique, *Mercure de France* (XIII 1895), p. 37.

da. It shows a keen insight to speak of 'Jésus' here—for we are only concerned here with the human being who was on earth at one time in history. On this human being all our attention is concentrated in this kind of works, whereas his divine office as the Messiah is ignored as well as His divinity. In contradistinction to this attitude Byzantine Art chiefly and pretty well exclusively paid attention to Jesus Christ's Divine nature.

db. 'A Byzantine Christ is a symbol. The Jesus of the modern painters is only literary, even though he should wear the most exact kiffyed. The former has an expressive form, the latter is nature, being imitated, that intends to be expressive.' Denis *Théories*, p. 10.

dc. He speaks about a photo of a Giotto in *Avant et Après*, p. 97: A Mary Magdalene disembarking at Marseilles. This probably refers to a fresco of the series of scenes from the life of Mary Magdalene in the Magdalene Chapel of the lower church of Assisi, represented in G. H. Weigelt *Giotto* (Klassiker der Kunst, 1925), p. 181.

dd. Cf. B. Dorival: Sources of the art of Gauguin from Java, Egypt and Ancient Greece, *Burlington Magazine* (XCIII, April 1951), p. 118. That he took photos of the Burubudur for works from Cambodja clearly appears from his letter to Bernard in 1889 in which he wrote (on the occasion of the World Exhibition at Paris) on the works exhibited in the Dutch-East-Indian Pavillion: 'Tout l'Art de l'Inde se trouve là et les photographies que j'ai u Cambodja se retrouvent là textuellement'. (*Lettres à Emile Bernard*, p. 66). (The whole art of India is found there and the photos I possess of Cambodja are found back again there literally). For in our opinion his term 'textuellement' means 'literally', exactly agreeing with, not merely as to style generally.

de. On the term modality cf. note cm, ch. VIII. Briefly we would describe the structure of a work of pictorial art as follows: First, a structure of an objective psychical qualification—oil-paint on canvas, applied in such a way that particular colours and lines are noticed in our sensory perception—in this bottom structure another one is founded, viz. one of an iconic qualification—for, the configurations of colours and lines given in sensory perception have been aranged in such a way that to the observer, to the human subject, they have an iconic-signifying sense, in short, that they render something, depict something—while, finally the iconic structure is the foundation of the aesthetically qualified one—and in the latter qualification we are confronted with the meaning and the peculiar nature of the work of art as such. However this may be, the iconic and the aesthetic aspects of a work of art are together the key-functions, which are closely interrelated, as we try to show in more detail in this part of our study. In connection with this, cf. Dooyeweerd, *Wijsbegeerte der Wetsidee* III, pp. 71 ff.; or ditto, *A New Critique of Theoretical Thought,* III, pp. 104 ff.

df. Here we have to deal with an anticipatory element within the iconic modality opening and expanding the latter and deepening its meaning. Cf. Dooyeweerd, *op. cit.* II, pp. 112 ff., and *A New Critique,* II, pp. 181 ff.

dg. This is a retrocipatory moment within the structure of the aesthetic modality. Cf. Dooyeweerd II *op. cit.,* p. 106; *A New Critique* II, pp. 181 ff.

dh. We are, e.g., referring to Weelkes 'As Vesta was from Latmos hill descending', of the anthology 'Triumphs of Oriana', 1601, published in honour of Queen Elizabeth (I): in it descent is musically characterized when the choir sings 'running down amain', while in the next line 'two by two' is sung by two voices, 'three by three' by three voices, and 'together' by the whole choir, etc.

di. Cf. my article 'Ontwerp ener aesthetica, *Philosophia Reformata* XI 1946, p. 144 where some more examples are given.

dk. 'Symbolism' is, properly speaking, an unfortunate term, as it is also used by the authors and artists we are discussing, and that in a very particular meaning. By this term 'aesthetical symbolism' we want to express that we are concerned with an element which is exclusively qualified by the aesthetic modality, although it is connected with the linguistic-iconic aspect of reality. A neologism like 'aesthetical iconism' seems awkward to us, for which reason we, after all, use the term 'symbolism', although placed between inverted commas.

dl. 'Instead of evoking our states of mind by means of the subject represented, the work itself must transmit the initial feeling, perpuate the emotion.' Denis *Théories,* p. 245.

dm. 'Suffice it to warn the visitor that Gauguin is a cerebral artist—I won't say, indeed, 'a literary man'—that he does not express what he sees but what he thinks by means of an original harmony of lines, by a drawing which is curiously comprised in an arabesque.' Gauguin: Préface inédite au catalogue de l'exposition des oeuvres d'Armand Seguin, *Mercure de France* (XIII, 1895), p. 222.

dn. 'It was natural that the synthesis should lead the artist to the symbol. Sacrifices and an order in the composition intended to make the author's thought intelligible, a liberation from the immediate dependence on direct observation, must inspire the artist with the wish to retain only those aspects of nature in which he read a significant allusion to that thought, and to unite those aspects in some great image, liberated from any verisimilitude (i.e. the naturalistic representation instead of the iconic rendering), as well as profoundly, that is to say vitally and artistically, true.' Morice *Gauguin,* p. 166.

do. From the way in which D. expresses himself it might appear that the term was by no means unusual. It was a current metaphor, which D. defines more closely, however, giving it a sharply outlined meaning.

dp. 'There is a kind of emotion which is very particularly proper to painting ... There is an impression which results from such an arrangement of colours, lights, and shadows, etc. ... This is called the music of the picture. Before knowing what the painting represents you enter a cathedral and you find yourself placed at too great a distance from the picture for you to know what it represents, and often you are caught by this magical harmony: sometimes the mere lines have this power ... Here is the true superiority of painting to any other art, for this emotion is directed to the most intimate part of the soul ... To what would be the spectacle of nature painting adds this element which verifies and selects, the soul of the painter, his particular style.' Delacroix: *Oeuvres littéraires* I, p. 63.

dq. 'A painting by Delacroix placed at too great a distance for you to judge of the charms of the outlines or the more or less dramatic quality of the subject penetrates you already with supernatural delight ... And when you come nearer, the analysis of the subject will not deprive you of anything and will not add anything to your primitive pleasure whose source is elsewhere and far away from any secret thought. I can invert the example. A well-drawn figure penetrates you with a joy that is entirely alien to the subject. Voluptuous or terrible, this figure only owes its charm to the arabesque it cuts out in space.' *L'Art Romantique,* p. 18/19.

dr. 'A good way to judge whether a painting is melodious is to look at it from a distance great enough for us not to understand the subject or the lines. If it is melodious it already has a meaning and it has already occupied its place in the repository of the memories.' *Cur. Esth.,* p. 92.

ds. 'There are gay and playful tones, playful and sad ones, rich and gay tones, rich and sad ones.' Ditto.

dt. 'Music ... (depicts) human feelings in a super human way, because clothed in golden clouds of gay harmonies it depicts all the movements of our emotions in an incorporeal form over our heads.' W. H. Wackenroder: Die Wunder der Ton-kunst, in Tieck und Wackenroder: *Phantasien über die Kunst* (1799, Deutsche National-Litteratur 145, Stuttgart o.J., p. 58), quoted by Abrams *Mirror and the Lamp,* p. 50 (in English).

du. 'And thus also is the state of affairs with respect to the mysterious stream in the depth of the human heart, language tells and names and describes its changes in an alien material; —music springs forth in ourselves ... in the mirror of the tones the human heart learns to know itself, by them feeling learns to feel.'

Ditto, p. 71, quoted by Abrams *op. cit.,* p. 93. Abrams deals elaborately with the question we are talking about here.

dv. This metaphor in connection with art had occurred at a much earlier date already. Cf. M. H. Abrams: *The Mirror and the Lamp,* pp. 32 ff. —where this term is even used in the title of the book. The metaphor goes back to a very old Neoplatonic tradition.

dw. 'A work of art is only really a work of art if like a mirror it reflects the psychological emotion experienced by the artist in the presence of nature or in that of his dream. This emotion can ultimately be only a pure sensation: a sensation of a particular harmony of lines, of a symphony determined by colours.' Aurier, article on the Salons of 1891, *Mercure de France* (III, 1891), p. 37.

dx. For we admit the existence of 'musicality' in this sense of aesthetic symbolism, but we deny the supposed correctness of the subjectivistic application of this phenomenon.

dy. 'Think also of the musical rôle that will henceforth be played by colour in modern painting. Colour is vibration just like music, and is in the same way able to attain to that which is most general and consequently most vague in nature, viz., its interior form.' Malingue CLXX.
In this letter Gauguin quotes from Delaroche's article, consequently he makes the latter's words fully his own. That article—*D'un point de vue esthétique à propos du peintre Paul Gauguin*—was also copied by him in his *Avant et Après,* p. 33, with this passage on page 40.

dz. '. . . sounds, colours, words have a wonderfully expressive value apart from any representation, apart even from the literal meaning of the words.' M. Denis: *Sérusier,* Paris 1942, cited by Agnes Humbert *Les Nabis,* p. 15. The pronouncement is Sérusier's.

ea. See note ai. Chapter VII.

eb. 'Yes, I know, we are only vain forms of matter—but very sublime for having invented God and our soul. So sublime, my friend, that I will give to myself this spectacle of matter, having consciousness of being, and yet throwing itself forcibly into this dream, which it knows it is not, singing of the soul and all similar divine impressions that have accumulated in us from the earliest times and proclaiming these glorious lies in the face of the Nothingness which is the truth. Such is the plan of my book, lyrical and such will probably be its title, the Glory of the Lie, or the Glorious lie. I will sing it as one who is despairing'. Letter to Cazalis, March 1866, cited by Michaud *Message poétique,* p. 172.

ec. This existentialistic terminology admirably fits in with Mallarmé's views, whom we may call a precursor of this twentieth century movement in many respects.

ed. 'Poetry is the expression of the mysterious sense of the aspects of existence by human language restored to its essential rhythm: thus it endows our sojourn with authenticity and constitutes our sole task.' Michaud *Message poétique,* p. 197.

ee. 'At present we need mysticism, and mysticism alone can save our society from brutalization, from sensualism, and utilitarianism. The noblest faculties of our soul are being atrophied ... on account of positive science we shall have returned to pure and simple animality. We must react. We must again cultivate the superior qualities of the soul. We must again become mystics. We must learn again what is love, the source of all understanding.' Aurier *Oeuvres,* p. 201.

ef. 'Their definitions are based on the theory of direct inspiration. To release this 'interior self' by imitation, this 'divine spark' that exists in the human personality, to enjoy this 'intuition', this profound insight into things resting on a 'spiritual illumination', those 'relations of an exceptional nature with the denizens of an invisible world', to possess 'the inner vision of the principle of the reality of this world', these are the hopes of the adepts.' A. Viatte: *Les sources occultes du romantisme 1770-1820,* I (Le Préromantisme), (Paris, 1928), p. 18.

eg. 'A great many souls looking down on the beaten paths sought new or neglected roads. Born under the protective shadow of a church or in the absence of any creed, they combine their doubt with religious anxiety.' A. Viatte: *Les sources occultes du romantisme 1770-1820,* I (Le Préromantisme), (Paris, 1928), p. 19.

eh. 'A book, an art-object, a musical phrase, pure thought as such ... are eternalizations of the self. We make as many means of them to disengage our I-ness from the contingences and also in this manner, and as soon as it escapes from these contingences, the self comes back ... to the hearth of the absolute, to the metaphysical place of the Ideas, to God.' Morice *La littérature,* p. 30.

ei. To a Greek of the Platonic School only the world of the ideas was the true reality, all other things were merely their adumbrations—recall Plato's myth of the cave in which man looks at the shadows of true events and takes them to be 'authentic'. What is relative and transitory thus only has a derived kind of reality at the most.

ek. 'Since it concerns the attainment of the absolute, must not poetical language try to find the necessary symbols that escape from any relativity? Michaud *Message poétique,* p. 327.

el. 'And indeed, from these three fundamental virtues liberty, order and solitude there immediately results a feeling of unlimited power, which is the adviser himself of the Infinite; immediately the soul acquires certainty about its own eternity in this exceptional solitude and that there is not death and no birth, and that veritable life is to be one of the conscious centres of the infinite vibration.' Morice *La littérature,* p. 367.

em. 'For, if things visible are the figures of things invisible, the essence of man near to the divine and endowed with harmony arranges and transforms nature in accordance with his supremacy to make it express his own supernatural origin.' Bernard: Ce que c'est que l'art mystique, *Mercure de France* (XIII, 1895), p. 29.

CHAPTER IX:

a. 'And they are called savages? They sing, they never steal . . . they do not murder. Two Tahitian words characterize them: Iorama (= good day, good-bye, thank you, etc.) . . . and Onatu (= I don't care, it does not matter, etc . . .) and are they called savages?' Malingue CXVI (1891).

It is remarkable that Gauguin never alludes to classical antiquity in this connection—a proof that he had got estranged from any kind of classicism which idealized Greco-Roman antiquity. The only author who refers to the anything but idyllic and ideal conditions really existing among the Tahitian population, is Th. Craven: *Modern Art, The Men, the Movements and the Meaning* (New York, 1940), p. 133 passim.

b. 'I have a great many worries and if it was not necessary for my art (of this I am sure), I would at once leave.' Malingue CXXVII.

c. 'his imagination has its starting point and its references in what is real.' Morice *Gauguin,* p. 190.

d. 'Paul Gauguin was in reality rather a decorative painter than a symbolistic one; for in none of his pictures there ever appeared any idea.' *Lettres à Emile Bernard,* p. 62.

e. 'His imagination up to now a prisoner of reality had been awakened and desired to express itself in the images of which the great masters have availed themselves. Suddenly he realized how very vain it was to attach oneself to the transitory aspects of his time.' . . . 'to the summary knowledge of the palette and the current practices he opposed the great science of art; to the false styles he opposed form; to the anemia of methods he opposed force; to the immediate subjects the great common places of humanity . . . no longer a beautiful Parisian woman at her toilet but a nymph watched by a satyr . . .' E. Bernard: Louis Anquetin, *Gazette des Beaux Arts* (1934, I), p. 117.

f. 'the most rigid and . . . the one which I want to keep or to sell dear'. Malingue CXXXIV. Now in the A. Conger Goodyear Collection, reproduced in almost every book on Gauguin.

g. 'A young girl of the South Sea islands is lying on her stomach showing part of her frightened face. She rests on a bed adorned with a blue 'paréo' and a bright-chrome yellow sheet. A violetpurple background strewn with flowers resembling electric sparks: a slightly strange figure stands on the side of the bed. Attracted by a form, a movement, I paint them without any other pre-occupation than to make a study of the nude. As such it is a slightly indecent study of the nude, and yet I want to make a chaste picture of it by giving the Pacific spirit, its character, its tradition. The 'paréo' intimately connected with the existence of a Pacific islander I use as the top of the bed. The sheet made of a material like the bark of a tree must be yellow because this colour suggests something unexpected for the spectator; because it suggests the light of a lamp, which enables me to

71

avoid the effect of a lamp. I want a slightly terrible background. Violet has been thoroughly indicated. This is the musical part of the painting fully exhibited.

'What can an entirely naked Pacific girl on a bed do in such a position? Prepare herself for love? This is indeed in her character, but it is indecent, and I won't have it. Sleep? That would be the end of the amorous action, which is also indecent. I only see fear. What kind of fear? Certainly not the fear of a Susan surprised by the greybeards. This does not exist in Oceania.

'The Tupapau (the spirit of the dead) has been entirely indicated. For the South Sea Islanders this means constant fear. At night they always have a lamp burning. Nobody walks about on the roads unless with a lantern and even then they go several of them together. Once I have found my Tupapau, I get entirely attached to it and make it into the motif of my painting. The nude is relegated to the second plan.

'What can an apparition be to a woman of the Pacific Islands? She does not know about the theatre, nor does she read any novels, and when she thinks of death she necessarily thinks of somebody she has already seen. My ghost can only be any simple woman. The decorative sense induces me to sprinkle flowers on the back-ground. The flowers are the flowers of the Tupapau, phosphorescences showing that the ghost is occupied with you. These are Tahitian beliefs.

'The title 'Manao Tupapau' has two meanings: either she is thinking of the ghost, or the ghost is thinking of her.

'To recapitulate. The musical part: horizontal undulating lines, harmonies of orange and blue, connected by yellows and violets, their derivative tints, brightened by greenish sparks; literary part: the spirit of a living human being connected with the Spirit of the dead. Night and Day. This genesis has been written for those who always want to know the why and the wherefore. In the other case it is simply a study of an Oceanian nude.'

From Notes Eparses, cited by Robert Rey *Gauguin,* p. 38.

h. 'All this is beside painting, one will say. Who knows? Perhaps not.' *Lettres à de Monfreid,* p. 102, March 12, 1897.

i. Of course the traditional manner of naturalism was equally iconic, but those means had become so familiar that they were no longer experienced as such—this is why we can formulate the issue as we did.

k. Toorop 'Klanklijnen' (lines representing sounds)—e.g., in his 'Drie Bruiden' (reproduced B. Polak, *Fin de Siècle,* ill. 24 and 26).

l. We are referring to the poetic language which uses motifs derived from antiquity and which has obtained from the 15th century till the present day—e.g. Giorgione (cf. P. Fehl: The Hidden Genre, a Study of the Concert Champêtre in the Louvre, *Journal of Aesthetics and Art Criticism* (XVI, 1957), p. 153—in our time, e.g. in Anquetin, etc.

m. The whole of this study, inclusive of this chapter, had been written before the publication of the special Gauguin issue of the *Gazette des Beaux-Arts,* in March 1958, marked the 98th year, dated January-July, 1956. The article by

G. Wildenstein—L'idéologie et l'esthétique dans deux tableaux—clés de Paul Gauguin—discusses the same work especially from the viewpoint of the motifs used that have been borrowed from older paintings by Gauguin himself; this article is only an additional support for our thesis. Wildenstein leaves the problems with which we are occupied entirely undiscussed.

n. 'I have finished a philosophical work on this theme comparable to the Gospel . . . I think it is good.' *Lettres à de Monfreid,* p. 119 ff., Feb. 1898.

o. 'That my words may clothe the brilliant forms of dreams which they adorn with images, flamboyant and descending on you . . . Do you understand the destination of humanity by means of this visible thought? from where it comes and where it goes to . . . Do you understand . . . such spectacles would take away and tear to pieces your intelligence . . . you understand?' Balzac *Séraphita,* p. 429.

p. 'A figure . . . lifts up its arms into the air and astonished, looks at these two personages who dare to think of their destination.' *Lettres à de Monfreid,* p. 119 ff., Feb. 1898.

q. The influence of Carlyle's work on Gauguin becomes all the more probable when we notice how clear the direct relation to Carlyle is in the case of an artist who temporarily worked under the strong impression of Gauguin's art and ideas. Thus the Danish painter Willumsen left France in 1892 for Norway where he made a few more or less symbolic paintings inspired by the mountains near Jotunheimen and the North Cape, entirely viewed after the manner of Carlyle, and in the frame, some figures to render the latter's thoughts of humanity—cf. *Sartor Resartus,* p. 242 ff, where Teufelsdrockh asks himself if this most important idea could never be painted. Cf. also, in the same work pp. 180 ff. See also O. Hølaas: J. F. Willumsen, *Kunsten Idag* (XLIV, Oslo 1958, 2), pp. 13 ff.

r. Carlyle derives his image from the sign of the Lord's presence during Israel's journey through the desert, Exodus 13 : 21.

s. *Sartor Resartus,* p. 68.
Carlyle had had a Christian education and no doubt he knew Bunyan's *Pilgrim's Progress* thoroughly. There is perhaps in this utterance a reminiscence of Bunyan's introduction, in which occurs:
'This book it chalketh out before thine eyes
The man that seeks the everlasting prize:
It shows you whence he comes, whither he goes.'

t. Both works were written almost simultaneously, without influencing each other, but only agreeing in that they derived from the same sources. Carlyle's work dates from 1831, Balzac's was written between 1833 and 1835.

u. From the comparison he makes between Melbourne and Sydney with London in a letter to Mette we must conclude no doubt that Gauguin had once been in England with her. He also knew English Children's Books about 1880 (cf. D. Sutton: The Gauguin Exhibition. *Burlington Magazine* (XCI, 1949), p. 285 and

73

note 26). He must have had some knowledge of English, but there is no proof of more than this 'some'.

v. In spite of his criticism Taine appears not to have escaped from the inspiring influence of Carlyle's *Sartor Resartus.* He wrote a French imitation of this work: *Opinions de M. Frédéric-Thomas Graindorge... publiées par H. Taine, son exécuteur testamentaire* (1867). It is a characteristically French trait that in this book Mr. Graindorge was not, like Teufelsdröckh an incomprehensible philosopher, but an amiable epicurean, making all kinds of remarks on the girls, the mistresses and the balls of Paris.

w. In view of this state of things we do not think it correct that in America Gauguin's work now bears the title: 'Where do we come from? What are we? Where are we going?' (In reproductions and in the texts relating to it produced by the M. Harriman Gallery, New York, 1936). The title had better be rendered by: 'Whence? What? Whereto?' or: 'Whence? What? Whither?'

x. 'Puvis explains his idea, yes but he does not paint it. He is Greek' ... 'whereas I myself am a savage. Puvis will entitle a picture 'Purity' and in explanation he will paint a young virgin with a lily in her hand—a well-known symbol, so it is understood. Gauguin will paint a landscape under the same title with limpid waters with not any stain of civilised man, perhaps one personage. Without my entering into details it is clear that there is a whole world of difference between Puvis and me. As a painter Puvis is a lettered man, whereas I am not a lettered man but perhaps a man of letters.' Malingue CLXXIV.

y. 'Here, close to my cottage, in complete silence, I dream violent harmonies in the natural perfumes that intoxicate me. A refined delight of I don't know what holy horror which I presume in the immemorial. The past, the fragrance of joy which I inhale in the present. Animal figures, of a statuesque rigidity:
'I do not know what ancient, glorious, religious flavour in the rhythm of their gestures, in their rare immobility. In their dreamy eyes the surface is blurred by an unfathomable enigma. And it is night—peace everywhere. My eyes are closed in order to see without understanding it the dream in infinite space which recedes in front of me, and I have a feeling of the doleful march of my hopes.' Malingue CLXX.

z. 'that which has not been expressed' ... 'it follows implicitly from the lines without colours or words, it has not been materially constituted.' Malingue CLXX.

aa. In this large picture:
        'Whither?
    Close to the death of an old woman,
    A strange stupid bird concludes.
        What?
    Daily existence.
    The man of instinct asks himself what all this means.
        Whence

Source.
Child.
Communal life.
'The bird concludes the poem by comparing the lower being with the intelligent being in this great whole which is the problem announced by the title.

'Behind a tree two sinister figures enveloped in clothes of a sad colour near the tree of knowledge make their note of dolour caused by this very science in comparison with the simple beings in a virginal nature that might have been a paradise conceived by man abandoning themselves to the bliss of living.' Malingue CLXXIV.

ab. In Morice's *Gauguin,* p. 113, the text is printed in three columns side by side, in the part of this letter which contains the indication of the contents of the three parts of the title. This is how Gauguin had it in his letter, logical, clearly arranged, and explanatory. Cf. the reproduction of this part of the letter in G. Wildenstein: L'idéologie et l'esthétique dans deux tableaux clés de Gauguin, *Gazette des Beaux-Arts* (98th year, Jan.-July 1956), p. 132.

ac. We are confronted in it with a very old tradition, connecting with the direction of handwriting and the way in which the illustrations, done in miniature in the scrolls were unrolled, in the literal sense of the word. Cf. A. C. Soper: The Illustrative Method of the Tokugawa 'Genji' pictures, *Art Bulletin* (XXXVII, 1955), p. 1.

ad. 'Look for harmony . . . that with you everything breathes peace . . . Avoid the pose in movement. Each of your personages should be in a static condition . . . Apply yourself to the silhouette of each object.' Gauguin *Avant et Après,* p. 55.

ae. 'putting oneself in the hands of one's Creator is annulling oneself and dying.' *Avant et Après,* p. 224.

af. 'The idol is there . . . forming part of my dream in front of my cottage with the whole of nature, reigning in our primitive soul, the imaginary consolation of our sufferings (mind this 'imaginary') in what they imply of vagueness and of the incomprehensible with respect to the mystery of our origin and our future.' Malingue CLXX.
Also in his writing which was begun in these same years and was entitled 'Esprit moderne et le catholicisme' (in the Museum at St. Louis, Mo., U.S.A., at the exhibition of French drawings from American collections in Boymans—Van Beuningen Museum, 1958, cat. no. 172) he occupied himself with this subject. Thus on the first page he wrote in the Dedication to Morice, 'D'où venons-nous, que sommes-nous, où allons-nous? L'éternel problème qui nous punit de l'orgueil—ô Douleur tu es mon maître—Fatalité que tu es cruelle et toujours vaincu je me révolte—La raison reste: folle sans doute mais vivante—Et c'est alors que la frondaison commence.' (Whence? What? Whither? The eternal problem that punishes our pride—Oh, Sorrow, thou art my master—fate, how cruel thou art, and always vanquished I revolt—Reason remains: foolish, no doubt, but alive—And then the foliage begins to come out'. This book has not yet been published.

ag. 'And then you know that if the others have gratified me with a system, I myself have none and I will not be condemned to it. To paint as I like, bright to-day, dark to-morrow, etc.... for the rest, an artist should be free or he is not an artist. *Lettres à de Monfreid*, p. 109, July 14, 1897.

ah. '... if a work of art were something accidental, all these notes would be useless.' *Avant et Après*, p. 24.

ai. 'all rays to the vital centre of my art.' *Avant et Après*, p. 24. Cf. Baudelaire Cur. Esth., p. 102: 'Rien n'est plus impertinent ni plus bête que de parler à un grand artiste, érudit et penseur comme Delacroix, des obligations qu'il peut avoir au dieu du hasard. Cela fait tout simplement hausser les épaules de pitié. Il n'y a pas de hasard dans l'art, non plus qu'en mécanique.' (Nothing is more impertinent or stupid than talking concerning a great artist, a scholar and thinker, such as Delacroix, of the obligations he may be under to the god of chance. This simply evokes only a shrug of the shoulders out of pity. There is no chance in art, no more than in mechanics).

ak. Delacroix still thought he could use photography (e.g. of nudes) as 'mots d'un dictionnaire'. Cf., e.g., *Journal* 21 May, 1853.

al. 'The machines have come, art has gone, and I am far from thinking that photography would be propitious to us' ... 'As to myself, I have withdrawn very far, farther away than the horses of the Parthenon ... to the 'dada' of my childhood, the good old hobby horse.' *Diverses Choses*, quoted by Morice *Gauguin*, p. 224.

am. 'Finally there is at present a beautiful effort which stems less from the previous epoch than from the romantics'. *Lettres à de Monfreid*, p. 134, Dec. 1898.

an. 'the mysterious centre of thought'. Cited Morice *Gauguin*, p. 153.

ao. 'Where does the execution of a picture begin and where does it end? At the moment when the extreme feelings are fusing together in the deepest part of being, at the moment when they burst and all thought is thrown out like lava from a volcano, is not there a breaking forth of the work that is suddenly created, savage if you like, but grand and of a superhuman aspect? The cold calculations of reason have not preceded this outburst but who knows when the work was begun in the depth of being? unconsciously perhaps?' *Lettres à de Monfreid*, p. 121, March 1898.

ap. 'I have wanted to establish the right to venture anything: my capacities have not yielded a great result, but the machine has been launched after all. The public does not owe me anything because my pictorial work is only comparatively good, but the painters who profit from this liberty nowadays owe me something.' Quoted in Morice *Gauguin*, p. 243.

aq. 'the shackles of verisimilitude'. *Lettres à de Monfreid*, p. 183, 17 November 1901.

ar. 'the academic bias' . . . 'the symbolistic bias, another kind of sentimentalism.' Ditto.

as. 'A cross, flames, that is it, symbolism'. Ditto, p. 104, April 1897.

at. Carlyle's Teufelsdröckh went through all this already in his youth: 'Thus already Freewill often came in painful collision with necessity' (*Sartor Resartus*, p. 122).

au. In the article on the American dramatist Harcoland, by C. Tigell, in *Mercure de France* (XIII, 1895), p. 290, we find the following quotation from one of the dramatist's works: 'Les lois sont la honte de l'humanité. Le premier législateur qui osa endiguer les torrents de l'âme attenta sinistrement à la liberté morale, le premier juge fut le coupable. Voici la ligne à suivre! pourquoi tenir cet hypocrite langage au nouveau-né et l'arracher dès l'aurore à sa spontanéité ou le plonger dans le canal des généralités asservies? . . . L'homme libre aide à l'harmonie; l'homme esclave la contrarie . . .' (Laws are the shame of humanity. The first legislator who dared to fence in the torrents of the soul committed a sinister assault on moral liberty, the first judge was the culprit. This is the policy we should follow! why should we talk in such a hypocritical way to the newly born and from the first moment of their day tear them loose from their spontaneity, in order to plunge them into the canal of servile generalities? . . . Free man is a support to harmony; enslaved man is the opposite).

av. The dots are Gauguin's.

aw. I know, like everybody, and as everybody will ever know, that two and two make four. It is a far cry from convention and intuition to understanding: I subject myself, and like everybody I say: Two and two make four . . . But . . . that bores me, and deranges very much my reasoning.' *Avant et Après*, p. 5.

ax. We are not concerned here with the tendency which was probably indirectly influenced by Sérusier and whose greatest master was Mondriaan; but we are dealing with the other non-figurative movement leading to Manessier, etc.

ay. 'It was, therefore, necessary, while taking into account the efforts made and all the researches, even the scientific, to think of a complete liberation, to break windows, at the risk of cutting one's fingers, to leave it to the next generation to resolve the problem in general, from now on independent, loose from any fetters. I do not say definitely, for there is question exactly of an art without end, rich in techniques of all kinds, fit to translate all the emotions of nature and man, appropriate for every individual in any period in joys and in sufferings.

'For this purpose one had to throw oneself into the battle body and soul, the battle against all the Schools, all of them without any distincion, not only by disparaging them, but by something else, insulting not only the officials, but also the Impressionists, the Neo-Impressionists, the ancient and the modern public. No longer to have a wife and children who disown you. What does insult matter? What does misery matter? All this as far as the conduct of man is concerned.

77

'As to the work, a method of contradiction, if you like, to attack the strongest abstractions, to do all that was prohibited, and to reconstruct more or less happily without fear of exaggeration, even with exaggeration. To learn anew, then, once known, to learn again. To conquer all diffidence, whatever ridicule it may raise. Before his easel a painter is no slave, neither of the past, nor of the present, neither of nature, nor of his neighbour, He, and again he, always he.' *Racontars d'un rapin,* (1951), p. 75. Rotonchamp *Gauguin,* p. 208. Morice *Gauguin,* p. 244.